Leaders in the Historical Study of American Education

LEADERS IN EDUCATIONAL STUDIES

Volume 3

Series Editor:

Leonard J. Waks
Temple University, Philadelphia, USA

Scope:

Leaders in Educational Studies provides a comprehensive account of the transformation of educational knowledge since 1960, based on rich, first-person accounts of the process by its acknowledged leaders.

The series provides unique insights into the formation of the knowledge base in education, as well as a birds-eye view of contemporary educational scholarship.

The initial volume, *Leaders in Philosophy of Education: Intellectual Self Portraits*, contains personal essays by 24 leading philosophers of education fromNorth America and the United Kingdom. The second volume, *Leaders in Curriculum Studies: Intellectual Self-Portraits*, contains similar essays by 18 leading curriculum scholars. The current volume on historians of American education contains essays by 25 leaders in this field. Volumes on other fields of educational scholarship are now being prepared.

Until the 1950s school teachers were trained for the most part in normal schools or teacher training colleges. The instructors were drawn from the teacher corps; they were not professional scholars. Those offering classes in so-called 'foundational disciplines' in education were not trained in these disciplines. Educational scholarship was generally weak and cut off from contemporary work in the so-called 'parent' disciplines. Professors relied on textbooks featuring out-of-date, dumbed-down knowledge.

In the late 1950s plans were made to bring a higher level of professionalism to school teaching. In the United States, the remaining normal schools initially became state colleges, and eventually state universities. In the United Kingdom, the training colleges were initially brought under the supervision of university institutes; eventually teaching was transformed into an all-graduate profession.

Commentators on both sides of the Atlantic argued that if education was to become a proper field of university study educational scholarship itself wouldhave to be transformed. Scholars were recruited into educational studies fromsocial sciences and humanities disciplines to contribute to teacher education and to train a new generation of educational scholars in contemporary research methods.

Under their influence the knowledge base for education has been completely transformed. In addition to major accomplishments in philosophy, history, sociology and economics of education, interdisciplinary work in educational studies has flourished. The series documents this transformation.

LEADERS IN THE HISTORICAL STUDY OF AMERICAN EDUCATION

Edited by

Wayne J. Urban
The University of Alabama, Tuscaloosa, USA

SENSE PUBLISHERS
ROTTERDAM/BOSTON/TAIPEI

A C.I.P. record for this book is available from the Library of Congress.

ISBN: 978-94-6091-753-0 (paperback)
ISBN: 978-94-6091-754-7 (hardback)
ISBN: 978-94-6091-755-4 (e-book)

Published by: Sense Publishers,
P.O. Box 21858,
3001 AW Rotterdam,
The Netherlands
www.sensepublishers.com

Printed on acid-free paper

Cover photo of Lawrence Cremin, pioneer in the field of history of American education and president of Teachers College, Columbia University , courtesy of Teachers College.

TABLE OF CONTENTS

TABLE OF CONTENTS

PREFACE

The aim of the LEADERS IN EDUCATIONAL STUDIES series is to document the rise of educational scholarship in the years after 1960, a period of astonishing growth and accomplishment, as seen through the eyes of its leading practitioners.

A few words about the build up to this period are in order. Before the mid-twentieth century school teaching, especially at the primary level, was as much a trade as a profession. Schoolteachers were trained primarily in normal schools or teachers colleges, only rarely in universities. But in the 1940s American normal schools were converted into teachers colleges, and in the 1960s these were converted into state universities. At the same time school teaching was being transformed into an all-graduate profession in both the United Kingdom and Canada. For the first time, school teachers required a proper university education.

Something had to be done, then, about what was widely regarded as the deplorable state of educational scholarship. James Conant, in his final years as president at Harvard in the early 1950s, envisioned a new kind of university-based school of education, drawing scholars from mainstream academic disciplines such as history, sociology psychology and philosophy, to teach prospective teachers, conduct educational research, and train future educational scholars. One of the first two professors hired to fulfill this vision was Israel Scheffler, a young philosopher of science and language who had earned a Ph.D. in philosophy at the University of Pennsylvania. Scheffler joined Harvard's education faculty in 1952. The other was Bernard Bailyn, who joined the Harvard faculty in 1953 after earning his Ph. D. there, and who re-energized the study of American educational history with the publication of *Education in the Forming of American Society: Needs and Opportunities for Study* (University of North Carolina Press, 1960). Many of the most important works of scholarship in these fields since that time have been created in the spaces carved out by these pioneering leaders. The series has been exceptionally fortunate that Scheffler has provided the foreword to the volume on philosophy of education, and that Bernard Bailyn has written the foreword to the present volume.

This volume brings together 26 personal essays, with a Foreword and an Afterword, all by established historians of American education. The authors detail their early life experiences, first encounters with history and history of education, periods of serious study and early professional work, emergence as leaders, development of mature work, and reflections on the current challenges and opportunities in the field.

Previous volumes in the series have featured leaders in philosophy of education and curriculum studies. Those volumes brought together essays by leaders from North America and from the United Kingdom in roughly equal numbers. Early discussions with the editor of this book, Wayne J. Urban, convinced me that such a plan was not practicable for history of education. Philosophy and curriculum studies have generated broad interchanges across the Atlantic. Not surprisingly, historians of education have by contrast attended largely to developments in their own national societies and educational systems. Consequently, we decided to limit this volume to historians of American education, and to plan a future volume of intellectual self-portraits by leading historians in the United Kingdom and Europe.

A final word: since 1960 the history of education has established itself as an important and vibrant branch of scholarship. Continued success, however, is not guaranteed. Since the 1980s neo-liberal state regimes in North America and the UK have inserted themselves aggressively and directly into both the schools and teacher education programs. Under such watchwords as "excellence" and "academic achievement" they have sought to transform conventional teaching practices into those that merely result in measurable improvements on standardized tests. They have disparaged the intellectual contributions for education of scholars in humanities disciplines. State bureaucrats now demand that such "useless" studies be replaced with something more "practical" – although by this they do not mean something that will enhance the practice of teaching, but rather something that will transform it in accord with state demands. Serious inquiry in the disciplines of the humanities is not likely to contribute to that demand. Far from recruiting leading humanities scholars, as Conant and other university leaders did in the 1960s, today's university leaders are failing to replace those that are now retiring, and in many cases closing the programs that train such scholars. Let me express the hope that the works of contributors to these volumes will shine like beacons, lighting the way for future education scholars in what may be less favorable times ahead.

Leonard Waks
Temple University
General Editor

BERNARD BAILYN

FOREWORD

Group biographies are always interesting. Individual peculiarities, gossipy tales, failures and successes, beginnings and endings, seen in comparison with others, tend to grip one's mind. But grouped memoirs, revealing and obscuring, subjective and objective, anecdotal and narrative, are especially fascinating, and none that I have seen are as fascinating as the brief memoirs in this volume by leaders in the field of the history of education. In part the fascination lies in the incidental, unexpected details in the lives of these distinguished scholars that suddenly appear: Jurgen Herbst as a teen age recruit to Hitler's Wehrmacht, Carl Kaestle as a collegiate singer (The Whiffenpoofs), Maris Vinovskis as a mayoral campaign manager, Ronald Butchart as a sixth grade herring catcher, Michael Katz as an encyclopedia salesman, Patricia Graham sacked twice as a teacher en route to the Deanship of Harvard's Graduate School of Education and the Presidency of the Spencer Foundation. In greater part the fascination is the result of the writers' frankness, perspicuity, and literary skill in exploring the main passages in their intellectual and professional careers. And beyond all the personal details a major fascination lies in finding in these memoirs a vivid demonstration of education as a social process, the conceptual origins and early development of innovative scholarship, and the emergence of a segment of the American professoriate. But what is most striking for me is a paradox that seems to lie at the heart of these life stories.

None of these leading historians of education aspired to work in that field; some had never heard of it until well along in their professional lives, and many moved in "zigzag trajectories" (Larry Cuban) in and out of the field as their work developed in other areas, but dipping back into the field when it seemed propitious. And they are aware of this paradox. "Never," Harvey Kantor writes with a note of surprise, "when I was in high school and college [did it occur] to me that I would become a historian of education." Diane Ravitch's retrospective surprise is even broader: "It never occurred to me that I might one day be a professor, an academic, a historian of education." "An Accidental Historian," Michael Katz calls his memoir, "Serendipity in the Making of a Career." The careers of the others illustrate the paradox again and again. There were no luminous goals, no alluring models to catch one's interest. The memoirists approached what became their life's work from angles and with interests unique to themselves. And indeed it could hardly have been otherwise given the variety of backgrounds from which these scholars emerged.

They came from almost every corner of the nation and from a great variety of sub-cultures. They came from the South Bronx and from fishing towns in the far

Northwest; from recently built suburbs in the Midwest; from upstate New York and downstate California, and often, with striking frequency, they came from immigrant families – children and grandchildren of emigrants from all over Europe who had settled in places as different as Flatbush and Houston. Two were immigrants themselves, one from Wolfenbüttel, Germany, the other from Riga, Latvia, both of whom, remarkably, resettled first, via utterly different routes, in Nebraska. And their initial schooling was as different as their family origins. Several found the schools they attended miserable. "I did not like school," Graham writes, "I found the schoolwork dull and the ambience dispiriting and isolating" – and "high school was even worse." Many saw their schools as irrelevant to the world around them, and that irrelevance proved to be a spur to their ambitions. But others, a few, attended elite schools and enjoyed them. And the post secondary school career lines were equally unique. If plotted on a geographical/academic grid they would appear not as lines converging into patterns but as a criss-crossing tangle of complex routes through the vast, unstructured multiplicity of America's collegiate institutions. There were no privileged, designated, assured routes of access.

Yet despite the great variety of personal backgrounds, schooling and collegiate experiences, these 26 scholars ended in the same broad field of the history of education to which all have made major contributions. Somewhere in the course of their collegiate education or shortly thereafter they came to see the unique importance of the field and within it the possibility of personal achievement. In some cases the moment is recorded. "Education history," Vinovskis writes, "had been just another fascinating but small academic issue for me, now it became one of my two or three major intellectual pursuits." For some that recognition seems to have become obvious by the sheer impulses of scholarship and intellection, but in most cases a teacher, a colleague, or a friend pointed the way. "Why don't you go into the history of education?" Theodore Sizer suddenly asked Katz: "'History gives you great flexibility. People seem to like to hire historians as administrators.' I took his advice." And one of the most interesting aspects of these memoirs is how the career lines have intersected within this small group, how intra-generational contacts proved creative, how one memoirist became an inspiration, a guide, ultimately a collaborator with others: so Carl Kaestle with Maris Vinovskis, Vinovskis with Diane Ravitch, Roger Geiger with Hugh Hawkins, Mary Ann Dzuback with Ellen Lagemann. And at the center of these many interactive careers stands the remarkable figure of Lawrence Cremin at Teachers College.

He seems to be everywhere, ubiquitous, in these personal accounts. One finds it difficult to believe--it is astonishing--that Cremin could have had that many course assistants whose careers he inspired, could have given wise counsel to that many unsure aspirants, could have been involved in that many collaborative projects, and could have maneuvered that many appointments throughout the nation's sprawling educational system. But so it appears from these memoirs, as does the influence and inspiration of David Tyack at Stanford. His style and influence, it seems, were different from Cremin's – more personal, more intimate, more open and sharing, but he was equally inspiring and influential in his teaching, in his mentorship, and in the model he provided in his teaching and scholarship.

However inspired by immediate colleagues and friends or by key figures like Cremin and Tyack, these writers tell of a discovery, at some point, of the pivotal, unique position that the history of education holds in the world of historical scholarship, education, and public policy. "Being a historian of education," Diane Ravitch writes, "provides an excellent starting point to interpret and reflect on all kinds of debates [and] to explain how the past informs our decisions and discussions." "Without realizing it," Katz explains, "I had written about the links between past and present, that I was using history to interpret contemporary educational reforms." The field was found to be boundless: "defined as the study of culture and its transmission through time," Ellen Lagemann writes, "the history of education can open for study an almost limitless range of topics and can help one move through many different positions in academe and outside."

These are no isolated scholars, entirely removed from the current concerns of society. There are different emphases - some have been more deeply involved in history as such, others' concerns have been more broadly political or administrative. But all share a devotion to the belief that history is a key to understanding where we are in the vital field of education, and how one might best think about the policies that account for the shaping of minds and the transmission of culture in the great swirl of American life.

And there is something more. These memoirs – short, insightful, candid, and lucid – are themselves important documents in the history of education and scholarship. The authors' careers are part of the story they tell.

WAYNE J. URBAN

INTRODUCTION

This volume is the result of an invitation from Leonard Waks to me to solicit essays from leaders in the field of history of education about their personal and academic backgrounds and how they came to work in this field. It is the third in a series, preceded by volumes in philosophy of education and curriculum studies. Initially, like in the two predecessor volumes, the plan was to involve contributors from Great Britain, Canada, and Australia, as well as from the United States. The character of history of education as a field, however, made it more nationally distinct than the other fields. The content of the field followed national experience more in history than in philosophy or curriculum studies and so, rather quickly, Waks and I reached the decision to restrict this volume to the history of American education. This is not to say that there is not significant scholarship elsewhere in the world. In fact, the International Standing Conference for the History of Education (ISCHE) is a vibrant organization with European scholars standing solidly as its base with branches throughout much of the rest of the world. A separate volume involving European and other international historians of education might well be a possible next step in this series.

Restricting this volume to American educational historians did not mean relatively few contributors, however. I initially invited thirty scholars to contribute to the volume. Twenty six stuck with the project and their essays, along with this Introduction, a Foreword by Bernard Bailyn, and an Afterword by Kate Rousmaniere, comprise its pages. The careful reader of the essays may note that there are no minority contributors. This is a loss, since there are several minority scholars who have made their mark in the field of the history of American education. Three of the four scholars who were invited but did not complete their essays are minority scholars. Two agreed to contribute but were unable, for different reasons, to produce an essay and one never responded to the invitation. I am regretful that they were not able to contribute to the volume and hope that I was not somehow involved in the reasons behind this failure. The fourth invitee who agreed to contribute rather quickly chose to rescind that action, remarking, not too presciently I hope, that such an activity was best left to "old men" (and women?).

That leaves the twenty six men and women who did agree to provide essays for the volume. Their essays are presented alphabetically. There was some discussion of grouping them chronologically, by time in the field. The Series editor and I decided, finally, not to do this. If we would have done it there would have been three sections. The first would consist of six essays, by Sol Cohen, Geraldine Clifford, Patricia Graham, Hugh Hawkins, Jurgen Herbst, and David Tyack, all who made their mark in the field rather soon after it was enriched in the 1960s. The

W. J. Urban, Leaders in the Historical Study of American Education, 1–5.

enrichment came from mainly from two sources: American colonial historian Bernard Bailyn, who wrote a seminal volume *Education in the Forming of American Society* in 1960 and Lawrence Cremin, who from within the field answered Bailyn's invitation to make it more than the history of schools. Not all contributors to this volume followed this invitation, however. Some have concentrated their work on the history of schooling, while others have investigated non-school topics. Historians of higher education have followed their own divergent paths in their scholarship. What all contributors to this volume have accomplished, however, is that they have applied the same exacting standards of evidence and argument to their work that characterized the work of Bailyn and Cremin and that are dominant in the larger field of American history. It is the scholarly caliber of work in the history of American education that makes it a legitimate part of the larger American historical enterprise.

To return to the first six essays, three, those by Sol Cohen, Geraldine Clifford, and Patricia Graham, are the product of Lawrence Cremin's early doctoral students, either in an Ed D program at Teachers College or a history Ph. D. at Columbia University. All three authors acknowledge Cremin, though in distinctly different ways, and his personal influence is also acknowledged in David Tyack's essay. Hugh Hawkins and Jurgen Herbst came to the history of education from a program of study in a history department without any affiliation with an education school or department and, thus, with limited knowledge of Cremin and his work. Five of the six early contributors were presidents of the History of Education Society, the one who was not specialized in the area of the history of American higher education and was a frequent presence at history of education meetings during his career, and a member of the Board of Directors of the society for three years. Bernard Bailyn was personally important for at least three of our six early contributors. The backgrounds of the six testify to the profound influence that both Cremin and Bailyn had on the development of the field.

Thirteen of the twenty six essays comprise what might have been a second section of this volume. They are the work of scholars who came of age roughly a decade or more after the time that our initial group started out. Again, Cremin and Bailyn are quite influential for many of them. Barbara Finkelstein, Ellen Lagemann and Diane Ravitch were Cremin's doctoral students at the Columbia history department, as well as being involved at Teachers College. Harold Wechsler studied the history of higher education in the Columbia history department. Carl Kaestle started out as Cremin's student but, under Cremin's influence, transferred to Harvard to study with Bernard Bailyn. Harvard was prominent in the doctoral education of Michael Katz and Maris Vinovskis, though the former was in the Harvard education school while the latter was in the history department. Harvard was the institution of the undergraduate education of Donald Warren, who received his doctoral degree at the University of Chicago. Bailyn himself is mentioned in passing in the essay of William Cutler, who received his doctoral training at Cornell. The Ivy League clearly dominated in the education of these thirteen contributors, with Roger Geiger's training at Yale added to that of those already mentioned. Yet among these thirteen, a wider pattern also begins to emerge.

Wayne J. Urban studied at Ohio State in a doctoral program in education and Ronald Butchart completed his doctorate in history at the State University of New York at Binghamton. Urban and Butchart also had distinctly different undergraduate educations from the Ivy League influence which dominated in the first and second groups, though with a few exceptions. Urban's undergraduate degree came from an urban Jesuit university in the Midwest and Butchart's came from a Pacific institution. Larry Cuban grew up in western Pennsylvania and spent time teaching in Cleveland, Ohio and working as a school superintendent in suburban Washington, DC, before obtaining his doctorate at Stanford under David Tyack.

The eastern hegemony that characterized the educational background of the the first group and most of the second was less prominent in the final seven scholars who provided the essays for this volume. John Rury and William Reese got their doctorates at Wisconsin under Carl Kaestle, Lynn Gordon obtained her degree from Chicago, where Donald Warren of the second group also finished his doctorate, Jeffrey Mirel got his doctorate at the University of Michigan, after doing his undergraduate work at Ohio State. David Labaree did his doctorate with Michael Katz at Pennsylvania and Mary Ann Dzuback studied with Cremin and Ellen Lagemann at Teachers College and Columbia; both moved west for their first position, Labaree to Michigan State and Dzuback to Washington University in St. Louis. Harvey Kantor studied with David Tyack at Stanford and took a position at the University of Utah, where he continues to work. As the field developed, then, it moved a bit away from roots in the Northeast and westward, even to the Pacific Coast where Tyack trained a small but significant number of educational historians. Wisconsin came to rival, if not surpass, Teachers College and Harvard as a leading producer of educational historians when Carl Kaestle and Jurgen Herbst worked there, and Wisconsin's prominence continues with Reese, Michael Fultz, and Adam Nelson now on its faculty. Southern universities produced no contributor to this volume, but two of them now work in the South, Wayne J. Urban at the University of Alabama and Ron Butchart at the University of Georgia. American educational history, then, at least as judged by the background and work of the contributors to this volume, has become close to a national phenomenon, though it is a field that still has, and acknowledges, its roots in New York City and Cambridge, Massachusetts.

One final point might be made about the roots of the field. History of Education as a field antedated Cremin and Bailyn, though each of them criticized the scholarly weaknesses of the early contributors. R. Freeman Butts, who was Cremin's senior colleague at Teachers College and who represented the values of the generations of educational historians who preceded all three of these men, deserves mention not for his influence on the training of the contributors to this volume, though he was involved with many of the early TC-Columbia contributors, but for his commitment to the public schools of the United States as institutions worthy of study and preservation. Several of the contributors to this volume were friends of Butts who shared his values and have applied them in their historical studies.

In his Foreword, Bernard Bailyn modestly fails to address his own contribution to the education of many of the contributors to this essay, the reason he was asked to write the Foreword. In fact, all of them have been influenced by Bailyn's seminal *Education in the Forming of American Society*, though differently in many cases. In his Foreword, Bailyn notes the wide difference in backgrounds of the contributors, the immigrant roots of several and the actual immigrant status of two, Jurgen Herbst and Maris Vinovskis. Bailyn notes that careful and systematic exploration of the checkered backgrounds and career paths of the contributors would make a significant contribution to the field of group biography. In fact, he is struck by the diversity of those backgrounds as well as the scholarly accomplishments in the history of American education, as represented by the contributors to the volume. One aspect of those backgrounds that I would like to mention, but am unable to explore in depth is their Jewish ethnicity. By my count, ten of the twenty six contributors have some Jewish heritage. The ways that this heritage influenced their work, as well as the academic choices that led them to that work, are surely worthy of serious and sustained study.

David Tyack and Michael Katz deserve mention in this introduction for the seminal contributions they have made to the field of the history of American education. Katz's 1968 volume *The Irony of Early School Reform* was a landmark both methodologically and ideologically, sparking the radical revisionist view of the common school and its successor institutions as something less than the ideal of democracy that they were thought to be as well as the quantitative study of educational history that continues to enrich the field to this day. Tyack's 1974 volume, *The One Best System*, tempered but did not repudiate Katz's ideological influence while opening up the fields of urban educational history and educational administration to historical study. Patricia Graham and Geraldine Clifford were early contributors to the rise of women as subjects in the history of education, and their work animated that of a vibrant sub-field of both the history of education and of women's history. Many of the essayists in this volume have contributed to various studies in the history of educational policy, mainly federal educational policy. Diane Ravitch and Maris Vinovskis held high positions in the federal educational agency in the 1990s, a testimony to the value that one's historical perspective can have in doing non-historical policy work. At least three of the contributors consciously cast their essays as memoirs, thereby illustrating the links between educational history and the linguistic turn that characterized another movement in the field of history.

While individual mention of the substantive accomplishments in educational history of all of the contributors to this volume is outside the scope of this introduction, this is not to deny that each one of them has had a significant influence on the field, in numerous varied and stimulating ways. The net result is that readers of these essays will find herein an enormously diverse set of intellectual backgrounds and an equally remarkable and diverse set of accomplishments. The history of American education is a vibrant field in the early twenty-first century, and the chapters in this volume are a testimony to both the diversity and the intellectual quality of that field.

In her Afterword, Kate Rousmaniere recounts her own experience as consumer of the work of these contributors and student and, eventually critic, of that work.

She stresses the memoir aspect in several of the essays, notes the insularity that comes with a relatively small field such as educational history, and acknowledges the accomplishment of the contributors in spite of, and maybe partly because of, that insularity.

This brings me to the last consideration in this Introduction. What is likely to happen to a vibrant field that seems to be experiencing the loss of academic positions assigned to it? Historians of education have seldom found homes in history departments, though a few historians of higher education have found academic employment there. Historians of education were employed fairly routinely in education schools for much of the twentieth century. The experience of the past decade indicates, however, that this pattern is disappearing. Positions for historians of education now come in a variety of newer roles: as policy analysts, as diversity-oriented scholars and teachers, as independent scholars. Recovering older patterns of employment might be possible, though that seems increasingly unlikely as education schools drift toward behaviorist oriented teacher training programs and strategies. Maintaining employment possibilities for historians of education is a serious problem worthy of the serious attention of those in the field. The lack of pattern in the backgrounds of the contributors to this volume provides a ray of hope in that the unusual has been the pattern in the past. We can only hope that the future will present unusual opportunities for the unusual people who will be the historians of education of future generations.

RONALD E. BUTCHART

HISTORIAN DESPITE THE ODDS

My first contact with the history of education was inauspicious. I was a senior at a small college in Idaho's Treasure Valley enduring a required education course, a portion of which purported to cover the history of American schools. As a history major, I looked forward to that portion, expecting to gain some historical leverage on my own impoverished education. By the end of the course, I had reached the reluctant conclusion that the history of education must be one branch of my discipline that explained little, since it clearly did not explain the schools my friends and I had attended.

I spent twelve years in schools scattered across the Northwest, from fishing and mill towns on the coast through agricultural market centers in eastern Oregon and southern Idaho to a small college town south of Portland. My schooling bracketed the 1950s, when school-book mothers maintained impossibly clean houses in cocktail dresses, school-book fathers in suits came cheerily home from unexplained occupations, and school-book children in gender-appropriate clothing rode scooters down tidy streets. The only correspondence between the world of my school-books and my world was that the mothers, fathers, and children in the books were, like me, all pallidly white.

I was a latch-key child before America obsessed about latch-key children. So were nearly all of the children I knew. Our mothers and fathers both worked; they had little economic choice in the matter. My mother worked at a variety of office jobs, though, given her era's socialization, to the day she died she never recognized herself as a member of the labor force. My father labored as a teacher, carpenter, and fisherman until the Cold War-inspired revolution in science teaching finally pulled him back to high school chemistry labs in my final years of high school. If my parents' college educations put my family technically in the middle class, the economic realities of poorly paid waged labor put it solidly in the working class.

The working class and its children did not exist in our school books. The social aspects of American life deemed worthy of portrayal to American school children included, in my fifth grade year in Nampa, Idaho, the study of "community." To better understand our community, we visited a bank and a fire station. We wrote short pieces on our churches, though we never talked about the social class differences among them; we were tested on the geographical determinants of the placement of communities, though the explanations did nothing to explain Nampa, Idaho; we read that communities were places where cooperation and civility were valued, though the schoolhouse we occupied valued competition and hierarchy, maintained in the schoolyard in social relations that mocked civility. By the fifth grade, working class children had found that the best salve for the indignity of

W. J. Urban, Leaders in the Historical Study of American Education, 7–19.

being at the bottom of the academic hierarchy was to beat up the kids in the clean clothes. A skinny child, I avoided participating directly in the sport, but took no little vicarious pleasure in silently applauding from a distance. We were all schooled well, though the lessons we took from that schooling were not those enshrined in the year's learning objectives.

Every day, in every grade, as regular as clockwork, we rose, placed our hands over our hearts, and pledged our allegiance to the flag, "with liberty and justice for all." Our allegiance having been pledged to the nation-state, as regular as clockwork we and our teachers studiously avoided asking awkward questions about the flag or about the nation for which it stood. We memorized the names of explorers and the dates by which various colonies were founded but were not encouraged to enquire about those who already inhabited the lands on which the colonies lay. Our books and lessons celebrated the Spanish-American War yet fell silent on the subsequent American half-century subjugation of the Philippines. Slavery found a discreet place in our lessons, though its racial character was acknowledged only by indirection; abolitionism did not merit even that. There was no labor movement worthy of the name, no imperialism, and if poverty had been a problem once upon a time, it made no appearance in our lessons on the contemporary world.

> **Personal Favorites**
>
> "'Outthinking and Outflanking the Owners of the World': A Historiography of the African American Struggle for Education," *History of Education Quarterly* 28 (Fall 1988): 333–66.
>
> Butchart, "Spielberg's Amistad: Film as History and the Trivializing of History Teaching," *Teaching History: A Journal of Methods* 24 (Fall 1999): 63–70.
>
> Butchart, "Edmonia G. and Caroline V. Highgate: Black Teachers, Freed Slaves, and the Betrayal of Black Hearts," in *Portraits of African American Life Since 1865*, Nina Mjagkij, ed. (Wilmington, DE: Scholarly Resources, Inc., 2003), 1–13.
>
> Butchart, "Remapping Racial Boundaries: Teachers as Border Police and Boundary Transgressors in Post-Emancipation Black Education, USA, 1861–1876," *Paedagogica Historica* 43 (February 2007): 61–78.

Our third-grade social studies textbook, *Our Neighbors*, asked us to memorize the major crops of our neighbor, Mexico. We ate tacos and learned *La Cucaracha* and the Mexican Hat Dance, then went to recess and taunted our neighbors, the sad, shy little brown children of Mexican migrant laborers, as dagos and wet-backs. No teacher ever intervened or made our unthinking cruelty the subject of a social studies lesson about community. And even in that far-off world of the Pacific Northwest, with a minuscule black population, no lesson, no book, no teacher breathed a word to us of the condition of our young black peers in Alabama or Georgia or Mississippi. For we had already pledged our allegiance; we knew there was liberty and justice for all; nothing more needed saying.

I did not succeed in my classrooms. No teacher expected me to. Most were probably not even aware I was there, except when they reprimanded me for filling the tedium by socializing. I was part of that half or more of every classroom that falls on the wrong side of the bell-curve. Most of us on that slippery slope eventually began to just go through the motions.

I succeeded elsewhere. Like most of my friends, I was an entrepreneur by the sixth grade. I caught herring in Yaquina Bay to sell to the crab fishermen for bait; I sold the *Oregon Journal* to the sailors on the tramp steamers loading lumber off the docks in Newport, Oregon, all of whom tipped extravagantly and whose pin-ups, studied furtively as I prowled the ships' corridors, provided the sex education the school was loath to provide; I walked a double paper route after school. Entrepreneurship paid well outside of school but carried no cachet inside the school, even as the textbooks praised the entrepreneurs of historical fame.

I was also part of that half or more of every classroom that wanted to learn by doing rather than by memorizing. We figured out on our own how to make the money we needed to buy better clothes than our parents could afford; we figured out together how to turn the indignity of classroom invisibility into badges of honor to wear in defiance of the school's hierarchy of rewards; we worked together to construct tree-houses of scavenged lumber; we taught ourselves how to start campfires despite that damp climate's sodden fuel. In our classrooms, we wanted desperately to figure out how to solve problems, how to work together to understand our world, and how to move with some measure of dignity toward adult life. But figuring things out together took time from important classroom tasks. Besides, the answers were already known; the task was to memorize the true and only answers. To work with others, in those classrooms, was "cheating;" knowing the teachers' and textbooks' answers was wisdom.

And so by junior high school the left-hand side of the bell-curve ignored the authorized explanations of the meaning of assigned poetry, though we spent hours consuming the callow poetry of early rock music, assigning our own meaning to lyric and beat. We avoided memorizing the correct definition of democracy and failed the week's quiz, never thinking to wonder why our small commonwealths were not laboratories in democracy.

In the summer of 1957, at fourteen years of age, I earned the special "agricultural permit" that allowed me to drive on the secondary roads around Tillamook, Oregon. I drove fifteen milk cans to the cheese factory every morning, milked cows morning and night, and bucked bales of Timothy hay onto farm wagons and into hay mows. My eighth grade teacher lectured us sternly on the evils of rock music and assured us that none of us would remember Elvis Presley within two years, the only memorable words in that year's parade of lifeless classrooms. On a clear October night in that year, though, a group of us lay in someone's back yard, watching as Sputnik, or more likely its much larger booster rocket following close behind, moved slowly across the night sky. And although we knew the words, "Cold War," nothing in our eight years of schooling gave us any means to understand that war, or the symbolic importance of Sputnik, or why we were being taught to hate our peers whose nation, and the flag it flew, had put that satellite into orbit over our land.

Sputnik proved pivotal to my relationship to schooling. Sputnik unleashed unprecedented federal spending to reconfigure the "manpower" crisis that followed the Second World War. Those using the language of "manpower" in the mid-1940s had spoken fearfully of the nation spiraling back into the Depression once military production ceased and troops returned expecting jobs. Within a very few years, however, the crisis was redefined as the need to recruit and train legions of workers to power the next industrial revolution, the revolution arising from rocketry, telemetry, the earliest computers, and electronics. The G.I. Bill had begun to address that crisis in the late 1940s; Sputnik extended the response in myriad new directions, one of which was the National Defense Education Act. NDEA fueled a sudden demand for vastly more science and math in the public schools, revolutionized the teaching of both disciplines, and blitzed students with the message that they should stay in school to defend America.

I felt the impact of NDEA personally. On the one hand, the emphasis on science teaching, and particularly the sudden availability of virtually free, high quality retraining for science teachers, drew my father into teaching high school chemistry, prompting a move from Tillamook, where, by 1957, not one in ten students went to college, to a small city in the Willamette valley where, by 1960, three out of four went to college. On the other hand, the sudden spotlight on moving an entire generation into higher education aspirations to defeat the Soviet Union and man the third industrial revolution changed schools overnight. The tracking system did not fully abandon its social-class base, but it shifted dramatically to recruit many of us from the working class into middle-class aspirations. Weak teachers did not disappear, but teaching improved, probably both because many teachers were paid to return to college for further training and because the media and government expressed great faith in teachers to solve the looming manpower problem. And students heard from guidance counselors, assembly speakers, teachers, and the nightly news that they were the future of the nation and education was the route to that future.

In my freshman year of high school in Tillamook, my guidance counselor, relying on prior grades, my IQ, and a raft of other "scientific" test scores, had enrolled me in wood shop, mechanical drawing, English I (affectionately referred to by our teachers as "bonehead" English), physical education, a dreadful "civics" course, and remedial math—the curricular fare for children such as I for the prior five decades or more. In McMinnville a mere year later, another guidance counselor, ignoring my prior grades, my IQ, my test scores, enrolled me in college preparatory classes in biology, English, geometry, and history, relenting to my anxious pleas only in regard to a second year of wood shop. I was in a daze for a good month, knowing that I had no capacity for the expected level of effort and no grounding in the prior knowledge needed to succeed, and realizing at the same time that a good third of the class was in exactly the same situation—they, too, had endured bonehead English, remedial math, and the wasted hours of not bothering to memorize trivia for a despotic civics teacher. Yet our teachers never doubted our capacity and did not fret over the vast chasms in our understanding. They simply assured us that we could all do well.

So we did. In my last two years of high school I abandoned the crutch of wood shop, taking Spanish in its place. Two years of college prep algebra were bracing but the discipline's linear logic was a joy to master. College prep English lured us away from linearity and toward interpretation and ambiguity. College prep US History, taught by the football coach despite his contempt for the subject, for teaching, and for any student who did not play for him, captured many of us despite his best efforts. College prep chemistry, we quickly discovered, was algebra practiced in a lab. Our teachers, save only the football coach, invited us to explore, to dance with ideas, to learn in whatever ways worked for us.

I entered high school not certain I would bother to graduate and less certain why I should. I left high school determined to go to college, though even with a pretty good record for my last two years, I did not have the overall grades to attend the University of Oregon or Oregon State where, in 1961, tuition was free. So, with $500 in my pocket, earned in a summer of twelve hour shifts in a plywood mill on the Oregon coast, and a promise from my parents of a dollar or two a month as their budget allowed, I headed back to Idaho to attend a small private college. Thanks to Sputnik, I intended to major in chemistry, physics, and math.

My $500 covered tuition, room and board for one semester, with a bit left over, but not enough to make it through the second semester. I conferred with the registrar, assuming that I needed to take a leave of absence. He was dismayed that I was leaving. "But I am out of money," I explained. "Well, we will give you a grant," he replied. I had no idea what a grant was, though I knew I did not want to take student loans, having learned in my hardscrabble neighborhoods to distrust banks. It was then that I learned that the effort to move people like me through college to become a warrior in the Cold War extended far beyond improved teaching and encouragement in high schools. It extended as well to federal money in the coffers of even small colleges in the backwaters of Idaho.

The college's core curriculum enraptured me. Here were ideas; here was art and music; here were words arranged in stunning, exciting ways; here were fellow travelers—the authors I read, two or three of the professors, and a small group of fellow students. Not so with my major, though it took three painful semesters before I could admit that. Intermediate calculus bored and perplexed me; its linearity was joyless. Physics was cold and lifeless in the hands of the brilliant but largely inarticulate man who taught it. Inorganic chemistry might have been bearable except that our professor spent every class period leaning against the blackboard and lecturing inaudibly to the side window; his lab sessions, which he never attended, were excruciating affairs in which we wrote up reports that explained what should have happened, though it seldom did.

After three semesters, frustrated with science and math and earning low grades in them, yet intrigued by my liberal arts curriculum, decision time had come. Despite grants, I was poor and in danger of becoming poorer—grants, after all, could not pay for clothes or dates, and my parents' occasional contribution (always accompanied with a paternal, "Buy razor blades") did not extend far, even in that day when a soda to split with a date cost ten cents. I had no idea what I wanted to do with my life, except that it would be anything other than science and math.

So I dropped out of school, moved to Seattle for a year of work at various low-paying jobs, and haunted book stores and coffee houses. When I was not changing tires at a Firestone store or installing built-in vacuum cleaners for what turned out to be a scam operation, I was reading hungrily, desperate to understand the world unfolding around me. It was, after all, the early years of US involvement in Viet Nam, the radicalizing years of the civil rights movement, the dawning years of the student movement, and the uncoiling years of assassinations and violence. Nothing in more than a baker's dozen years of formal schooling had given me a single tool to understand any of that, except the tool of literacy that I had largely wrested from school rather than received from school.

I returned to college in the nick of time, literally intercepting the registrar on his way to the campus post office to respond to my Draft Board's inquiry into my student status. I thereby avoided a free trip to the rice paddies of Southeast Asia to fight for a cause I had come to loath. I returned with but one goal: to finally force my formal schooling to answer the questions it had sedulously avoided for more than thirteen years. I ended up with a history major, more by default than by design—I leveraged more ways of understanding my world through history than most other disciplines—and added teacher training when I grudgingly agreed that I needed something that paid once I graduated.

Thus it was that I found myself, a second-year senior, listening incredulously as an education professor lectured the history of education from an uninspired textbook. The lectures and the text smacked of fiction. They spoke of an institution as foreign to my school experience as Cal Tech was to the medieval University of Paris. They told of a compassionate institution steeped in democratic values where rich and poor met on terms of equality to be taught by artful, selfless teachers. The story moved seamlessly from poorly equipped eighteenth century district schools that earnestly imparted republican values through better regulated and more broadly available nineteenth century common schools to expansive twentieth century progressive schools in which every child's gifts were developed to their fullest capacity, classrooms examined social problems collectively, children's mental and physical health was monitored and improved, and masses of splendidly educated graduates moved annually into the welcoming bosom of a happy and prosperous society.

The story made no sense given what I was seeing of the world in 1966, much less given the ten different schools I had attended in eight different towns and cities. Neither the world nor the nation was happy or prosperous, though prosperity reigned amidst squalor in both places. The many schools I attended were not "Nurseries of Democracy," the title of one chapter in our textbook; they were dictatorial regimes in which the will of the governed was never consulted nor its consent solicited. They were not sites of inquiry, examination, and the nurture of penetrating minds; they were stultifying institutions that disparaged intellectual hunger, rewarded shallow cleverness, and insisted that there was only one right answer, whether in math, social studies, or art. They amplified a few of the gifts of those gifted with wealthy parents but assumed that the rest of us, the parentally ungifted, were also ungifted in all other ways and would remain that way. We were assumed to have differential capacities and we were differentially educated; worse, we were educated to only a small fraction of even those starved capacities. Thus ended, inauspiciously, my first encounter with the history of education.

I took my first teaching position in a rural high school on the Idaho-Oregon border. To keep salaries (and thereby taxes) low, the school found it expedient never to extend a contract beyond the first year. Only the shop teacher, the librarian, and the principal had been in the school more than a year; they had taught the parents of most of my students. I established a debate squad that competed successfully that year and gained sufficient notice to allow me to move to a high school in Boise after my contract expired.

The students at both schools were nearly indistinguishable from the young people I grew up with—bright but convinced they were academic dullards; disrespectful because they were disrespected and because they saw little in adults worthy of respect; competent and resourceful in frustrating and turning aside all efforts to cow and train them; tough, articulate, and funny; and painfully, desperately eager to talk about their world, to ask why, to challenge themselves, each other, and their teachers, to express their individuality and their creativity. We posed questions together, and reposed the questions when answers began to coalesce. We dove into history, into debate, into music, into books, to find multiple answers to our questions. We staged plays that asked more questions than they answered, then took our plays to the entire school. We sought out kindred spirits in the faculty and enlarged the circle of learners. We met early and stayed late. We wrote, we fought, we laughed, we organized. Here, I thought, is what school should be: students and adults together mobilizing every corner of the curriculum to explore authentic questions that originate with those who will soon inherit the earth. I witnessed passionate study, eager learning, engaged debate from young people, many of whom had once given up on their early dreams of mastering the codes of learning.

But those two schools were not intended for mastery and passion. The first short-circuited any possibility of transcendence by disrupting all continuity of teachers from year to year. The administration of the second decided that passionate, engaged classrooms lacked proper discipline, that some questions—particularly those about patriotism, race, war, class, authority, and hypocrisy—had no place in the secondary curriculum, and that the first task of a teacher was to teach the iron law of order, not the fine art of questioning. When a colleague was fired for having a noisy classroom, I and others left with her. She was undoubtedly the finest educator I have met. In one semester, she turned three classes of "low-level" sophomore English students into communities of learners who wrote, read, talked, composed poetry, argued with and supported each other, and flourished. Her classroom pulsated with intellectual energy. Its noise was the noise of young minds deeply and happily at work. Its noise became the administration's pretext for attacks on her and on us. Nothing in my misbegotten history of education class had prepared me for the school, the bright, tough kids that inhabited it, or the administrators.

So I left public education. I had learned immensely from the courageous young people that surrounded me for three years and I left them with an aching regret that still stings. I had learned immensely as well from administrators, not one of whom was courageous. I left because of the latter. And I did what, by then, came most naturally for me: I went back to school because I had questions. I initially tried to turn my back on the most burning questions, thinking I would forget public education entirely and study Russian history. But I had not planned ahead to go to graduate school; the bloodbath that prompted my exit did not happen until mid-April of my third year of teaching. Deadlines for applications had long passed. Through the intercession of my undergraduate major professor, I was accepted as a master's degree student at Northern Arizona University. NAU had no Russian history program. I chose US social history by default.

The Fates are contrarians. I had taken a history of education course and was convinced that the history of education was irrelevant; I had taught and wanted nothing more to do with public education. So my assignment at NAU was to serve as the assistant to Dr. Philip Rulon, resident historian of education. Fine. I would serve him well, but I would not take his graduate course in the history of education. I took graduate seminars on the Truman Era, the history of science, urban history, the American West, and other social history courses instead.

History majors were required to take an interdisciplinary quantitative research methods course taught by a young sociologist. One assignment required reporting on a book in our discipline that relied upon quantitative methods. I asked the faculty for suggestions; Rulon mentioned a new book that he had not read but had heard about, Michael Katz, *Irony of Early School Reform*.[1] I found it in the library that afternoon, began reading, forgot dinner, and left the library at midnight, having read all of it. Suddenly light flooded across the history of education. It had not been consensus and the gratitude of the masses, after all; it had been conflict, struggle, pitched battles over meaning and means, schools as a tool of power and control.

Personal Favorites in the History of Education

James D. Anderson, *The Education of Blacks in the South, 1860–1935* (Chapel Hill: University of North Carolina Press, 1988).

Merle Curti, *The Social Ideas of American Educators* (Totowa NJ: Littlefield, Adams, 1959).

Herbert M. Kliebard, *Schooled to Work: Vocationalism and the American Curriculum, 1876–1946* (New York: Teachers College Press, Columbia University, 1999).

Margaret A. Nash, *Women's Education in the United States, 1780–1840* (New York: Palgrave Macmillan, 2005).

Simultaneously, in my spring semester I signed up for the first African American history course ever offered at NAU, taught by Richard Davies, not a scholar of black history, but a committed teacher who prepared himself well for his new assignment. And light poured into yet another dark corner of my schooled universe. Here was a stunning narrative. Nothing in twelve years of the nation's sanctified social studies curriculum had hinted at this narrative. Nothing in five years of undergraduate study as a history major had prefigured this narrative. Nothing in that first sad exposure to the history of education had prepared me to contemplate what this narrative implied for the history of education in America. Nothing in a lifetime of pious and patriotic sermons by my former faith's evangelical preachers even acknowledged the existence of these people, much less the complicity of evangelical Christianity in their brutalized narrative.

Stunned, reeling, and angry, I cast about for a topic for my seminar paper. Rulon suggested that little had been done on the education of the freed people since a single book published in the 1940s by southern historian Henry Lee Swint.[2] That paper, naive and simplistic, planted the seed for nearly four decades of work around a core set of historical questions touching on ideology, agency, intention, modality, context, race, gender, and meaning.

When I entered my graduate studies, I had no idea why I was doing so or where it would lead me. All that mattered initially was to gain great distance from the public school. Yet I found myself writing a master's thesis on schooling on the western frontier. Faculty members began telling me I should go on for a doctorate. Though lacking a clear goal, I applied to and was accepted at four universities. I settled on the State University of New York at Binghamton, in part because it had just assembled a covey of social historians, in part because it offered a good assistantship. No one there worked in the history of education and there was no school of education. Neither mattered to me. Strong social history did. I studied there with Richard Dalfiume, a Truman-era and early civil rights era historian; Sarah Diamond and Mary Ryan, brilliant women's historians; Melvin Dubofsky in labor history; Charles Forcey in Progressive era history; Norman Cantor in medieval history. Tom Africa, in ancient history, taught a required historiography course and assigned Arnold Toynbee's twelve-volume study of history for my seminar paper while my compatriots digested single volumes. I was one of the few in the seminar who already had a master's degree and the only one not trained at a top-flight eastern school; he thought it well to test the upstart westerner particularly keenly.

Despite education's invisibility in the department, I was drawn inexorably back to the schooling of the freed people for my dissertation. None of the faculty felt competent to judge work in the history of education; I assured them it was social and ideological history impinging on African American history, not what they took to be history of education—they would be burdened with neither arcane pedagogical arguments nor citations to historians with suspect pedigree. The dissertation explored the conflicting ideological stances of the various northern groups that supported early black education, then traced the effects of those stances on actual practices in the South.[3] Cut by two-thirds, it became my first book.[4] That study, along with work published almost simultaneously by other scholars, sharply revised the work of Swint and other southern historians. Where they had condemned the freedmen's teachers as meddling carpetbaggers bent on punishing the South for slavery and the Civil War, we held the teachers up as heroic, if flawed, working toward greater black freedom in the post-slavery South.

Thus, in yet another arena, my status as an historian of education had inauspicious beginnings, for my scholarly training involved only one historian of education, Phil Rulon, not well known among scholars in the field and responsible for only one year's work. Nor did I go from Binghamton to a major university to work alongside colleagues in the field. Instead, I went to SUNY College at Cortland, a liberal arts school with a normal school heritage. On the strength of my three years teaching experience and my dissertation, I joined the Education Department as its only historian and one of just four teaching the social foundations of education.

Cortland was a teaching school. Faculty taught four courses per semester. If one wanted funds to travel to conferences, he taught a fifth course, usually offered in Utica, ninety miles from the campus. I always taught five courses. Administrators were surprised when faculty engaged in research and writing; colleagues were caustic, since those who did publish monopolized the merit pay pool. I published and presented papers regularly, including, early on, a few pieces that drew from my earlier interest in the history of education in the American West, along with essays on teaching history.[5] A course I devised on historical research methods culminated in a text on research methods in the history of education.[6] My course on the history of African American education, however, served as my primary muse, inspiring several papers and articles, most importantly "'Outthinking and Outflanking the Owners of the World,'" an historiography of black education as of the mid-1980s.[7]

Meanwhile, my research in those years focused increasingly on a question I had posed almost off-handedly in a footnote in my first book: what might we learn about early southern black education if we looked much more closely at a large sample of the teachers who taught among the freed people? What might that also teach us about teachers and teaching more generally in the nineteenth century? I began compiling the names of every teacher that I could identify as having taught among the freed slaves and seeking as much information on each as I could locate. About the time I published the historiographic essay, I published the first article based on that research, a study of several hundred teachers from New York State who worked in the South.[8] The article was framed by one of the more striking findings to come out of the research: the freedmen's teachers were not primarily the relatively affluent young white women who had dominated the narrative since 1903 when W. E. B. Du Bois penned his poetic lines about the calico-clad New England schoolmarms who dared to teach recently freed slaves.[9] The New York contingent of teachers included, prominently, a remarkably large minority of black teachers. They were significantly overrepresented among the teachers—in 1860 only two percent of New York's population was black. That article revealed as well that while women made up most of the white New York teachers, black men and black women participated in the work equally and expressed a more focused, race-conscious goal for their work.

My work on the freed people's teachers began to raise other sorts of questions. In their letters, for example, the teachers frequently commented on issues of classroom discipline, occasionally accompanied with comments on the inadmissibility of corporal punishment in their schools, often because they thought corporal punishment particularly odious when employed against those whose enslavement had been enforced by the lash. To understand the context of such comments, I began to look for scholarly overviews of the history of classroom discipline. I found vaguely nostalgic tales of dunce caps and salutary correction with the paddle, along with occasional descriptions of classroom life in particular periods. I found nothing, however, that explained the historical ideas and processes that linked disciplinary practices across time. So I took time out from my search for teachers' lives to write a history of classroom discipline, one version of which found life as a presidential address to the American Educational Studies Association, another as the introductory chapter to a book that explored the problems of classroom discipline in American schools.[10]

The detour into the history of classroom practices coincided with a change in location and professional obligations. The University of Washington hired me as part of the founding faculty of its new Tacoma campus and director of a new education program. My small faculty and I had to create a graduate teacher education program, recruit students, write curriculum, teach three courses per quarter, and participate in all aspects of creating a new university. In that setting I did not even have the advantage of fellow social foundations scholars such as I had in Cortland. For seven years, institution-building was ascendant. Scholarship languished.

I had just returned to my work on the freed people's teachers during a sabbatical when the University of Georgia offered me a position. For the first time in my career, I was working in the South, the home of the subjects of most of my work. Though a department head, my research accelerated. A large Spencer Foundation grant allowed me to assemble a cadre of doctoral research assistants who, directed as much by my wife as by me, pushed the Freedmen's Teacher Project forward. My data-base of nearly seven thousand teachers swelled to well over eleven thousand while the amount of information on individual teachers trebled. I began to understand that I had to revise myself and my fellow revisionists from the 1980s. The binaries of bad teachers/good teachers, dangerous zealots/heroic champions, destroyer of salutary race relations/protectors against re-enslavement, that had dominated the historiography for a century did not work when we took account of the practices, classrooms, motivations, pedagogy, and profiles of thousands of teachers.

I provided a glimpse into the contours of that revision in my presidential address before the History of Education Society in 2001, arguing in "Mission Matters" that the ways the teachers spoke about their work, the missions they described, explained much about how they taught and the length of their commitments to black education. Many of the northern white teachers expressed a surprising lack of interest in the freed people and their intellectual and social needs at the dawn of emancipation. Rather, their concerns were self-referential. They sought to be of service and to reap the spiritual rewards of that service; who they might serve and toward what ends carried little weight.[11] Papers presented before the International Standing Conference for the History of Education, some subsequently published in *Paedagogica Historica*, extended my self-revision. They explored the meaning for black freedom of the diversity of teachers who entered their schools, the impact on black learners of the mass of southern white teachers, many wearing Confederate gray into those learners' classrooms, and the effect on black intellectual striving of the Reconstruction-era campaign of terror against black schools.[12]

The culmination of nearly four decades of work, beginning with that master's seminar paper in Arizona, has just been published. *Schooling the Freed People: Teaching, Learning, and the Struggle for Black Freedom, 1861–1876* seeks to correct the assumption in most histories that schools for the freed people were the selfless gift of northern white largess. Education was, rather, the firm, insistent demand of the freed people, as often delivered by black teachers as by white. It draws on the lives and actions of over 11,600 teachers to understand teachers' motivations and their consequences, teachers' dispositions and their effects, teachers' commitments and their messages to wary young minds. It examines pedagogy and curriculum to understand the goals teachers had for the freed people while remaining aware that learners can wrest from schools the tools to achieve goals of their own.[13]

My next project is already taking shape in my mind. Suffice it to say that, like all of my work, it will try to make sense of the contradiction between the limitless possibilities of education and the extraordinary mis-education of most of our children, past and present. I hope that the next project will not take four decades to complete, though that may be the price of inauspicious beginnings.

NOTES

1. Michael B. Katz, *The Irony of Early School Reform: Educational Innovation in Mid-Nineteenth Century Massachusetts* (Cambridge: Harvard University Press, 1968).
2. Henry Lee Swint, *Northern Teachers in the South, 1862–1870* (Nashville: Vanderbilt University Press, 1941).
3. Butchart, "Educating for Freedom: Northern Whites and the Origins of Black Education in the South, 1862–1875," PhD diss., SUNY Binghamton, 1976.
4. Butchart, *Northern Whites, Southern Blacks, and Reconstruction: Freedmen's Education, 1862–1875* (Westport, CT: Greenwood Press, 1980).
5. Butchart, "Education and Culture in the Trans-Mississippi West: An Interpretation," *Journal of American Culture* 3 (Summer 1980): 351–73.
6. Butchart, *Local Schools: Exploring Their History* (Nashville: American Association for State and Local History, 1986).
7. Butchart, "'Outthinking and Outflanking the Owners of the World': A Historiography of the African American Struggle for Education," *History of Education Quarterly* 28 (Fall 1988): 333–66. This essay has been reprinted in M. J. Shujaa, ed., *Too Much Schooling, Too Little Education: A Paradox of Black Life in White Societies* (Newark, N.J.: Africa World Press, 1994), 85–122; and in Roy Lowe, ed., *History of Education: Major Themes* (London: Routledge, 2000).
8. Butchart, "'We Best Can Instruct Our Own People': New York African Americans in the Freedmen's Schools, 1861–1875," *Afro-Americans in New York Life and History* 12 (January 1988): 27–49. This essay was reprinted in Donald G. Nieman, ed., *African-American Life in the Post-Emancipation South, 1861–1900* (Hamden, CT: Garland Publishing, 1998).
9. W. E. B. Du Bois, *The Souls of Black Folk* (1903; rpt. New York: Modern Library, 1996), 27.
10. Butchart, "Discipline, Dignity, and Democracy: Reflections on the History of Classroom Management," *Educational Studies* 26 (Fall 1995): 165–84; Butchart, "Punishments, Penalties, Prizes, and Procedures: A History of Discipline in U.S. Schools," in *Classroom Discipline in American Schools: Problems and Possibilities for Democratic Education*, Ronald E. Butchart and Barbara McEwan, eds. (Albany: State University of New York Press, 1998), 19–49.
11. Butchart, "Mission Matters: Mount Holyoke, Oberlin, and the Schooling of Southern Blacks, 1861–1917," *History of Education Quarterly* 42 (Spring 2002): 1–17.
12. Butchart and Amy F. Rolleri, "Secondary Education and Emancipation: Secondary Schools for Freed Slaves in the American South, 1862–1875," *Paedagogica Historica* 40, no. 1&2 (April 2004): 157–81; Butchart, "Remapping Racial Boundaries: Teachers as Border Police and Boundary

Transgressors in Post-Emancipation Black Education, USA, 1861–1876," *Paedagogica Historica* 43, no. 1 (February 2007): 61–78; and Butchart, "Black Hope, White Power: Emancipation, Reconstruction, and the Legacy of Unequal Schooling in the U.S. South, 1861–1880, *Paedagogica Historica* 46 (March 2010): 33–50.

13. Butchart, *Schooling the Freed People: Teaching, Learning, and the Struggle for Black Freedom, 1861–1876* (Chapel Hill: University of North Carolina Press, 2010).

GERALDINE JONÇICH CLIFFORD

SERENDIPITY, OR SO IT WOULD SEEM

and in Melodious Accents I
Will sit me down & Cry "I! I!"
William Blake, Public Addresses

While teaching third grade in San Lorenzo, California, had I not been bored with
the given approach to teaching spelling - still a "big ticket" item in the elementary
school curriculum in the 1950s - I would probably not have turned my bundle of
possibilities toward the history of education. No obvious signs pointed there: not in
1954 when I graduated from college, nor in 1958 when I enrolled in a doctoral
program. Yes, I had enjoyed and done well in history courses; but I had liked and
met the modest demands of virtually every subject leading to a high-school
diploma, teaching credential, and two college degrees. (High school chemistry was
the exception, a fact disguised on my transcript because Mr. Strauss gave me a "B"
in exchange for my promise not to take his physics class.) And, yes, as early as my
second year of teaching I had given idle thought to becoming a professor: perhaps
a teacher educator, in some distant future.

Hence there was no way of predicting that the incidental fact of devising my
own method of teaching spelling (including drawing the study words, not from the
state's lists but from my pupils' personal "composition dictionaries") would
prompt a casual decision to write a masters-level course paper on the history of
spelling instruction. This resulted in my professor's proposal to forward my name
as a fellowship candidate to an eastern institution about which I then knew little
and cared less.

Life-history as a literary form and schooling as a coordinated effort of the polity
pretty much grew up together during the 19th century. In the following memoir – too
narrowly focused to qualify as autobiography – I weave together ("entangle"?) some
inner and outer facts, and what Stuart Bates[1] thinks essential, the "reconsideration of
recollections," with issues in education and themes in history that successively
captivated me: matters I researched, wrote, taught, and came to care about. From
this life-and-historiography self-scrutiny the reader might better place my work in
the field that I stumbled into some six decades ago.

"A PEDRO KID"

In the autobiography of his youth, *A Walker in the City*, Alfred Kazin wrote,
"Every time I go back to Brownsville it is as if I had never been away."[2] Back in
my home town for the 60th reunion of the Class of '49 of San Pedro High School,

in a downtown shop window I spotted a tee shirt. It read "You can take the kid out of Pedro, but you can't take Pedro out of the kid." The motto fits better than the tee shirt, expressing both the leaving and inability-to-leave-behind the place and persons of ones initial "knowing self." Like other working-class immigrant communities, San Pedro – it was Peé-dro to locals, not the Spanish Pay-dro – would lose many of its kids to other places, jobs, and life styles. The 3,000 Japanese went first, forcibly interned in 1942, an action that also removed most of the schools' highest achievers; they never returned.

As for the rest, with each generation social mobility would draw away a progressively greater share of the offspring of the fisher-folk who settled this harbor town. During my growing-up years, immigrant fishermen together with the wives and daughters who canned the fish made San Pedro, California the nation's largest center of commercial fishing.

We used to joke, about both the town and its one public high school, that "There are the Slavs, the Italians, the Portuguese, and the Americans." The "Slavs" were largely from Dalmatia, an outpost of Austria-Hungary when my maternal grandfather left Europe in 1900, and part of the new Yugoslavia when my father emigrated in 1920. Our Italian-Americans, like most nationally, were from southern Italy and Sicily. The smaller number of Portuguese came slightly earlier, the first in the 1870s, chiefly from the Azores – proud that their countryman, Juan Cabrillo (Cabrilho) claimed the area, now southern California, for Spain in 1542. As for "The Americans," in our insular view they were merely the remainder: overwhelmingly white, blandly "non-ethnic" as far as we immigrant kids could tell, and adherents of vaguely suspect Protestant churches. It wasn't until I went to college in 1950, living in a campus dormitory with Jews from Beverly Hills and Fairfax High, that I realized that San Pedro's "Americans" had indeed included Jews whose dry goods and clothing stores we had patronized.

Needing a harbor and armed with promises, Los Angeles persuaded San Pedro's voters to accept annexation in 1909. The since-neglected town, twenty-five miles distant from the city's commercial, cultural, and political centers, lay outside the wide-ranging streetcar system when most of the families I knew lacked cars. San Pedro High (SPHS) was, however, within the Los Angeles Unified School District,

---

Favorites from My Own Work

"Scientists and the Schools of the 19th Century: The Case of American Physicists," *American Quarterly* 19 (Winter, 1966): 667–685.

The Sane Positivist: A Biography of Edward L. Thorndike (Middletown, CT.: Wesleyan University Press, 1968, 1984).

"Words for Schools: The Applications in Education of the Vocabulary Researches of Edward L. Thorndike," in Patrick Suppes (Ed.), *Impact of Research on Education: Some Case Studies* (Washington, D.C.: National Academy of Education, 1978), 107–198.

"Marry, Stitch, Die, or Do Worse: Educating Women for Work in America," in Harvey Kantor & David B. Tyack (Eds.), *Work, Youth, and Schooling: Historical Perspectives on Vocationalism in American Education* (Stanford, CA.: Stanford University Press, 1981), 223–268.

---

regarded as one of the nation's most progressive, well-run systems. But, like the town, it was also apart. Academic "extras" were missing – French, beginning Latin for those who'' ignored" it in junior high, advanced literature courses – as were such extracurricular amenities as a swimming pool or football bleachers. Given SPHS's rather undernourished curriculum and the entry-level jobs the port provided, it was unsurprisingly said of those students who did not drop out at sixteen, that the colleges got only two small clusters: the boys who went to USC (the private University of Southern California) to play football and the girls who went to UCLA (the Los Angeles campus of the state university) to become teachers.

It was not that UCLA had once been the Los Angeles State Normal School, but that some 60 percent of my generation of women college graduates nationally earned a teaching credential, and another 13 percent took education courses. I hadn't even aspired to teach although my mother was a student at the state normal school in Bellingham, Washington in the late 1920s, when my father took a train northward, looking for a woman who "spoke his language" and could mother his two young children. Aside from her parents' having emigrated from the same Adriatic island that he had left, and a mutual familiarity with hardship, my parents had little in common: in temperament, interests, education. She had been a model student, valedictorian of her high school class, played the piano and violin well, and seemed headed for a least a brief career in a respectable profession. My father had received almost no schooling on his scenic but hard-scrabble home island – unlike my maternal grandfather who had been taught by the resident monks as a prospect for the Church. What Dad did have was intelligence, charm, shrewdness, intense ambition, and a tolerance for risk-taking – eventually bringing him annual honors as "top skipper" in the tuna fleet, raising his family into prosperity, and enabling him to send his children to any college and sponsor similarly ambitious relatives left in now-Tito's Yugoslavia He understood the instrumental value of education represented by his accountant, banker, druggist, and doctor, the maritime attorney and custom-house officials he dealt with, the men-in-suits at the oil company and ship chandlery where he provisioned the two versions of the purse seiner he had built and named "The Pioneer."

My father pitied the three brothers who remained in Komiza, while emulating the older two "pioneers" who preceded him to San Pedro. My seven San Pedro cousins, their immigrant parents all unschooled, included four college graduates: a journalist (the only woman among them), a chemist, an engineer, and an architect. Cousin Mary did it on her own, her brothers and cousins with the help of the "G. I. Bill" and the tuition-free state university. In part by being later-born, my father's five children (from two marriages) earned even more degrees; each spent some time in college and the three graduates earned doctorates: two in the hard sciences and one in "ultra-soft" education. Because their influences converged, and they modeled a well-honed work ethic, I cannot confidently weigh the relative contribution of my mother's quiet, non-directive example and my assertive father's competitive drive. While my closest school friends (like my older half-sister and two female cousins) took the "commercial" course, I stuck with the college-prep track but left for UCLA directionless. Once there, however, I was quickly surrounded by the early-marriage, high fertility norms that American culture set before even college women in the postwar years: "coeds" were to get "pinned" in the freshman year, and engaged in the next. I fell far short, however: becoming a reluctant teacher, later a purposeful university professor – still unwed!

Favorites from My Own Work (continued)

"Eve: Redeemed by Education and Teaching School," essay review of Redding S. Sugg, Jr., "*Motherteacher: The Feminization of American Education;*" Elizabeth Green, "*Mary Lyon and Mount Holyoke;*" & Barbara J. Harris, "*Beyond Her Sphere; Women and the Professions in American History,*" *History of Education Quarterly,* 21 (Winter 1981): 479–491.

"Daughters Into Teachers: Educational and Demographic Influences On the Transformation of Teaching into 'Women's Work,'" *History of Education Review* [Australia-New Zealand], 12 (1983): 15–28.

"'Shaking Dangerous Questions from the Crease': Gender and American Higher Education," *Feminist Issues,* 3 (Fall 1983): 3–62.

Ed School: A Brief for Professional Education, with James Guthrie (Chicago: University of Chicago Press, 1988).

"The Historical Recovery of Edyth Astrid Ferris," *Educational Researcher,* 17 (May 1988): 4–7.

"*Equality in View*": *The University of California and the Schools* (Berkeley: Center for Studies in Higher Education, University of California, 1995).

The imprint of this early on my subsequent career as a historian of education is twofold, at least. Like those second and third generation scholars who contributed so richly to researching and writing immigration history, I "inherited" a latent attraction to the subject of immigrants and schools. In 1963, when I found an entry in Bess Thorndike's diary that her husband's bedtime reading was the new multi-volume report of the Dillingham Commission, *The Children of Immigrants in School,* the reference was familiar; I was already reading casually on the subject in the primary and secondary sources in history and sociology. Later I probed more deeply: exploring the Commission's and other studies on the remarkable (I thought) representation of immigrant-origin women in the teaching profession, by making "Americanization" a prominent theme in the graduate social foundations courses I taught, and building a freshman "American Cultures" course that compared the school experiences of Italian, Mexican, and Native American youth with those of "mainstream" Americans.

When, by the late 1960s I began running across assertions that public schools in the United States had not been the great engine of social mobility or the essential ingredient in realizing "The American Dream," I was skeptical, at least where the children of immigrants were concerned. The personally grounded part of Diane Ravitch's rebuttal of the "radical revisionist" group of educational historians resonated with me, despite the differences in our backgrounds – Ravitch raised in Houston, a Jew from an intellectually and culturally distinguished family, product of an expensive eastern women's college. We had each found our own public school experiences, and those of our "kith and kin," at odds with the pessimistic conclusions that, by the 1970s, swept across the historiographic landscape, enthralling our students and animating our professional meetings. Although I knew Sol Cohen, I was unaware of his theory: that Diane Ravitch was offering the public defense of the common school ideal that Larry Cremin – our common mentor– had declined to give.[3]

TO MORNINGSIDE HEIGHTS VIA MARACAIBO

Wilbur Dutton was the first university professor to whom I was more than a name on a "blue book. Around 1952, my college roommate agreed to represent UCLA's secondary-school student teachers at a weekend meeting of the California Teachers Association, and I was dragooned to represent the elementary school cohort. Dutton was the faculty sponsor, and we three went to Asilomar in his car; it was my first professional meeting in education. In 1956, after two years of teaching in northern California, I returned to UCLA to earn a master's degree in education, a promise made to my father in exchange for his not belaboring my decision to take my first teaching job five hundred miles from home. The one-year program was strictly prescribed, and included Dutton's course on the elementary school curriculum; for him I wrote the aforementioned essay on the pedagogical history of spelling. At one of his office hours Dutton mentioned another UCLA graduate, Walter H. MacGinitie, then holding the Macmillan Fellowship: a one-year, non-renewable grant to a doctoral candidate in language arts or the psychology of reading (Walter's specialty) at Teachers College, Columbia University. As Dutton thought I could handle either option, would I like to be recommended? Flattered, I agreed. Teachers College responded to him that it would be better not to select two UCLA products in succession, but I was encouraged to reapply. While I never did so, unknown to me the gears had been set in place.

An equally portentous event of that master's year was the required two-semester course in the history of education: taught as a prolonged memory exercise, using a narrow, school-based approach. I was not converted to the subject, but noted that Education faculty and students were still abuzz about the dynamic young New Yorker who had spent his summer vacation teaching Southern Californians the history of American education. His name was Lawrence Cremin; his text was "Butts and Cremin" (not the mimeographed syllabus used by the regular professor).[4] Cremin did not examine by multiple choice questions of fact (Where was Pestalozzi's first school?), but asked his students probing essay questions that would relate educational to other social and cultural institutions.

I did not file Cremin's name in memory, however, since my intention was to use teaching to explore the wider world. Two years of experience and a master's degree qualified me for the schools run by the U.S. military branches for children of servicemen stationed abroad. With job offers from the Army (plus Los Angeles and Santa Monica, my "safety nets"), I was waiting to hear from the Air Force when informed of a well-paid position in a private American school in Venezuela. My application to Escuela Bella Vista was accepted so quickly that it preempted other options. Able to read Spanish fluently, I was unknowingly positioning myself to learn a great deal about the diverse intersecting of education and politics – dramatic, clamorous, even revolutionary lessons: not insulated by the cotton-wool of my own culture, but living and working in a third-world nation that resented Yanqui pride, power, and proclivity to interfere in Latin American affairs.

The school where I taught in 1957–58 was part of the large (20,000?) American community drawn to Lake Maracaibo after Marcos Pérez Jiménez awarded oil leases to more foreign companies; there were, we heard, 10,000 operating wells on the "lake" during my time there. The Venezuelan parents whose children constituted 40 percent of enrollment at "the American school" did not think it the best school in the then small city of Maracaibo; that honor went to the Jesuits' (boys) school or perhaps the Shell ("British") School, run by the Shell Oil Company. Formerly owned and operated by Creole, a subsidiary of Standard Oil of New Jersey (later Exxon), Escuela Bella Vista's attraction to ambitious, "modern" locals was that it offered their sons a smoothed way into and through the petroleum engineering and related programs at the state universities of Oklahoma or Texas; with our "American school" naturally being coeducational, some of their sisters also enrolled.

These were my first mini-lessons in comparative and international education, quickly dwarfed by the fall-out from three events of far broader meaning. On September 23, 1957, days after our school year began, nine African American students entered Central High School in Little Rock, Arkansas, a result of the 1954 *Brown v. Board of Education* ruling on racial segregation in public education. The world watched as President Eisenhower sent an Airborne Battle Group from Kentucky to Little Rock and took control of the Arkansas National Guard from the segregationist governor, Orville Faubus; these troops provided escort and peace-keeping services throughout 1957–58, amidst battles in the courts and on the streets. Next, on October 4, 1957, headlines and television news added "Sputnik" to our vocabulary when the Soviet Union successfully launched the first satellite into orbit, throwing the United States into a crisis of "catch up" and recrimination. Immediately, and for months and years thereafter, America's schools and teachers – We! – absorbed much of the blame for this "Cold War disaster."

The third challenge to any remaining complacency began in Venezuela itself. Ten years after seizing power, General Pérez Jiménez decided to legitimate his presidency by holding a popular plebiscite at the end of 1957. For us the eventual upheaval began quietly when the national ministry of education directed that, with the country's other schools and universities, our two-week Christmas break would be extended throughout December. The school's oil-company contacts explained that, since revolutions in Latin America "begin in the universities" – ignited by university students' protests – the dictator's strategy was to disperse university students, disguising his motives as a generous gift to all students and their families: a month-long opportunity for recreation, time with family, travel to the country's beauty spots, etc. I was in Quito, Ecuador with four fellow teachers when, on January 1, 1958, the local newspapers reported a failed *coupe d 'e'tat* in Venezuela. We returned to Maracaibo the next day, living under martial law and then a gradually relaxed curfew after a nearly bloodless transfer of power in late January made democracy in Venezuela possible. As Americans the fact that the United

States offered Pérez Jiménez sanctuary added to our collective sense of unease, even humiliation.

During that teaching year in Venezuela I feasted on a rich diet of social, cultural, and political events in which education figured – but without the intellectual tools to grasp more than surface facts. Did I decide, therefore, to go immediately where I might acquire such tools? Not at all. Merely wishing a more temperate climate for teaching small children and craving new sights, I applied to Escuela Campo Alegre, the American (International) school in Caracas for the 1958–59 school year. Fate intervened when Teachers College officials tracked me to Maracaibo; I was called from a faculty meeting by a telegram offering me the Macmillan Fellowship for a fully-funded year of study. Postponing further travels in Latin American by a year in Manhattan sounded just fine. Excused from my commitment to Campo Alegre– "Come when you finish there; nothing they teach you will make you less valuable to us" – I accepted T.C.'s offer. I was utterly oblivious to the possibility that this momentous year's worth of formless questions about education and society might get some answers in New York: not the only answers, of course, nor perhaps the best. But, on reflection, I was about to begin the process of approaching my truer self: one more intrigued by question-making than answer-giving; one more likely to think of schooling as a complex of researchable "realities" rather than of solvable "problems."

"EUREKA" - A DIRECTION!

Favorites from Other Historians
Lawrence A. Cremin, *The Transformation of the Schools: Progressivism in American Education, 1876–1957* (New York: Knopf, 1961).
Larry Cuban, *How Teachers Taught: Constancy and Change in American Classrooms, 1890-1980* (New York: Longman, 1984).
Merle Curti, *The Social Ideas of American Educators* (New York: C. Scribner's Sons, 1935).
Nancy Hoffman, *Woman's "True Profession": Voices from the History of Teaching* (New York: McGraw-Hill, 1981).
Richard Hofstadter, *Anti-Intellectualism in American Life* (New York: Knopf, 1963).

"It's too late to get into Professor Cremin's seminar; it's already filled." These words, overheard from the next table in TC's cafeteria, ended my supper. Midway through my first semester I was already certain about two things. Despite the expectation of the fellowship committee, essentially Professor Emeritus Arthur Irving Gates (the royalties from his widely-adopted school readers funded the Macmillan Fellowship), I decided against any more work in language arts, my Fellowship specialty; I found these and other courses in the Curriculum and Teaching Department, as taught by the senior faculty, to be thick on "process" and thin on substance, grist for the mills of Arthur Bestor, Jacques Barzun, and Admiral Rickover. Lincoln Steffens' *Autobiography* (1931) has him entering the University of California with a set of examination questions to put to the faculty[5]; I was less confidently rebellious, merely electing to spend my final New York semester in the company of chosen professors: Elizabeth Hagan, whose newish book on testing with Robert Thorndike I had been assigned as a paid test-item writer during my UCLA master's program; Miriam Goldberg who taught a course on the gifted (whether gifted students deserved special attention was a popular issue); and Lawrence Cremin. The door to his spacious, book-laden office wide open, I approached the great man, asked for a place in his seminar, noted my UCLA connection, and answered his questions. Agreeing to give me one of the fifteen places, Cremin added that while he denied no student a seat in his large lecture class, those admitted to his seminars and colloquium were expected "to pull their own weight."

The seminar's exclusive topic during the 1959 spring term was the progressive education movement, the subject of his nearly completed next book.[6] Each student, mostly doctoral candidates in the several social foundations fields, was to become "the expert" on one of fifteen figures whom Cremin had identified. I drew Edward L. Thorndike, not one I would have chosen – and never regretted it. I had encountered Thorndike's name frequently but casually, starting with an undergraduate course in educational psychology, and used his *Children's Dictionary* in my teaching. My week came to chair the seminar and discuss Thorndike's career and a designated work, and I clearly recall commenting on the seeming contradiction of his atomistic theory of learning with a grandiose vision of a science of education, an article of faith that explicitly guided his wide-ranging investigations. This seminar presentation grew into my 1961 Ed.D. Dissertation: "Edward L. Thorndike and the Scientific Movement in Education, 1898–1918."[7]

After a seminar session where I casually noted my dissatisfaction with the worn-out progressivism I sensed at TC, Cremin asked to see me, "at your leisure." Lacking such, I nonetheless took this as a command, wondering if I might be one of those not pulling her own weight. Instead, he asked me to consider becoming his doctoral student. Then followed some self-questioning and consultation about whether I would be too young and inexperienced to pass myself off as a doctor of education. And how was I to pay for my post-fellowship studies? I wouldn't ask my father's help and a

Favorites from Other Historians (continued)
Polly Welts Kaufman, *Western Teachers on the Frontier* (New Haven: Yale University Press, 1984).
Leon Litwack, *North of Slavery: The Negro in the Free States, 1790-1860* (Chicago: University of Chicago Press, 1961).
Barbara Melosh: *"The Physician's Hand": Work, Culture, and Conflict in American Nursing* (Philadelphia: Temple University Press, 1982).
Jonathan Messerli, *Horace Mann: A Biography* (New York: Knopf, 1972).
George W. Pierson, "The M Factor in American History," *American Quarterly* 14, Supplement (Summer 1962): 275–82; "A Restless Temper," *American Historical Review*, 62 (July 1964): 969–89.
David B. Tyack, *The One Best System: A History of American Urban Education* (Cambridge: Harvard University Press, 1974.

teaching assistantship wouldn't suffice, but Arthur Gates generously reasserted his offer of a part-time research position at his Institute of Language Arts, despite my change of fields. During my two-years at the Institute I travelled around the metropolitan area giving the revised Gates-McKillop Reading Diagnostic Tests to individual children, then developed the norms and wrote the examiner's manual. Not directly relevant to my historical thesis, like my upbringing, teaching experiences, and life abroad, this too left its mark on large pieces of my subsequent career as a scholar, writer, and teacher.

ANOTHER IMPROBABILITY: BERKELEY

My having been a teacher helped bring an offer from one of New Jersey's former normal schools, but my youth and lack of college-teaching experience raised doubts at the other institutions that were advertising in 1961 for a historian of education or "social foundations person." I flunked my first interview, at the University of Wisconsin, for being "too academic." (I later ruefully wondered if any of the Madison folk were still around when Jim Guthrie and I, both former K-12 teachers, brought out *Ed School*, where we lambasted the leading education departments for distancing themselves from "the field.")[8] Meanwhile Larry Cremin finessed the experience issue by directing Sol Cohen to spend the upcoming summer working on his dissertation so I could teach Sol's history and social foundations classes at the University of Massachusetts. With that soon-to-be event on my resumé and Larry's nagging of TC's placement director, I was offered an acting assistant professorship at the new graduate school of education at the University of California at Santa Barbara, another former normal school; the school was deanless that year, hence the "acting" title attached to all new faculty "hires." My assignment included supervising two student teachers, two offerings of the required course in "School and Society" for future teachers (where I shone), and only one course in the history of education – the other taken over by the department's audio-visual instructor who, having lost his student helper, used his faculty seniority to "get my course." Looking ahead, I put myself back on the market. I was interviewed at UCLA – rejecting the position that later went to Sol Cohen – and got an offer from Berkeley, without interview, on the basis of Arthur Gates' recommendation to his former student, another reading expert, David H. Russell. My appointment would be in the Division of Elementary Education, and my principal teaching the required credential course, "The School and American Society"; this resulted in the only textbook I wrote, *The Shape of American Education* (1975), heavily dependent on Larry Cremin's formulation of the defining characteristics of American education: publicness, diversity, universality, and breadth.[9] I was also named one of three instructors (they weren't taking any chances!) of the required "Social Foundations" graduate course – with comparativist Joseph Fischer and sociologist Martin Trow; both became personal friends and Martin's work influenced my later teaching and writing in the history of higher education.

UCLA and Teachers College provided examples of women faculty, a number with tenure; Berkeley did not. In September 1962, I was the lone woman on a tenure ladder faculty of about 45, not counting (for they did not "count") an equal size group of supervisors of teacher education, some two-thirds of them women. I later learned that Education had not recommended anyone for tenure, except Arthur Jensen, since 1938, and had last promoted a woman to tenure in 1927. Would that information have mattered? Aroused any latent feminist instincts? "No" to both. My task seemed clear: to teach as well as I could while turning my inadequate dissertation into a solid biography of Edward Lee Thorndike. As a publishing scholar at Berkeley – "Berserkeley" soon became a fixture on the "Six O'Clock News" and a magnet, even to Education, for liberal and radical students from around the world – I simply assumed I would have a choice of offers when Berkeley's tenure clock ran out on me. It never did, thanks in some measure to a Guggenheim Fellowship, an award never before given to a woman in educational studies, with an unsolicited offer from Barnard College being "extra credit." So, by 1967 I neither expected, nor wanted, nor had to depart Berkeley; my colleagues and the campus had accepted my right to be and to remain. And I then married Bill Clifford, a political and labor movement activist and "history junkie."

Jack London, not the famous author but Berkeley's professor of adult education, asked more of me. A life-long feminist, he insisted that, as an academic woman in a misogynous institution, I was obliged to motivate and mentor our then small complement of women students. Unlike the fictional Janet Mandelbaum, a Harvard English professor in Amanda Cross's *Death in a Tenured Position*, I did not disavow any such interest or intention; neither did I seize the baton.[10] Through the 1970s, by inclination and invitation I still followed themes flowing from "Thorndike & Co.," especially psychology as pedagogy's "science" and the broader history of educational research. I focused on tracing influences on schooling precisely – in actions, not exhortations, and wrote several reviews faulting historians for conflating curricular and teaching realities with their rhetorical wrappings.

Biography-writing is the clearest link of my work, from first to last. Having neglected Thorndike-the-person in my dissertation, I plunged into the literature on biography as history and art, then on life-writing more generally, including the emerging collective biographies of marginalized groups. Intrigued by works like Oscar Handlin's *The Uprooted* and Bell Irvin Wiley's *The Plain People of the Confederacy*, I was leaving "great man" history for "history from the bottom up": seeking the presence, voices, and contributions to educational history of those (mostly) "blameless, not uneventful but quite unimportant lives," using author and critic Elizabeth Bowen's phrase.[11] I proposed this new research agenda for myself in the early '70s, and it became the theme of my presidential address to the History of Education Society: "Saints, Sinners, and People" – less a scold of the radical revisionists than the title implied.[12]

Teachers, mostly women, were "the little people" of the profession – schooling's "Anonymous Americans" to borrow Tamara Hareven's title. Researching and writing about women teachers and, by extension, the schooling of girls and women, drew me easily into all that went with it: reading feminist scholarship, joining a few Berkeley faculty women to promote Women's Studies from "program" to "major," accepting the suggestion of Maresi Nerad, one of those foreign students drawn to Berkeley, that I teach an experimental course, later cross-listed with Women's Studies, on women and higher education. Gender became a category of analysis in much that I taught and wrote through the next quarter century, helped enormously by the reference advice of a former student, Suzanne Hildenbrand. I accumulated massive personal-history sources for my post-retirement book project: "Those Good Gertrudes": The Woman Teacher in American History. But it was an essay, "Marry, Stitch, Die, or Do Worse,"[13] for a conference at Stanford commissioned by Lana Muraskin, another former student, and published in an edited volume in 1981, that brought forth from David Tyack something like these concluding words: " I think, Geraldine, you have now found your own voice."

NOTES

[1] E. Stuart Bates, *Inside Out: An Introduction to Autobiography* (Oxford: Basil Blackwell, 1936, 1937), Vol. 2, iv.
[2] Alfred Kazin, *A Walker in the City* (New York: Grove Press, 1958), 5.
[3] Diane Ravitch, *The Revisionists Revised: A Critique of the Radical Attack on the Schools* (New York: Basic Books, 1978).
[4] R. Freeman Butts and Lawrence A. Cremin, *A History of Education in American Culture* (New York: Holt, 1953).
[5] Lincoln Steffens, *The Autobiography of Lincoln Steffens* (New York: Harcourt, Brace, 1931).
[6] Lawrence A. Cremin, *The Transformation of the School: Progressivism in American Education, 1876-1957* (New York: Knopf, 1961).
[7] Published as Geraldine Jonçich, *The Sane Postivist: A Biography of Edward L. Thorndike* (Middletown, CT.: Wesleyan University Press, 1966).
[8] Geraldine J. Clifford and James W. Guthrie, *Ed School: A Brief for Professional Education* (Chicago: University of Chicago Press, 1988).
[9] Geraldine J. Clifford, *The Shape of American Education* (Englewood Cliffs, NJ: Prentice-Hall, 1975).
[10] Amanda Cross, [Columbia University Professor Carolyn Heilbrun], *Death in a Tenured Position* (New York: Dutton, 1981).
[11] Oscar Handlin, *The Uprooted: The Epic Story of the Great Migrations That Made the American People* (Boston: Little, Brown, 1951); Bell Irvin Wiley, *The Plain People of the Confederacy* (Baton Rouge: Louisiana State University Press, 1943); and Elizabeth, Bowen, "Autobiography As an Art," *Saturday Review of Literature*, 34 (March 17, 1951): 9–10.
[12] Geraldine J. Clifford, "Saints, Sinners, and People: A Position Paper on the Historiography of American Education," *History of Education Quarterly*, 15 (Fall 1975): 257–271.
[13] Geraldine J. Clifford, "Marry, Stitch, Die, or Do Worse," in Harvey Kantor & David B. Tyack (Eds.), *Work, Youth, and Schooling: Historical Perspectives on Vocationalism in American Education* (Stanford, CA.: Stanford University Press, 1981), 223–268.

SOL COHEN

MEMOIR

A Mosaic of Memory

Sam: "If I knew such things would never be,
I would have tried to remember better."

Barry Levenson, *Avalon*, Tri-Star Pictures, 1990

PART I.

It is afternoon in a condominium in Westwood, Los Angeles, CA, a few miles
south of UCLA, where I am writing this memoir. UCLA will be shuttered this
Holiday Season from Dec. 21-Jan. 4. Faculty and staff are on mandatory furlough.
I note these facts in the self-disclosure spirit of the memoir genre and to remind
readers that, as Michel De Certeau put it,[1] "historical writing is always embedded
in a particular time, a particular place, a particular institution, and 'rooted in a
particular situation.'" These are the environs in which this memoir is being written
– this time, this place, this institution, and in this particular situation.

One of the most important developments in the post-WWII discipline of history
is the growing acceptance of memoir and autobiography, what French historians
call *Ego-Histoire*,[2] as a reputable genre of historiography. Memoir is a fascinating
but most problematic, even treacherous genre. The blatant subjectivity of self-
narrative challenges our normal traditions of "objectivity" and is scary. Though I
vow to be as truthful as possible, skepticism should abound. What follows is part
autobiography, but mostly memoir. The memoir will be in the form of a mosaic,
made up of bits and pieces of a disorderly life stitched together to construct a
narrative to support the idea of what I used to be, or have become, or imagine what
I have become.

I was raised in the South Bronx, New York City, the son of an uneducated and
unskilled manual worker who immigrated to the United States from a village in
Poland during the early years of the Great Depression. I spent my entire youth in
the streets of the South Bronx; the street was my domain. School rarely interrupted
my street idyll. There were neighborhood public elementary schools and libraries,
and a decent public high school. But I was a "dropout" before the term had been
invented. Back then, books never captured my imagination, or attention. Our antipathy
through high school was mutual. I could have said, "I sit with Shakespeare and he
winces." But my mother made sure that I went to school clean, appropriately
dressed, and with a warning to behave, the three cardinal virtues teachers looked

W. J. Urban, Leaders in the Historical Study of American Education, 33–44.

for in their students in the old days. I was rewarded with "B's." I never planned for college, never even thought about college, and utterly clueless I was admitted to City College of New York (CCNY), as every high school student with a "B" scholastic average was, regardless of how dumb, unmotivated, or uneducated we were. I graduated with a BA, not the first educational miracle to occur at CCNY. Work (aside from waiting tables during the summer in Catskill Mountain resorts in Sullivan County, a few hundred miles north of NYC) didn't appeal to me, so to please my mother, who complained that I was becoming a "good for nothing," I enrolled in the MA program at Teachers College, Columbia University (TC). After a few pleasant years I earned my degree and teaching certificate, and became a high school social studies teacher. I subsequently moved to an apartment in Manhattan, near TC. My high school teaching degree from TC became my passport out of the Bronx. Mine is no epic saga, but an old story, the familiar American Jewish immigrant experience, except in my case, the rise through diligence not aptitude, from humble origins to the respectable middle class. For many like me, leaving the Bronx meant social advance and liberation, for others, a sense of dislocation and social alienation. Since I'm pretty much immune to confessional impulses, I will not linger on the biography part of this memoir.

However, before I allow myself to actually begin this memoir, I must confess to readers, both as a mark of my respect for their credulity, and as a way to innoculate the work against possible criticism, that my memory is notably suspect among those who know me best. I believe that readers will agree with me that the *sine qua non* of any "memoir" is at least a reliable memory. This being said, I have made provisions to guarantee some fidelity in my account. Before my office at UCLA was shuttered, I gathered as many documents: notes, letters, articles, announcements, brochures, papers, and so forth, as I could. Nevertheless, it is still up to my suspect memory to help me remember many of the events and persons I shall write about. Now I endeavor in earnest, and against all my limitations, to finally begin this memoir. But, one more caveat: however I describe these events and persons, let the reader beware it is just my description and not necessarily the case in question. But I seem to be getting ahead of myself. I've begun the memoir with my conclusion. So let me return to my introduction.

When I accepted the invitation to contribute to this volume, I vowed that if I were going to write a memoir I would tell the truth, the whole truth, and nothing but the truth. But I soon discovered how naïve this was. For some events I had more material than I could reasonably include in my narrative, and for others too little. Thus, in order to maintain the integrity of my tale, I had to select, omit, fudge or manipulate evidence, privilege one thing and downplay another, and decide whether to withhold or disclose "secrets," as historian Luise White points out in her provocative and fascinating "Telling More: Lies, Secrets, and History."[3] Inevitably, I had to resort to fictionalizing for the sake of the story, as poet and essayist Andrew Hudgins maintains we have to do, in his equally provocative and enlightening, "An Autobiographer's Lies."[4] What a paradox - to tell the truth we may have to conceal "secrets" and indulge in "lies" and utilize all the artifices of fiction at our disposal. How else but through fictional embellishment or invention could I give my muddled life some coherence, unity, intelligibility, meaning, and make myself a possibly interesting or stimulating, even omniscient character? (As one of my students, Pablo Torres, remarked - when we write ourselves into history, can we be faulted for being generous with ourselves?)

Part of the delight and excitement of writing this memoir is that I can bypass my pre-Hayden White years of innocence when I was in training to become a historian, and the discipline of history boasted that it approximated a science: document–based, factual, committed to objectivity, and intolerant of personal perspectives,[5] and shift my priorities to literary-based historiography. I gravitated towards Hayden White because he makes historical writing (and reading) so unique and fascinating. Now, writing this memoir, as another one of my students, Hugh Schuckman, reminds me, I can experience first-hand the opportunities as well as the traps and pitfalls offered by narration, emplotment, modes of representation, tropes and other rhetorical embellishments that White encouraged us to employ when he declared the historical profession in bad shape "because it has lost sight of its origin in the literary imagination." In the interest of appearing scientific and objective, history "has repressed and denied itself its own greatest source of strength. ... History belongs to the literary genre of narrative, understood in the Aristotelian sense of the emplotment of represented actions."[6] The historian's choice of emplotment, White insisted, "is essentially a literary, that is to say fiction-making operation."[7] My seminar on historiography agreed that White argues from a passionate commitment to history as a humane discipline. That what White hopes to achieve is not so much a complete redressing of the field of historiography, but to offer, as Jevdet Rexhepi, one of the students in the seminar explained, "an 'impetus toward refinement'" in terms of how we discuss and frame historiography and how we set about constructing our historical accounts.

PART II.

It would be tedious for me to write once more about Lawrence A. Cremin, progressive education and "the transformation of the school," or Cremin's three - volume, *American Education (1970–1988)*, or the "revisionist" or "theory" wars of the 1970's and early 1980's. However, in this memoir, the editor *will* expect it, readers *should* expect it, so I will have some fresh material about Professor Cremin ("Larry" to everyone who knew him). I assume most readers know that I was once Larry's TA. Readers may be interested to learn how I became his TA. So far as the "theory" wars of the 70's and 80's, they led to a far-reaching turn in my career and changed my life, as I will explain later.

While teaching high school, to keep myself out of trouble while living in Manhattan, I had begun taking a few courses at TC at night, including Larry's History of American Education course. Who should I meet in the class but Morris I. Berger (Mark), a smart kid from my old neighborhood, one of my Sunday night poker-playing buddies of whom I had lost track, and who was now indeed Larry's TA. Meeting Mark in Larry's class was strictly luck; as serendipitous as what happened next. Mark had just received an offer of a position as an Assistant

Professor of Education, to teach philosophy of education, at the State University of New York at Albany (SUNY-Albany), and the Dean wanted him up there immediately (Mark had just completed a dissertation on the history of the social settlement movement in New York City. But influenced by philosophers of education, Philip H. Phenix and James E. McClellan, both hired by TC in the mid -1950's to join Larry and senior professor, R. Freeman Butts, in Foundations of Education - Mark had dedicated himself to philosophy of education). Now Mark had to tell Larry he was leaving. I can imagine the conversation between Mark and Larry.

Mark: Larry, guess what? I was just offered a position as an Assistant Professor of Education at SUNY, Albany. They want me to begin right away.

Larry: It's only mid-semester. You're not going anywhere until you've read and graded my final exams and term papers (there would have been about 125 or so, of each).

Mark: Larry, Albany wants me right now.

Larry: OK. Get me someone to replace you and you can go.

Mark: Don't move, Larry. I'll be right back.

Mark ran to the large auditorium where Larry's class was being held, found me, and taking me by the arm, dragged me into Cremin's office, and announced "Here's your new TA, Larry. Sol Cohen." Cremin stared at me. I don't think he was very impressed, but he was not going to read exams or term papers. He had some Ph. D. candidates in the pipeline, but apparently none was interested in history of education. He was desperate for a TA. With a nod to Mark, and never asking for credentials or a resume, never asking anything about me, said "ok." That was my interview. Things were happening so fast; I was in a daze. I don't recall saying a word, only thinking, how did I get here? What am I doing here? Then Mark told me, "You'll have to quit high school teaching and enroll as Larry's Ph. D. student. I'll fill you in later." One day, Mark was gone and I was Professor Cremin's TA, no longer a high school social studies teacher but one of Larry's Ph.D. candidates in history of American education. That's just about the way it happened - the beginning of my new life as TA for Lawrence A. Cremin, soon to be the most celebrated faculty member at TC, and the foremost historian of American education of his time.

I spent three or four years as Larry's TA (I TA'd for his History of American Education and History of Education in Western Culture courses). I kept office hours, read and graded all term papers and final exams, carried his books to class, his coat and umbrella after class, and called the airport to tell them to change the path of planes while he was lecturing (this latter may be imaginary, or one of Mark's jokes, like my memory of resistance to being exploited - coming to the lecture hall early and writing on the board, "I rebel," and Larry coming into the room and saying "erase that," which I immediately did).[8] As a young man, Larry was possessed of movie-star good looks, always impeccably dressed, his Phi Beta Kappa key flashing on his vest, enormously self-confident, a spellbinding lecturer, and an easy grader - the Bell Shaped Curve, with a very soft curve. No one ever failed; no one ever complained. After class, it was my job to escort Larry to the 116th Street subway station, and keep his fans, the class "groupies," away from him.

Did I serve Larry well? Did Larry serve me well? These are difficult questions. I am reluctant to even try to give an answer. If I were to attempt an answer it would have to be along the lines of the cliche: "It was the best of times, it was the worst of times." Larry secured for me my first position at the University of Massachusetts, Amherst, where, while teaching "foundations of education," I sweated over my dissertation. As my dissertation advisor, Larry was a bitter disappointment. He was not inclined to bother with me or, perhaps he couldn't spare the time to bother with me. His attitude seemed to be either I could do the dissertation or not, he didn't care. But once I finished the dissertation--it absorbed four years of my life-- Larry had it published by Teachers College Press, and when I subsequently resigned at U. Mass., he secured my appointment at UCLA. But I was scarred by the dissertation experience and for years afterwards, I could not communicate with Larry at all.

I never got to know Larry personally or socially. I understand that better now. We were from different worlds. My patrimony was "new" immigrant, from the Bronx, no less, with all the linguistic, cultural, and social deficiencies the name, or epithet, "the Bronx" conjures up. Larry was born into the "old" highly cultured German-Jewish immigration, and enjoyed a privileged upbringing. I must have embarrassed him. We never enjoyed a meal together or lingered in his office before or after class to chat. And then, Larry was gone on leave frequently. His Bancroft Prize-winning, *The Transformation of the School: Progressivism in American Education, 1876–1957*, had come out in 1961 and he was in demand as a lecturer by seemingly all of education's professional organizations, or he was in demand as a lecturer or visiting professor at one or another other elite university. I did get to know his replacements, John S. Brubacher, and Martin S. Dworkin, pretty well. I TA'd for both when Larry was away, as well as for Professor Butts.

Professor Brubacher, a prolific textbook writer, had recently published, with Willis Rudy, *Higher Education in Transition: A History of American Colleges and Universities, 1636–1956*.[9] Brubacher was what my colleague, Carlos Torres, humorously calls a "travelling scholar." But aren't we all? A tall, courtly gentleman, Brubacher seemed to be retired from the University of Michigan, and was so easygoing and mellow–he gave the impression he was at TC on holiday. He required of our class in History of American Education a little reading and less writing, and during class simply talked about his new book. But after class, Brubacher was a delight. He'd take me to a bar on 120th Street for a few beers and amusing gossip about faculty he knew or had known (he seemed to know everybody who was anybody in higher education- he had taught at Yale, before he left for Michigan), although he stayed clear of gossiping about TC faculty, no matter how much I egged him on. That semester, I didn't learn much beyond what was in *Higher Education in Transition*, but I enjoyed Professor Brubacher's company and have fond memories of him. For the first time, I could recognize a professor as a real person.

That brings me to Martin Dworkin, a most unusual man. I might say that Martin gave me a compensatory education, supplying me with much needed quantities of intellectual etiquette, as well as linguistic and cultural capital of which I was painfully under-endowed and Martin had plenty to spare. Martin was also Bronx and CCNY, but he was a true student, soaking up knowledge at CCNY where he achieved his BA, then receiving his advanced education, though not a higher degree, taking courses in social sciences and the humanities at The New School for Social Research from some of the most brilliant emigres from Europe then teaching there.

Martin was also taking courses at TC in the mid- or late-1940's, ostensibly to prepare himself to become a doctoral candidate. But Martin was way beyond sitting in classes like a dutiful student writing papers and taking exams; he was already a published photographer, poet, and film critic. At TC, he met Larry, then a doctoral student working on his dissertation on the Common School. Martin, who was always in teaching mode, encouraged Larry and helped him formulate his thesis and write the dissertation. When Larry completed and published his dissertation, and joined the TC faculty in Foundations of Education in about 1949, he secured appointments for Martin to take over his courses when he was away on leave. That's how I became Martin's TA. I came with the courses. Larry had an encyclopedic mind, especially for history of education, but his learning seemed to be bounded in breadth and depth by the two textbooks-- *A History of Education in American Culture*, and *A Cultural History of Western Education*. My impression was that Larry was getting a crash course from Martin in the latest developments in the social sciences, the humanities, and mass communications and popular culture.

Martin was the first intellectual I had ever known. His poems, photographs, and film criticism were being published in such journals as *The New Republic*, *The New Leader*, and *The Progressive*.[10] And Martin was an extraordinary teacher. In the Cultural History of Western Education course, students were thoroughly immersed in the Classical Tradition anchored in ancient Greece. He thought the Greeks had discovered the secret of the good life - *paideia* - which Larry would later emphasize in his own lectures. In the History of American Education course, a few years before Larry (and Bernard Bailyn) borrowed the idea, Martin had already formulated a new way of thinking about education that went beyond schools and formal pedagogy to include film, newspapers, and radio. Indeed, Martin was teaching that all the agencies, institutions, and creations of culture and society educate.

Though Martin thought me an ignoramus, we spent quite a bit of time together. Especially after class, Martin gave me private tutoring, discussing the latest print, performance, and visual arts happenings in Manhattan--theater, concert, ballet, modern art, photography, books and literary criticism, and of course, film criticism, to which he devoted most of his time. Martin loved to walk. He would walk me home after class, (home was now a room in one of those huge apartments on 120th Street), still talking a blue streak. Some afternoons, he took me along to special screenings of movies. But Martin was difficult company: he was an intellectual bully and a bad listener, speaking to me as if he were pounding knowledge into my head. I always left his presence wiser in knowledge but feeling diminished in my confidence as a scholar, which is why, though I was out of my depth, floundering, I never could ask Martin to help me with my dissertation.

From time to time, when I was at U. Mass., and then later on when I moved to UCLA, I'd hear about Larry and Martin. Larry was on the expressway to the top. He became the Head of Foundations when Professor Butts retired, and was obviously in line to be the next President of TC, and I heard he had become President of TC in 1974 (1974–1984). I heard that Martin was teaching two courses he had developed; "Aesthetics in Education," and "Education, Ideology, and Mass Communications." I also heard that Martin had helped Larry organize TC's Institute of Philosophy and Politics of Education (1965). Many years later, in the mid-1990's, after Larry's death in 1990, when I was working on a memoir of Larry, I learned that Larry had, in 1978, abruptly ended Martin's appointment at TC. Larry's old friend, mentor, and colleague of thirty years, was left without a job, retirement benefits, or even so much as a letter of commendation.[11] What happened between Martin and Larry? What was Larry's tenure as President of TC like? Secrets. Some day, the veil of secrecy may be lifted on Martin's story, on what happened between Martin and Larry, as well as on Larry's tenure as President of TC by some of the former TC faculty or doctoral candidates who were privy to these events at the time.[12]

PART III

About the "revisionist" wars or "theory" wars of the 70's and early 80's of which no one inside the history of American education needs to be reminded, and no one outside of the history of American education probably cares, I will be brief, although they were, as I indicated above, a turning point in my career and in my life. By the late 70's and early 80's, I had become disgusted with the coarse antics of the "revisionists." I, and other historians of education in the U. S., agreed that Michael Katz's debunking of what Colin Greer called "the great school legend"-- free public schools, open and accessible to all, the shining example of American Exceptionalism--was a necessary supplement to Lawrence Cremin's reigning Heroic narrative of the rise of the public school. But the revisionists wouldn't relent. They wanted the discipline cleansed of anyone who still or had ever supported Larry's version of the rise of American public education, and made meetings of the History of Education Society (HES) and Division F (History and Historiography) of AERA, a hell. I served a term as President of HES while all this was going on, but I had already begun to slip away from HES, Division F, and the field of battle to concentrate on new currents in historiography and methods of historical research. If I made a clean break with HES, however, I had no idea where to go or who might be interested in my work or where it might lead. At this point, luck intervened again. Richard (Ritchie) Angelo, Professor of Education at the University of Kentucky, and sometime participant in HES and Div. F, entered my life. Now it was Ritchie who advised and taught me. Ritchie had already disengaged from the internecine quarrels over the history of the public schools and, under the influence, notably of Hayden White, had struck out on a new path. I followed him.

I first came across Ritchie in 1981 through an Essay Review he published in *History of Education Quarterly*. The books reviewed were eminently forgettable, but what Ritchie made of them, through a close reading *not* of the facts or the evidence or the argument adduced by the authors of the books at hand, but of *how* the books were written - of the language, metaphors, figures of speech, the apparatus of *writing* itself. Ritchie's way of reading, his, what my student, Schuckman, calls, the "excavation of discourse," was so original, so extraordinary, so remarkable, I had to write him. Subsequently, Ritchie sent me a half-dozen more of his papers and book reviews. It seemed to me, as a Soviet film director is reported to have remarked upon seeing Eisenstein's *Strike* (1925): "All that we've been doing up to now is baby stuff." Using, for the most part, White's literary approach to reading - the "excavation" of the stylistic and rhetorical aspects of the writing of the text, of which he was a master, Richard produced some of the most memorable papers, reviews, and essays I've ever read on education, and they beg to be expanded into a book.[13]

In the early 1980's, Richard and I were both having difficulty getting published in the *History of Education Quarterly* or even getting a paper past the guardians of Division F of AERA. My first efforts at cultural history, the literary turn, and postmodernism, were pathetic attempts at reading and writing like Richard Angelo, and were rejected. But that Division F's referees rejected Richard's work? That was unforgivable and I gave up on Division F and AERA. Ritchie also had some distinctive ideas about paper presentations with which I was wholly in accord. What Richard was interested in, advocated and practiced, was a "criticism of recognition" rather than the ordinary "criticism of rejection"; he was an advocate of the "open hand, not the fist."[14] When, in 1983, Richard suggested that we attend the Joint Conference of the recently organized Canadian History of Education Association (CHEA) and the American History of Education Society, to be held in Vancouver, British Columbia, I readily agreed.

I can still recall the exhilaration I felt at that meeting. I remember the CHEA officers and members - totally professional, yet so civil, so welcoming; my sense was that of a community getting together as friends as well as colleagues and scholars. Sessions had Chairs and sometimes "Chair / Commentators," but knives were sheathed. The camaraderie, the atmosphere at the sessions, was what Richard and I had hoped for: the open hand, not the fist. I had found a home. At the Vancouver meeting (CHEA meetings were shortly to become biennial meetings), papers on historiography were welcome. I did a paper on language and educational change titled "Language, Vocabulary, and Communities of Discourse: Reflections on Educational Innovation," at a session chaired by Charles Burgess, while Richard, at a different session, with Wayne Urban as Chair/Commentator, delivered "Ironies of the Romance and the Romance of Irony: Some Notes on Stylization in the History of Education since 1960," the paper which introduced many in the audience to the work of Hayden White.[15] My paper was incorporated some years later into a chapter in my *Challenging Orthodoxies*[16] as were some of the other papers I read at CHEA conferences in the late 80's and 90's. From 1983 to 1996, I attended and delivered papers at all the biennial meetings of CHEA. In fact, many of the papers I first delivered at CHEA conferences were subsequently published as research papers or book reviews, or as Review Essays in CHEA's new journal, *Historical Studies in Education/Revue d'Histoire de l'Education (HSE/RHE)*.[17]

Although Richard had reservations about making a commitment to CHEA, I joined CHEA, finally becoming a member of the international community of historians of education. I met and got to know, from the Canadian contingent-- J. Donald Wilson, William Bruneau, J. D. Purdy, Neil Sutherland, Ruby Heap, Diane Purvey, Alison Prentice, Paul Axelrod, Brian Titley. I also encountered many other international scholars at CHEA meetings, including Marc Depaepe and Frank Simon from Catholic University, Leuven, Belgium, co-editors of *Paedagogica Historica: International Journal of the History of Education,* who were later to mean so much to my career, as well as Roy Lowe, Manchester University, England, and Yuval Dror from Israel. I renewed acquaintances with colleagues and historians of education from the U.S. - William Reese, Wayne J. Urban, James M. Wallace, Richard Altenbaugh, Charles Burgess, and C.H. (Toby) Edson.

Though I hadn't thought about it as "networking," what an ugly term, that's what I was doing. In 2004, I was preparing to stand for Professor Step VI, officially the top of the tenure ladder at UCLA. The Department of Education at UCLA was then research-driven. Publication of research papers and essays in refereed and prestigious journals and letters of recommendation from internationally renowned scholars, not books - I had a book, *Challenging Orthodoxies* – counted heavily now. I didn't have a huge stack of articles, (or any large grants) but thanks to *HSE/RHE* and the *History of Education Quarterly,* where after a long hiatus I had been given an opportunity to publish again by Richard Altenbaugh and Robert Levin, I had a handful of solid research articles and Book Review Essays in my CV.[18] Now, Marc Depaepe and Frank Simon of *Paedagogica Historica*, intervened in my career. Both Marc and Frank attended all the biennial meetings of CHEA and I had gotten to know them and their work very well; they shared my interests in new developments in historiography. In 2005, I was invited to edit, in conjunction with Depaepe, an issue of *Paedagogica Historica* devoted to "History of Education in the Postmodern Era," which was widely noticed in England and Western Europe. Simon and Depaepe then secured an invitation for me to contribute to an issue on "The Writing of History" in the international journal, *Studies in Philosophy and Education,*[19] the only American historian of education so honored.[20] Consequently, when I came up for promotion, I was able to choose my referees, not only from acclaimed scholars in the U.S., but from internationally acclaimed scholars in Canada, the U. K., and Europe. The circle of friends, advisors, readers, and correspondents I could call upon made me confident of my promotion. The referee's praise-- UCLA faculty can see redacted copies-- was most embarrassing. My promotion to Step VI gave me the security and freedom I had never possessed before and confirmed for me that I was a major historian of education.

PART IV

That I have not published in the last few years is not due to "academic fatigue" (Professor Torres' term), but due to some surgery for which I am still in rehab. But my ailments will no longer stop me from writing when given the opportunity. In fact, just as I was writing this memoir, *HSE/RHE* invited me to review John E. Conklin's, *Campus Life in the Movies* (McFarland, 2009). Nor have the usual aches and pains stopped me from teaching.

What an exhilarating time to be a historian. One of the great joys of history is its ability to absorb new approaches. I have taken full advantage of the liberalization of historiography. My undergraduate course--dealing with the representation of high schools, teachers, and adolescence in American movies, emphasizes reading these films as "text" in history of American education, with Richard Angelo's paper on "Professing the History of Education after Textualism," as our guide. My graduate seminar, "Special Topics in Methods of Historical Research and Writing: Romantic Disorder," begins with Peter Novick, *That Noble Dream,* Ranke's seminar and document-based historical methodology, then moves on to a lengthy discussion of Hayden White. Then, emulating White, we analyze the "The Content of the Form" of several recent histories of American education, followed by Roger Chartier's "Four Questions for Hayden White."[21] Weekly seminars devoted to gender and history, film, photography, then biography, autobiography, and memoir, follow. In addition to Novick, White, and Chartier, students read, and write substantial critical pieces on Anne Firor Scott, Susan Sontag, Alan Trachtenberg, Bill Nichols, Robert Rosenstone and, of course, Hudgins.

PART V

I conclude this memoir for now. There are endless versions of a life and career and perhaps there will be other installments from time to time. So far as this tale, there are some lessons to be sure. We must acknowledge, as I observed when I began this memoir, that we are bound by certain practical limitations-- of time, place, and professional situation. Within these constraints I have disclosed as much of the truth (or of "secrets") about my life and career as I wanted at this time to share. In practicing our discipline, and trying to live up to its "noble dream," we are also bound by certain theoretical constraints. Our foundational terms such as truth, objectivity, and reality are contested. It seems clear that any effort at doing history today under the guise of scientific principles without considering issues of narrative, emplotment, tropes, invention, and other rhetorical embellishments and literary artifices, seems naïve or quaint. Indeed, literary invention can enhance reality and deepen the emotional truths of our histories more so than the literal truth. Finally, if history teaches us anything we must not rest assured with our current inclinations. Or rather, our own inclinations will be suspect at a future time, and thus we should endeavor to make them suspect in our present time, if only in principle. Hudgins writes, "autobiography is in some ways a translation of actuality onto the page and in other ways a selective and imaginative re-creation of it." Readers should keep in mind the provisional nature of our characterizations of events, agents, and agencies, a caution that especially resonates in the genre of memoir.

NOTES

[1] Michel De Certeau, *The Writing of History* (New York: Columbia University Press, 1992), 58

[2] Jeremy D. Popkin, "Historians on the Autobiographical Frontier," *American Historical Review* 104, (June 1999.)

[3] Luise White, "Telling More: Lies, Secrets, and History," *History and Theory* 39 (Dec. 2000).

[4] Andrew Hudgins, "An Autobiographer's Lies," *American Scholar* 65 (Autumn, 1996).

[5] Peter Novick, *That Noble Dream: the 'Objectivity Question' and the American Historical Profession*, Chicago: University of Chicago Press, 1988).

[6] Hayden White, *Tropics of Discourse: Essays in Cultural Criticism* (Baltimore: Johns Hopkins University Press, 1978), 99. And see White's *The Content of the Form: Narrative Discourse and Historical Representation* (Baltimore: Johns Hopkins University Press, 1987).

[7] White, *Tropics of Discourse*, 85. Responding to an e-mail inquiry from Schuckman, White generously replied: " During the sixties it occurred to me that historical writing had to be treated as writing first and foremost...This meant studying discourse theory. ...The rest, as they say, is history." Jan. 26, 2009.

[8] Larry finally hired Philip Eddy, one of his doctoral students in philosophy of education, to help me.

[9] John S. Brubacher and Willis Rudy, *Higher Education in Transition* (New York: Harper & Row, 1958).

[10] Dworkin's essays on film and education were original, far ahead of their time, and remain relevant. E.g., "Toward an Image Curriculum: Some Questions and Cautions," *Journal of Aesthetic Education* 4 (April 1970).

[11] Sol Cohen, "Lawrence A. Cremin: Hostage to History," *Historical Studies in Education / Revue d'Histoire de l'Education* 10 (Spring 1998).

[12] Martin Dworkin died on March 22, 1996, at the age of seventy-four. See Bernard J. Looks, *Failed Friendships: A Memoir of Martin S. Dworkin* (New York: Xlibris, 2005). Dr. Looks also published a volume of Martin's poems: *Unfinished Ruins* (New York: YBK Publishers, 2002).

[13] Richard Angelo, "Myth, Educational Theory, and the Figurative Imagination," *Philosophy of Education*, (1978 Yearbook, ed., Gary D. Fenstermacher); "The Freedom We Have in Mind," Review Article, Maxine Greene, *Landscapes of Learning, Educational Theory* 28 (Winter 1979); "A Sense of Occasion," Essay Review of R. Freeman Butts, *Public Education in the United States* and Geraldine Joncich Clifford, *The Shape of American Education, History of Education Quarterly* 21 (Fall, 1981); "Ironies of the Romance and the Romance with Irony; Some Notes on Stylization in the Historiography of American Education Since 1960," *Educational Theory*, 40 (Fall 1990); "Professing the History of Education After Textualism", unpublished paper delivered as a "Fireside Chat," AERA, Div. F, San Francisco, March, 1989; "Drugs, Sex, & Rock 'n Roll: Youth and Instruction in Contemporary Film," Delivered at the Annual Meeting of the Ohio Valley Philosophy of Education Society. Oct. 15, 1987. There are a handful more papers, but I couldn't locate them.

[14] Angelo to Cohen, August 30, 1984

[15] Angelo, "Ironies of the Romance and the Romance with Irony. . . ."

[16] Sol Cohen, *Challenging Orthodoxies: Toward a New Cultural History of Education* (NewYork: Peter Lang, 1999).

[17] "Traditions of American Education", *Historical Studies in Education / Revue d'histoire de l'education*, 12 (Spring and Fall 2000); "History, Memory, Community," Ibid. (Fall 2004).

[18] Sol Cohen, "An Innocent Eye: The 'Pictorial Turn, Film Studies, History," *History of Education Quarterly* 43 (Summer, 2003).

[19] Sol Cohen, "An Essay in the Aid of Writing History: Fictions of Historiography," *Studies in Philosophy and Education* 23 (Sep.-Nov. 2004).

[20] Thomas S. Popkewitz, Barry M. Franklin, and Miguel A. Pereyra, eds. *Cultural History and Education* (New York: Routledge, 2001) . The editors note: "Cohen's ideas have had more impact in Europe than in his home country." This is not news to me, of course. But it was the path I chose, for reasons discussed above.

[21] Roger Chartier, *On the Edge of the Cliff: History, Language, Practices* (Baltimore: Johns Hopkins University Press, 1997) and Novick, *That Noble Dream.*

LARRY CUBAN

TEACHER, SUPERINTENDENT, SCHOLAR

The Gift of Multiple Careers[1]

I am a teacher. Others might classify me as an "educator" since for nearly a half-century, I have also been a superintendent, a teacher educator, an associate dean, and an historian of education. But it is teaching—not administration or research—that has defined my adult life. Teaching has permitted me to be a lifelong learner, a persistent questioner, performer, writer, and friend to former students and colleagues.

In teaching, I have had moments when odd tingles ran up and down my back as students' thoughts and mine unexpectedly joined and became one; moments when listening to students forced me to rethink a prized idea after I had closed the door; moments when it became clear that my students had touched me deeply. These moments I treasure.

Less treasured moments are those that left me numb with the repetitiveness of teaching one high school class after another or the nagging truth that the voice I heard coming out of my mouth glazed students' eyes and caused their heads to droop onto desks. Other moments left me sad when I knew in my heart that I had failed to reach some students. There were times when bright students stopped coming to class and dropped out of school despite my visits and phone calls to their homes.

Teaching has also spilled over to the rest of my life. I look everywhere for lessons that can be taught and learned. I approach situations and think: How can I get my point across? What can I learn from this person? Over the years, my wife, daughters, and dear friends have had to endure the questions, pauses, the indirect and direct teaching style over dinner, pillow talk, and during vacations.

Moreover, teaching history and trying to understand the educational past has forged my core personal and professional values. Knowledge of the past has shown me that both constancy and change mark human affairs. Through an historian's eyes, the present has deep roots in the past. Thus, for nearly five decades, teaching in general and history in particular have been paramount in my life. Yet random chance has also played a crucial role in my becoming and staying a teacher.

The third son of Russian immigrants, I saw that my brothers who had to work during the Great Depression to provide family income and then serve the country in World War II lacked the chances that I had simply because I was born in the 1930s and they were born in the 1920s. Like many other sons of immigrants I clutched at the American Dream. Because sheer chance made me the third son, I was too young to serve in World War II and, as luck would have it, I had polio as a

W. J. Urban, Leaders in the Historical Study of American Education, 45–54.

child and was declared physically unfit to serve in the Korean War. Therefore, I finished college and became a teacher in the mid-1950s, first in the Pittsburgh area and then Cleveland's Eastside where I landed a job as a young white teacher of mostly black students.

In Cleveland, I was a politically and intellectually naïve 21 year-old teacher eager to push my unvarnished passion for teaching history onto urban students bored with traditional lectures and note taking. At Glenville High School, I invented new lessons and materials in what was then called Negro history. My success in engaging many (but not all) students in studying the past emboldened me to think that sharp, energetic teachers (yes, like me) creating and using can't-miss history lessons could solve the problem of disengaged black youth.

It was also at Glenville, not four undergraduate years at the University of Pittsburgh or, later at Case-Western Reserve University where I got my Masters in history, that I encountered someone who engaged me intellectually. Oliver Deex, Glenville's principal, a voracious reader and charming conversationalist, introduced me to books and magazines I had never seen: *Saturday Review of Literature*, *Harpers, Atlantic, Nation,* and dozens of others, which he often lent to me.

> **Works of Mine that I Favor:**
>
> *To Make a Difference: Teaching in the Inner City* (New York: The Free Press, 1970).
>
> *How Teachers Taught*, second edition (New York: Teachers College Press, 1993).
>
> *The Managerial Imperative and The Practice of Leadership in Schools* (Albany, NY: State University of New York, 1988).
>
> "Reform Again, Again, and Again," *Educational Researcher* 19 (January-February, 1990).
>
> *Tinkering toward Utopia* (with David Tyack) (Cambridge: Harvard University Press, 1995).
>
> *Oversold and Underused: Computers in the Classroom* (Cambridge: Harvard University Press, 2001).
>
> *How Can I Fix It: Finding Solutions and Managing Dilemmas* (New York: Teachers College Press, 2001.

Deex often invited to his home a small group of teachers committed to seeing Glenville students go to college. When we were in his wood-paneled library, a room that looked as if it were a movie set, he would urge me to take this or that book. At our rushed lunches in high school or in his office after school, we would talk about what I read. I have no idea why he took an interest in the intellectual development of a gangly, fresh-faced, determined but naïve novice, but his insistent questioning of my ideas and gentle guidance whetted my appetite for ideas and their application to daily life and to schools.

After teaching seven years at Glenville, I was nearly finished with a doctorate in American history at Case-Western Reserve and had already written chapters for a dissertation on Negro leadership in Cleveland. I had an offer in hand to teach U.S. history at a Connecticut college and another offer to stay in public schools. I was at a fork in my career and had to choose.

I took a one-year job in 1963 as a master teacher in history in a federally funded project located in Cardozo High School in Washington, D.C. to train returned Peace Corps volunteers to teach in ghetto schools, then euphemistically called "inner-city." It was a big risk to move my family for only a year to D.C. but I was eager (and, yes, ambitious) to join those idealists drawn to Washington in the Kennedy years who wanted to end urban school dropouts by transforming classrooms, using the community as a resource, and reach higher goals than improved test scores.

Federal policymakers in those Kennedy-Johnson years framed the problem of low-performing urban students dropping out of school as having too few skilled and knowledgeable teachers who could create engaging lessons. The pilot Cardozo Project in Urban Teaching was a teacher-driven, school-based, neighborhood-oriented solution to the problem of low-performing students. Master teachers in academic subjects trained recently returned Peace Corps volunteers to teach while drawing from community resources. Once trained, these ex-Peace Corps volunteers would become crackerjack teachers who could hook listless students through both creative lessons drawing from their knowledge of ghetto neighborhoods and personal relationships with students and their families.

A series of unexpected events (e.g., unstable annual funding for the project) forced me and the family to trek back to Cleveland each year to seek a regular teaching job and scratch out summer income as I gambled on the roulette game of whether or not federal dollars would be released to continue the program. As luck would have it, the Project got funded each year and I continued to teach at Cardozo High School and eventually directed the program.

Directing the project and coping with uncertain funding opened my eyes about how politically and bureaucratically complicated it is to engage students, raise academic achievement, and involve parents and residents in improving their schools. The intersection between a school, the students, community, and organizational bureaucracies became concrete to me and other teachers as we spent time with families, in Cardozo neighborhoods.

But it took four long years for me and other advocates to convince the D.C. superintendent and school board that this program for recruiting and training Peace Corps returnees was a decided benefit to a district that had to scramble every year to staff all of its classrooms. The superintendent and board finally agreed to take over the program in 1967 re-naming it the Urban Teacher Corps and expanding it from recruiting and training 50 new teachers a year to over a hundred annually.[2]

After this exhilarating but exhausting experience with a federally funded program, I returned to teaching history in another D.C. high school. I wrote a book about these experiences and created with co-author Phil Roden a series of U.S. History paperbacks for urban students.[3] After I taught at Roosevelt High School, the D.C. deputy superintendent invited me to head a new department aimed at revitalizing the entire District's teaching corps. I was now a reformer responsible for a system-wide program located in District headquarters from which I worked closely with the superintendent and school board members.

The school board and superintendent had defined the problem of poor schools and low-performing students as one where teachers' knowledge and skills were under-developed and needed bolstering. The organizational solution they adopted and one I convinced myself was worthwhile, was professional development for the entire D.C. staff. But school reform from the district office perch looked very different than from hands-on work in Cleveland classrooms, working at Cardozo High School with Peace Corps returnees, and teaching history in D.C. high schools.[4]

After two years in the downtown district office, I grew weary of seeing aggressive policies pushing system-wide changes get shot down time and again by headquarters' staff or get strangled by fierce racial politics. Fundamental changes had recently occurred in D.C governance with a newly elected mayor, city council, and school board leading to a take-no-prisoner brand of racial politics in which I was a bit player who grew tired of playing that game. I voluntarily returned to the classroom, "demoted without prejudice," my transfer notice read.

Here I was in my mid-30s, again a high school history teacher but no longer interested in college teaching. For nearly a decade, then, I had seen up close how the District of Columbia schools eagerly embraced reform after reform and proceeded to bury each one in bureaucratic channels or alter the policies so much as to become unrecognizable when they appeared at the classroom door. My experiences had convinced me that system-wide problems needed system-wide solutions unimpeded by racial politics and bureaucrats protecting their turf. Maybe, I thought, I might be able to supply those solutions as a superintendent. Was I now an older but still innocent and ambitious educator? Yes, I was.

To become an urban superintendent I had to get a Ph.D. So after returning to a university as a middle-aged graduate student with family in tow, I got a doctorate. Because I had a Masters in history from Case-Western Reserve and because I had scrounged a research grant while teaching high school to write about the D.C. reform effort to transform the central office, I sought out graduate fellowships that would concentrate on history of school reform. Here again, chance played a large part in what I ended up doing. I had applied to three graduate schools and two offered no financial aid. But through the efforts of David Tyack, Stanford University did.

The two years I spent at Stanford were powerful intellectual experiences for me. I had told David Tyack, my adviser then, (years later my teaching colleague, co-author, and dear friend) that I wanted to get the doctorate swiftly and find a superintendency.

With an abiding interest in history, I pursued courses that Tyack taught in the history of education but also studied political science, organizational sociology, and the economics of education. It was an intellectual feast for anyone interested in history of education and the social sciences. The work of Michael Katz, Joel Spring, Samuel Bowles, Herbert Gintis, Carl Kaestle, and David Tyack, some of it tinged by a version of neo-Marxism, other works advancing new theories of bureaucracy and organizational decision-making, had shaken mainstream historians of education. The early 1970s were exciting times for scholars of education.

If motivation and readiness are prerequisites for learning, I had them in excess. My experiences in Cleveland and D.C. public schools were rich but specific and non-theoretical. Moving from being a teacher to a researcher–for Stanford didn't train administrators, they prepared doctoral students to be researchers—I had to embrace analytical thinking over personal involvement, generalizations over particular facts. Through graduate work I discovered connections with the past, seeing theories at work in what I had done and, most important to me, coming to see the world of schooling, past and present, through political, sociological, economic, and organizational lenses. These analytic tools drove me to re-examine my teaching and administrative experiences. Informative lectures, long discussions with other students, close contact with a handful of professors, and working on a dissertation about three big city superintendents (Chicago, San Francisco, and Washington, D.C.) before and during their struggles over desegregation made the two years an intensely satisfying experience. I gained new insights and transitioned, uneasily to be sure, from a teacher to a researcher but without losing my footing in schools and classrooms.

David Tyack's patient and insightful prodding through well-aimed questions turned archival research and writing the dissertation into an intellectual high. I learned from Tyack to frame historical questions into puzzles to be solved, even (and sometimes, especially) if they ran counter to accepted interpretations of contemporaries and historians.

Organizational theorist Jim March opened up a world that meshed with my experiences. From March, I learned the importance of looking at organizations and their environments in multiple ways, of learning to live with uncertainty, of the tenacious hold that rationalism, not randomness, has upon both policymakers and practitioners, and of understanding that ambiguity and conflict are part of the natural terrain of organizational life.

So whenever I read about superintendents and principals who found their graduate preparation either insufferable or inadequate, I recall how different my experiences were. Those two years at Stanford turned out to be first-rate preparation for the next seven years I served as a superintendent.

After being turned down by 50 (not a typo) school boards, I lucked out when a reform-minded (and risk-taking) school board appointed me school chief in Arlington, Virginia, a city of around 160,000 population at that time, just across the Potomac from Washington, D.C. For seven years I worked within a district becoming culturally diverse and shrinking in enrollment as its test scores declined. The school board and I had defined the central problem as the public's loss of confidence in the district ever reversing the downward spiral in academic achievement as minority children increased. Fortunately, Arlington had a strong tax base to operate schools. Close superintendent oversight of each school's performance with measures assessing progress toward five basic school board goals (e.g., increased academic achievement, critical thinking skills, growth in the arts and humanities, and community involvement) was the objective. The board and I believed that steady pressure on school staffs wedded to ample support of teachers and principals, would lift achievement, reach the goals we set, and renew community confidence in its schools. State test results marched steadily upward, local metrics on other goals showed improvement, and parent surveys documented growing support for Arlington schools.

Within that big picture, however, school board and superintendent policy initiatives of closing small schools and launching innovations aimed at making incremental changes in both school practices and the culture of the system stirred up fierce political conflicts, particularly during two economic recessions. Heading a complicated organization with multiple stakeholders inside and outside the system stretched my skills and knowledge to a breaking point. During crises I learned the hard way about managing dilemmas and the political and organizational tradeoffs between prized district goals in negotiating those tradeoffs.

In 1980, a newly elected school board took office and was eager to reduce school spending. They wanted a school chief more in sync with their values than I was. I completed my contract in 1981 and departed for Stanford to teach graduate students and do research.

In those seven years as superintendent, I learned the difference between problems that can be solved and unsolvable dilemmas that have to be well managed. I found out that reforms needed jump-starting in a system but once initiated had to be prodded, elaborated, massaged, and adapted as they entered schools and were put into classroom practice. Yes, I did learn that problems of low achievement were intricately connected to what families and students brought with them to schools, what teachers did in their classrooms, how principals worked in their schools, and how boards and

> **Works that have Influenced my Thinking:**
>
> Seymour Sarason, *The Culture of the School and The Problem of Change* (Boston: Allyn and Bacon, 1971).
>
> Philip Jackson, *Life in Classrooms* (New York: Holt, Rinehart, and Winston, 1968).
>
> David Tyack, *One Best System* (Cambridge: Harvard University Press, 1974).
>
> Joseph Weizenbaum, *Computer Power and Human Reasoning: From Judgment to Calculation* (San Francisco: W.H. Freeman, 1976).
>
> Dan Lortie, *Schoolteacher* (Chicago: University of Chicago Press, 1975).
>
> Walter Powell and Paul DiMaggio (Eds.) *The New Institutionalism in Organizational Analysis* (Chicago: University of Chicago Press, 1991).
>
> Richard Neustadt and Ernest May, *Thinking in Time: The Uses of History for Decision Makers* (New York: The Free Press, 1986).

superintendents finessed (or fouled up) the intersecting political, social, and economic interests of various stakeholders inside and outside the schools. I learned how historical events combined with organizational and political factors to shape leaders' actions in wrestling with problems. Most of all, my years as superintendent made me allergic to those who offered me fairy tale solutions—kissing a frog to get a prince--to the problem of low-performing schools reaching multiple goals. I returned to academia fully aware of the world in which districts, schools, and classrooms operated.

I came to Stanford on a five-year contract as an associate professor fully intending to return to an urban superintendency. In 1985, I applied for a half-dozen posts and made the short list each time but was not selected school chief. It became clear that my plan to return to a superintendency wasn't working. When the

Stanford School of Education Dean asked me if I wished to seek tenure as a full professor (I had written three books in the five years I was on contract) I agreed to be reviewed since I would be shortly job-less. The University granted me tenure in 1986. Clearly, in my mind, I had wanted another shot at a superintendency and had failed. It was surely an accident that I ended up a tenured professor, a piece of luck that I have had no regrets over.

As a university professor since 1981 I have sought through my teaching, research, and writing to improve schooling through historical studies aimed at policymakers, administrators, and practitioners. I have been deeply interested in the nexus between policy and practice and how reformers, eager to alter what teachers do daily, have often gone astray and unknowingly repeated the errors earlier generations of school reformers had made in disrespecting teaching and teachers.

I returned to Stanford as a veteran practitioner who had framed and re-framed the problems of disengaged students, tired teachers, and lousy academic achievement. In seeking solutions, I had looked, at first, to classroom, then, school, and finally system-wide solutions without ever losing sight of the importance of the teacher. I wanted deep changes in a district and a community but saw that byte-sized increments over time were necessary to achieve gigabyte reforms both inside and outside schools. This chastened, far more humble, reformer also learned that hoopla-driven innovations, particularly those applicable to schools and classrooms--were highly contingent on savvy leadership, luck, and certain conditions being in place including adequate funding. When these conditions were absent, a reform had a short, happy life and, poof, disappeared.

In the two decades I spent at Stanford thinking, teaching, and writing about school reform, I now had the precious time to pursue policy and practice questions that I could not as a high school teacher and superintendent. Why, for example, did the high school classrooms in which I sat in the late-1940s seem so similar to the ones I observed in the 1980s as a superintendent? Why do some reforms stick and others disappear like bird-tracks in sand? Why so much drama about new technologies in classrooms and so few teachers using the equipment? Why is it so hard to fundamentally change schools with large numbers of poor children? Why do schools focus on test scores rather than other, larger civic and social goals? These, and many more policy-driven questions, often requiring me to examine the past, were anchored in decades of classroom and administrative experiences.

In returning to Stanford after being superintendent, I easily resumed the connection I had forged with David Tyack when I was a student years earlier. Then it was an advisor/advisee relationship, but with my return to Stanford, it blossomed into an enduring collegiality and strong friendship.

Because of Tyack's extensive knowledge of the Bay area and his love of the outdoors, we started biking together including day and week-long trips. We shared doctoral students, worked on committees together, and team-taught (for ten of those years) a history of school reform course. In that course, we covered three intense periods of school reform in the 1890s–1920s, the 1960s, and between the early 1980s and late 1990s.

We worked well together on both the personal and professional levels. He delved into the history of past policies designed to alter institutions and worked through their anticipated and unanticipated consequences. While I pursued a similar strategy, I was also keenly interested in tracing the varied histories of contemporary policies aimed at influencing classroom practice. So our intellectual interests converged when we taught the course. It was also in that course that the ideas in *Tinkering toward Utopia* were developed, tried out on graduate students, refined, and eventually mapped out.[5]

The intellectual give-and-take between two historians of education who are excited about a subject, teach it together, and want to collaborate on a book is a fascinating process. Here is what I remember of how we conceptualized the book between 1989 and 1991.

Shortly after we developed the graduate course, we received a Spencer Foundation grant to do a history of school reform. By 1991, we had prepared a rough outline of the book and had divided up the chapters according to the research we had done and wanted to do on this book.

During this time Tyack and I had resumed our bike rides. We would drive to the base of Kings Mountain Road, park the car, and bike up 5.5 miles to Skyline Drive. Usually, it would take us an hour and a half, including water breaks, to do the climbing and about a half-hour for the descent to the parking lot and car.

During those 90-odd minutes of climbing Kings Mountain we talked through particular chapters, mentioning sources to use, and noting the perspectives of other historians of education. As we climbed to Skyline, there was much heavy breathing, numerous water breaks, and numerous occasions to talk as we pedaled upward. The ride down was fast but we continued to talk as we rode down the mountain with brakes squealing.

On the way home, in the car we would continue the discussions of different points in a chapter, particularly sources that each of us should look into. After I would get home, I would type up a draft memo of the key ideas we had discussed, what views we had expressed, sources we mentioned, and any interpretations that had molded the give-and-take during the bike ride. I sent the memo to Tyack and within a day, he would add to, amend, and occasionally delete points in the memo and then I would type up the final copy of the memo that would become a guide to each of us working on a chapter draft. We mapped out the entire book in this manner.

It was a genuinely exciting experience to have these conversations about issues in school reform while we were also jointly teaching the course. Generally, we knew where our interpretive history of school reform would fall in the world of education historians. We had depicted Americans' faith in education as an ill-fated panacea to unrelenting national difficulties. We documented the perennial practice of policymakers "educationalizing" economic, social, demographic, and political problems, that is, delegating to schools the task of solving serious issues. We pointed out endless cycles of crisis, utopian demands, and subsequent disillusionment. By examining historically the intersections between policy and practice and the impact of organizational and political factors on both, we had carved out a centrist niche between those historians of education on the political right and left. Harvard University Press published *Tinkering toward Utopia* in 1995. Since then, Tyack and I have diverged in our writings but we have continued to read each other's drafts before publication.

After 1995, much of my writing has been on the nexus between policy and classroom practice, often including an historical background to the particular policy issue I was investigating. In *Why It is So Hard To Get Good Schools* (2001), *Oversold and Underused* (2001), *Powerful Reforms with Shallow Roots* (2003), and *The Blackboard and the Bottom Line* (2004), historical context surrounded policy issues revealing again and again both change and continuity over time and their connection to classroom practice.[6] In *Partners in Literacy* (2007) Sondra Cuban and I wrote about the historical and contemporary use of technology in public schools and libraries in cultivating literacy.[7]

A recent study I completed examined Austin Independent School District (AISD) over the past half-century as it struggled with the continuing legacy of a once-segregated city in its low-income, minority schools. *As Good As It Gets: What School Reform Brought To Austin* (2010),[8] like many of my studies, puts the decade-long tenure of AISD's Pat Forgione in its historical context showing the many positive changes that have occurred in the district and the continuing issues of poverty and race in chronically low-performing schools.

I close this intellectual autobiography of a teacher who moved in and out of teaching and administration, on a zigzag trajectory ending in becoming an accidental scholar/practitioner. I have been and remain deeply committed to teaching and writing policy history in order to understand better how and why school reform policies, past and present, seldom achieve their intended outcomes in altering classroom practices and reaching the goals of ever-higher standards of literacy, civic engagement, career preparation, and moral growth. A touch of idealism perhaps even innocence still rattles my bones since I believe that better crafted policies, respect for teachers' expertise, stronger community partnerships and, yes, even a little bit of luck, will improve student learning toward these ends in urban, suburban, and rural schools.

NOTES

[1] I thank Sondra Cuban, Janice Cuban, and Lillian Miller for their helpful comments on an earlier draft of this intellectual autobiography. Of course, any slips and errors are my responsibility.

[2] In 1966, the U.S. Congress had authorized the National Teachers Corps, based on the model we created at the Cardozo High School. I served on the Advisory Board for the National Teacher Corps. In 1981, President Ronald Reagan ended federal funding for the Teacher Corps. There is a similar punch line to the story of the Urban Teacher Corps in the District of Columbia. In 1971, after four years of recruiting and training teachers in this school-based program, a new superintendent abolished the program.

[3] Larry Cuban, *To Make a Difference: Teaching in the Inner City*, 1970 (New York: The Free Press, 1970); Larry Cuban and Phil Roden (eds.) *The Promise of America*, volumes 1–5 (Glenview, IL: Scott Foresman, 1971, second edition, 1975).

[4] I described and analyzed these District of Columbia experiences, particularly in the Cardozo Project in Urban Teaching in *To Make A Difference: Teaching in Inner City Schools*. Those experiences at Cardozo High School, in the District of Columbia bureaucracy, and as superintendent in Arlington are also described in Larry Cuban, *The Managerial Imperative: The Practice of Leadership* (Albany, NY: State University of New York Press, 1988).

[5] David Tyack and Larry Cuban, *Tinkering toward Utopia; A Century of Public School Reform* (Cambridge: Harvard University Press, 1995).

[6] *Why It is So Hard To Get Good Schools* (Cambridge: Harvard University Press, 2001), *Oversold and Underused* (New York: Teachers College Press, 2001), *Powerful Reforms with Shallow Roots* (ed. with Michael Usdan) (New York: Teachers College Press, 2003), and *The Blackboard and the Bottom Line* (Cambridge: Harvard University Press, 2004)

[7] Sondra Cuban and Larry Cuban, *Partners in Literacy: Schools and Libraries Building Communities through Technology* (New York: Teachers College Press, 2007).

[8] Larry Cuban, *As Good As It Gets: What Reform Brought to Austin* (Cambridge: Harvard University Press, 2010).

WILLIAM W. CUTLER, III

ONE OFFICE, OR TWO? MY DOUBLE LIFE AS A HISTORIAN OF EDUCATION

On October 4, 1957 the Soviet Union launched a satellite into earth orbit, a scientific and political achievement that soon led to less disruption above than below. An eleventh grader at the time, I was studying American history with a teacher who had the presence of mind to forgo whatever lesson he had planned for October 5th in favor of a spontaneous discussion of this historic event. I don't remember what was said, but the consequences of that launch would turn out to be far greater for me than I knew then. As life course analysis convincingly shows, demography, culture, and history interact to shape individual lives. Had I been born five years before or five years after 1941, Sputnik's impact on me would have been far different because I would have graduated from college just as its significance was beginning to be felt, or so long after that other events would have overshadowed it.

As a freshman at Harvard College in 1959, I enrolled in a brace of science courses for pre-med students. Having similar aspirations, my roommate and I took them together. He ended up becoming an anesthesiologist, but as the grades on my transcript made abundantly clear, my interests and talents lay elsewhere. Lecture courses with Bernard Bailyn, Frank Freidel, William L. Langer, and a junior tutorial with then graduate student Gordon S. Wood gave me a hint. Written under Wood's direction, my senior thesis on the Massachusetts Governor's Council from 1765 to 1774 convinced me that I liked doing historical research and taught me that I could do it well. But even as late as the first semester of my senior year I was still undecided about my future. A private meeting with Professor Bailyn did not help. Seated at the far end of his enormous office in Widener Library, he did nothing to build my confidence or dispel my doubts. Discouraged, I decided to apply for a master's degree in secondary education. American military involvement in Vietnam was just beginning, so being drafted was not something that I was particularly worried about. Instead, I was focused on buying some time until I could figure out what I wanted to do with my life.

At this point "history" intervened because one of the four universities to which I applied for a master's degree in education made me an offer I could not refuse -- a National Defense Education Act Fellowship. It came with full tuition remission for three years and an annual stipend that started at $2200. The School of Education at Cornell University had four of these fellowships to award, one of which could be mine if I would accept admission to its doctoral program in the Foundations of Education. At the time, I knew very little about the federal law that had been enacted five years before in direct response to the Sputnik launch. What's more, I

W. J. Urban, Leaders in the Historical Study of American Education, 55–67.

knew nothing at all about the field for which I was being offered this attractive fellowship. Perhaps this is not surprising. Several years later, one of my secondary school teachers asked me what "Foundations" was; he had never heard of it. Having completed my PhD by then, I could tell him that it was an interdisciplinary field in the philosophy and history of education that mainly served undergraduate programs in teacher education. To this day I am not sure whether he understood because he was not certified to teach in the Massachusetts public schools. He had learned his craft on the job at a private school that hired teachers with bachelor's degrees in the liberal arts.

Selected Personal Publications
Parents and Schools: The 150-Year Struggle for Control in American Education (Chicago: University of Chicago Press, 2000).
The Divided Metropolis: Social and Spatial Dimensions of Philadelphia, 1800-1975, co-edited with Howard Gillette, Jr. (Westport,CT: Greenwood Press, 1980).
"Oral History: Its Nature and Uses for Educational History," *History of Education Quarterly* 11 (Summer 1971: 184-194.
"Status, Values and the Education of the Poor: The Trustees of the New York Public School Society, 1805-1853," *American Quarterly*, XXIV (March 1972): 69-85.

In the mid 1960s philosophers were the leading lights in Foundations of Education. Scholars like Theodore Brameld and B. Othanel Smith predominated. However, some historians had begun to distinguish themselves in the field by then, led by R. Freeman Butts and his student at Teachers College, Lawrence Arthur Cremin, whose pioneering study of progressive education won the presti gious Bancroft Prize in 1962.[1] At Cornell, philosophers D. Bob Gowin and Robert Ennis ran the Foundations Department with the help of historian Frederick H. Stutz, who devoted most of his time to being dean of the university's School of Education. Gowin and Ennis encouraged me to become a philosopher, but they acquiesced when I made it clear that if Foundations was to be my field, history would be my discipline. Encouraged to work with faculty in the History Department, I registered for some of its graduate classes. Former president of the Organization of American Historians Paul Wallace Gates accepted me into his research seminar, treating me like one of his own graduate students. I took two courses with intellectual historian David Brion Davis who could not have been more aloof. But I did not hesitate when I was asked to be one of his teaching assistants for a large undergraduate lecture course in which he needed some extra help. Davis gave me the chance to speak to this class on the history of progressive education, and my confidence received a boost when I discovered that I could command a large lecture room. The director of the Cornell Oral History Program, Gould P. Colman, introduced me to this research methodology at a time when it was relatively new. Under his direction, I conducted two sets of oral history interviews, one on the politics of public education in Ithaca in the 1950s and the other on the history of progressive education. I did the latter with Katharine Ann Taylor, who served for many years as the headmistress of Boston's elite Shady Hill School. Encouraged by the editor of the *History of Education Quarterly*, Henry

Perkinson, I published there for the first time (1971) on oral history in the history of education.[2]

The topic that I chose for my dissertation at Cornell turned out to be both a blessing and a curse. A study of the New York Public School Society, it plunged me into the history of urban public schools, an important topic that I have since then often pursued. Two other graduate students were working on similar projects at the time, one under Cremin at Teachers College and the other, Carl Kaestle, under Bailyn at Harvard.[3] Harvard University Press published Kaestle's dissertation in 1972.[4] My dissertation led to the publication of an article in the *American Quarterly* that was judged the best to appear in that journal in 1972.[5] It prompted kudos from Merle Curti, one of the first historians to study the history of American education, and the Jacksonian specialist Edward Pessen who taught for many years at NYU.[6] But perhaps because it dealt with the backgrounds and motivations of the Society's trustees, it never attracted much attention among those historians of education who were focused on refuting the so-called liberal interpretation of American public education first advanced by Paul Monroe and Ellwood P. Cubberley.[7] This interpretation was still very much alive in the works of Butts and Cremin. Rejecting the argument that the history of American public education was a story of democracy, opportunity, and progress, these historians -- the so-called revisionists -- argued that it was all about class bias and the reproduction of economic inequality. The revisionists dominated the field in the early 1970s, and while the hegemony of their neo-Marxist interpretation came to an end soon enough, my article never found a prominent place in this body of scholarship.

When my *American Quarterly* article appeared, I was in my fourth year as a tenure-track faculty member in the Departments of History and Foundations of Education at Temple University. Coming out of graduate school, I had found many openings for tenure-track faculty in Foundations of Education. Comprehensive universities with large programs in teacher education were hiring. A few research universities were looking, too. I interviewed for a position in the School of Education at UCLA, where Sol Cohen had gone after teaching briefly at Cornell. I had taken his seminar on the history of progressive education in my second year in graduate school. His new dean, John Goodlad, offered me a job as an assistant professor of Foundations at an annual salary of $10,000. This was, he said, the best he could do. Deciding not to go to the West Coast, I accepted instead the offer of a joint appointment at Temple. What convinced me to accept Temple's offer was the prospect of working in both a History and a Foundations department. It seemed at the time like the best of both worlds. I soon discovered, of course, that this was not necessarily true. After more than forty years in two departments, I can say unequivocally that the pluses of my joint appointment have far outnumbered the minuses. But I certainly did not know when I made my decision what I was getting myself into.

Most historians of education work today in Schools or Colleges of Education. Given the highly differentiated nature of the modern university, their close association with educational practitioners and policy makers will surely continue for the foreseeable future. According to John Rury, historians of education like their counterparts in other applied disciplines (e.g. law and medicine) should accept this fact and "be attentive to the interests and concerns of their nonhistorian [sic] colleagues."[8] But whether they work in an applied field or not, the best historians I know pay close attention to non historians, borrowing insights and ideas from scholars in such related fields as sociology, anthropology, and political science. If my personal experience is any indication, it is also true that historians of education who do not work exclusively in a School or College of Education have many options and opportunities.

Selected Personal Publications (cont.)

A Preliminary Look at the Schoolhouse: The Philadelphia Story, 1870–1920," *Urban Education*, VIII (January 1974): 381–399.

"Cathedral of Culture: The Schoolhouse in American Educational Thought and Practice since 1820," *History of Education Quarterly* 29 (Spring 1989): 1–40.

"Symbol of Paradox in the New Republic: Classicism in the Design of Schoolhouses and Other Public Buildings in the United States, 1800-1860," in *Aspects of Antiquity in the History of Education*, F-P. Hager, et al., eds., International Series for the History of Education, Vol. 3 (Hildesheim, Germany: Bildung und Wissenschaft im verlag August Lax, 1992), 163–76).

"The History Course Portfolio," *Perspectives: American Historical Association Newsletter* 35 (November 1997): 17–20.

Not long after I came to Temple, the university's College of Arts and Sciences established an American Studies Program. In its original configuration it featured a service learning component that paid Temple undergraduates to work as interns in local arts and culture institutions. Had I not been a member of the university's History Department I would not have had the chance to participate in the curriculum and governance of this program. I would not have become the president of the mid Atlantic chapter of the American Studies Association or the chair of the program committee for the ASA's Bicentennial Meeting. This international conference brought scholars from the United Kingdom and the United States to Philadelphia in the fall of 1976. Without it, I would not have become the co-editor of *The Divided Metropolis: Social and Spatial Dimensions of Philadelphia, 1800–1975* that Greenwood Press published in 1980. This book included several papers originally given at the Bicentennial Meeting and some new essays, including my own.[9] My association with Temple's American Studies Program also led to other professional opportunities in international education. Between 1985 and 1991 I co-directed six summer institutes funded by the Fulbright Commission and the United States Information Agency that taught themes in American Studies to a grand total of 209 teachers of English and history from forty-seven countries. My background in the history of education gave me a special bond with many of those who attended these institutes, but it alone would not have justified my leadership role. As a direct result of my work in them, I spent more than a month in Algeria in the spring of 1989, lecturing on topics in American Studies and American education. Arriving there during Ramadan, I soon learned some basic truths about the difference between the Islamic and the Christian worlds.

Several chapters in *The Divided Metropolis* explored themes in the history of Philadelphia's built environment. My own included an analysis of the conceptualization and construction of the Benjamin Franklin Parkway, a Beaux Arts boulevard built in Philadelphia between 1908 and 1918 to connect the city's downtown with Fairmount Park. Home to the Philadelphia Museum of Art, the Franklin Institute, and for many years the headquarters of the School District of Philadelphia, it was and still is an avenue devoted to public memory, civic pride, and cultural education. Its many objects of public art tell a story of both consensus and conflict in the history of Philadelphia.[10] By the time I began work on *The Divided Metropolis*, I had already discovered the city's rich resources on the history of school architecture. Published between 1913 and 1939, Franklin D. Edmunds' eight volumes documenting the school buildings of Philadelphia convinced me that there was much to be learned from a historical study of the material culture of American education.[11] When Dana White invited me to contribute to a special historical issue of *Urban Education*, I wrote an essay that examined both the development of urban school design in Philadelphia and the politics of locating new city schools.[12] My finding that its middle class received preference when new schools were built or old ones enlarged dovetailed nicely with what other historians (e.g. the revisionists) were saying at the time about the history of urban schools.

My article in *Urban Education* was the first of three that I published on the subject of school architecture. The piece best known to most people in the field appeared in the *History of Education Quarterly* in 1989.[13] It explored the relationship between school architecture and school administration as well as the role of the schoolhouse in civic and moral education. Twenty years after it appeared, the History of Education Society programmed a retrospective session at its annual meeting in Baltimore on recent developments in the history of school architecture. My work on this topic reached an international audience in 1991 when I gave a paper on the impact of the Greek Revival movement on American school and civic architecture at the annual meeting of the International Standing Conference on the History of Education (ISCHE) in Zurich, Switzerland. This essay subsequently appeared in the conference proceedings, edited by Fritz-Peter Hager and Jurgen Herbst, among others.[14] A professor at the University of Zurich, Hager was well known in Western Europe as one of those responsible for the formation of ISCHE. I first met him when he invited me to include Zurich on a lecture tour I made in the winter of 1991, speaking on the history of American culture and education at several universities and teachers institutes in Germany and Switzerland. His graduate students proved to be an attentive audience for my lecture in English on the history of American school reform. But lectures in English were not taken for granted the following summer at the ISCHE meeting in Zurich where some participants complained loudly about the requirement that all presenters speak in either English or German. Hager himself spoke at length in German at a plenary session whose audience included many who, I am sure, did not understand a word he said. Using the German I learned in graduate school, I managed to get just his general drift!

*****

When I arrived at Temple University in the fall of 1968, it was expanding rapidly. Three years before it had joined Penn State and the University of Pittsburgh as one of Pennsylvania's three state-related research universities. A commuter school in the heart of one of America's most distressed urban areas, Temple was now in a position to improve its campus, expand its faculty, and enlarge its student body. Between 1965 and 1970 the university hired dozens of faculty. I joined a Foundations Department that included well-known philosopher James E. McClellan, Jr., who came to Temple from Teachers College, and Michael H. Moscow, an economist who subsequently went on to a distinguished career in finance and banking.[15] Many other departments at Temple added prominent scholars. Barak Rosenshine took a position in Educational Psychology. My colleague for thirty years, Allen F. Davis left the University of Missouri to become a member of Temple's History Department. Even after 1970, Temple continued to bring in prominent faculty. The Foundations Department welcomed Leonard Waks, the general editor of the series in which this book appears.

Selected Favorites
Philippe Aries, *Centuries of Childhood: A Social History of Family Life*, translated from the French by Robert Baldick (New York: Random House, 1962).
Lawrence A. Cremin, *American Education: The Colonial Experience* (New York: Harper and Row, 1970).
Jack Dougherty, *More than One Struggle: The Evolution of Black School Reform in Milwaukee* (Chapel Hill, NC: University of North Carolina Press, 2004).
Ira Katznelson & Margaret Weir. *Schooling for All: Class, Race, and the Decline of the Democratic Ideal* (New York: Basic Books, 1985).
Michael B. Katz, *Class, Bureaucracy and Schools: The Illusion of Educational Change in America* (New York: Praeger Publishers, 1971).

But the good times were short lived. A tuition driven institution popular with first-generation college goers, Temple was especially vulnerable to political, economic, and demographic forces over which it had little or no control. Even as one administrator was predicting that Temple's College of Education would some day soon need more than twice as many faculty members as it had at the time, the tide was turning.[16] The recession of 1973 slowed the growth of the university's state appropriation and in time the disappearance of baby boom applicants forced the administration to accept the fact that enrollment growth at Temple would not be unending. Such developments, though still incipient, probably were on the minds of at least some in the Temple administration when I came up for tenure. As a joint appointee, I came before two separate personnel committees, one in Arts and Sciences, the other in Education. My joint appointment presented a special problem. Facing two reviews in two colleges, I was in double jeopardy. The challenge in History was especially daunting. With seventy-three full-time faculty members, Temple's History Department was the largest in the country at that time. Eight of its junior members came up for tenure in 1973. The department's leaders knew that they could not keep all eight no matter what their credentials. When the review process was over, four remained; fortunately, I was one of them. The following year five more came up, only one of whom got good news when the review process ended.

By the late 1970s, Temple's enrollments were falling rapidly, eventually dropping more than ten per cent. The university's president, Marvin Wachman, and his closest advisors knew that they had to make some difficult decisions. When I first heard the word "retrenchment," I did not know what it really meant. As I learned in due course, it meant much more than layoffs. It meant a crisis of confidence and years of mistrust between the faculty and the administration at Temple. Layoffs occurred in 1982, beginning with staff but quickly reaching into faculty ranks. Part-time and non tenured professors were the first to go, but tenured faculty soon followed, especially in the College of Education. Its enrollments had dropped so much, the administration said, that some departments would have to be either downsized or completely eliminated.[17] The Foundations Department was one of those slated to go. Two of its faculty received layoff notices; one left Temple for a non tenure-track job at Penn State while the other accepted a transfer to another position at Temple, teaching general education courses to freshmen. I did not receive a layoff notice, perhaps because I held tenure and rank in two departments. The elimination of my position in Foundations of Education would not have affected my position in the History Department. So I was left alone -- in more ways than one. The Foundations Department soon disappeared, its courses and degrees assigned to a new department called Educational Leadership. Its faculty also included those who had previously taught in the Departments of Educational Administration and Urban Education. They had been downsized, but enough of the "ed. admin." faculty remained for them to dominate the new department. By the end of the decade, I was the only "Foundations" person in that department. My work there consisted almost entirely of teaching a "core" course in the history and sociology of education to master's and doctoral students from all over the College of Education. I enjoyed teaching this course, but it was not what got me out of bed in the morning. My work in international education had flourished by then, and it was to this that I chose to devote much of my energy.

The impact of retrenchment on Temple did not end once the layoffs were over. By 1982 Temple had been an organized campus for nearly a decade, its faculty represented by the Temple Association of University Professionals (TAUP), which was then an AAUP local. When the layoffs came, the administration adhered to the TAUP contract, applying its language on the procedures for retrenchment. Somehow Temple and TAUP renegotiated without incident in 1983, but when this contract came up for renewal three years later, bargaining did not go so smoothly. The university had a new leader by then, Peter J. Liacouras. The former dean of Temple's law school, he had not initiated retrenchment, but as president he did nothing to reverse it. Dissatisfied with the university's contract offer and still smarting from the retrenchment episode, TAUP walked out at the beginning of the fall semester. There is no such thing as a good strike, but some are worse than others. This one was bad -- as adversarial as it could be. The president of the university and the president of the union engaged in a nasty public relations duel. I walked the picket lines at the university's main campus. I did it again four years later when the Temple faculty went out again. Salary and benefits were the ostensible issues, but the memory of retrenchment had not completely faded. Along with many of my colleagues, I was not yet ready to place my trust in the leadership of Temple. Most of us were picket line veterans by then because the Temple faculty had not changed much since 1982. Unlike the first strike, which lasted less than ten days, the second dragged on for almost a month, prompting some faculty to return to work before a deal was made. The bitterness that resulted from such decisions did not disappear any time soon.

Selected Favorites (Cont.)

David Labaree, *How to Succeed in School without Really Learning: The Credentials Race in American Education* (New Haven: Yale University Press, 1997).

Lawrence W. Levine, *The Opening of the American Mind: Canons, Culture, and History* (Boston: Beacon Press, 1996).

Jeffrey Mirel, *The Rise and Fall of an Urban School System* (Ann Arbor: University of Michigan Press, 1993).

Julie A. Reuben, *The Making of the Modern University: Intellectual Transformation and the Marginalization of Morality* (Chicago: University of Chicago Press, 1996).

David B. Tyack, *The One Best System: A History of American Urban Education* (Cambridge: Harvard University Press, 1974).

Laurence R. Veysey, *The Emergence of the American University* (Chicago: University of Chicago Press, 1965).

In the 1980s, I was a not a leader of the faculty union. That would come twenty years later, but in the aftermath of retrenchment there was never any doubt in my mind that I would support the union if and when a strike came. I had openly participated in the organizing efforts that led to the union's certification in 1973, overcoming my initial fears that such activity might jeopardize my career by labelling me a trouble maker in the eyes of the admini-stration. Even while serving for six years (1979–1985) as an assistant and then an associate dean of the university's Graduate School, I continued to pay union dues though I was technically out of the bargaining unit.

Today that would not be tolerated, but at that time nobody said I could not do it. My decision to work as an administrator was driven in part by the prospect and then the reality of faculty retrenchment. If my professorial job was going to be eliminated, I thought, my resume should include something that might allow me to stay at Temple in another capacity or move as an administrator to another institution. Toward the end of my stay in the Graduate School I actually applied for positions in the administration of graduate education at a couple of other schools, but nothing came of these applications, and I know now that this was for the best. When a new Vice President for Graduate Education and Research told me in 1985 that I would have to leave the Graduate School so he could trim his budget, I made the transition back to faculty status with no resistance and no regrets.[18] But my time in the administration of graduate education was not without collateral benefits. In the summer of 1980, I went to Bendel State, Nigeria to evaluate applicants for an on-site master's program that the College of Education established there to give underemployed Temple professors new opportunities. This trip gave me my first practical lessons about life in the under developed world.

In 2001 I was elected president of TAUP. I served for six years, leading the union while David Adamany was Temple's president. The university's Board of Trustees chose Adamany to succeed Liacouras in part because he had been president of Wayne State University, an urban institution much like Temple. His relationship with the faculty union at Wayne State had been rocky at best, and when he arrived in North Philadelphia, there were more than a few on the Temple faculty who believed that he had been hired to break the Temple faculty union. Whether that was true or not, it can be said with absolute certainty that Adamany wanted to leave his mark on Temple. Taking charge of every aspect of university policy and practice, he made the president's office like the eye of a needle. Needless to say, this approach to university leadership discomforted many members of the faculty. It reinforced my belief in the value of a union contract, a feeling that was, I think, widely shared across the university.

The TAUP contract that had been in force when I became union president expired in October 2004. I knew going into the negotiations for a new agreement that this would be a struggle. President Adamany had a long list of contract changes that he wanted to make, many of which were designed to shift the balance of power at Temple. Since he did not trust the faculty in many of the university's schools and colleges to make wise decisions about such important matters as tenure and promotion, he proposed structural reforms that would increase the administration's power. Beginning in June 2004, the negotiations for a new contract bogged down almost immediately. While talks continued, both sides engaged in a public war of words that often became very hostile. By the time a new agreement was reached -- five months after the expiration of the old contract -- the mood at Temple was somber. For me, the whole experience was a practical lesson in the politics of education, a subject that I had been teaching for more than thirty years but which for me had now become much more than a matter of scholarship.

My education in the politics of education took a new turn in my penultimate year as president of TAUP. In the spring of 2005 the Pennsylvania General Assembly adopted a resolution that called for the creation of a select committee charged with investigating the academic climate for students on the campuses of the commonwealth's public colleges and universities. Inspired by the work of conservative author and lecturer David Horowitz, the committee conducted a series of hearings across the state, one of which took place at Temple. Horowitz himself appeared at this hearing, testifying that Temple was a bastion of liberal, even left-wing sentiment, whose faculty deliberately silenced conservative students. To achieve a balance between liberal and conservative opinion he called for a hiring regimen that would make political opinion a criterion for faculty employment at public colleges and universities. Drawing upon my knowledge of the history of education, I testified against such a quota system, arguing instead that in American higher education all ideas had been welcome since the development of the concept of academic freedom, but that none had ever been or should be guaranteed a place in the curriculum. Whether my testimony had any effect is certainly open to question. What can be said for sure is that the select committee's final report died a quiet death in the Pennsylvania General Assembly. At Temple, on the other hand, the hearings had an immediate impact. In the summer of 2006, the university's Board of Trustees decided to require a reference on all university syllabi to its new policy on student academic freedom, a policy that drew heavily from the ideas of David Horowitz.[19]

*****

My work in the 1980s on the history of school architecture taught me something about the importance of the relationship between schools and their constituents. Because all schools are public buildings, their appearance matters to many people -- not just those who use them. Schoolhouses serve their respective communities as symbolic reminders of the significance of American education. Working from this insight, it was a natural step for me to undertake a study of the relationship between parents and schools. At the time I began to research this topic, the historiography of American education had entered a new and promising phase. Moving beyond the debate between the liberals and the revisionists, scholars like James Anderson, Paul Peterson, William Reese, and Barbara Solomon had pushed those in the field to think more broadly. They had shown how historians of education might better incorporate race, ethnicity, region, and gender into their work, giving recognition to a wider array of stake holders and interest groups. Parents are and always have been an important element in American education. But as I discovered as I worked on this project, parents have been more than just another interest group. They have represented the home and the community and all that these vital institutions mean in America. Taking his cues from Bernard Bailyn, Lawrence Cremin had successfully shown in 1970 how important these institutions were to education in early America.[20] This important point got lost in the second and third volumes of his trilogy on the history of American education -- perhaps because these massive volumes lacked a sharp focus. In *Parents and Schools: the 150 Year Struggle for Control in American Education* I concentrated on it.[21] The book actually began as a study of early childhood education, but the more I read, the more I came to appreciate not just the educational significance of the home and the community but also the importance of the school's relationship to them. Service on my local school board while I was writing the book helped to shape my thinking, demonstrating first hand just how political the relationship between the home and the school can be. It underscored for me as well the significance of the schoolhouse because when parents came before the board to complain, it was often about the physical condition of the schools.

When *Parents and Schools* appeared in 2000, I was in the midst of a fellowship at the Carnegie Foundation for the Advancement of Teaching (CFAT). In part because of my joint appointment, my career has taken many twists and turns over its full length. But teaching has been a constant, whether to undergraduates in a basic survey course or doctoral students writing dissertations. It was not difficult for me to say yes, therefore, when educational historian Nancy Hoffman, then working in the Provost's office at Temple, asked me to join the university's team participating in a teaching project funded by the Pew Charitable Trusts and the now defunct American Association for Higher Education. It brought together teams of scholars in history and other fields to develop protocols for the peer review of teaching. The brainchild of educational policy maker Ernest Boyer and Stanford professor Lee Shulman, this work took on a much larger profile when Shulman followed Boyer as president of CFAT. In 1998 Shulman opened the Carnegie Academy for the Scholarship of Teaching and Learning, a multi-faceted program that included fellowships for academics interested in learning more about how to make their teaching a public act and how to relate teaching to learning. In my fellowship year (1999–2000) I joined historians Lendol Calder (Augustana College), T. Mills Kelly (George Mason University) and David Pace (University of Indiana) as well as scholars from such diverse fields as music and mathematics in a year-long study of my own and their teaching. Making college teaching more transparent and effective through systematic reflection and documentation was our common goal. It was an exhilarating experience that led in turn to several publications and a term for me as the director of the Teaching and Learning Center in the College of Liberal Arts at Temple.[22]

*****

In one of my last acts as president of the Temple Association of University Professionals, I persuaded the university's administration to offer a phased retirement program to senior faculty. Like so many other American colleges and universities today, Temple was then and still is an institution that could easily lose nearly half of its faculty to illness, death, or retirement in just a few years. When I worked on this benefit, I did not necessarily have myself in mind, but the program soon turned out to be right for me. It allows me to work half time for two years, giving me the chance to lay the groundwork for the two research projects I have in mind for full-time attention after the end of my teaching career. Focused on the relationship between citizens and schools, one is a direct outgrowth of my previous work on parents and schools. So my professional life will change in the near future, but it will not end. I look forward to whatever the future holds.

NOTES

[1]   Lawrence A. Cremin, *The Transformation of the School* (New York: Knopf, 1961)
[2]   "Oral History: Its Nature and Uses for Educational History," *History of Education Quarterly* 11 (Summer 1971): 184–194.
[3]   Julia Agnes Duffy, "The Proper Objects of a Gratuitous Education: The Free-School Society of the City of New York, 1805–1826," unpublished PhD dissertation, Teachers College, Columbia University, 1968. Since both Duffy and I were doing research in New York City in the mid 1960s, I approached her advisor, Lawrence Cremin, about attending a session of his seminar at Teachers College so Duffy and I could both report on our respective projects. Cremin said no.

[4] Carl F. Kaestle, *The Evolution of an Urban School System: New York City, 1750–1850* (Cambridge: Harvard University Press, 1973).

[5] "Philosophy, Philanthropy, and Public Education: A Social History of the New York Public School Society, 1805–1853," unpublished PhD dissertation, Cornell University, 1968; Status, Values, and the Education of the Poor: The Trustees of the New York Public School Society, 1805–1853," *American Quarterly* 24 (March 1972): 69–85.

[6] Merle Curti to Professor [William] Cutler, Madison, Wisconsin, April 4, 1972, which is in the possession of the recipient. Edward Pessen, *Riches, Class, and Power before the Civil War* (Lexington, MA: D. C. Heath & Co., 1973), xx & 269.

[7] Lawrence A. Cremin, *The Wonderful World of Ellwood Patterson* Cubberley (New York: Teachers College, 1965), 25–26, 40; Milton Gaither *American Educational History: A Critique of Progress* (New York: Teaches College Press, 2003), 95–97.

[8] John Rury, "The Curious Status of the History of Education: A Parallel Perspective," *History of Education Quarterly* 46 (Winter 2006): 597.

[9] "The Persistent Dualism: Centralization and Decentralization in Philadelphia, 1854–1975," *The Divided Metropolis: Social and Spatial Dimensions of Philadelphia, 1800–1975* (Westport, CT: Greenwood Press, 1980), 249–284.

[10] As a result of this work, I developed a walking tour of the Benjamin Franklin Parkway that I have sometimes used in my courses on the history of urban education at Temple. In 1997 this tour was part of the program for the annual meeting of the History of Education Society, which met in Philadelphia that year.

[11] F. D. Edmunds, *The Public School Buildings of the City of Philadelphia, 1745–1918.* Volumes 1–8. (Philadelphia; School District of Philadelphia. Board of Public Education, 1913–1939).

[12] "A Preliminary Look at the Schoolhouse: The Philadelphia Story, 1870–1920," *Urban Education* 8 (January 1974): 381–399.

[13] "'Cathedral of Culture': The Schoolhouse in American Educational Thought and Practice since 1820," *History of Education Quarterly* 29 (Spring 1989): 1–40.

[14] "Symbol of Paradox in the New Republic: Classicism in the Design of Schoolhouses and Other Public Buildings in the United States, 1800–1860," in *Aspects of Antiquity in the History of Education*, F.–P. Hager, et al., eds., International Series for the History of Education, Vol. 3 (Hildesheim, Germany: Bildung und Wissenschaft im verlag August Lax, 1992), 163–176.

[15] Moscow was president of the Federal Reserve Bank of Chicago from September 1994 to August 2007.

[16] Notes he left in the files of the university's Graduate School from the early 1970s document his estimate that the College of Education would need more than 400 faculty within a decade.

[17] For the administration's side of this story, see Marvin Wachman, *The Education of a University President* (Philadelphia: Temple University Press, 2005), 152–156.

[18] From 1968 to 1979 I had two offices, one in the History Department and one in Foundations Department. When I entered administration, I gave them both up, but upon my return to the faculty in 1985 I decided that having two offices was less a benefit than a burden. The Foundations Department was gone, and most of those with whom I was working closely were in the College of Arts and Sciences. From that time till now, I have had but one office, located in the History Department.

[19] Horowitz is the author of the "Academic Bill of Rights," which served as a model for the new academic freedom policy at Temple. His books include: *The Professors: The 101 Most Dangerous Academics in America* (West Lafayette, IN: C-Span Archives, 2006) and with Jacob Laskin, *One Party Classroom: How Radical Professors at America's Top Colleges Indoctrinate Students and Undermine Our Democracy* (New York: Crown Forum, 2009). He is the founder of Students for Academic Freedom, an organization supported by such conservative groups as the American Association of College Trustees and Alumni.

[20] Lawrence A. Cremin, *American Education: The Colonial Experience* (New York: Harper and Row, 1970).

[21] *Parents and Schools: The 150-year Struggle for Control in American Education* (Chicago: University of Chicago Press, 2000).

[22] See, for example, "The History Course Portfolio," *Perspectives: American Historical Association Newsletter* 35 (November 1997): 17–20. This essay was later republished on the AHA's web site.

MARY ANN DZUBACK

BECOMING A HISTORIAN

Educational Choices, Sponsored Mobility, and Institutional Challenges

My interest in history of education did not emerge until I was well into adulthood. Yet it was singularly shaped by a broad range of educational experiences, in my family and the schools and colleges I attended, and as a teacher, working with infants through high schoolers and then as a teaching assistant with graduate students prior to receiving the interdisciplinary Ph.D. in history and education. I knew little about academic life, though, and did not have the kind of competitive ambition I had seen among some of my fellow students in graduate school. For that reason, sponsored mobility by mentors and colleagues became a critical means of better understanding the profession and the field. By sponsored mobility, I mean casual mentoring and networks among peers that grew into strong friendships.

Growing up, I attended six elementary schools, one junior high school and five high schools, and then two colleges to complete undergraduate education. My father was a successful engineer, who, with a growing family of six children, two with a chronic disease, decided to use his training and skills to pursue a career in sales of engineering equipment, which was more lucrative than design in the 1950s, and required frequent family moves. After being in so many schools, the idea of the academic life held little appeal for me when I finished college. I had switched from science to education after one year in college and a two-year hiatus, during which time I'd begun to run a day care center in my rural community. More importantly for my interest in education, I read John Dewey in an educational philosophy class I audited. Encountering *Democracy and Education* and *School and Society* in this class, along with a number of arguments for alternative schooling in the early 1970s, was a revelation. I understood then that education wasn't entirely shaped by institutions, that individual agency plays a key role in what is learned and how it is learned, and that institutions that nurture growth and more growth as Dewey argued, would have greater or, perhaps, more direct impact on students than most of the schools I had attended.

In my experience as a middle-class, white, successful student, I had become disenchanted with the ways schools seemed to be institutionalizing students—to strive for the grades, credit hours, test scores, and other measurable outcomes of the schooling experience in the United States. Costs of these measures included intellectual disengagement, institutional cynicism, and, occasionally, a sense of entitlement, particularly for those successful at gaming the system. To counter these effects, I had become interested in existential philosophy in high school and

W. J. Urban, Leaders in the Historical Study of American Education, 69–80.

tried to focus on the learning, rather than the grades. In the end, I was simply tired of school by the time I got to college. My favorite classes had been those that presented serious intellectual challenges, high expectations, and the support to meet them. Madame Martin in French, where I encountered Sartre and Camus for the first time; Ms. Dawson and Father Rowley in English composition, grammar, and literature; Sister Jean-Patrice in math; and Bill MacLenathen in American history and government were my favorite teachers. Moving from school to school was not easy. But my parents chose each location for the quality of its public schools, with the exception of one town in rural New York, where they had no choice, given the location of my father's most recent promotion. There, I begged to go to the local Catholic high school after one semester at the regional public; they acceded because they were feeling a little guilty about the last move—from a school I loved.

My Own Favorites

Mary Ann Dzuback, "Berkeley Women Economists, Public Policy, and Civic Sensibility." In *Civic and Moral Learning in America*. Ed. Donald Warren. (New York: Palgrave McMillan, 2006).

Mary Ann Dzuback, "Creative Financing in Social Science: Women Scholars and Early Research." In *Women and Philanthropy in Education*. Ed. Andrea Walton. (Bloomington: Indiana University Press, 2005).

Mary Ann Dzuback, "Gender and the Politics of Knowledge." *History of Education Quarterly* 43 (Summer 2003): 171-195.

I remember at each new school going through a period of difficult adjustment, not only socially, but also in dealing with a whole new set of expectations, depending on the school district. My mother, a southern woman who understood life through stories and had volumes to tell, had a particular formula she used when she was encouraging me to give each new school, teacher, and subject my best. It went something like this: "Mary Ann, you have got to understand how important education is to our family. Your Dido [paternal grandfather] left the Carpatho-Rusyn Mountains and his village— his family farm and land and gave up his inheritance—to come to this country so his children and grandchildren could obtain an education. [I found out later that he actually left, in part, to avoid conscription in the Austro-Hungarian army.] Your Baba left her mother and sisters to join him so that their children—your father and aunts—would have better opportunities. And look: all three of your aunts finished college. Your Dido would not pay for your father to go to college—only the girls, so your father worked his way through the first two years, and then finished on the G.I. Bill after he'd served in the Navy during the war. You can do anything, *anything* you want to do with an education. Don't let this math/chemistry/French class hold you back. If you work hard enough, you can learn it and get a good grade." If that didn't work, then she told me her own story of growing up in Tennessee and Georgia, about how her father refused to help pay for her college education. With the encouragement of her high school principal, who told her she was too smart to stop her schooling, she took out a loan and enrolled in the local college, but had to drop out to work to pay off her debt, and then never finished. That story and my father's high expectations usually kept me going.

My family members' struggles and my own to adjust to each new town and school helped me to understand in some visceral way about marginality. I do not know whether my Baba was literate, even in her own language. She rarely had a book in her hands, except for the hymnal and liturgy for the Carpatho-Rusyn Greek Orthodox church she and my grandfather helped to start in Bayonne, New Jersey. It is the first church I remember. Attending services there as a child was akin to stepping into another world from the suburban neighborhood in which my parents lived, where our neighbors were mostly Catholic and Protestant and all the other kids' grandparents spoke English as their first language. My maternal grandparents did not finish high school in their rural Georgia town, and my grandmother, whose father was a minister in the Church of God, tried to fill us, unsuccessfully, with Pentecostal teaching when we visited their home in Chattanooga, Tennessee, every couple of years during the summer. I remember seeing southern segregation and being completely perplexed; "why are there two bathrooms for women," I'd ask, "one white and one 'colored' . . . what does that mean?" My mother explained racism to me and my brothers and sisters, but it did not make sense to us. And the racist comments I heard from beloved relatives made even less sense, given their normal tendency toward civility. I was visiting in Tennessee when the 1964 Civil Rights Act passed. Watching the announcement on television, I was the only one cheering in my great uncle's living room. My mother had done volunteer work on race relations with the National Council of Christians and Jews in the Chicago area where we lived then, and I had begged to march with Martin Luther King, Jr., when he came to Chicago, but my father had said I was too young. These experiences seemed to set me apart in my mind from most of the children I played with, and contributed to the feeling of always being the "new girl" with the strange last name and the almost bipolar consciousness I felt moving between grandparents, churches, regions, and schools.

When I dropped out of college and moved to northern New Hampshire, my parents were devastated; my father had had high hopes for a career in medicine or science for me. But when I was invited to return to school by the president of the local college, and provided the resources (NDEA loans, scholarships, grants) to finish, I felt very fortunate, even though the college was not the kind of institution my parents had in mind. It was an experimental college, very non-traditional, but it had a profound intellectual influence on me. It was there I was introduced to Dewey, read anthropology, as well as theories of human development, and studied teaching and learning, while living in a cabin in the woods, heating with a wood stove, hauling water, reading by kerosene lamp, and running the day care center on the side. At this college, which no longer exists, I first confronted interdisciplinary teaching and learning, and came to understand, though vaguely, that knowledge is constructed and produced in particular ways, depending on institutional structures and organizations. I was part of a learning community that alternately functioned poorly and well. There were serious students, including myself, and lost souls, who otherwise didn't seem to fit into any kind of academic structure. The worst moments for a pragmatist like me were those interminable community meetings that lasted sometimes into the early morning hours and focused on governance, curriculum, and programs. They seemed to be dominated by the male members of the community and were often marked by charged disagreements between the *wunderkind* young president Leon Botstein and the counter-culture faculty he had recruited. The best moments were in classes, in my case run mostly by female faculty members, but also the occasional male (in psychology and anthropology), while writing my senior thesis as an upper division student, and in my debates with President Botstein about what constituted the most important knowledge and education in a rural mountain community. I thought we should have cows and a maple sugaring operation in addition to the academic curriculum; he was preoccupied with stretching a thin budget to obtain a piano, beef up music, languages, and the rest of the academic curriculum, and attract interesting faculty. Needless to say, he prevailed. But the conversations were instructive.

My Own Favorites (continued)

Mary Ann Dzuback, "Gender, Professional Knowledge, and Institutional Power: Women Social Scientists and the Research University." In *The 'Woman Question' and Higher Education: Perspectives on Gender and Knowledge Production in America.* Ed. Ann Mari May. (Cheltenham, UK: Edward Elgar, 2008).

Mary Ann Dzuback, "Women and Social Research at Bryn Mawr College, 1915-1940." *History of Education Quarterly* 33 (Winter 1993): 579-608.

Mary Ann Dzuback, "Women, Social Science Expertise, and the State." *Women's History Review* (UK) 18 (February 2009): 71-95.

I considered graduate school upon finishing (my whole family attended the outdoor ceremony as we graduates trotted barefoot up to get our degrees), but decided I needed more real world experience first. So I spent a year as a nanny for my friends Karen and Joe Wilcox's children, while also deciding *not* to pursue graduate training in family counseling. Then I taught for a few years in an alternative school started locally by friends; teaching at Coppermine School was enlightening, particularly the challenge of matching creative content to equally creative pedagogy. I relied extensively on my co-teachers for advice and criticism. We kept meticulous track of every student's progress in a joint daily journal. And we navigated together the unpredictable group parent meetings where we had to balance, for example, the parent who wanted to teach astrology with the parent who was constantly vigilant to protect her child from racism with the parent who wanted us to focus on providing a loving environment. We worked continually to create and maintain a sense of community among the children and were quite successful. We also saw astonishing academic gains, with some students jumping a grade or two and others (including my two stepsons) testing well in all subjects. But the school closed for lack of continued funding, and I left New Hampshire for other adventures, including substitute teaching in a number of locations.

I landed in New Jersey, where I'd gone after landscaping (and subbing) in California and living in the UK for a short period. Leon Botstein, with whom I'd stayed in contact and who became a close friend, suggested I reconsider graduate school and think about Teachers College, Columbia (TC) or the Bank Street School. I was taken by the vast number of different kinds of courses at TC and its connection to Columbia, so I applied to TC's Master's program in curriculum theory. I chose curriculum theory because the school district where I was teaching was a top district in the state, with well educated and dedicated teachers, a fair amount of wealth in the community, and many disengaged students in the classes I encountered. I thought maybe the problem was the curriculum and what I believed was lack of innovation and pedagogical variety, particularly in comparison with the Coppermine School and the high level of student engagement there. In graduate school I came to understand that my diagnosis was quite uninformed and simplistic.

Teachers College at that point was teeming with Master's enrollees. Fortunately my advisor agreed with my plan to select courses for the faculty, rather than the subject matter. Together we constructed a challenging semester of courses, including history, philosophy, developmental psychology with an emphasis on critical theory, a required course in teaching, and a course in reading systems. I was completely hooked, and decided after the first year to move from a Master's to a doctoral program, but this advisor, with whom I had hoped to work, was leaving for Yale Divinity School. In the meantime, I'd taken Larry Cremin and Ellen Lagemann's History of Education and then Education and Public Policy courses and Ellen had hired me for the summer to do some historical research on the history of nursing for a book she was editing. She gave me my first publishing opportunity—a bibliographic essay reframing the history of nursing as a profession. She also hired me as the teaching assistant for both the history and the public policy courses, an arrangement that continued for the next five years. In addition, she helped me choose a Ph.D. program, given my interests, and I chose history.

History appealed to me for a number of reasons. First, in the Cremin-Lagemann course, the focus was on education broadly conceived. We read social and intellectual history, institutional history, history of philanthropy, as well as primary published materials. I became intrigued by the ways knowledge has been constructed. Second, the research I'd done for Ellen Lagemann involved locating sources, solving problems, and thinking through the process of reorganizing bodies of research to see the topic in new ways. I really loved the research process. Spending hours in the library and reading musty, dusty materials was both satisfying and absorbing. Finally, history seemed more grounded to me than my other alternative, philosophy. Working with real (past) lives and institutions, using documents to piece together enough evidence to construct a narrative analysis, seemed more satisfying than analyzing ideas alone.

I had to take many extra history courses, some in the Graduate School at Columbia's history department, to make up for the lack of a history major as an undergraduate. The more I read, the more I wanted to focus on knowledge production in higher education, particularly during the period when research became increasingly important in shaping both academic disciplines and American higher education institutions. This was sharpened by my research for Ellen on *Private Power for the Public Good.* [1] Douglas Sloan's course in history of higher education and his gentle guidance in choosing a dissertation topic, as well as his graceful writing, led me to ask him to supervise my dissertation work, as Ellen Lagemann was not yet in a position to supervise PhD students at Teachers College—that came a couple of years later. But I continued to do occasional research for her on *The Politics of Knowledge*,[2] which furthered my interest in the social and intellectual structures contributing to the development and organization of knowledge.

By then, I'd also been offered a research assistantship with Larry Cremin on his third volume of the *American Education* trilogy and some of the preliminary work on *Popular Education and Its Discontents*.[3] He was moving from the presidency of Teachers College to the presidency of the Spencer Foundation, so I worked as his research and office assistant and had a minor position at the Foundation. I had been hesitant to take the position—I remember complaining to Ellen about "schlepping books from New York to Princeton" (where Larry had a sabbatical year while beginning in the Spencer presidency), but she persuaded me that this would be a good thing. I had no career ambitions, I just wanted to finish my dissertation. Being connected with Spencer helped to broaden my understanding of education research, and enabled me to meet some very interesting scholars, including Ralph Tyler, William Julius Wilson, Pat Graham, and many others. I was moved to read their work in my spare time and began to grasp in ways I had not before, the field in which I was becoming a scholar.

With Ellen's support, Larry's ebullient encouragement, and Douglas's calm willingness to talk through some of the stumbling blocks, I completed my dissertation on Robert Hutchins and the University of Chicago under Hutchins's leadership. Douglas had suggested I consider focusing on an academic leader as a way of anchoring my interest in the history of the organization of knowledge. I chose to focus on Hutchins, rather than Alexander Meiklejohn or some other academic innovator, because Hutchins became president of one of the premier research universities in the country in 1929, the period following rapid growth in the establishment of modern research universities between the 1870s and the 1920s.

Works that Have Influenced Me

Ellen Fitzpatrick, *Endless Crusade: Women, Social Scientists, and Progressive Reform* (New York: Oxford University Press, 1990).

Hugh Hawkins, *Pioneer: A History of The Johns Hopkins University, 1874-1889* (Ithaca: Cornell University Press, 1960 [1984]).

Linda K. Kerber, *Toward an Intellectual History of Women: Essays* (Chapel Hill: University of North Carolina Press, 1997).

Gerda Lerner, *The Creation of Feminist Consciousness: From the Middle Ages to Eighteen-Seventy.* (New York: Oxford University Press, 1993).

Robyn Muncy, *Creating a Female Dominion in American Reform, 1890-1935.* (New York: Oxford University Press, 1991).

Margaret Rossiter, *Women Scientists in America: Struggles and Strategies to 1940.* (Baltimore: Johns Hopkins University Press, 1982).

Joan Wallach Scott, *Gender and the Politics of History.* (New York: Columbia University Press, 1988).

I was particularly interested in Hutchins's reputation as an intellectually motivated university president and in the ways his presidency seemed to work in contradiction to the idea of the modern, research-oriented university in the United States. Douglas encouraged me to read a number of biographies of university presidents, many of which were more hagiography than history. Hugh Hawkins's volume on Charles W. Eliot was an exception.[4] Hawkins's study served as a loose model for me, one that I did not use in the dissertation as well as I might have. I was not happy with the dissertation, and decided that I could take the extensive primary research I had already done, build on it, and develop a more fine-grained analysis of the impact Hutchins had on the university and on higher education, the reasons for the responses he evoked in members of the university community, and his place in the pantheon of university presidents. Fortunately, my dissertation committee offered me some solid guidelines for significantly revising the dissertation to turn it into a book.[5]

Unfortunately, the job market was terrible in 1987 for historians of education. There were three jobs open that year and one had already been promised to a more senior scholar. I applied for the other two, which brought me to Washington University. I had done some research on St. Louis for Ellen Lagemann, specifically on Henry Pritchett, who had a faculty appointment at the University in the 1880s, and the scientific and philosophical community in which he found himself in St. Louis. And I heard from others that Ray Callahan had been the previous historian in the Education Department before he retired.[6] But otherwise I knew nothing about the University or St. Louis. Once on campus, I made contact with fellow historians in the history department and found that being in a department of education in a college of arts and sciences had many benefits. All of my history courses were easily cross-listed and I began working with both graduate and undergraduate students interested in American history, particularly late nineteenth- and early twentieth-century social and intellectual history and, of course, the history of education. My colleagues in the education department seemed to appreciate having a historian present and, although my teaching load was heavy (two courses per semester with up to 100 students in each, with no teaching assistants), I was able to get to work on the book within months of the transition.

Taking the comments of the dissertation committee and a generous Spencer Foundation Small Grant, and continuing conversations about the book with Larry Cremin, whom I occasionally saw in Chicago or New York on my research trips, I spent three years completely rewriting the book. I reread Ellen Lagemann's *A Generation of Women,*[7] and Cremin's *American Education* volumes, focusing on the educational biographies, which led me to examine more closely Hutchins's early life, family, church, school, college, and military experience, and career to understand the variety of experiences that had a transformative, educative influence on him. I remember spending one summer in a house in New Hampshire, wrestling with the chapter on the reform of the college at the University of Chicago, which became two chapters, one on the curricular changes and one on Hutchins's interactions with faculty. After I wrote it, I sent it off to Harold Wechsler for comments, and got pages of suggestions back, which were very helpful in the revisions. Harold had completed his graduate work at Columbia, too, and we'd worked with some of the same people, including Walter Metzger. He was so encouraging in those early years, I felt very lucky to have him as a professional colleague and friend.

In fact, by then, I had been attending the History of Education Society meetings for a few years. The first was the meeting at Stanford, where David Tyack led some colleagues on a hike in Palo Alto. I didn't go on the hike, as I'd combined the meeting with a visit with family. But I did meet David Angus, one of the discussants on my paper. I had heard he could be tough, but he was very kind to me. In those early years of membership, I came to understand better the whole concept of sponsored mobility, although I think it was more akin to active collegiality. Because I found no other historians of education at my own university, except for the historian of medical education Kenneth Ludmerer, whom I met later and who became a friend, the meetings grew in importance. It was the one place I could hear about new work being done in the field, converse with people who were interested in talking about teaching history of education, and share my work with colleagues who understood it and always made helpful suggestions for improving it. There were only a few hundred of us working in this area, and the affirmation of the annual meeting helped me to better grasp the contours of the field and the key issues emerging in new scholarship. The meetings also afforded me the opportunity to begin to participate in the process of not only finding a place for myself, but also helping others to do the same. Just as my colleagues had nominated me for positions, pushed me to take on more leadership, and shared their insights about the state of the field, I began to do the same for others. It was such a satisfying dimension of becoming and being a historian of education. Bill Reese, John Rury, Jeff Mirel, Linda Eisenmann, Harold Wechsler, Lynn Gordon, Wayne Urban all became both friends and mutually supportive colleagues in this process, and it has been a delight to meet their students, read their work, and collaborate with them on various professional projects in the History of Education Society.

While I was working on the Hutchins book, and doing research at the University of Chicago at Regenstein Library's Special Collections, I was also developing a keen interest in women's history. This interest first emerged while I was working on the bibliographic essay for the nursing book, but I set it aside to finish the dissertation. I had read about nursing as a women's profession, the ways nursing opened to women who had few other options in the late nineteenth century, and the power and status dimensions of those professions that became dominated by women by the late nineteenth century—nursing, social work, and teaching. And my teaching in the history of schooling and American education more broadly fostered my interest in marginality in institutions.

I thought my second project might focus on teaching, but while working on Hutchins I kept finding letters and documents related to women on the faculty of the University of Chicago and became intrigued by the question of how they had gotten there. One, in particular, interested me: Mary B. Gilson, an economist who had written Hutchins complaining about how her department colleagues held meetings at the Quadrangles Club on campus, and attended conferences, and had never invited her to anything. She claimed she felt virtually invisible to them. About a month later she wrote back to him thanking him—she suddenly started receiving invitations and began to be included in her colleagues' activities. I found other women economists (most in the School of Social Service Administration), and a historian, along with the occasional graduate student. I also noted that, when Hutchins and the faculty of particular departments discussed the qualifications of someone for a faculty appointment, the language was vague. Assessments of quality seemed to rest on unarticulated assumptions, the recommendations of faculty in the department, and scholars in the field. Most of the hiring was done by recruitment, in a profession that claimed to be meritocratic.

I started reading whatever I could find on the history of women in higher education, starting with Rosalind Rosenberg's *Beyond Separate Spheres*, then Penina Glazer and Miriam Slater's *Unequal Colleagues* and Geraldine Clifford's *Lone Voyagers*, and working back to Mabel Newcomer's *A Century of Higher Education for American Women* and Thomas Woody's *A History of Women's Education in the United States* and Barbara Solomon's *In the Company of Educated Women*.[8] These works detailed the development of women's higher education and charted the enormous difficulties women with Ph.D.s had faced trying to find positions in academic institutions as scholars. I was curious about these women at Chicago I kept finding and how their experiences squared with the women portrayed in these other studies.

I remember talking with Ellen Lagemann about my interest in academic women and she suggested that, if I were to pursue this, I would have to begin doing archival research at the women's colleges, where many of them obtained academic positions. I spent part of one summer traveling around to different college archives to see what was there. I didn't have enough money to spend a lot of time in each place, but I learned enough to apply over the next few years for a Spencer Foundation grant, a Frederick B. Artz grant to work at Oberlin College Archives, where one economist had taught, a Rockefeller Archives grant to examine material on women scholars' projects in social sciences, and a Washington University faculty research grant. I feel very fortunate to have been awarded funding from all of these places. The largest grant came from Spencer, under Patricia Graham's leadership. The funding enabled me to take a sabbatical, finish most of the archival research, and write Part One of a three-part book. The writing, as with many projects, went very slowly, and slower still when I returned to full-time teaching and committee leadership in my department. I have spent 17 years on the project and am still not done. To my regret, I allowed too many university obligations to interfere with writing and had to take a number of summers to deal with both professional and family obligations, rather than writing. But I have published articles out of this research and I do plan to finish the book.

As I worked my way through the secondary literature and archival materials, I decided the focus should be on women academic social science scholars between 1890 and 1940. I chose to focus on women in the academic social sciences for a few reasons. First, women were not marginal in numbers in higher education by 1890, which is the starting date for my study, but they were marginalized in a variety of ways, even in coeducational institutions, as Lynn Gordon amply demonstrates.[9] They were also marginalized on higher education faculties, except at most of the women's colleges, as Patricia Palmieri argues in the case of Wellesley.[10] Second, the period of 1890 to 1940 was a critical period for the development of academic social science in the U.S. and Europe. Empirical research was largely conducted by male university faculty beginning in the late 1880s and 1890s. In fact, scholarship of any kind in Europe and the U.S. was considered men's work. Women might participate in the transmission and consumption of knowledge, but the production of knowledge was a male enterprise. Yet women had been involved in social science in the context of social reform and social welfare education, policy, and practice since the 1880s in the United States, and then in Britain and Germany by the turn of the century. As Mary Jo Deegan argues, Jane Addams introduced social research at Hull-House on specific problems in Chicago in the 1890s, which was modeled in part on social survey research in Britain, and influenced in part the orientation toward social science research in the early years at the University of Chicago.[11]

Third, universities in the U.S did not generally offer rigorous graduate education in any disciplines, but especially in the social sciences until the 1880s. Women were not admitted to doctoral programs until the 1890s; before that incipient female scholars who pursued graduate training went to Europe, principally Germany, Switzerland, and then Paris. When male faculty and university presidents began to accede to pressure from women and to see a need for graduate training for faculty at the women's colleges, they opened graduate programs to women. Women's enrollment in all the social science disciplines increased significantly throughout the 1900s, 1910s, 1920s, and 1930s, and when women could not find work in research university faculties, they did so at women's colleges, a few co-educational colleges, some state universities, and, in rare cases, newly emerging research universities. Academic positions for women declined somewhat in the 1930s, opened briefly in the 1940s during World War II, and then closed again until the late 1960s and early 1970s, again under pressure from feminist academic scholars. Yet even during the so-called quiet period of the mid-1940s to the mid-1960s, as Linda Eisenmann argues, debates about the need for and purposes of higher education and professional work for women continued.[12]

I was curious about how earlier women scholars made the transition from social reform to academic research and the kinds of impacts their scholarship had on the developing social sciences. I also was interested in exploring their impact on the institutions in which they did find a place on the faculty, as scholars as well as teachers. Ellen Lagemann's essay "Looking at Gender: Women's History," pointed to the need to move beyond rendering women visible to examining the impact of gender on institutional cultures.[13] Part of my project was to render women visible in the academic social sciences and among higher education social science faculty in this period, as Mary Jo Deegan has done with women sociologists in *Women in Sociology*, but I was also concerned with examining the kind of gender challenge women presented to both the developing disciplines and the institutional cultures they encountered, as in Bonnie Smith's work on *The Gender of History*.[14]

At this point in the project, I have come to understand that, although women continued to be marginalized in a multitude of ways in the disciplines included in my study--anthropology, economics, history, political science, and sociology--and in some of the institutions, they did have an impact on institutional culture and they were able to produce scholarship, albeit more slowly than they might have with more support and recognition. In many cases, women who were able to gain some footing in colleges and research universities made places for other women in their institutions. Many received mentoring from their male colleagues and doctoral advisors. And a good number of them participated in local, state, and national policy-making through their research contributions. They had access to both institutional funding and philanthropic foundation funding, though not on the scale of their male colleagues. I have found most intriguing the ways they learned to navigate these institutions, negotiate for recognition as faculty and scholars, and persist in the face of repeated gender discrimination.

The very language of academic research was gendered, in the assumptions of what constituted strong scholarship in these disciplines and who might be considered a good scholar. It permeated academic searches, differential expectations regarding the duties and roles of women and men faculty, negotiations over salary, assessments of scholarly production and competence, and even who was allowed into the libraries and the "faculty club." And all of these processes changed over time, depending on the number of women in a department or institution, the attitudes of administrators and other faculty, the ways a particular department or research unit perceived changes in the discipline, and the ways those perceptions reflected anxiety about institutional status. One issue became clear: even as scholars and administrators were claiming that the research enterprise of higher education institutions and educational access was growing increasingly meritocratic in the first four decades of the twentieth century, which was a major justification of academic freedom and academic professionalization, this was not actually the case. Investigating the experiences and impact of women in this gendered environment has potential to change the ways we see higher education and scholarship in American society and American history.

I remember when I had been working on the project off and on for about four years, someone who heard me present a paper on my research said "It must be so interesting working on women who were your predecessors." Oddly enough, I had not initially thought of the project in that way—I had seen it as a historical problem, understanding gender, marginality, and the academic development of social science scholarship during this period. Over time, I came to see it in part through the lens of my own experiences, although it might be more accurate to say I was seeing my own experience through the lens of the research. I understand in deeper ways how higher education cultures develop and change and how previously marginal groups can change institutional cultures, their policies, practices, and operating assumptions. Fortunately, the historical research on women and gender in higher education has grown significantly over the past fifty years since Mabel Newcomer's *Century of Higher Education for Women*. Although it began as a story of "expansion and exclusion," as Patricia Graham argued in 1978,[15] and the scholarship on gender and higher education has broadened and deepened, there is still much to be explored. Rendering women visible has made the institutional cultures themselves more visible, which is one of the major aims of research on women and gender.

NOTES

1 Ellen Condliffe Lagemann, *Private Power for the Public Good: A History of the Carnegie Foundation for the Advancement of Teaching* (Middletown, CT: Wesleyan University Press, 1983).

2 Lagemann, *The Politics of Knowledge: The Carnegie Corporation, Philanthropy, and Public Policy* (Middletown, CT: Wesleyan University Press, 1989).

3 Lawrence A. Cremin, *American Education: The Metropolitan Experience, 1876–1980* (New York: Harper & Row, 1988) and *Popular Education and Its Discontents* (New York: Harper & Row, 1990).

4 Hugh Hawkins, *Between Harvard and America: The Educational Leadership of Charles W. Eliot* (New York: Oxford University Press, 1972).

5 Mary Ann Dzuback, *Robert M. Hutchins: Portrait of an Educator* (Chicago: University of Chicago Press, 1991).

6 Raymond Callahan, *Education and the Cult of Efficiency: A Study of the Social Forces that Have Shaped the Administration of the Public Schools* (Chicago: University of Chicago Press, 1962).

7 Lagemann, *A Generation of Women: Education in the Lives of Progressive Reformers* (Cambridge: Harvard University Press, 1979).

8 Rosalind Rosenberg, *Beyond Separate Spheres: Intellectual Roots of Modern Feminism* (New Haven: Yale University Press, 1982); Penina Migdal Glazer and Miriam Slater, *Unequal Colleagues: The Entrance of Women into the Professions, 1890–1940* (New Brunswick: Rutgers University Press, 1987); Geraldine Joncich Clifford, ed., *Lone Voyagers: Academic Women in Coeducational Institutions, 1870–1937* (New York: The Feminist Press, 1989); Mabel Newcomer, *A Century of Higher Education for American Women* (New York: Harper & Brothers, 1959); Thomas Woody, *A History of Women's Education in the United States* (2 vols. New York: The Science Press, 1929); Barbara Miller Solomon, *In the Company of Educated Women: A history of Women and Higher Education in America* (New Haven: Yale University Press, 1985).

9 Lynn Gordon, *Gender and Higher Education in the Progressive Era* (New Haven: Yale University Press, 1991).

10 Patricia Ann Palmieri, *In Adamless Eden: The Community of Women Faculty at Wellesley College* (New Haven: Yale University Press, 1995).

11 Mary Jo Deegan, *Jane Addams and the Men of the Chicago School, 1892–1918* (New Brunswick, NJ: Transaction Press, 1988).

12 Linda Eisenmann, *Higher Education for Women in Postwar America, 1945–1965* (Baltimore: Johns Hopkins University Press, 2006).

13 Lagemann, "Looking at Gender: Women's History," in John Hardin Best, ed., *Historical Inquiry in Education: A Research Agenda* (Washington, D.C.: American Educational Research Association, 1983).

14 Mary Jo Deegan, ed., *Women in Sociology: A Bio–Bibliographic Sourcebook* (New York: Greenwood Press, 1991); Bonnie G. Smith, *The Gender of History: Men, Women, and Historical Practice* (Cambridge: Harvard University Press, 1998).

15 Patricia Albjerg Graham, "Expansion and Exclusion: A History of Women in Higher Education in America," *Signs: Journal of Women and Culture in American Society* 3 (Summer 1978): 759–773.

BARBARA FINKELSTEIN

LIFE AT THE MARGIN OF POSSIBLITY

Learning Along the Way

I have crafted a life of scholarly work that has taken form and shape in the small spaces of everyday life where people get a sense of who they are, what they hope to become, and what might be available for them in life. "There is no "plotted narrative here-- -not a linear story that shows "how one thing led to another and those to a third and then and then and then...." [1] This chronicle of my life is a "show and tell" of particular "events, encounters, and chance discoveries." It arrays "...a variety of facts and battery of interpretations" [2] that tells something about living in history and discovering how history lives. Mostly it is about learning along the way. [3]

FRIDAY NIGHT DINNERS AND MESSAGES FROM HOME

Growing-up-learning went something like this: I was born in Brooklyn, New York in 1937 and lived on Westminster Road in Flatbush, just three blocks from Brooklyn College. Every Friday night for the next eighteen years, in the company of more than twenty aunts, uncles, cousins, and assorted friends, we celebrated the Sabbath. Our Bubby, the family matriarch, chased the girls out of the kitchen in this way. "Get Out of the Kitchen. You're in America now." Pop, as the family patriarch, spoke and muttered prayers which some neither understood nor heard. All of us however, absorbed Bubby's deepest beliefs: that kindness was God-given and that a "lie for peace" was benevolent. Those of us in the youngest generations watched fathers and uncles slip out to eat non-kosher food, smoke, seek real estate opportunities, and otherwise re-interpret the cultural and social rules that had governed their lives. Friday night dinners, it seems, were spaces-in-between, sites of learning that straddled the intersections between the Old World and the New, newcomers and natives, young and old, the past and the future.

In 1941, the family joined a diaspora from urban Brooklyn to near-by suburban Great Neck where the power and influence of the Jewish community was on the rise. [4] Great Neck in the 1940's and 1950s became home to a relatively affluent Jewish community where women looked after family households, built and joined volunteer networks, took charge of child-rearing, and organized domestic life around the dinner table, the radio, the synagogue, the schools, and the informal social networks where young people communicated and learned their place in the world. Men typically commuted, held community offices, provided material support for their immediate families and for European relatives seeking to immigrate to the U.S. No matter what its status in an evolving social hierarchy, the Jewish community was riveted to news about the rise of Adolph Hitler, the expansion of Nazi power, and the rising tide of anti-Semitism in Europe, a family matter for many and a community building focus for all.

Personal Favorites

"Casting Networks of Good Influence: The Reconstruction of Childhood in the United States," in M.Hawes and N. Ray Hiner, eds., *American Childhood: A Resource Guide and Historical Handbook* (Westport CT: Greenwood Press, 1985), 111–153.

"Education Historians as Mythmakers." *Review of Research in Education* 18 (Washington, DC: American Educational Research Association, 1999): 255–297.

"Perfecting Childhood: Horace Mann and the Origins of Public Education," *Biography* 13 (1990): 6–21.

Regulated Children/Liberated Children: Education in Psychohistorical Perspective (New York: The Psychohistory Press, 1989).

"Revealing Human Agency: the Uses of Biography in the Study of Educational History," in Craig Kridel, ed., *Writing Educational Biography: Explorations in Qualitative Research* (New York and London: Garland Publishing, Inc.), 45–59.

My mother was a master of women's separate sphere, a graduate of Smith College, a closet socialist, and an avid consumer of child-rearing advice literature. She was a cultural standard-bearer and specialist in social etiquette and entertainment. She was also, like many women of her generation, a lady-in-waiting. My father was a successful paper bag salesman and manufacturer, a Republican, an heir to powerful traditions of patriarchy and commerce, and the ultimate ruler of our household. I had a second mother, Rosetta Buggs who joined an urban migration from North Carolina in search of opportunity. Rosie became a love rock and a companion. We cheered for Jackie Robinson and became avid Brooklyn Dodger fans. We saw discrimination in action and I learned to hate it. My sisters and I went to Tunis Lake, a socialist summer camp, where we learned labor songs, lived in communal solidarity, and railed against injustice as we discovered or experienced it.

Notwithstanding the experiences in our "Commie" camp, the social messages of the household were clear and unambiguous: study hard, learn to type, play the piano, go to temple, absorb high culture, try a competitive summer camp, try a socialist camp, be smart, but not too smart, go to Smith, train to be a teacher, marry well and wealthy—maybe a doctor, remain chaste, avoid vulgar displays of wealth, don't pierce your ears, don't smoke, behave yourself in school. These messages reverberated in the movie theaters, in the schools, in the books that we read, the songs that we heard, and in the woman-less, mind-numbing histories that we had to memorize. The litany of parental advice was reinforced at my sister's graduation from Smith College, in 1955, when Adlai Stevenson, the commencement speaker, exhorted members of the graduating class to make use of their education and sustain civilization by placing Classics on the bedside tables of their husbands – not apocryphal – I was there. Thus schooled in the power of patriarchy and the ideals of socialism, the practices of capitalism, philanthropy, charity, and social welfare, I graduated from Great Neck High in 1955 and began a momentous two year journey, not to Smith, but to the University of Wisconsin at Madison where I began to question the taken-for-granted assumptions of the world into which I was born.

DISCOVERING AN HISTORICAL STATE OF MIND

My life at Wisconsin was transformative. I discovered the uses of the mind as a way to understand the things I cared about in life. I learned to reflect on the world around me. I found a pathway to independence, a way to re-imagine the meaning of things. The occasion for this epiphany was entirely accidental, a matter of good luck really. Professor George Lachmann Mosse brought an historical intelligence into my life when, in his much-venerated course in European Cultural and Intellectual History, he enlarged the terrain of history and of life as I knew it at the time. A brilliant and charismatic lecturer, an historian of immense social and political insight, an impassioned teacher, Mosse grounded history in the bedrock of human experience. He "peopled" history in powerful ways. He brought memorable individual and group stories into view, not so much to put a face on history nor to decorate history with interesting vignettes, but to reveal an array of excruciating dilemmas that shaped what individuals and groups could do, know, imagine, believe, and choose as Nazi Germany emerged. He placed his own life and that of his opulent and influential family on view in the matrix of European Anti-Semitism. He chose to chronicle, among other things, the critical moment when they had to choose whether to stay or go, live as exiles abroad, or use their considerable resources to sustain their social, political, and cultural advantage in an increasingly hostile Germany.

As he dramatized the contours of his family's reasoning and their ultimate decision to leave, Mosse revealed the underbelly of German cultural beliefs, political habits, and social practices that enabled the rise of a Fascist state. He understood the shape of both good and evil. He made matters of daily life the very stuff of history and the stuff of history a matter of daily life and living. He demonstrated that it was possible to refract history through the experiences of individuals and groups while, at the same time, to situate the meaning of daily life in the bedrock cultural, political, social, and economic circumstance. [5]

Professor Mosse's historical turn initiated me into what has become a relentless, life-long commitment to the study and craft of cultural/intellectual history, and the uses of biography and autobiography as a way of recovering history and making sense of the world. His small honors seminar was a revelation and a privilege--the best course I have ever had. As I was to learn later, he was one of a handful of historians who "...blurred the boundaries between political, intellectual/cultural, and social history."[6] In 1957, he was for me, the man of the moment for what lay ahead: a life transition, a coming to terms, with the conflicting claims of academic, social, and domestic life that framed the choices women could make. The Wisconsin experience softened the ground for the cultivation of my passion for the history of education.

I transferred to Barnard in 1957, knowing that it was a woman's college where the life of the mind was cherished and nurtured, the cultural riches of New York City were immediately available, and the supply of eligible bachelors was plentiful. It was also a place of excruciating personal conflict and turmoil. Like many women of my generation, I was caught in a complex web of contradictory prescriptions and aspirations— between the traditions of domesticity that I had learned at home, and the pursuit of an intellectual life that appeared at the time, to be out-of reach, and out-of- mind, and almost unimaginable. I did not know then, as I was to learn along the way that the choice of a demanding professional career could be counter-cultural, politically constrained, and psychologically challenging—at least for many middle class women. Nor did I know exactly what I was doing when, as a senior history major at Barnard, I decided to take a master's degree in the teaching of history and get married.

The choices were safe ones that became subversive. I did what I was told to do -- Become a teacher! "Marry a doctor!" But the lessons that I had learned at Wisconsin persisted. My new companion, Jim Finkelstein, was a doctor, but a doctor with a difference. He was an interdisciplinary academic who navigated the boundaries between hard science and clinical medicine. He liked smart women. He respected the life of the mind. Like me, he had rejected suburban life and elevated matters of the mind above matters of money. He took pleasure in the weirdness of my master's program which included a seminar in Nineteenth Century Romantic History taught by Jacques Barzun and Lionel Trilling which I completed during our honeymoon in Mexico.

CIRCLING BACK AND MOVING ON

The year of my graduation, 1959, was momentous, not only because I got married, and gathered up a teaching credential. It was also the year of The Cremin, and a transformative encounter with the history of education. Cremin was a brilliant and charismatic teacher, a rising academic star, and an inspired platform speaker. The content of his big lecture class in the Foundations of Education reflected the traditions of his mentor – R. Freeman Butts. Cremin had a distinct style! He was a master storyteller, a weaver of tales, an exemplary scholar-teacher who enlarged the concept of schools as something more than a compulsory experience for children. The course revealed a professional focus and a reason to enter a doctoral program a year later.

In 1961, Teachers College was an extraordinary place to study education. It was a face-to-face world of intellectual encounter, argument, and critique. The faculty comprised an interlocking circle of scholars, historians, philosophers, comparative educators, sociologists, anthropologists, political scientists, and curriculum theorists, who examined education from multiple angles and discipline-based perspectives. The interdisciplinarity of the program echoed the intellectual excitement that Professor Mosse had inspired.

I arrived on Larry Cremin's doorstep at a captivating moment, when the history of education as a field of study exploded. There were orgies of revisionism that expanded the boundaries of the field, produced alternative historical narratives and whole new ways of thinking about the meaning and importance of education and education history. The explosion of creativity also generated sub-communities of scholars who championed the relative benefit of one or another approach to education history. A reception at Geraldine Clifford's home during an Annual Meeting revealed the creativity and turbulence of the field, and a certain quality of aggressive advocacy for one or another approach. Seating and standing preferences were symbolic. In one room, there were the more traditional practitioners who explored the history of public schools as seedbeds of opportunity, civic learning, and democratic and humanitarian reform. In a second room was a rising generation of historians who focused on the emergence of schools as hegemonic institutions, instruments of social control, and structures of inequality. A third less visible and physically dispersed group were intellectual historians exploring processes of cultural transmission and the nurture of cultural and political habits in the crucible of families, churches, museums, libraries, taverns, and newspapers, as well as in schools. The history of education was a field in motion, a bubbling cauldron, which nurtured in me a life- long preference for synthesis and historiographical critique.

Within the evolving universe of education history, I discovered that the field was bereft of studies of classroom practices. I had been impressed with Merle Curti's *Social Ideas of American Educators* as a form of social history that documented the importance of biography as a way to ground and analyze the contours of political and social belief among serial generations of education reformers.[7] I was much taken by the creativity and power of Ruth Miller Elson's book *Guardians of Tradition: American Schoolbooks in the Nineteenth Century,* a masterful study of textbook content as an index of political belief, moral exhortation, and social and cultural practices. I learned that textbooks functioned as powerful message systems which amplified and legitimized race-based hierarchies and American exceptionalism. There were portrayals of the virtues and rewards of hard work but not of inherited privilege. Nor were there portrayals of conflict and war.[8]

I found it odd then, as I do now, that the interests of historians of education, no matter what their sub-specialties or points of view, typically stopped at the schoolhouse door. I thought then as I do now that historians of education somehow didn't get to the heart of the matter in education – the places where teachers taught and young people learned. Thus perplexed, I left Teachers College.

MOVING ON AND FINDING A WAY

I completed my dissertation seven years later – at a distance from Teachers College. The process was gradual, slow going, and non-linear. We moved to Washington, D.C. in 1963. Jim took up a fellowship at the National Institutes of Health and I began to juggle multiple careers as a mother, wife, civil rights activist, lecturer, and dissertation writer. Our daughters, Donna and Laura, were born in 1964 and 1965, almost precisely at the moment when the Civil Rights movement had come, big time, to Washington, D.C. Donna participated in the March on Washington in utero and Jim developed a relationship with the D.C. bail-bondsman in order to secure the release of incarcerated friends. In 1968, I took a job as a lecturer at the University of Maryland, where I became culturally and politically schooled in an anti-intellectual, racist, sexist, and anti-cosmopolite university culture.[9]

I experienced first-hand the workings of an intricate cultural apparatus that pinned women into lower paid jobs, children into institutional corners, and people of color into hierarchal "pigmentocracies," to use Nelson Mandela's marvelous concept. I became a dedicated feminist and took to the streets and lawns of College Park and the Pentagon to protest the war in Vietnam. Together with Jim and assorted friends, we founded The Little School—a pre-school for children under three. I engaged in a monumental struggle to reconcile my life as a mother, scholar, teacher, social activist, graduate student, and rising professor.

As a mom, I became a participant-observer and decision maker who had learned to love learning, and hoped that my daughters could, as I had done, find places for their imaginations to soar. I had learned to think of schools as networks of association, structures of authority, and places of learning and did my best to find good schools for Donna and Laura.

Favorite Works that Influenced Me

Phillipe Ariès, *Centuries of Childhood: A Social History of Family Life* Robert Baldick, trans. (New York: Alfred A. Knopf, 1962).

James Axtell, *Natives and Newcomers: The Cultural Origins of North America* (New York and Oxford: Oxford University Press, 2001).

John W. Blassingame, *The Slave Community: Plantation Life in the Antebellum South* (New York, Oxford: Oxford University Press, 1972;

Jill Kerr Conway, "Perspectives on the History of Women's Education in the United States," *History of Education Quarterly* 14 (Spring, 1974): 1–13.

Clifford Geertz, *The Interpretation of Cultures* (New York: Basic Books, 1973, revised and enlarged edition, 1979).

I discovered a new community of colleagues, mentors, scholars, and life-long friends at the Library of Congress, a world populated by social, cultural, intellectual, and political historians who explored the terrains of childhood, youth, the family, and education in their work. I had access to a treasure trove of primary sources – autobiographies, memoirs of teachers and students, the observations of foreign travelers, obscure works of school reformers, pictures of classrooms, textbooks, and portraits of instructional technology. I became schooled in the experiences of nineteenth century classrooms by the very people who inhabited, observed, and represented them.

Schools came into view as powerful structures of persuasion, templates of experience, and message systems that reverberated in the small spaces of every-day life where teachers taught and children learned. I had learned, more or less, to decode the message-systems inscribed not only in textbooks, but in the behavior and practices of teachers within classroom walls. I had found a way, in the footsteps of Professor Mosse, to populate the world of education history with children, youth, teachers, families, and local community leaders. I learned that teaching repertoires remained stable over time, but the uses of literacy might not.

Governing the Young revealed the emergence of schools as spaces in between— way stations between the small world of family, community, church, and school, and the larger and evolving worlds of commerce, politics, cultural production, and nation-building. They were sites of communities-in-the making, not only projects for the architects of public education, the socializing notions of school reformers, or the institutional imaginings of social, political, economic, and cultural leaders. They were also places where teachers and students could learn who they were and what they could aspire to be. [10]

Without quite knowing it at the time, I had learned that it was possible to write an historical narrative ethnographically. I learned to understand schools not only as political, economic, and social watering holes, but as playgrounds and/or prisons of a sort, where teachers and students could and sometimes did, craft worlds of their own in a dazzling multiplicity of ways. I learned that schools were places of possibility and of constraint. I learned to see them as networks of association that refracted the centralizing tendencies of modern life in different ways. I had also learned along the way, to situate my life and the lives of my children in the bedrock of history.

LIVING AND LEARNING IN CONVERGING WORLDS

When I completed *Governing the Young* in 1970, my life was once again in transition. Donna and Laura went off to elementary school. I became an assistant professor at the University. I tried as best I could to make sense of the multiple, intersecting, intertwined, and often disjointed communities within which I lived my life. I tried to stitch together the threads of a complex life as mother, professor, teacher, scholar, civil rights activist, and child advocate.

For the next fifteen years, I lived in the worlds that I studied and studied in the worlds that I lived. I was a mother who began to study the history of childhood, youth, and the family and a child advocate who studied the history of child rearing and the evolving contours of child abuse and school discipline. I was a teacher who studied the history of teaching and learning in families and local communities. I was a feminist who began to study the history of women professionals and the contours of professionalism as women defined them. I lived in the company of historians, militant women, community activists, scholars, students, and teachers who took aim at the cultural assumptions, political practices, socio-economic hierarchies, and legal precedents embedded in traditions of education history and inscribed in the habits of mind and association of everyday life in schools and localities across the country.

Governing the Young, with its focus on teacher behavior elicited little interest in the world of education history scholarship. I discovered rather quickly that the history of childhood, like the history of teacher behavior did not have a congenial home in the field. Undeterred, I am proud to say, I set out quite deliberately to find ways to import the history of childhood into the history of education as a field of study.

I began to focus on the learning as well as the teaching end of things – taking threads from here and there in an exploding and evolving universe of knowledge.[11] I tried to understand the historical circumstances within which serial generations of diverse young people learned to imagine, know, believe, aspire and find a place in the world. I began to study how young people learned who they were, what they hoped to become, and how they made sense within the small spaces of everyday life in families, communities, and schools.

Luckily for me a new journal, the *History of Childhood Quarterly* had emerged and so too had the Psychohistory Press, both the brain children of psychohistorian Lloyd deMause. Both became watering holes for child-focused historians who would ultimately stretch the boundaries of education history as a field and a craft. Within the new worlds of childhood history, I discovered a forward looking scholarly domain that didn't inscribe the kinds of culture wars that I had learned to avoid.

It seemed natural to convene a community of historians who had interests in the intersections of childhood and education history and were prepared to contribute to the preparation of an edited book. Within the pages of *Regulated Children/ Liberated Children: Education in Psychohistorical Perspective* were nine essays that explored constructions of childhood as reflected in the small spaces of life where teaching and learning went on, and evolved over time. It was as Anthony F.C. Wallace suggested in his review of the book in *History of Education Quarterly*, "a stage setting exercise…with a focus on how parents, teachers, poets, psychoanalysts, psychologists, educators, and school reformers…perceived the child as a developing human being."[12]

My own essay in the book, "Reading, Writing, and the Acquisition of Identity in the United States 1790–1860," is a personal favorite, along with several subsequent biographical studies. I learned what it meant to be a girl of privilege growing up in a city and learning the constraints of being female and rebellious as Elizabeth Cady Stanton had done. "Oh how I wish you were a man," her father mused on more than one occasion. I learned what the acquisition of literacy could mean to generations of enslaved African Americans who had to "steal" an education and, after emancipation, gathered together and built a scaffolding on which to construct public education in the South. I learned how the children of laboring and dependent classes, who, as they went to schools, learned to read, write, and labor in atmospheres of relentless regulation, and commonly learned to hate schools and resist schooling. I learned that school reformers like Horace Mann developed exquisite education sensibilities in the complex learning environments growing up on a farm in proximity to a hat-manufacturing town.[13]

My article in *Regulated Children* was a personal favorite for other reasons as well. I had learned to think about the history of education comparatively across boundaries of race, class, gender, generation, and location. I learned to think about the rise of formal education culturally, as a chapter in the history of human consciousness, the evolution of social practices, the shaping of belief and aspiration, and the construction of new forms of association and communication at the intersection of tradition and change.

Over the course of three decades, from 1956 when I had discovered cultural history at the University of Wisconsin to 1986, when *Governing the Young* was accepted for publication, I had become a full professor and traversed the boundaries between the past and the future as all historians do. I had stood on the shoulders of pioneering women and historians and tried to push up the sky for Donna, Laura, and the legion of students and young faculty who would come my way. I had lived through an almost civil-rights revolution in the U.S. I could see a new generation of education historians coming over the horizon. I celebrated the emergence of a more expansive *History of Education Quarterly* that not only extended the borders of the field, but helped to create a kinder, gentler community of education history scholars who honored all kinds of work.[14] Over time, a dazzlingly diverse array of historians would recast the field to go beyond the exploration of social structure and political and economic determinacies. Some focused on the fate and experience of young people, women, and teachers, as they struggled to find a dignified place in the world. For my own part, I had crafted an approach to education history that focused on cycles of teaching and learning and the uses of biography to study history and reveal the ways in which the power of circumstance and terrains of freedom intersected.[15] I came to understand that historians of education studied the hard structures of modern life, but typically ignored the hidden underbelly of human creativity, social and political action, and transformative possibility in the array of learning communities, unless of course they were biographers and community historians. I discovered that the weight of tradition fell as heavily on historians as it did on the lives of the less privileged, and have spent a professional life time crafting historiographical critiques to make the point.[16]

I could go on about all of the publications, historiographical and otherwise, that accompanied these efforts. I could map out the genealogy of *Governing the Young* and its arrival as a book in 1989, thirty years after it was completed. I could chronicle the applications of work that I loved to do: peopling education history with teachers, learners, and previously unacknowledged groups; preparing historiographical critiques; editing books focused on creative, innovative, and ignored worlds of scholarship; and publishing work on teaching as a profession, mothers and fathers as tutors for a rising generation, and public policies designed to regulate the lives of children and youth, teachers and students, mothers and women professionals. But these are stories for another day, not only mine, but those of a rising generation of historians who have constructed a corpus of extraordinary historical work that reveals among other things, the fate and experience of young people not only as victims of circumstance, or repositories of cultural imposition and social control but as active agents of social change and sometimes powerful historical actors as well.

CROSSING BOUNDARIES OF PLACE: LEARNING NEW WORLDS

In 1983, Donna and Laura had gone off to College, our private sphere was quiet, my career was on solid footing, and I had completed a line of historical work on teaching and learning in the nineteenth and early twentieth centuries. It seemed a logical extension of previous work to apply what I had learned to the study of contemporary cultures. The place became Japan. Oral history and ethnography became the tools.

The timing was perfect. In both Japan and the United States, commitments to internationalization and globalization had become a focus of public life, school reform, and civic learning. Opportunities for access to Japanese and U.S. schools proliferated. Non-profit foundations created funding strategies that privileged the development of Japan-in-the-schools initiatives and support for cultural exchanges. We jumped all over the opportunities and created the Mid-Atlantic Region Japan-in-the-Schools (MARJiS)—a program designed to combine academic and experiential learning and to enhance the quality of Japan-related instruction and research in the United States, and also of U.S.-related research and education in Japan.

MARJiS became a beehive of activity. It convened networks of scholars, researchers, educators, historians, policy makers, and social advocates who were committed to the transformation of education policies, practices, and perspectives. It created transcultural education experiences which we hoped had the potential to transform schools, transcend stereotypes of nationality, race, class, religion, education level and gender, and discover and strengthen connections between people of different cultures, nations and generations.

My life as a Pacific border crosser presented a series of firsts: learning to take joy as well as frustration in the daily company of strangers; unpeeling the meaning of strange encounters when people in possession of alternative habits of heart, mind, and association try to learn from one another; discovering that U.S. teachers teach history in relation to causes, effects, and changes over time, while Japanese teachers teach history as young people discover it in local communities and experiences of still living elders; doing field work in Japanese schools and communities where oldcomer and newcomer children co-mingle and Japanese young people learn how to navigate the world. I discovered how creative teachers could transform what they learned in Japan and the U.S. into publishable and rigorous instructional materials, lesson plans, and travel narratives. There were other firsts: singing in Karaoke bars with the titans of discipline-based studies of education; comparing Japanese and U.S. cultures in pockets of Japanese life where teaching and learning go on: sushi bars, coffee shops, restaurants, subway platforms, bullet trains, family dinners, and crowded offices; chuckling when my grandson Brian was swarmed by a gaggle of giggling Japanese girls doing English language homework at the Peace Park in Hiroshima and asking him "Do you like Peace?"

There were scholarly firsts as well, some of them terrifying: first woman to serve as a keynote speaker and discussion leader at the Annual meeting of the Sapporo Seminar in American Studies where Japan's most distinguished American Studies and education scholars and all American Fulbrighters gathered together to learn; first to deliver a paper on multicultural education and diversity advocacy at the Sociology of Education annual meeting in Japan; first to become a confidant of high achieving Japanese women who saw no particular utility in the strategies of U.S. feminists to further their opportunities in Japanese academia; a first time senior fellow at the University of Tokyo who was willing to speak out-loud about disjunctions between what faculties knew and what female students wanted to learn; a touching first when the Imperial House of Japan honored me beyond words, by awarding The Order of the Rising Sun to celebrate the work that we had done in Japan and the United States.

Among the more dispiriting yet inspirational firsts was the discovery of an invisible Japanese minority – the Burakumin—who, when I arrived on the scene, were breaking traditional taboos against public confrontations and portraying Japan as a discriminatory state. Burakumin are an indigenous, status degraded Japanese minority community who are linguistically and racially Japanese, but have been subject nonetheless to cruel and incomparable forms of bigotry.[17] I learned from Burakumin people that the world was not flat, not even in a nation described recently as a "habitus of homogeneity" by Harumi Befu, a reigning expert on Japanese diversities.[18]

From that moment to this, I have had a passion to amplify the voices of Burakumin. I felt honored then as I do now that Burakumin scholars, social activists, teachers, school reformers, and museum curators have permitted me to cross over what a witness described as "The river with no bridge."[19] They have created opportunities for me to collect oral histories about the meaning and contours of discrimination as four generations of Burakumin have lived, experienced, and made history. They have made it possible to work with film-makers, community leaders, museum curators, fire-eating political and social activists, and specialized research institutes. I lived in the houses and communities of scholars, teachers, school reformers, parents, human rights advocates, and a rising generation of young people who have learned to "speak up and speak out," to advance human rights education, and to re-create and dignify Burakumin identity. My Burakumin colleagues constructed opportunities to put me on the lecture circuit, arranged for appearances on national broadcasting networks and scholarly panels, and solicited articles that explore the contours of diversity policies in the U.S.

I believe and hope that I have been well used. Every participant in every MARJiS seminar has lived and learned in Burakumin communities and returned the favor by hosting scores of Burakumin scholars, teachers, and school reformers seeking to understand the practices of multicultural education in American schools. Others have identified Burakumin as important actors in the forming of multicultural education agendas and the advancement of human rights in Japan.[20] Still others have organized professional development seminars focused on the cultural productions of Burakumin film-makers, novelists, curriculum makers, and students.

Newer on the scene are comparative studies of cultural education and diversity policies and practices in majority-minority schools and communities in Japan and the U.S.[21] I am beyond fortunate to have a new-age, brilliant research partner, woman, and friend, University of Tokyo professor Ryoko Tsuneyoshi. We study sites of teaching and learning that are outside the educational mainstream and wonder what the study of schools at the margins can reveal about the limits and possibilities of public schooling, a traditional structure in a fast-evolving world.

LIVING IN HISTORY

I have heard Martina Navratilova remark that what matters in life is not what you do, but what you finish, a hard lesson for someone like me who prefers to begin things rather than end them. I will still explore the history of children, youth, and education. I will remain an unapologetic critic of education history and an engaged transcultural scholar and educator. I will fashion oral histories that can amplify the voices of individuals and groups who would otherwise be lost to history. I will still travel into the small corners of the world to discover how people learn to make sense of things. I will still think historically about bashing discriminatory boundaries, living in and fashioning mind-expanding environments, discovering previously un-imagined communities, and creating teaching and learning environments within which a rising generation can shine and then, and then, and then....

NOTES

1 Clifford Geertz, *After the Fact: Two Countries, Four Decades, One Anthropologist* (Cambridge: Harvard University Press, 1995), 1.
2 Ibid, 3.
3 Mary Catherine Bateson, *Peripheral Visions: Learning along the Way* (New York: Harper Collins 1994)
4 Judith Stein, *Inventing Great Neck: Jewish Identity and the American Dream* (New Brunswick: Rutgers University Press, 2006).
5 Jeffrey Hurt, "The Historian as Provocateur: George Mosse 's Accomplishments and Legacy," *Yad Vashem Studies* 29 ,Shoah Resource Center: The International School for Holocaust Studies, (2001), 18.
6 George L. Mosse, *Confronting History: A Memoir*, with a Foreword by Walter Laquer, (Madison: The University of Wisconsin Press, 2000).
7 Merle Curti, *The Social Ideas of American Educators* (New York: Charles Scribner, 1935; Pagent Books, Inc.1959 for the special chapter on the "Last Twenty-Five years.").
8 Ruth Miller Elson, *Guardians of Tradition: American Schoolbooks of the Nineteenth Century* (Lincoln: University of Nebraska Press, 1964).
9 I owe an enormous debt of gratitude to my friend and colleague Donald R. Warren, who when he became chairman of my Department reversed two decades of discrimination and disrespect and created a congenial environment, and a modicum of dignity for me.
10 Barbara Finkelstein, "Governing the Young: Teacher Behavior in Popular Primary Schools in Nineteenth-Century United States, " (Unpublished Dissertation, Teachers College, Columbia University 1970). The published book appeared almost 20 years later. *Governing the Young: Teacher Behavior in Popular Primary Schools* (London and New York: The Falmer Press, 1989).
11 For examples, see: *Phillipe Ariès, Centuries of Childhood: A Social History of Family Life* Robert Baldick, trans. (New York: Alfred A. Knopf 1962); Lloyd deMause, "The Evolution of Childhood," in Lloyd deMause, ed., *The History of Childhood* (New York: The Psychohistory Press, 1974); Richard Sennett,*The Uses of Disorder:Personal Identity and City Life* (New York: Alfred A. Knopf, 1970); Anthony F.C. Wallace, *The Death and Rebirth of the Seneca* (New York: Alfred A. Knopf,

1970); John W. Blassingame, *The Slave Community: Plantation Life in the Antebellum South* (New York: Oxford University Press, 1979 [1972]).,

12 Anthony F.C. Wallace, *History of Education Quarterly* 22 (Summer 1982): 245–247.

13 Barbara Finkelstein, "Reading, Writing, and the Acquisition of Identity in the United States: 1790–1860 in Barbara Finkelstein, ed., *Regulated Children/Liberated Children: Education in Psychohistorical Perspective* (New York: The Psychohistory Press, 1979) 114–140. See also Finkelstein, "Perfecting Childhood: Horace Mann and the Discovery of Public Education in the United States, *Biography* 13 (1990): 6–21; "Life at the Margins of Possibility Nineteenth Century Literacy Stories," *Bulletin of the Center for American Studies*, no. 16 (University of Tokyo: Center for American Studies 1993): 11–19.

14 It was a rewarding moment when HEQ editors enlarged thematic emphases to "include the history of education, both formal and informal, including the history of childhood, youth, and the family."

15 Barbara Finkelstein, "Revealing Human Agency: The Uses of Biography in the Study of Educational History," in Craig Kridel, ed., *Writing Educational Biography: Explorations in Qualitative Research.* (New York and London: Garland Publishing, Inc. 1998), 45–59.

16 For example, see: Barbara Finkelstein, "Education Historians as Mythmakers." *Review of Research in Education* 18 (Washington, DC: American Educational Research Association, 1999) : 255–297.

17 For centuries, Burakumin were confined to residentially and psychologically walled-off villages and ostracized because of their association with leather-crafting and other occupations believed to be "abundantly polluted." Burakumin people have been an invisible minority who are being ripped from obscurity by a courageous and vociferous Burakumin minority who have "come out" and traveled the world to discover ways to do justice for their people and revise the Japanese course of study to include histories of Japanese minority groups and the study and practice of human rights education in the schools.

18 Harumi Befu, "Foreigners and Civil Society in Japan," *Bulletin of the International House of Japan* 56, no.2, (2009): 22–34.

19 Sue Sumii, *The River with No Bridge* tr. By Susan Wilkinson. (Rutland Vermont and Tokyo Japan: Charles E. Tuttle, 1989).

20 Barbara Finkelstein, Joseph Tobin, and Anne Imamura, (eds.) *Transcending Stereotypes: Discovering Japanese Culture and Education* (Yarmouth, Maine: Intercultural Press, Inc. 1991).

21 Barbara Finkelstein, "Educating Strangers: A Comparison of Cultural Education Policies and Practices in Japan and the U.S." in Y. Hirasawa and Y. Tomoda, eds., *Patterns of Value Socialization: A Comparative Study* (Osaka Japan: Osaka University Press 1998), 95–125.

ROGER L. GEIGER

BECOMING A HISTORIAN OF HIGHER EDUCATION

It is indeed a great honor to be invited to contribute to the history volume of the Leaders in Educational Studies series. As historian of higher education I am probably best known for the *Knowledge* trilogy that traces the evolution of American research universities through the twentieth century. I have also written on nineteenth-century colleges, and since 1993 I have had the privilege of editing the *History of Higher Education Annual*. Most of my writings on higher education have a historical dimension, and this has included many pieces that qualify as contemporary history. However, I remain a historian by training and choice, as the following essay will show.

Professing the history of American higher education at a major research university no doubt optimizes my microscopic contribution to the welfare of mankind. This judgment, I hope, reflects neither hubris nor complacency, but rather a balanced appraisal of the endowments that have allowed me to accomplish what I have and a temperament that would have precluded success in other lines of endeavor. Among my disqualifying traits would be a distrust of authority, reinforced no doubt by coming of age in the 1960s, and an inability to follow directions, let alone orders. I was not born to lead, or even manage. Instead, I am what once was called 'inner-directed.' I have a large quotient of intellectual curiosity and a need to internalize knowledge to satisfy my own understanding. The predominance of this disposition steered me along the twisted path to the history of universities. However, having the time and fertile intellectual settings to nurture my interests was indispensable, and this luxury was made possible by being associated with great universities.

My lifelong attachment to universities began in 1960 when I entered Michigan State University, then in the midst of frenetic expansion. There I experienced mass higher education long before I learned what that term signified: living in high-rise barracks, walking with throngs of fellow students from one lecture hall to another, and experiencing fairly modest academic standards. My professors at MSU were rather good, but the context produced a profound sense of anomie. After one year I transferred to the University of Michigan. In suburban Royal Oak where I attended high school, my contemporaries either went to MSU, U of M, or someplace weird. Initially, I had been intimidated by Michigan, but after my freshman year at MSU I was ready for greater intellectual stimulation.

One semester of physics and calculus at U of M (poorly taught) ended my formal STEM education. I had lost interest in those fields, but more importantly, I wanted to learn so many other things that the university offered. I had a romantic notion that I could obtain a true liberal education, a chimera not abandoned until I

W. J. Urban, Leaders in the Historical Study of American Education, 95–106.

finished a Ph.D. in intellectual history. But first I became an English major, probably my weakest subject. For the remainder of my undergraduate career I happily immersed myself in literature and was pretty oblivious to what I would eventually do for work. So, I naturally went to graduate school. However, there I discovered that the professional study of English literature, then under the hegemony of the new criticism, was far less interesting than my undergraduate literature courses. Finishing the master's degree, I managed to talk my way into the History Department, chiefly because the graduate advisor agreed with my misgivings about literary criticism (he used the term "idiotic"). Three reasons loomed large in this fateful decision: English was a dead end for me; I had favored a historical approach to criticism, which was now beyond the pale; and Cazzie Russell & co. were about to lead Michigan basketball to unprecedented glory. 1965 was no time to leave Ann Arbor. And there was still so much to learn.

Some of My Favorite Articles

Roger L. Geiger, "The Ten Generations of American Higher Education," [revised] in R. O. Berdahl, P. G. Altbach, and P. J. Gumport, eds. *Higher Education in the Twenty-First Century* (Baltimore: Johns Hopkins University Press, 2010 [3rd edition]); Chinese translation: *Peking University Education Review* 4, 2 (2006): 126–45.

Roger L. Geiger, Essay Review: "American Malaise: Lagging College Attainment in the United States," *American Journal of Education* (August 2010).

Roger L. Geiger, "Ivy League" in David Palfreyman and Ted Tapper, eds., *Structuring Mass Higher Education: the Role of Elite Institutions*, (London: Routledge, Taylor & Francis, 2008), 281–302.

Roger L. Geiger, "Demography and Curriculum: the Humanities in American Higher Education, 1945-1985," in David A. Hollinger, Ed., *The Humanities and the Dynamics of Inclusion Since World War II* (Baltimore: Johns Hopkins University Press, 2006), 50–72.

Roger L. Geiger, "The Reformation of the Colleges in the Early Republic, 1800-1820." *History of Universities* XVI, 2, (2000): 129–182.

For my one-year master's degree in history I took a hodge-podge of courses. My interest was European history, but no one advised me that this required proficiency in a European language (I could barely read French, my most detested college subject). I was nonetheless accepted into the doctoral program and advised to pursue my degree directly. This was good career advice considering the booming market for faculty, but I was getting tired of going to school. Instead, I took a position as instructor of history at Northern Michigan University. In the Fall of 1966 I began teaching NMU freshmen the History of Western Civilization, 90 percent of which I had never studied. I had just turned 23 years old.

NMU in the late 1960s represented another dimension of mass higher education. Deluged with unsophisticated, first-generation, baby-boomers from Michigan's Upper Peninsula, enrollments had doubled in only a few years. The History Department also doubled its faculty the year I joined. The students were assigned a dreadful text for Western Civ, while the instructors drew lectures from R. R. Palmer's marvelous survey. New faculty members throughout the university were products of Jencks and Riesman's Academic Revolution, and ill-suited for their mission in the wilderness.[1] Many, in fact, departed when I did after my two temporary years. I returned to Ann Arbor to earn the credential for a university history teacher. Ironically, it would take nineteen years to obtain a faculty position. By then, my aspirations were considerably higher.

The University of Michigan offered an extraordinarily rich setting for doctoral education. The History Department was one of the best in the country. The department itself was a ferment of activity, and legions of fellow doctoral students were another source of ferment (in both senses). Still, I found key concepts in other fields. Most extraordinary was the group of sociologists and social historians that clustered around Charles Tilly. I belonged with neither, but was introduced by my good friend John Merriman. Every Sunday night, Chuck and his historian-wife Louise hosted an open seminar in their house where students, faculty, and visitors presented their work. Chuck readily agreed to sit on my doctoral committee, and provided helpful advice for what was pretty much a self-directed project. At one point he told me to look at Thomas Kuhn's *Structure of Scientific Revolutions*, a work that shaped my dissertation and much subsequent work. Kuhn also dovetailed with a more eclectic group organized in the Center for Conflict Resolution that was exploring what Derek de Solla Price had announced as the "science of science." From their meetings I learned basic concepts of the sociology of science that informed my thinking about disciplines and universities.

My dissertation traced the development of sociology in France from positivism to the Durkheimians.[2] I distinguished three different approaches that laid claim to a science of society. Emile Durkheim triumphed by incorporating the positivist tradition, establishing a true paradigm, and achieving institutionalization in the university. This study set my style for subsequent work: the history of ideas firmly grounded in historical context; employment of social science concepts; and an emphasis on the role of institutions. I had no inkling of how important the latter would become.

Looking again at this study after many years, it seems clear that I should have quickly turned it into a book. It still represents a contribution to the origins of sociology—the roots of the Durkheim school as well as its context and rivals.[3] The study was well-received in France, where the Maison des Sciences de l'Homme included a Groupe d'études durkhiemiene. I was told that my dissertation was repeatedly stolen from the Maison's library. I did publish two articles in the *Revue française de sociologie*.[4] Why not a book? I assumed at the time that my study needed more work, which was partially true, but I greatly overestimated this hurdle. In retrospect, what I badly needed at this juncture was encouragement and guidance, and I received neither. Moreover, I was demoralized by the abysmal job market.

In 1972 I joined the largest cohort of history Ph.D.s ever graduated. The academic hiring boom of the 1960s was over; intellectual history was moribund, European little better; and the affirmative action machinery was powering up. I managed to do some irregular teaching at Michigan branches in Dearborn and Flint, and in the Michigan History Department. I also benefited from a summer postdoc from the Deutscher Akademischer Austauschdienst that gave me a remarkable opportunity to discuss the history of sociology with eminent scholars at German universities. Eventually, I had a few interviews for not-very-good jobs, but by then I had developed a disposition toward scholarship that no doubt saved me. One administrator asked, how would I choose between 100 percent teaching or 100 percent research? What was the wrong answer for him actually foreshadowed my future. John Merriman, now an assistant professor of history at Yale, informed me that a research group was looking for a postdoc to study French higher education. I knew little about the French system after Durkheim, but one could always sound smart by saying, 'nothing has really changed.' In 1974 I joined a group Burton R. Clark had assembled to study comparative higher education. This move effectively ended any possibility of a job in a history department (although the Yale department, probably the best in the country, gave me a courtesy appointment). What the field of higher education entailed, I had no idea.

Some of My Favorite Articles (continued)
Roger L. Geiger, "The Era of the Multipurpose College in American Higher Education, 1850-1890," *History of Higher Education Annual* 15 (1995): 51–92.
Roger L. Geiger and I. Feller, "The Dispersion of Academic Research in the 1980s," *Journal of Higher Education* 65 (May/June, 1995): 336–60.
Roger L. Geiger, "Science, Universities and National Defense, 1945–1970," *Osiris* 7 (1992): 94–116.
Roger L. Geiger, "Democracy and the Crowd: The Social History of an Idea in France and Italy, 1890–1914," *Societas* 7 (1977): 47–71.
Roger L. Geiger, "Markets and History: Selective Admissions and U.S. Higher Education Since 1950," Review Essay, *History of Higher Education Annual* 20 (2000).

Yale in some ways fit its stuffy and staid reputation, but it was an enormously rich and stimulating environment. Instead of reading Derek Price and R. R. Palmer, I attended their seminars. Our research group was part of the Institution for Social and Policy Studies, where Charles Lindblom presided over weekly lunchtime seminars.[5] An unending succession of lectures, research groups, visiting speakers, and regular gatherings like the ISPS lunches supplied a surfeit of intellectual fodder. Moreover, people were seriously interested in ideas. Postdocs like me were at the bottom of the pecking order (after undergraduates and doctoral students), but our ideas nevertheless received full hearing. Anyone who was a Yalie, even temporarily, was accorded respect; but not necessarily agreement. Ideas were subject to honest and frank criticism.

Embarking on the study of comparative higher education was like earning a second Ph.D., and also took about as long. Bob Clark had recently become a comparativist with a study of the Italian professoriate, and was then beginning a general analysis of *The Higher Education System* (1983). But there was no central theme to our eclectic group. Nor was it clear what a postdoc was supposed to do beyond making a seminar presentation each semester. Research and publish were the imperatives. But what? I soon resolved to write a history of the French university in the Third Republic. However, after limited progress, I discovered the perils of living on soft money. Our patron, the Lilly Foundation, shifted its interest to smaller, unstudied, systems. But I was also learning to adapt. With one morning in the Yale library I became an 'expert' on Belgian higher education. My postdoc was renewed but, like my previous studies, the fruits of my labor were merely additional articles.

My adroitness was tested again when patrons lost interest in comparative higher education, per se, and could only be persuaded to support thematic studies. Fortunately, Bob Clark was a genius at translating the vague penchants of foundation officers into tangible academic projects, which in this case emerged as international perspectives on private higher education. I had no particular interest in this subject, but I did have some insights. Belgium had developed parallel public and private universities, both funded by the state; and France retained vestiges of a private sector. Americans, aside from our research group, were quite ignorant of the huge private sector in Japan. Here was material for a comparative study of private higher education.[6] No sooner had I embarked on this study than Bob Clark, whose stature in comparative higher education was little appreciated at Yale, was awarded the Allan Cartter Chair in Higher Education at UCLA. Luckily, my study of private sectors fit with the nascent Program on Nonprofit Organization, or PONPO, the first organized research group to study this field.

PONPO was the brainchild of law professor John Simon—a leader in the foundation world, pioneer in the study of nonprofits, and a revered member of the Yale Pantheon. PONPO brought together scholars from all the social sciences to analyze fundamental organizational questions pertaining to foundations, health care, cultural institutions, and, infrequently, education. In this enormously stimulating setting, excellent scholarship established a new field of study.[7] Being there certainly enriched my own study, *Private Sectors in Higher Education: Structure, Function, and Change in Eight Countries*.[8] This work depicted three paradigms of private sectors and compared them to the complex private sector in the United States. Yet, it took years to find a publisher. Reader reports were generally positive, but the ms. was plagued with rookie mistakes. After two or three turndowns, Bob Clark offered key advice, and wrote a preface as well. With this stamp of approval, the University of Michigan Press offered a contract. The book was well ahead of the times. Private higher education has since become far more important internationally, and my study is still considered a seminal treatment of the topic.

Writing *Private Sectors* left me with several firm impressions. First, writing the historical material came easily, but sociological analysis did not. My talents as a scholar seemed to lie with history. Second, history was not hopeless. There seemed to be a need and appreciation for the history of higher education, particularly when the past could be connected to the present, (something academic historians were generally loath to do). Third, the most fascinating institutions encountered in the entire study were the private American research universities.

About the same time, Stanley Katz visited PONPO and presented work that he had been doing on the history of foundations. He sketched the pivotal role that the Rockefeller and Carnegie trusts had played in fostering research in American universities. This talk implanted a seed in my brain that soon germinated. One morning driving to the office it hit me: there was need for a history of American research universities in the twentieth century. Laurence Veysey's magisterial study declared that American universities had assumed their definitive form by 1910. Story over. In fact, there was a complex and fascinating story to tell of their development up to World War II, and another story afterward. John Simon was both encouraging and helpful. A proposal to the Andrew W. Mellon Foundation was favorably received and funded.

Books that I Have Found Particularly Helpful or Inspiring

Burton R. Clark, *Places of Inquiry: Research and Advanced Education in Modern Universities* (Berkeley: University of California Press, 1995).

J. David Hoeveler, *Creating the American Mind: Intellect and Politics in the Colonial Colleges* (Lanham, MD: Rowman & Littlefield, 2002).

Thomas Kuhn, *The Structure of Scientific Revolutions* (Chicago: University of Chicago Press, 1962).

Charles E. Lindblom, *The Market System* (New Haven: Yale University Press, 2001).

Henry May, *The Enlightenment in America* (New York: Oxford University Press, 1976).

I knew little of the history of American higher education, but I did understand universities, scientific organization, and nonprofits. Finally, I had a topic that suited me. Still, with great trepidation I sent early drafts to Hugh Hawkins. His generous comments gave me all the confidence I needed. In fact, research and writing went smoothly, except for one thing. The level of detail (and primary sources) needed to produce an original, analytical account proved greater than I had anticipated. It soon was clear that the project would take much longer. I decided to conclude a first volume at 1940. A contract with Oxford University Press seemed to validate that decision. But Hugh Hawkins warned that if I stopped there I would probably never finish.

However, the topic of research universities since World War II was all the more relevant to funders. Grants from the Ford Foundation and Lawrence Cremin at Spencer launched the second volume, and Mellon later provided additional support. In all, I spent thirteen years at Yale on soft money, advancing from a postdoc to a 'senior research scientist.' This may be a record for a historian. I was exceedingly fortunate to have this opportunity, or opportunities. Yet, being a full-time researcher has drawbacks, even in an environment as congenial as Yale's. Research projects require a narrow focus, which tends to become narrower over time. Yale's incomparable library collections were less helpful for post-1945 research, and that period was a kind of no-man's land, beyond the focus of historians and prior to the interests of social scientists. I consequently welcomed the opportunity to move to Penn State in 1987 with no regrets.

The university I joined was in the early stages of a transformation from a bureaucratic, lethargic land-grant to one of the top fifteen public research universities, although I cannot say I recognized this at the time. The position I filled was chiefly charged with teaching the history of higher education in the Higher Education Program. The Center for the Study of Higher Education was supposedly the research arm, and its members did little teaching. At least some of the faculty looked askance at my complete ignorance of the profession of higher education administration as taught in such programs, but as a mere historian I was apparently tolerated. Despite my background in grantsmanship, I was never asked to participate in a Center project, nor did I wish to. I continued to obtain grants but had them administered elsewhere. Still, here was the stable base I had long been seeking. I was told originally that Penn State was a good place to do your work— and it has been for me.

My maturation as a historian of higher education at Penn State occurred in three spheres of endeavor. The first has been the ongoing study of research universities, past and present. Initially this meant finishing *Research and Relevant Knowledge*, and later completing the *Knowledge* trilogy with *Knowledge and Money* (2004).[9] Second, assuming the editorship of the *History of Higher Education Annual* in 1993 thrust me from the periphery to the center of the field. And third, *American College in the Nineteenth Century* (2000)[10] was the fruit of focused research and teaching, but also provided a key to interpreting the history of American higher education.

The titles of the *Knowledge* trilogy reflect the forces that transformed academic research in each of the three eras. In *To Advance Knowledge*, foundation initiatives were the dominant influence, chiefly intended to advance basic sciences in the universities. After World War II, federal support predominantly served to support research relevant to the mission agencies that provided the funds. Since 1980, and more so since 1995, incremental additions to the research economy have been predicated on pecuniary expectations of economic growth or commercial payoffs. Completing *Research and Relevant Knowledge* brought home the perils of writing contemporary history. I reached the end of the ms. around 1990, but it took me more than another year to actually finish. The ideological polarization of those years followed fault-lines that extended back to the 1960s. But these issues were extremely difficult to incorporate without sounding partisan. Carrying history up to the present day can be a thankless task, especially if the catchphrases of current controversy cannot be transcended. Historians should try to distance themselves from polarizing issues by establishing a more elevated and general platform on which to stand.

Few would regard *Knowledge and Money* as history, and aside from several passages it is not. Rather, it might be described as temporal analysis, intended to document and analyze change over time. Temporal analysis identifies the nature of change and argues that 'in this case' it appears to have been affected by such-and-such circumstances. Often this amounts to applied social science, since processes analyzed in these disciplines can provide key elements of explanation. But social mechanisms operate in specific contexts that also need to be identified. For example, in the book I wrote with Creso Sá, *Tapping the Riches of Science: Universities and the Promise of Economic Growth*,[11] the underlying force for change was the expectation that university research will produce innovation and technology-based economic development. Significant changes have occurred in corporate-sponsored university research, state policies to promote economically relevant research, the evolution of university patenting and licensing, and the organization of research in universities. And these changes are manifested somewhat differently in each locus.

Books that I Have Found Particularly Helpful or Inspiring (continued)

Robert A. McCaughey, *Stand Columbia: A History of Columbia University in the City of New York, 1754–2004* (New York: Columbia University Press, 2003).

Samuel Eliot Morison, *Three Centuries of Harvard* (Cambridge: Harvard University Press, 1936).

Laurence R. Veysey, *The Emergence of the American University* (Chicago: University of Chicago Press, 1965).

Gordon S. Wood, *The Radicalism of the American Revolution* (New York: Knopf, 1992).

Early in 1992 Harold Wechsler asked me if I would be interested in assuming the editorship of the *History of Higher Education Annual*. This journal was launched in 1980 as a collective project among a small band of scholars. It had been sustained almost single-handedly by Harold's efforts to edit, publish, and distribute it. I had recently had a good experience as section editor for the Pergamon *Encyclopedia of Higher Education*—a section equivalent to a 500-page book.[12] I was both flattered and intrigued. To take this on, though, Penn State would have to provide a graduate assistant to handle subscriptions, etc. But obtaining support for an additional graduate student interested in history was itself a strong inducement. For managing the journal I would also need the help of Roger Williams, my first doctoral student at PSU, author of a landmark study of George Atherton, and a brilliant administrator. Everything fell into place, and we began by publishing the 1992 volume, which Harold edited. I introduced myself to the *Annual* community by contributing the first version of the "Ten Generations of American Higher Education." This essay reflected my course on the history of American higher education. It was intended to summarize the existing literature for purpose of discussion and also propose a hypothetical structure. Three *Annual* stalwarts published commentaries that were generally favorable, although with significant quibbles. Subsequent versions of this essay have appeared in a popular higher education reader, most recently in 2010.[13] This is easily my most widely read contribution to the history of higher education. Perhaps more important, it has given me a vested interest in the interpretation of all eras of American higher education. Most recently, this interest has prompted a reevaluation of the most recent generation.[14]

Editing the journal has brought challenges and frustration, but has ultimately been deeply satisfying. It has acquainted me with the entire range of scholarship in this field in ways that have enhanced both my own work and my understanding of the subject. A crucial responsibility of this position has been eliciting the contributions of other scholars in this field—for reviews, articles, and advice. In this respect, the journal remains a collective effort of a small, and at times I fear, precarious community. I believe the journal is an important resource in sustaining the history of higher education as a quasi- or sub-discipline, rather than a collection of isolated scholars and studies. During the sixteen years that I have been editor, a generational turnover has taken place. Keeping abreast of evolving subject matter, styles, and interpretations is an ongoing challenge.[15] Certainly, one of the most satisfying aspects of this job is assisting young scholars, whose dissertations produce much of the fresh empirical scholarship.[16] Not only is constant renewal essential for the journal, for me it serves as an antidote to academic senility.

After its first decade at Penn State, the *Annual* faced difficult circumstances. The university and my department reneged on support for the journal assistant (so much for the promises of departed administrators). The chores of arranging for printing, mailing, and accounting had been performed heroically, most recently by assistants Susan Richardson and Christian Anderson (now Associate Editor), and were absolutely essential. At this juncture, Irving Louis Horowitz visited campus, and in our first conversation offered to incorporate the *Annual* into Transaction Publishers. He had already agreed to republish *To Advance Knowledge* and *Research and Relevant Knowledge*, for which I was exceedingly grateful.[17] Regarding the *Annual*, I was in no position to bargain; but there was nothing to bargain about. Irving is an incomparable combination of hyper-prolific scholar and publishing entrepreneur. He has built Transaction Publishers into a robust business without any compromise of intellectual integrity. He expected me to retain complete editorial control and also to uphold the journal's high academic standards. As businessman, he changed the name to *Perspectives on the History of Higher Education* to better fit the Transaction format, but the change dovetails with my own wish to be more open to material linking history with contemporary issues. Teaming with Irving has taught me that practices have to change with the times as well as ideas.

In the history of American higher education, the nature of the college in the nineteenth century was long the unresolved issue. The traditional interpretation depicted the colleges as hopelessly dominated by classical languages and denominational myopia, and thus ripe for modernizing reforms. A group of revisionists, some of whom founded the *Annual*, vociferously exposed the shortcomings of this view, but offered only partial findings to replace it. For a number of years I taught this controversy to my classes, but was never happy with the residual uncertainties. After *Research and Relevant Knowledge* was finished, I worked intermittently on this topic for the rest of the 1990s. The first piece of this puzzle was published in 1995 as "The Era of Multipurpose Colleges."[18] This study integrated data compiled for the Bureau of Education *Reports of the Commissioner of Education* and numerous institutional histories with a multi-source examination of collegiate evolution in Ohio. In some ways it completed the picture suggested by Brad Burke's demographic study, *American Collegiate Populations,* which had first used the term "multi-purpose." The colleges of the latter nineteenth century were flexible and pragmatic while clinging to a classical core. But they were also inherently limited when confronted with the academic revolution.

The second piece crystallized after the appearance of a student memoir written at Princeton in 1853. This intriguing document prompted a review of mid-century student writings. A dramatic evolution occurred during the century from institutional policies of submission and control of students to a rich, student-led extracurriculum.[19] Clearly, this was one of the most important dynamics of American higher education in this era—a central facet of the history.

These findings stimulated my curiosity about the earlier period. This resulted in a detailed study of the colleges in the first two decades of the century, which had been a neglected subject. What became clear was that American colleges reached their lowest ebb around 1800, not in the later 'antebellum' colleges. The reconstruction of the classical curriculum that followed provided a pedagogical and cultural basis for later developments, rather than stifling them. The rise of theological seminaries deflected ministerial training away from the colleges, permitting the growth of a secular curriculum.[20] The denominational colleges that proliferated after 1820 built upon this base.

By the end of the 1990s I had the material to write a history of the nineteenth-century college, but I did not have the time. I was committed to the study that became *Knowledge and Money*, including a 2000 sabbatical at the UC Berkeley Center for Studies in Higher Education. As a compromise, I assembled *The American College in the Nineteenth Century*. This collection of articles, mostly from the *Annual*, illustrated many of the points I wished to make. They were tied together with an Introduction that sketched a new interpretation of the period.[21] In addition to the three points described above, two other conditions were critical to understand this evolution.

First, the traditionalist/revisionist muddle was chiefly due to the objectification of a single antebellum college. In fact, three distinct versions emerged by the 1830s. In the Northeast, leading colleges achieved considerable academic advancement as well as nurturing autonomous student extracurricular life. In the South, state universities dominated higher education for the benefit of a social-political elite, while evangelical religious colleges played a lesser role. West of the Appalachians, the expansive dynamics traced in the "Multipurpose Colleges" reigned, producing those distinctive institutions.

Second, the prevailing antebellum/post-bellum dichotomy was quite misleading. The mid-century was characterized by pre-modern institutional forms. These included multipurpose colleges, separate affiliated schools of science, "female" colleges, proprietary professional schools, and normal schools. These forms, as such, were doomed by 1890 to eventual extinction. Of course, some survived as institutions—or evolved—but only by changing their fundamental nature.

Now, a decade later, I return to the challenge of creating a narrative history of American higher education, not just for the nineteenth century, but for its entire span. Historians who seriously contemplate this kind of endeavor tend to emphasize either its desirability or impossibility. Ideally, a narrative history should synthesize as much of the extant knowledge as possible. It must also impose order on this material in the form of interpretation. However, interpretation implies selection and exclusion. I cannot resolve this conundrum, but neither do I intend to be defeated by it. The parlous state of our field calls forth the effort. The proliferation of studies appears to be increasing fragmentation instead of convergence. As a consequence, our field has become increasingly irrelevant to the mainstream of American history (if there is such a thing) and neglected by the intelligent reading public. The history profession is of course itself beset by fragmentation, but integrating narratives are still being written. Two recent examples by giants of the field testify to the invisibility of higher education. Gordon Wood practically omits the colleges, citing Donald Tewksbury's long discredited 1932 study. Daniel Walker Howe cites a better selection of authors (as well as Tewksbury!), but only three from the last quarter century.[22]

We may never return to the era of Richard Hofstadter, who made higher education central to the country's intellectual and social development. And American historians may now be too specialized to care. But higher education probably ranks as highly among public concerns now as at any time since the 1960s. Surely the time is ripe for telling this important and fascinating story.

How to proceed? Institutions of higher education essentially exist to prepare young people for their adult lives. Chiefly, this involves expectations about occupations and culture. These expectations connect the colleges directly with American society, and are thus in constant evolution. Universities are also institutions of the *highest* education, and as such are affected to varying degrees by the advancement of knowledge. Culture, careers, and knowledge have thus been the dominant factors that have shaped American colleges and universities over time and have linked them with other dynamics of American society. This inclusive perspective does not explain the history of those institutions, but rather indicates what questions to pose. I hope to spend the next few years trying to answer those questions.

NOTES

[1] Christopher Jencks and David Riesman, *The Academic Revolution* (Chicago: University of Chicago Press, 1968).

[2] Roger L. Geiger, "The Development of French Sociology, 1871–1905," Ph.D. Diss. University of Michigan, 1972.

[3] My dissertation chapter on Gabriel Tarde (ibid.), was recently critiqued by Barbara Czarniawska, "Gabriel Tarde and Organizational Theory" in: Adler, Paul (ed.) *The Oxford Handbook of Sociology and Organization Studies: Classical Foundations.* (Oxford: Oxford University Press, 2009), 246–267.

[4] Roger L. Geiger, "La sociologie dans les écoles normales primaires: Histoire d'une controverse,' *Revue française de sociologie*, XX (janvier-mars 1979): 257–67; idem., "Rene Worms et l'organisation de la sociologie," *Revue française de sociologie*, XXII (juillet-sept. 1981): 345–60.

[5] Lindblom's 2001 book, *The Market System* (Charles E. Lindblom, *The Market System: What It Is, How It Works, and What to Make of* It [New Haven: Yale University Press, 2001]) was a key to concluding *Knowledge and Money*. Reading it I could still hear his voice.

[6] My colleague, Dan Levy, had embarked on his definitive study, *Higher Education and the State in Latin America: Private Challenges to Public Dominance* (Chicago: University of Chicago Press, 1986), and preceded me in transitioning to the Program on Nonprofit Organizations.

[7] For PONPO's early work see, Walter W. Powell, ed., *The Nonprofit Sector: a Research Handbook* (New Haven: Yale University Press, 1987).

[8] Roger L. Geiger, *Private Sectors in Higher Education: Structure, Function and Change in Eight Countries* (Ann Arbor: University of Michigan Press, 1986).

[9] Roger L. Geiger, *To Advance Knowledge: The Growth of American Research Universities, 1900–1940* (New Edition, Transaction Publishers, 2004, First Edition, Oxford University Press, 1986); *Research and Relevant Knowledge: American Research Universities Since World War II.* (New Edition, Transaction Publishers, 2004. First Edition, Oxford University Press, 1993); *Knowledge and*

Money: American Research Universities and the Paradox of the Marketplace. (Stanford: Stanford University Press, 2004.

[10] Roger L. Geiger, ed., *The American College in the Nineteenth Century* (Nashville: Vanderbilt University Press, 2000).

[11] Roger L. Geiger and Creso M. Sá, *Tapping the Riches of Science: Universities and the Promise of Economic* Growth (Cambridge: Harvard University Press, 2008): see, www. tappingtherichesofscience.info.

[12] Roger L. Geiger, "The Institutional Fabric of Higher Education," in Burton R. Clark and Guy Neave, eds., *Encyclopedia of Higher Education*, 4 vol., Pergamon, (1992), II, 1031–1278.

[13] "The Historical Matrix of American Higher Education," *History of Higher Education Annual*, 12 (1992): 7–34; most recently, "The Ten Generations of American Higher Education" in Philip G. Altbach, et al., eds. *American Higher Education in the Twenty-first Century*, 2nd edition, (Baltimore: Johns Hopkins University Press, 2010).

[14] Roger L. Geiger, "Postmortem for the Current Era: Change in American Higher Education, 1980–2010," in Ellen Lagemann and Harry Lewis, eds., *For Whom and For What? The Future of U.S. Higher Education in a New Age of Scarcity*, publication in progress.

[15] For an overview of writings on the history of higher education, most published since I became editor of the *Annual* in 1993, see Christine A. Ogren, "Sites, Students, Scholarship, and Structures: the Historiography of American Higher Education in the Post-Revisionist Era," in William J. Reese and John L. Rury, eds., *Rethinking the History of American Education* (New York: Palgrave Macmillan, 2008), 187–222.

[16] The *Annual* began the publication of abstracts of dissertations on the history of higher education in 1994, a service continued in *Perspectives*.

[17] *To Advance Knowledge* was published by Oxford University Press as a trade book, reviewed by the *New York Times Book Review*, and displayed in quality book stores. *Research and Relevant Knowledge* was issued at more than twice the price, relegating it to the library market. It consequently received little notice, and few scholars were able to own it. Republication by Transaction Publishers in paperback has made both titles readily available.

[18] Roger L. Geiger, "The Era of Multipurpose Colleges in American Higher Education, 1850–1890," *History of Higher Education Annual* 15 (1995): 51–92.

[19] Roger L. Geiger with Julie Ann Bubolz, "College as it was: Review Essay," *History of Higher Education Annual* 16 (1996): 105–15; expanded version republished in *College in the Nineteenth Century*, 80–90.

[20] Roger L. Geiger, "The Reformation of the Colleges in the Early Republic, 1800–1820," *History of Universities.* XVI, 2 (2000): 129–182.

[21] "Introduction: New Themes in the History of Nineteenth-Century Colleges" in Roger L. Geiger, ed., *The American College in the Nineteenth Century* (Nashville: Vanderbilt University Press, 2000), 1–36.

[22] Gordon S. Wood, *Empire of Liberty* (New York: Oxford University Press, 2009); Daniel Walker Howe, *'What Hath God Wrought?'* (New York: Oxford University Press, 2008).

LYNN D. GORDON

THE PERSONAL IS THE POLITICAL AND THE PROFESSIONAL

I always wanted to investigate and write about the past. At age eleven, fascinated by ancient history and classical mythology, I decided to become an archaeologist. In high school I took four years of Latin from a wonderfully enthusiastic teacher. I enjoyed the language for its own sake, but also thought of it as a tool for my future profession. But when I discovered how much hard science, not to mention physical labor, was required for archaeology, I shifted my focus to the era of written records that could be examined in the comfort of an air-conditioned library. I briefly considered a career in journalism, as a foreign correspondent, but although I considered myself a good writer and liked the image of myself dashing around the globe wearing a faded trench coat, I wanted the opportunity to study issues in more depth than daily deadlines would allow.

I attended a Seven Sisters college, specifically Barnard, in the middle of New York City, where the "action" was (for the same reason, my parents tried to interest me in non-urban schools). A college that admitted only women--smart women-- intrigued me. As a female with intellectual and professional ambitions, not typical for a high school student at that time, I wanted to meet other women who shared my interests. My wonderful and adoring grandfather, who read Tolstoy's short stories to me when I was very young, encouraged and supported me, paid for my first year at college and suggested I do graduate work at the Sorbonne.

During my four years at Barnard I took courses from an impressive group of female faculty. What I learned in their classes, and the example set by their lives and careers, led me to ask questions I later addressed as a scholar. Women's history was not then recognized as a legitimate field in American history; it could be a topic, but not a subject. Ironically, Annette Baxter taught one of the earliest women's history courses at Barnard, but it never occurred to me to take it. Professor Baxter and her husband sometimes spoke to students, encouraging them to contemplate both marriage and career instead of either/or. This was a revelation to me. A devout admirer of Betty Friedan (*The Feminine Mystique* came out in 1963, when I was in high school), I had absorbed Friedan's insistence on women having careers, but she didn't have much to say about combining those careers with marriage and family.[1] I only got to know Professor Baxter after graduation, when I was in the early stages of my career. She was a mentor for several Barnard women who became professional historians, including Carol Berkin, Linda Kerber, Paula Fass and Estelle Freedman. Tragically, in 1983, Annette Baxter and her husband died in a fire at their home.

My knowledge of Latin, I reasoned, would be of great help if I specialized in medieval history, so I took additional Latin courses in college. I had the good fortune to study with Nina Garsoian, a specialist in the history of the Byzantine Empire. Professor Garsoian, a dynamic lecturer, and, even for Barnard-Columbia, an exceptionally brilliant scholar, was my first female role model. I had never before met or even heard of a woman with an academic career. I wanted to be a Byzantinist, like her, and eagerly sought her advice. She was most cordial, although I was hardly a star student, earning only a B minus in her class. Byzantine history lost its charm when I learned how many additional languages I would have to learn, but Nina Garsoian's influence and example have remained with me.

Gordon Personal Favorites:

Gender and Higher Education in the Progressive Era (New Haven: Yale University Press, 1990).

"Education in the Professions," in Nancy Hewitt, ed., *A Companion to American Women's History* (Oxford, UK: Blackwell, 2002).

"Why Dorothy Thompson Lost Her Job: Political Columnists and the Pres Wars of the 1930s and 1940s," *History of Education Quarterly* 34, 2: (Summer, 1994).

"Race, Class, and the Bonds of Womanhood at Spelman Seminary, 1881–1923," *History of Higher Education Annual* 9 (1989).

With a new focus on Western Europe in the Middle Ages, I "declared" a history major. At that time, Columbia and Barnard had a complex agreement about sharing or not sharing classes. It was well-known at Barnard that certain Columbia professors would not open their classes to women students. I envied my Columbia friends the Contemporary Civilization and Humanities core courses they were required to take; we had no such entrée into Western civilization at Barnard. But we did have access to Columbia's medievalists; most of my history courses were co-educational. Assigned, in one of those classes, to write a paper on King John of England and the Magna Carta, I surprised myself (and undoubtedly the professor) by struggling with the primary sources and coming up with an interesting and well-defended thesis. I no longer remember what I argued in that paper, but keenly recall the pleasure of a successful research effort.

Although I completed a history major with a specialty in medieval history, by senior year my intellectual interests had changed. The sixties happened, and like many college students, I got caught up in the excitement of participating in a new kind of politics. As a freshman, I joined Friends of SNCC, established when African American activists decided that SNCC itself should be a "blacks only" organization. We raised money for SNCC and sought signatures on petitions asking the Democratic party to recognize the legitimacy of the Mississippi Freedom Democratic party. Fannie Lou Hamer's life and work inspired me, as they did many others.

Ted Gold chaired Friends of SNCC; he was dynamic, decisive and full of optimism. By 1970, he had a darker outlook. A member of the Weather Underground, he died in an explosion from bombs the group was making in the basement of a Greenwich Village townhouse. But during my first two years in college it was not unusual to be a member of both SDS and the Columbia-Barnard Democratic Club, as I was. We thought the system could be made to work by appealing to American ideals and values. The war in Vietnam proved us wrong.

I never made Ted Gold's journey; my own "radicalism," even by the end of the sixties, was never more than tentative. I was not in one of the Columbia buildings raided by the police in May 1968 and I was not arrested that spring, when so many of my classmates were. I was, nevertheless, thoroughly disgusted with the "system" and the ineffectiveness of protest in ending the war. How could those massive marches on Washington D.C., in which I participated, produce such meager results? I still wanted to be a historian, but of twentieth century America. I especially hoped to learn more about the relationship between public opinion and American foreign policy. How, in a democracy, could elected officials ignore the wishes of their constituents, not to mention the deaths of young American men. Financial issues prevented me from attending graduate school immediately, and I looked for a way to earn some money, while putting my ideals into practice.

I decided that the mass psychosis afflicting my fellow citizens could only be alleviated by educating American youth about issues and causes. I was particularly struck by how little my high school history courses had taught me about racism, civil rights, imperialism and the destruction of Native Americans. In 1967 and 1968, I volunteered to lead reading groups for high school students, but this activity, although enjoyable, had its limits in terms of influence. In preparation for a (temporary) career as a high school social studies teacher, I enrolled in Professor Patricia Graham's seminar on secondary education. That year I learned there was a "history of education." Although the class ranged over many issues, a key focus was school integration. We studied the *Brown* decision, white flight, red-lining, busing, tracking and their impact on both students and teachers. I got as excited about a paper I wrote on tracking in the Washington D.C. school system as I had about my work on the Magna Carta. We did our student teaching in the public and private schools of New York City and discussed with each other the triumphs and travails of that experience.

After a truly dreadful year teaching ninth grade social studies and English at a private school in the Bronx, where the students were barely literate and the faculty/administration refused to acknowledge that this was the case, I landed a plum job at a suburban junior high school in Amherst, New York, near the future SUNY Buffalo campus. During my four years teaching seventh and eighth grade social studies I made two important discoveries: first, students and their parents had absolutely no interest in a revised version of American history, one including African American and Native American history, and casting doubt on the wisdom of various governments and presidents. I did not give up on presenting a "new" American history, but my efforts did not produce the political awakening I hoped for among my students. More important, perhaps, was my discovery of some central issues in the history of American education. As a new teacher, I was assigned not the weakest students, but honors classes. Puzzled, but not complaining about my good fortune, I asked for honors classes in subsequent years and always got them. Purely by chance, I read Richard Hofstadter's *Anti-Intellectualism in American Life.*[2] As someone whose life revolved around books and education,

I found Hofstadter's arguments about the anti-intellectual character of schools shocking, but eye-opening. Now I understood why honors students were considered a problem; my fellow teachers preferred students who asked fewer questions and were not intellectually demanding.

By 1973, when I entered graduate school in history at the University of Chicago, I had traveled a long way from archaeology and medieval history. My intellectual questions and research interests in the history of education and the relationship between foreign policy and public opinion arose from my political concerns. At Chicago, however, only "the life of the mind" mattered, i.e. inquiry and research undertaken for their own sake, unconnected to "presentist" concerns. I did not change my interests, but I learned to keep my mouth shut about my reasons for choosing these fields.

In the 1970s, the historical profession was rapidly changing its focus and developing new methodologies. I had little interest (and certainly no aptitude) for quantitative history and did not enroll in the course provided by the department. Social history fascinated me; studying "ordinary" people seemed like a way to pursue the questions that interested me. At the time, however, social historians tended to define themselves either as quantifiers or theorists. I took a social history class with a new young faculty member, only to find myself overwhelmed by classroom debates over the appropriate Marxist theories for studying the working class, peasants, non-literate and minority populations. I felt as though I were back at Barnard, attending an SDS meeting.

I was fortunate to study with Akira Iriye, a pioneer of the cultural approach to American foreign relations, but, as I should have known, the sources were not yet available to study public protest and government response during the Vietnam War. I decided to work with Arthur Mann, a historian of American social reform, immigration and ethnicity. Although a reserved and intimidating figure, he was unfailingly kind and helpful to me. My paper for his seminar on Progressive Era social reform in Chicago dealt with the anti-child labor movement. While researching this topic, I made an interesting discovery. The leaders of that movement and so many other social justice causes at the turn of the century were women. Although I grew up in the Chicago area, I had only heard Jane Addams's name in passing and knew nothing of her impact on the Progressive Era. As I found out more not only about Addams, but also about her colleagues, Florence Kelley, Sophonisba Breckinridge, Edith Abbott, Margaret Dreier Robins, Grace Abbott and others, I discovered an interesting pattern. Many of these women had activist parents, all were college-educated, and all felt an imperative to be useful and professionally productive. The crucial role of women reformers, particularly those associated with the settlement houses, in Progressive Era social movements, is, by now well-known. In the early 1970s, however, I had discovered something new, and my seminar paper was published in *Social Service Review*.[3]

My interest in women of the Progressive Era deepened. Not only was this uncharted research territory, but also, these women bore a certain resemblance to women of my own day. Although hardly hippies, they critiqued social injustice and war, became politically active, and most were, if not feminists, suffragists. Just when I was looking for a dissertation topic, two journalists published books on women's higher education: Liva Baker, *I'm Radcliffe, Fly Me* and Elaine Kendall, *Peculiar Institutions*.[4] Both authors depicted the Seven Sisters colleges as educational institutions for the wealthy and frivolous. Of course I resented the stereotyping of women's college graduates, but it also seemed to me that Baker and Kendall were, simply, wrong. Many women reformers and professionals had attended women's colleges between the 1870s and 1910s. These schools had been instrumental in nurturing their students' desire to effect social change.

In the archives of both single sex and co-educational colleges and universities, I discovered ample evidence to support my thesis. From their founding through the 1910s, women's colleges in particular provided an environment rich in opportunities for students' intellectual, social and political development. Students founded organizations dedicated to fostering social change and had many connections to off-campus social movements. Newspapers, yearbooks and other documents affirmed women students' desire to make their mark on the world. Even the notoriously conservative Southern white women's colleges (I studied Sophie Newcomb College of Tulane University and Agnes Scott College, just outside Atlanta) created expectations for purposeful work and activities among their graduates. In contrasting the lively and dynamic student life at women's colleges with the more constricted campus activities of "co-eds," my work contributed to the on-going debate about the value of single sex education for women.

> **Gordon Influential Volumes**
>
> Joyce Antler, *Lucy Sprague Mitchell: The Making of a Modern American Woman* (New Haven: Yale University Press, 1987).
>
> Lawrence A. Cremin, *American Education: The Colonial Experience, 1607-1783* (New York: Harper and Row, 1970).
>
> Richard Hofstadter, *Anti-Intellectualism in American Life* (New York: Knopf, 1963).
>
> Michael Schudson, *Discovering the News: A Social History of American Newspapers* (New York: Basic Books, 1978).
>
> Kathryn Kish Sklar, *Catherine Beecher* (New Haven: Yale University Press, 1973).

While writing a dissertation and then turning it into a book, I puzzled over the persistence, even in the scholarly literature, of characterizations of women college students as flighty young girls, mostly interested in social status, clothes and parties (e.g. Helen L. Horowitz, *Alma Mater*).[5] For a long time, college attendance by women sharply curtailed their marital prospects; around half of the first generation of college women (from the 1860s through the 1890s) never married. And even as late as 1910, when marriage rates for college women approached those of women in the general population, college graduates married significantly later and had small families, a trend that continues today. Under those circumstances, why would women consider higher education unless they had serious goals. Investigating this puzzle, I looked at articles written about women college students around the turn of the century. In addition to the ever-present warnings that educated women would never marry, I found a genre of writing about "college girls," both in books and popular magazines. In the pages of the *Ladies' Home Journal*, one of the most widely-read publications in the country, pictures of college girls as Gibson Girls, modern and athletic, but also beautiful and ladylike, abounded. Articles about women college students, particularly at the Seven Sisters colleges, featured young women partying and playing, and by no means doing anything that might be construed "unfeminine." My favorite picture showed a Gibson Girl/college girl studying (one of a very few pictures depicting an educational activity) with a rose draped over her book. In an article I wrote for *American Quarterly*, I argued that such images deflected concerns about the emergence and growing social impact of the New Woman. A social historian's approach (investigation of women's actual behavior on campus) allowed me to demonstrate both the inaccuracy of these images and their cultural significance.[6]

While I was working on my manuscript, the *History of Education Quarterly* asked me to review some recent books on the history of college students' activism. One of these books traced the organizational history of SDS, arguing that a more or less straight line connected that group to the Intercollegiate Socialist Society, founded in 1905. I disagreed, pointing out, in the review, that differences among the various eras of student activism were far more numerous and significant than any continuities, imagined or real.[7] For some time I had realized that students' political involvements fluctuated according to the political climate off campus. Not surprisingly, perhaps, the three most visible eras of student activism occurred during the Progressive Era, the New Deal period and the 1960s. So what happened, especially to women students, in less reform-friendly times? If I examined campuses during the 1920s, 1940s, 1950s or 1980s, would I too conclude that women college students were not serious about anything except their social lives?

I had little interest in doing additional research on the campus experiences of college women, especially since Paula Fass's intriguing book, *The Damned and the Beautiful* (1979) suggested that student activism did not disappear, but became a less prominent theme in the 1920s, an argument that made sense to me and probably applied to other decades as well.[8] But my question persisted, albeit in a somewhat different form: if women who graduated from college and entered the work force during reform eras benefited from a liberal political climate, what happened to them when that was no longer the case.

For some time, historians of American women had puzzled over the decline, particularly in the 1920s, in the numbers of women entering the professions, the rise in the marriage rate of college women, and the dearth of feminist activity following passage of the 19th Amendment. Indeed, the period between 1920 and the 1960s came to be considered "the doldrums" in women's history. Some attributed this to the implosion of the feminist movement over issues of social class during the struggle, in the 1920s, to pass the Equal Rights Amendment. Others wrote about the rise of "compulsory heterosexuality" and increased pressure on women to marry and have families. Still others maintained that reform, feminism and women's professionalism continued into the 1920s, only to be shut down by the Great Depression and then World War II. And, in a compelling book on women in the professions after 1920, Patricia Hummer argued that the post-suffrage ethos of equality pushed women doctors and lawyers, in particular, into direct competition with their male colleagues—a competition they lost. Women had, perhaps, been better off when they claimed professional legitimacy based on their unique gender-based qualities of caring, moral integrity and suitability to deal with women clients/patients.[9]

After many twists, turns and false starts, I decided to write a biography of a mid-twentieth century professional woman: journalist Dorothy Thompson (1893–1961). Born during the late Victorian era, a college graduate, and active in the suffrage movement, Thompson exemplified the New Woman of the early twentieth century. She had a distinguished forty-year career as a foreign correspondent, columnist and public figure. Yet both Betty Friedan in the 1960s and Anna Quindlen in the 1990s accused Thompson of opposing feminism, encouraging women to remain in the home, while she herself garnered satisfaction and public recognition from a professional career. Dorothy Thompson was indeed a complex figure, and often reversed herself on important issues, including feminism. I'm working on a journal article relating her changing views on gender to difficulties she experienced as a New Woman growing up in a changed world. The views Friedan and Quindlen found so offensive stemmed not from hypocrisy, but regrets about her own choices in life.

As a historian of education, I had additional reasons to write about Dorothy Thompson. Lawrence Cremin's *American Education: the Colonial Experience* demonstrated the multiple ways education occurred in society.[10] Cremin's analysis of the impact of newspapers on the American Revolution renewed my interest in public opinion and foreign policy. By exploring Thompson's role in educating the American public about the dangers of fascism and Nazism during the 1930s and 1940s, I could finally address questions I'd had since the 1960s.

When I began research for the biography, Lawrence Cremin and then Patricia Graham were presidents of the Spencer Foundation. There I found support for my work and acknowledgment that my questions could legitimately be addressed within the history of education. Similarly, my colleagues and friends in the History of Education Society listened patiently to my presidential address, in which I discussed the ambiguous position of newspaper columnists *vis a vis* both the public and the publishers in the 1930s.[11]

At home, however, teaching history in a school of education, my project encountered quizzical looks, and concerns, from administrators, that I was no longer centrally concerned with education. This situation had little to do with me personally, but reflected the school of education's "mission" to effect reform in the community's elementary and secondary schools. A historian, they believed, could only be useful if she wrote about public education; even higher education was only of marginal significance. Those of us with backgrounds in the disciplines came together in a department/program of higher education administration: three historians, a philosopher, and a legal scholar.

Within a year or two, we realized that the strategy of creating our own department and what was, essentially, a foundations program for the school of education, did not make us any more "relevant" in the eyes of our deans. Our colleagues, who had doctorates in education, argued that their multi-disciplinary training qualified them to teach history, sociology and philosophy to students in a school of education. Our experiences were part of a national trend, in schools of education, to move away from liberal studies. Two of our department's faculty left for other institutions, one retired, and two, including me, moved across the campus to the College of Arts and Sciences.

The move had many benefits. I no longer had to justify my research interests, I had colleagues to talk to about my work, and was encouraged to teach whatever I wanted. Dorothy Thompson's expertise in Central and East European politics and history led me to read intensively about those regions, and, eventually to co-teach a course on European nationalism and ethnic conflict with a colleague in European history. The Thompson project also made it necessary for me to study twentieth century Jewish history, the history of the Arab-Israeli conflict and American policies toward the Middle East. Thompson, a non-Jewish Zionist, became deeply involved in the European refugee crisis of the 1930s, advising FDR on the issue, and writing an influential article on the subject in *Foreign Affairs*.[12] Following the war, however, she turned against Zionism and campaigned vigorously, first against the establishment of Israel, and then on behalf of improved relations between the United States and the Arab countries.

I thoroughly enjoyed expanding my intellectual horizons this way. My colleague and I got a small grant to visit Eastern Europe and collect materials for a course on the Holocaust, as well as a larger grant to develop a course in Modern Jewish history. Additionally, in summer 2006, I received a fellowship to attend a seminar on the Arab-Israeli conflict, taught at the Hebrew University in Jerusalem; in summer 2010, I've been accepted into a program, run by Brandeis University, to prepare academics for teaching the history of Israel.

In truth, being pushed out of the school of education allowed me to think both more widely and more deeply about my work, without worrying about "fit." My research questions have not changed all that much over the years. I'm still working on the educative relationship of journalists with the American public, and how that relationship influenced foreign policy. My next project will explore the affect of American public and journalistic opinion on United States policies toward Israel.

In the twentieth century, schools of education alternated between promoting discipline-based research and focusing on professional issues of concern to educators. My graduate education and early career occurred during one such "swing;" during those years, a school of education seemed an appropriate, even ideal, place to work. By teaching aspiring educators, I fulfilled a long-held political goal of influencing the K-12 social studies curriculum, if indirectly. In the 1990s, the emphasis and mission in schools of education changed, and I left. Did the shift in goals and values improve or weaken schools of education? Over the past fifteen years I've thought and read a great deal about this question, without coming to any conclusions. Although I can't decide what to think about the larger issues, I consider myself fortunate to have a new and different institutional home. With or without the label "historian of education," I found a way to do the intellectual work that matters to me.

NOTES

[1] Betty Friedan, *The Feminine Mystique* (New York: Dell, 1963).

[2] Richard Hofstadter, *Anti-Intellectualism in American Life* (New York: Vintage, 1963).

[3] Lynn D. Gordon, "Women and the Anti-Child Labor Movement in Illinois, 1890–1920," *Social Service Review* 57 (June 1977): 228–248.

[4] Liva Baker, *I'm Radcliffe, Fly Me* (New York: Macmillan, 1976); Elaine Kendall, *Peculiar Institutions* (New York: Putnam, 1976).

[5] Helen L. Horowitz, *Alma Mater* (Amherst: University of Massachusetts Press, 1993).

[6] Lynn D. Gordon, "The Gibson Girl Goes to College: Popular Culture and Women's Higher Education in the Progressive Era," *American Quarterly* 39 (Summer 1987): 211–230.

[7] Lynn D. Gordon, "In the Shadow of SDS: Writing the History of Twentieth Century College Students," *History of Education Quarterly* 25 (Winter 1985): 131–39.

[8] Paula S. Fass, *The Damned and the Beautiful: American Youth in the 1920s* (New York: Oxford University Press, 1977).

[9] Patricia Hummer, *The Decade of Elusive Promise: Professional Women in the United States, 1920–1930* (UMI Research Press, 1979).

[10] Lawrence Cremin, *American Education: the Colonial Experience, 1607–1783* (New York: Harper Collins, 1972).

[11] Lynn D. Gordon, "Why Dorothy Thompson Lost Her Job: Political Columnists and the Press Wars of the 1930s and 1940s," Presidential Address 1993 *History of Education Quarterly* 34, 2, (Summer 1994): 281–303.

[12] Dorothy Thompson, "Refugees: A World Problem," *Foreign Affairs* 16 (April 1938): 375–387.

PATRICIA ALBJERG GRAHAM

FROM THE WABASH TO THE HUDSON TO THE CHARLES

Born in the depths of the Depression, February 9, 1935, to Victor and Marguerite Hall Albjerg, I seemed a miracle to them for I was incontrovertibly healthy. I was their fourth child, and the only one who lived. Our home was West Lafayette, Indiana, a town of less than 2500 residents focused entirely on Purdue University with only the Wabash River and several Indian battle fields providing diversion. We lived in a rented upstairs apartment over our landlords.[1]

In such a small town we knew nearly everyone. Soon I came to know the one school that served us all as well, Morton School. It was the only one in West Lafayette, which at that time did not permit Negroes, as they were then called, to live in town. They had to live across the Wabash in larger Lafayette, as did most Jews before World War II. Roman Catholics had no church in West Lafayette and hence no parochial school for their children. West Lafayette boasted only Methodist and Baptist churches. Despite this profound limitation on the diversity of its enrollment, Morton School thought of itself an all-encompassing "common school," a mistake made by many Hoosier educators, including Paul Monroe, Ellwood Patterson Cubberley, Otis Caldwell, Lewis Terman and Charles Prosser.

I did not like school. In that era of progressive education "creativity" and "popularity" were seen as the goals, both elusive for me. As a little girl with thick glasses, heavy straight hair in braids, good at reading with a large vocabulary and absolutely no talent athletically, artistically, musically, or socially, I found the schoolwork dull and the ambiance dispiriting and isolating.

While school was never a place that I found academically compelling, neither was most of college nor was some of graduate school. What I did find gripping was reading and the discussions, mostly about history and contemporary affairs, that accompanied meals at home. Both my mother and father had PhD's in history from the University of Wisconsin. My father but not my mother was an eminently successful professor of history at Purdue, an institution that valued engineering, science, agriculture and regarded history as a lowly "service department." Both published quite extensively, sometimes together and sometimes separately, rare occurrences for Purdue history faculty. My mother, who had been chair of the history department at Alabama State College for Women in Montevalo before her marriage, regularly sought a teaching position at Purdue but was rebuffed by the department. Finally in the late 1950s she was hired – most happily - by the Dean of Women's Office as the only person on the staff at that time who had a PhD and who was married or a mother. Who knew which attribute was more important? The

W. J. Urban, Leaders in the Historical Study of American Education, 117–127.

lesson of limited job opportunities for married women PhD's in small Indiana towns impressed me vividly.

While my academic education was heavily driven by my experiences at home, my social education depended on my experiences at school. When forced to take my first standardized test sometime in elementary school, I encountered questions of standard English usage, presumably the subject of classroom study. As I pondered the question of objects of prepositions (is it "between you and I" or "between you and me"?), I recalled only my mother's repeated correction of my language. I had no recollection of any teacher ever having mentioned these matters. And so it was for most of my classmates; teachers could focus on stimulating our creativity and social engagement and need not bother with the basics, which were provided at home.

If elementary and junior high school had been beset with social dilemmas, high school was even worse and even more frustrating. My grades were fine, and my participation in extra-curricular activities extensive. I was elected to this and that and co-editor of the school newspaper, but I wanted out of that confining environment of 76 fellow classmates, most of whom I had known since first grade. So, one day in the fall of my senior year when I had turned 16, I went to the school library, looked up the Indiana Superintendent of Public Instruction's report, and discovered that I was old enough to quit and had taken enough courses to receive a diploma. I went immediately to Principal Carl Hammer's office, told him I was quitting and that I was entitled to a high school diploma. By 5 pm I had a job in the stenographic pool in the Purdue Agricultural Economics department. I reported all this to my parents that night at dinner, a tumultuous occasion. The justification I offered for this action was to earn money to go away to college. The following September I entered the Integrated Liberal Studies (ILS) program at the University of Wisconsin, Madison on a scholarship.

Madison terrified me. I knew no one there, and the academic work expected of me was of a caliber that I had never encountered. For the first time the curriculum became both compelling and demanding. I was on my own, and I was very frightened that I would not be able to manage. But manage I did, ending the year with marks that put me in the freshman academic honorary society. However, my father had become ill, and at Christmas my mother and I decided that I should return to Purdue the following year to help.

September 1953 found me back in my bedroom in West Lafayette and enrolled as a sophomore at Purdue. The classes were, as I feared, mostly uninteresting. To improve the situation I returned to my high school interest, journalism, and volunteered to work on the Purdue student newspaper, the Exponent. My first afternoon there I was assigned to help the "issue editor," Loren Graham, and we married two years later, September 6, 1955. On that day he was commissioned an Ensign in the US Navy, graduated as a chemical engineer from Purdue (and editor of the Exponent), and I graduated as an English major, social studies minor with a secondary school teaching certificate. Just as I had not liked high school much, neither did I like college much and therefore I completed my college degree in three years, thereby fulfilling my parents' condition that I could not marry until I had graduated from college.

Norfolk, Virginia was the next stop where Loren was assigned to a destroyer and spent 29 of the next 36 months of active duty at sea. I looked for a job to pay off the $2500 debt that we had accumulated in college. Unsuccessful at finding a journalism job (I turned down the only one I was offered, to edit Royster Guano's internal newspaper, the Poop Sheet), most reluctantly I looked for a teaching job. Deep Creek High School, an all-white school in segregated Virginia serving the youngsters of mainly poor families living in Deep Creek and the Dismal Swamp, hired me at $2250 as the eighth grade English and social studies teacher with a fifth course in drama for the high school seniors who could not pass the English course. The high school drop-out rate was seventy-five percent. Like my beginning experience in Madison, again I was terrified but not by the academic demands. Rather, like most beginning teachers, I had no idea how to manage a classroom, let alone how to help the children learn. In addition, I was furious that I was back in the institutional setting, school, that I had repeatedly tried to escape or ignore.

Somehow I managed to get through the fall and by Thanksgiving my eighth graders and I were getting along well, and some were beginning to read and a few were even reading well. By spring my unlikely drama class had coalesced, and the students won the district one-act play contest and went on to take second place in the state competition in Charlottesville and return two trophies to the barren Deep Creek High School trophy case. I was fired at the end of the year because I was pregnant.

Deep Creek fundamentally changed me. I opened one of my books with a discussion of it and returned to it again briefly in a later book.[2] I reported on improvement in education in Deep Creek under the leadership of a long-term principal (a tenth grader when I taught at Deep Creek) and of federal action bringing desegregation and support for improved instruction.[3] What Deep Creek fundamentally taught me was that school, which I had largely disdained, was for some children their only hope of developing the skills and values that they needed for successful adulthood. For me those skills and values came largely from my home, but for the Deep Creek children the school was a principal provider. I had never thought of that.

With my husband largely absent on his US Navy destroyer, as a pregnant woman I did one of the few things society permitted such persons to do: I went back to school. Since I could again live at my parents' home, I sought a master's degree at Purdue. One required course was in the history of education. We had a textbook, a heavy gray book with the title in red and filled with small print. The teacher always referred to it as by "Butts and another man." It was too expensive for my budget, and before the first test, I read it in the reserve room of the library. After the first test, I never read it again since the test only required regurgitation of the lecture material. Very dull material, I thought.

While his destroyer plunged about the sea, my husband improbably wrote that when he left the Navy, he wanted to study Russian history and become a professor. This would require money so I resumed teaching, this time at Maury High School in Norfolk. And at the end of the year again I was fired. Termination this time, however, was not personal but institutional. Norfolk closed its schools in 1958 rather than admit six black students into the white high schools. I could not understand it.

September, 1958 brought us to New York City where my husband enrolled in the PhD program in Russian history at Columbia. I again reluctantly sought a school job, having failed to find one with the Girl Scouts or with publishing firms. On a rainy day while exploring our new neighborhood on the Upper West Side, I knocked on the door of a brownstone that identified itself as St. Hilda's and St. Hugh's School. A nun opened it, settled me in the hall while I explained that I sought a teaching job. She told me to wait for a bit until the headmistress, the Reverend Mother Ruth, could see me. Mother Ruth needed a history teacher, and the school also ran a nursery school which would take our two year old, Meg. I taught half time for $2500 a year, five history classes a day (10th grade American, 11th grade European, Civics, AP American, AP European) and the baby in the nursery. It was a Godsend.

This assignment presented a new challenge. Though my parents were both historians and my husband aspired to be an historian, I was not. I had a serious knowledge-deficit in what I was supposed to be teaching, and after the first chaotic year with excellent students who fundamentally taught themselves (unlike most of my previous students), I recognized for the first time in my life that I really needed some substantive academic work in a subject for which I was responsible. My husband's Danforth Foundation fellowship was limited to men, but it provided tuition for wives to take courses, as the brochure shrewdly but bluntly described, "so the husband would not outgrow his wife intellectually and divorce." While I did not want that either, my most immediate need was for some courses in history. Loren agreed and after studying his fall schedule for 1959 volunteered Thursday, 4–6 pm as the time he could baby-sit, and I could take a class.

Columbia University's History Department had one course that term in the Thursday, 4–6 slot. Taught by a new faculty member on social and educational issues in America since 1865, it was a seminar, and I needed the professor's permission to enroll so I went to see him. Upon my arrival he quizzed me about my background in history and then inquired what work I had done in the history of education. Startled, I recalled my insubstantial Purdue class, mentioned it, and he inquired, "what did you read for that course?" I knew enough not to mention the color of the binding, which was about all that I recalled, and finally mumbled, "a book by Butts and some other man." The professor's face reddened, and then with exquisite tact suggested that if I were to take his course, I would need to do some other reading that summer and rattled off a dozen basic texts. I left, headed straight for the library to check the name of the second author besides Butts. As I feared, it was Lawrence A. Cremin, the professor with whom I had just spoken.

Academic year 1959–60 brought profound changes to my family's and my life. Having completed the dozen books Cremin recommended by August 1, I wrote and asked for suggestions of more reading. He replied that I should take a vacation (the last time he ever suggested that to me!) and I was admitted to his year-long seminar. In this seminar, I wrote a long paper on the history of the Progressive Education Association, a topic closely related to Cremin's book-in-progress on progressive education.[4] When I had arrived in the fall, he had lost his teaching assistant for his big survey course in the history of education that he gave at Teachers College and asked me to serve in that capacity, thereby forcing me quickly to cover all the material in that course. Meanwhile, I had been made head of the History Department at St. Hilda's and St. Hugh's. That spring Loren was selected as one of a dozen American students to spend the following year studying at Moscow State University. Late that spring Cremin had a fundamental talk with me about my plans startling me by urging me to take my written and oral examinations for the PhD that fall before Meg and I expected to join Loren in Moscow. I was staggered that he thought I could prepare adequately in that short period of time, but he simply said that if I failed, I could always retake the exams later. To my even greater surprise, I passed the fall exams and received my PhD in 1964.

My enthusiasm for the Progressive Education Association was at best limited. It did become the topic of my first book but it was not initially helpful in securing a teaching position.[5] We moved to Bloomington, Indiana where Loren was offered an assistant professorship of history in 1963, but I was unable to find a teaching position. The history department expressed nepotism concerns and progressive educators in charge of the school of education found me to be "too liberal artsy." I, of course, feared that I was repeating my mother's sad employment history at Purdue. Finally I was hired as an "executive assistant" (aka secretary) for the organization that then administered the US/Soviet Academic Exchange Program which had sent Loren to Moscow. When Loren was offered an appointment at Johns Hopkins and told his dean at Indiana that he might accept because his wife was not happy in her job at Indiana, Harold Shane, dean of the school of education at Indiana to whom I had referred somewhat derisively in my dissertation, called me on a Sunday morning and said that he had been asked to hire me "in order to keep your husband at Indiana." I accepted with alacrity. A year later Loren was offered a visiting position that became a tenured professorship at Columbia. Fortuitously for me, Geraldine Joncich Clifford, my graduate school friend then teaching at University of California, Berkeley, had just turned down a position at Barnard College to direct its education program, and the Barnard administration went back to Larry Cremin for another suggestion, and he mentioned me. I got the job.

Very little prepared me to be a "teacher educator," unless the fervor of my dissatisfaction with my own 18 credit hours of education courses counted. My vivid memories of Deep Creek forced me think about how we prepared beginning teachers, usually in settings that were thought to be "ideal" but where they stood absolutely no chance of getting a first job. The first job, at least in New York City, was likely to be in a low-functioning public school where family and community supports were often lacking. If one got a private school job, it was not likely to be in one of the several excellent ones in New York. Hence, I thought we needed to prepare future teachers to be able to cope effectively with the students they were likely to face. The late sixties were chaotic, particularly in New York, where strikes closed schools three years in a row, an early lesson in "professionalism" for my beginning teachers. In spring, 1968 Columbia completely shut down, overwhelmed by striking students (and faculty) protesting both the university's and the nation's policies. As an aspiring academic, one wondered about the viability of educational institutions.

By fall, 1968 I was finally offering a course in the history of American education (in the Barnard history department despite the skepticism of some of its senior members). I had also agreed to write a book in which I tried to explain regional differences in American educational practices and the roles that class, religion, gender and race played in several communities in different regions.[6] Further, I attempted to unite both schools and colleges historically though I was disappointed when the chapter on Amherst was eliminated from the final version.

At Barnard, however, I was primarily considered not an historian of education but rather the administrative director of the Education Program, which had now expanded to include Columbia undergraduates. Barnard's new president, Martha Peterson, responded to Princeton president Robert Goheen's request for a woman faculty member interested in education to advise on their impending coeducation by recommending me. The most important element of this arrangement was that I would return home at the end of the year. In short, this was Barnard's lend lease program to Princeton. Fall,1969 saw the Grahams moving to an apartment on the grounds of the Institute for Advanced Study, where Loren was appointed a fellow for the year. I biked to Nassau Hall at Princeton where initially no one sought my assistance. I got a lot of research done, including the Princeton chapter, for my *Community and Class in American Education*.

Ultimately with the cooperation of the new provost (William Bowen) and the new dean of students (Neil Rudenstine), Goheen agreed that I should attempt to answer the question, "What changes, if any, are needed to make Princeton as good a place for its girls as it has been for its boys?" My answer was women professors, of whom there had been none prior to 1969. Women faculty, I believed, would keep the issue of women students' needs alive better than any short-term administrative remedy. Initially many at Princeton did not believe that any women could meet their elevated standards for faculty appointments, but forty years later with Shirley Tilghman as president, Nancy Weiss as long-term dean, and a number of women faculty and administrators Princeton is quite different. My experience at Princeton led me to write what I suspect is my most frequently cited paper, on women in the academy, just as I returned to Barnard.[7]

The time at Princeton, the situation of Barnard and Columbia, and my mother's and my professional experience shifted my research interests to the experience of women in academic life. By 1970 the women's movement, particularly in New York City, bubbled, and two of my Barnard colleagues, Catharine R. Stimpson and Kate Millett were deep in the midst of it. My former graduate school colleague, Gerda Lerner, and I joined a group of "New York City Women Historians," and we met regularly to discuss our professional and sometimes personal issues. I joined Hanna Gray, Page Smith, and Carl Schorske on the ad hoc committee of the

American Historical Association chaired by Willie Lee Rose investigating the professional circumstances of women historians (not good, we found), and upon Willie Lee's serious illness, I became chair of the permanent committee. Meanwhile Columbia faced a challenge about discrimination against women faculty from the federal Office of Civil Rights, and I joined several other faculty at the request of the then president, William McGill, to investigate the salaries of men and women. Initially two distinguished colleagues, Nina Garsoian in history and Cheng T. Wu in physics, joined me (a deep skeptic about fairness in academe), and, of course, we discovered significantly lower salaries for women. All this "activism" led me back to my research question, and soon I began gathering data on the historical participation of women in American higher education and had a large box of IBM punch cards coded for various women. In 1972–73 I received a Guggenheim fellowship for a proposal to write a book on the subject, which I never did, though I published several papers on the subject, including one that appeared in *Signs*.[8]

My life took a profound turn in 1974 when I left Barnard most reluctantly to begin a "commuting marriage" when I accepted the deanship of the Radcliffe Institute and a professorship at Harvard. My professional life was taking a determined administrative tilt, but the opportunity to improve the professional circumstances for gifted women that the Radcliffe Institute offered seemed compelling. By February, 1977 Radcliffe and Harvard signed a "non-merger, merger agreement," which I thoroughly supported, had worked hard to achieve, and which eliminated the Radcliffe Institute of which I was dean. The afternoon we were signing the agreement I was interrupted by a phone call inviting me to come to Washington to consider the position of Director of the National Institute of Education in the new Carter administration. I accepted, took a public service leave from Harvard, never expecting to return, and remained in Washington until 1979. I did return, however, because Loren accepted a professorship in history of science at MIT and later at Harvard, and we both drove back to Cambridge.

The intense administrative experience first at Radcliffe in the negotiations with Harvard and then in the federal government helped me to understand some of the forces that affect educational change, something that my prior reading in the history of education had not done. Most of the history of education I had then read had been about educational ideas or about famous educators who had those ideas. Little dealt with the implementation of those ideas or about the forces that brought these changes, something many began to call "educational policy." As I returned to the faculty of the Harvard Graduate School of Education, I decided that my next book would focus on the history of the federal government's role in education. Before I could get it written (but with 200+ fascinating – to me – pages on the Smithsonian, the Morrill Acts, national university controversies), Derek Bok, president of Harvard, convinced me to become Dean of the Harvard Ed School, and I did not finish the book.

As the first woman in Harvard's history to be dean of a school, I learned a great deal about how higher education functions. When universities like Harvard were willing to have such low-status faculties as schools of education, they have typically concentrated their efforts on schooling of the children they would like to have as their undergraduates. That has meant preparing teachers and administrators for the finest affluent districts, typically in the second half of the twentieth century those in the suburbs. Most, including Harvard, dropped focus on the schools by the last third of the twentieth century and shifted their attention to "policy" and social science research, both thought to be of higher status among their arts and science colleagues.[9] Many including Yale, Johns Hopkins, Duke, and Chicago, closed their schools of education altogether. Harvard came perilously close, and when I became dean, the Ed School had not been able to make a tenured appointment since 1974. It did not resume such appointments until 1985 (with Sara Lawerence-Lightfoot) when Bok and the Harvard Corporation regained confidence in it. This was due largely as a result of a shift in focus to prepare graduates to understand and improve schooling, particularly for those most needing it in poor communities.

These experiences led me to write *SOS: Sustain our Schools*, which incorporated explicitly some of my personal experiences and implicitly what I understood historically about the evolution of schooling in the United States and the various roles of families, communities, government, higher education, and business in fostering it. I also wrote it to be sure that I still had the taste for historical research and writing as I envisioned leaving the deanship and returning fulltime to the professoriate. That destiny, however, was not to be.

Larry Cremin's sudden death in September 1990 unexpectedly propelled me from the Board of the Spencer Foundation to its presidency. I resigned as dean at Harvard but retained my professorship part time while I took on the Spencer position, also part time.

Again in an administrative job, I tried to use what I had learned as an historian to determine what we needed in future educational researchers. My overwhelming sense was that we needed a new generation, better prepared than we had been and able to cope with the extraordinary demands of improving educational practice. Money is certainly an important lubricant in solving problems, but it does not solve them by itself. Ideas are also necessary and determining where to find the best ideas, who to support to investigate them, and convincing researchers to do so in a timely fashion is challenging indeed, particularly when one rarely knows whether the ideas and money are truly having a beneficial effect upon education. And one certainly cannot accept the accolades of the fund-seeking community as a reliable indicator of one's work.

In 2000 I was 65 years old and resigned at Spencer. I returned to Harvard in September and taught my "Finding a Researchable Question" course with David Tyack and Elisabeth Hansot, who were visiting that fall. Loren had retired in 1999, having successfully recovered from brain tumor surgery, an experience that reminded both of us that we would not live forever and that there might be some activities yet to enjoy that fulltime employment precluded. In 2001 I also retired from Harvard though with the title "research professor." Rather to my surprise I also agreed to write another book on the history of education for the Annenberg Institutions of Democracy series, the first piece of writing I had ever undertaken when I did not have a full time job.[10] In it I attempted to explain what our educational institutions had been expected to do and what they had actually done over the last century.

"Retirement" brought the opportunity to participate on governing boards of various organizations (Josiah Macy Jr. Foundation, Center for Advanced Study in the Behavioral Sciences, American Academy of Arts and Sciences, American Philosophical Society, Central European University, Smolny College of St. Petersburg State University, Carnegie Foundation for the Advancement of Teaching), thereby broadening my professional network considerably and deepening my understanding of the strengths and frailties of academic institutions. My professional life has consistently brought me into contact with many leading scholars, and I have tried to persuade many of them to explore and improve education. I have come to realize how extraordinarily fortunate I (and many of them) have been, first to be born into a family and in a community that was rich in intellectual resources, which I absorbed without recognizing most of them. When my colleagues and I succeeded, we thought it was the merit system at work, often not recognizing either the advantages our environments provided or the disadvantages that many other talented individuals faced in less salubrious settings. For me schooling was the spice to the stew of education, not the sustaining stew itself. But for many others schooling provided the primary educational sustenance, and frequently that schooling was woefully inadequate. In the United States schools serving the poor and racial minorities were most likely, though not always, to be inferior to ones serving the affluent and white students. In short, students needing good schools the most got the worst schools while students needing good schools the least got the best ones.

Educational policy makers have identified this problem but have not solved it. Better ideas on how to improve educational practice are needed, but they are in short supply. These are issues that should tax the intellects and energies of our finest scholars. For those less fortunate in the circumstances of their birth than I, we need imaginative, rigorous, supportive institutions to educate them. We do not have them now.

While education cannot guarantee an informed citizenry that acts wisely, I believe that improving our educational institutions for everybody remains our best hope of maintaining and improving our society. In both my scholarship and my other professional activities I have tried to do so.

BIBLIOGRAPHIC MUSINGS

Wayne Urban, the distinguished editor of this volume, requests the authors to list the dozen or so books that have shaped our scholarship. Since such a list does not quite fit my experience, I have offered some alternative "musings."

Within the text of this essay I have noted my debt to my thesis advisor, Lawrence A. Cremin, whose professional support for me was remarkable. While a graduate student working on progressive education as he was writing *The Transformation of the School*, I came to realize that the progressive education movement as he defined it (1875–1918) seemed to me really two movements, the early one serving primarily immigrant and poor children and the latter one reaching middle class and affluent ones. This insight came to me when I unexpectedly discovered Scott Nearing's *The New Education* while I was writing my thesis.[11] Cremin's three volume magnum opus, *American Education: The Colonial Experience* (New York: Harper & Row, 1970), *The National Experience* (New York: Harper & Row, 1980, and *The Metropolitan Experience* (New York: Harper & Row, 1988) is a superb compilation of scholarly resources in the history of educational institutions and individuals.

As has been true for so many other historians of education, my intellectual debt to David Tyack is enormous, not only for his fluid and thoughtful prose, but also for his and Elisabeth Hansot's willingness to participate in extended and deep conversations about our field often while walking in beautiful places. Conversations, such as those with David and Elisabeth, have helped me to define questions that I subsequently investigated.

So also have fiction, biographies and memoirs broadened my understanding of issues that were often obscure in the archives. For example, the portrait of the 14th century Scandinavian woman portrayed by Sigrid Undset in *Kristin Lavransdatter*, which I read in the New York: Knopf, 1966 edition, inspired me to think about women's roles in ways I had never considered. Similarly Simone de Beauvoir's four volume autobiography, *Memoirs of a Dutiful Daughter* (New York: Harper & Row, 1958), *The Prime of Life* (Cleveland: World Publishing, 1962), *Force of Circumstance* (New York: Putnam, 1965), and *All Said and Done* (New York: Putnam: 1974), and one of her autobiographic novels, *The Mandarins* (Cleveland: World Publishing, 1956) further extended my understanding of the variety of women's experiences. Sara Lawrence-Lightfoot's biography of her mother, Margaret Morgan Lawrence, *Balm in Gilead* (Reading, MA: Addison-Wesley, 1988) and Sissela Bok's biography of her mother, *Alva Myrdal: A Daughter's Memoir* (Reading, MA: Addison-Wesley, 1988), extended my appreciation of these women's accomplishments through education, both formal and informal.

A journalist, Richard Kluger, wrote the book that I have found most useful in attempting to understand the history of school segregation in America, *Simple Justice* (New York: Knopf, 1976). The contrast between what Kluger describes there and what John Dewey prescribes in his inimitable prose in *Democracy and Education* (New York: Macmillan, 1916), *The Child and the Curriculum* (1902) and *The School and Society* (1899), reprinted in Martin S. Dworkin, ed., *Dewey on Education* (New York: Teachers College Press, 1959) continues to be a challenge to all of us who would like to bring the best of Dewey's educational practice to all Americans. Christopher Jencks and his many co-authors clarified the consequences of poor schools for poor people in *Inequality* (New York: Basic Books, 1972), which he had hoped to entitle "The Limits of Schooling."

Two recent works have impressed me deeply: Claudia Golden and Lawrence Katz's historical analysis using considerable quantitative data, *The Race Between Education and Technology* (Cambridge, MA: Harvard University Press, 2008) and Jonathan R, Cole, *The Great American University* (New York: Public Affairs,

2009). Both are examples of the continuing tradition of superb American scholarship about education.

Finally, my greatest education has come from my work as a professor (with nearly forty successful doctoral advisees, only some of whom were interested in the history of education) and as an administrator. As a Harvard professor and dean, I listened to and read carefully the written work of persons we were considering for appointment and promotion, among them Jerry Murphy, Noel McGinn, Sara Lawrence-Lightfoot, Kurt Fischer, Howard Gardner, Carol Gilligan, Catherine Snow, Anthony Bryk, Marvin Lazerson, Richard Murnane, Richard Elmore, Gary Orfield, Robert Peterkin, Carol Weiss, Patricia Cross, Susan Moore Johnson, John Willett, Judith Singer, Eleanor Duckworth, Vito Perrone, Robert Kegan, Robert Sellman, Katherine Merseth, Julie Reuben, Richard Chait and Kate Elgin. What a magnificent education these students and faculty provided! Later as president of the Spencer Foundation I read a good many more fascinating research proposals and participated in lively conversations with our fine staff and advisory committees as we evaluated which ones to recommend to our Board. From all these experiences has come the conviction that Richard Hofstadter may be correct in reporting on the tradition of American anti-intellectualism, but there is still remarkably strong intellectual activity surrounding studies of education in America from which I have benefited.

NOTES

[1] The assignment given was to write an "intellectual autobiography." My work as an historian of education has been fundamentally shaped by the experiences of my life. Those adventures have given me the questions I have chosen to pursue as a researcher. While grappling with the historical circumstances of contemporary dilemmas, I have been vastly aided by the work of others. No book helped me more than Richard Hofstadter, *Anti-Intellectualism in American Life* (New York: Knopf, 1963), for I understood from reading it that the effort to bring a vibrant and challenging education to all children flew in the face of reigning American antipathy toward "useless learning." I have found that to be true, and have explored the consequences of those difficulties with the education of girls, and women, of ethnic minorities, and of the poor.

[2] Patricia Albjerg Graham, *SOS: Sustain Our Schools* (New York: Hill and Wang, 1992).

[3] Patricia Albjerg Graham, *Schooling America* (New York: Oxford, 2005).

[4] Lawrence A. Cremin, *The Transformation of the School* (New York: Knopf, 1961).

[5] Patricia Albjerg Graham, *Progressive Education: From Arcady to Academe* (New York: Teachers College Press, 1967).

[6] Patricia Albjerg Graham, *Community and Class in American Education* (New York: John Wiley, 1974).

[7] Patricia Albjerg Graham, "Women in Academe," *Science* 25 (September 1970): 169: 1284–1290.

[8] Patricia Albjerg Graham, "Expansion and Exclusion: A History of Women in American Higher Education," *Signs* 3 (Summer, 1978): 760–63.

[9] I wrote about this phenomenon in "A View from Within," *Oxford Review of Education* 34 (June, 2008): 335–348.

[10] Patricia Albjerg Graham, *Schooling America* (New York: Oxford, 2005),

[11] Scott Nearing, *The New Education* (New York: Row Peterson, 1915).

HUGH HAWKINS

SCHOLARSHIP AND FELLOWSHIP

Like most middle-class families, mine valued education. We respected and admired our teachers in the Kansas and Oklahoma railroad towns where I grew up. All four of my older siblings went to college, and although the family lacked today's intense concern, there was much talk about college life. My father, a railroad dispatcher, had gone to work after the seventh grade, but he solemnly told me to get all the education I could: "It's the one thing they can never take away from you." My mother had graduated from Washburn Academy in Topeka and took pride in saying that with a little summer tutoring, she could have enrolled in Washburn College as a sophomore. Instead, she married my father.

Restless in high school, I decided to finish a year early, taking summer school classes while living with relatives in Denver and Washington, D. C. I found that the large, impersonal city high schools offered new challenges, but enjoyable ones. Like two of my siblings, I enrolled at Washburn, but after one semester moved on to DePauw in Indiana, my first choice all along. There I majored in history, but in my senior year felt strongly drawn to philosophy.

It made sense, however, to apply to graduate programs in history, and in 1950 I entered Johns Hopkins University. I had learned that its stature came from more than its medical school. At DePauw Professor Coen G. Pierson, in an informal seminar about the historical profession, had emphasized Hopkins's pioneering role in producing history Ph.D.s. Later, at the competition for Rhodes Scholarships in New Orleans, among the group of disappointed aspirants who went out to drown our sorrow, I chatted with a graduate student from Hopkins. The Ph.D. program there, he assured me, put greater emphasis on writing than on teaching, an appealing notion, since I often thought of myself as writer—a journalist and perhaps a novelist. One DePauw professor told me that since Hopkins offered the new specialty of "intellectual history," I might be able to indulge my interest in philosophy there. When Hopkins awarded me a fellowship with full support and no teaching duties, I had no hesitation in accepting.

I found that indeed Hopkins downplayed courses and urged graduate students to delve into original sources and produce written scholarship. Among the history department's four full professors, all major figures, my mentor was Charles A. Barker, a leader in the development of intellectual history and a founder of the American Studies Association. Though he never attained the stardom of his colleague C. Vann Woodward, I feel fortunate that Barker was my *Doktorvater*. Students joked about his laborious lecture style and mixed metaphors, but his bluff manner and lack of pretense worked well with me. His long comment on my first research paper ended forever my tendency toward rigid categorization. He

W. J. Urban, Leaders in the Historical Study of American Education, 129–141.

surprised me once by saying, "Of course it's you students that we are preparing to take over these professorships." Somehow that future role had scarcely occurred to me.

Barker let me indulge my philosophical interests with a research paper on the pragmatists and a course in American philosophy under Victor Lowe. Urged to find a dissertation topic, I toyed with the idea of a biography of the seminal pragmatist Chauncey Wright. Then, one day in his office, Barker handed me two recent studies of single colleges by Thomas LeDuc and Walter P. Rogers.[1] He assured me that though the history of higher education had been largely ignored by the profession, these works indicated fresh possibilities. The early Johns Hopkins University, despite its importance, had never been adequately treated, and besides, "just down the hall," Frieda Thies, doyen of the collections in the Lanier Room, had organized the papers of Daniel Coit Gilman, the university's first president.

Partly because of cautionary tales about students who kept delaying the dissertation, and partly because the two books attracted me with their historical acumen and literary skill, I committed myself to the suggested project. Finding immense pleasure in perusing original documents, I brushed off teasing by fellow students that I was doing "local history with a vengeance." With so much anti-Communist hysteria directed at universities, I considered it far from irrelevant to be exploring their role.

Representative Works of My Own

"Edward Jones, Marginal Man," in *Black Apostles: Afro-Americans and the Christian Mission from Revolution to Reconstruction,* eds. David Wills and Richard Newman (Boston, G. K. Hall, 1982), 243–53.

Railwayman's Son: A Plains Family Memoir (Lubbock, TX.: Texas Tech University Press, 2006).

"The University," in *Encyclopedia of the United States in the Twentieth Century* (New York: Scribner's, 1996), vol. 4, 1819–39.

Fascinated by the eccentric J. J. Sylvester, the university's first professor of mathematics, I wrote him up in considerable detail, presenting the result at the department's main seminar.[2] Should I submit a master's thesis on Sylvester? No, Barker counseled, reminding me that Hopkins focused on the doctorate and awarded the master's mostly as a terminal degree.

Although my summer in Europe in 1952 raised some faculty doubts about my scholarly seriousness, the university's financial support continued. A good deal of my energies went into Students for Academic Freedom, a Hopkins group founded to combat McCarthyism, sponsoring a debate between Dirk Jan Struik and Ernest van den Haag, as well as lectures by figures like David Riesman. We also collected evidence to aid the defense of Owen Lattimore, McCarthy's earliest target.[3]

In spite of such diversions, I worked my way through the Gilman Papers document by document and found an additional trove left in the bowels of the library. At the conveniently nearby Library of Congress, the J. Franklin Jameson Papers, especially his diary, helped me capture much of the flavor of time and place. In the fall of 1953 I hit my stride in producing chapters. It helped that I had decided the founding and first year of the university were important and complex enough to justify a dissertation. The supportive chairman of the department, Sidney Painter, encouraged me with the comment that even this might be too much.

During 1953–54, while Barker was away teaching in Lebanon, Woodward supervised my work. I had all along aspired to imitate his prose, whose freshness and clarity all his students admired He warned me not to bog down in the lives of the trustees, and in marginal comments he complimented my occasional well-turned phrase.

When it came time for my final orals, with Barker still absent, Woodward shepherded me through. On this occasion I proved that I knew very little of the general history of education. I could barely identify the Lancastrian system, which the dissertation mentioned in passing, and drew a blank when the distinguished humanist Kemp Malone asked me who had founded the University of London. With a teasing smile he commented, "He's still there." (Some months later the officious gatekeeper, identified as "the beadle," allowed me to view the fully dressed skeleton of Jeremy Bentham, a relic which is brought out to preside over a banquet each year. "Sheer vanity," the beadle huffed.)

When I stepped outside the examining room, I heard a wave of loud, shared laughter. I judged this to be better than dead silence or low murmurs and indeed I had passed.

The military draft caught me a few weeks after receiving the degree. Beginning in July, 1954, I served as an enlisted man, thus technically a Korean War veteran, although I served in Germany. The pain of this surprising development was all the greater because I had been hired for an internship in the American Studies program at Amherst College. I admired that program's "Problems in American Civilization" series and in fact had used these booklets in cramming for the Hopkins general exam.

Although as a soldier I managed a good deal of travel around Europe and improved my Ph.D. German, I felt lucky when a cost-cutting measure moved my discharge date up to May, 1956. Chiefly through Woodward's influence, I obtained an instructorship at Chapel Hill. My year there offered many satisfactions, including the start of lifelong friendships with my officemate Robert Moats Miller and with Morton and Phyllis Keller. Still, when the chair of Amherst's American Studies program, George Rogers Taylor, called to offer not a one-year internship, but an instructorship with possibilities of staying on, I balanced pros and cons and decided I ought to accept.

Amherst's Problems in American Civilization course, required of all sophomores, sought to teach the art of decision-making. It made no claim to be a survey course. Students heard and read conflicting approaches to selected aspects of American culture (slavery as a cause of the Civil War, the Americanness of Walt Whitman, the steel strike of 1919). After submitting brief papers defending their chosen position on the topic at hand, they participated in "seminars" (more properly discussion sections), in which twelve to fifteen students argued the issues. What students lost in faculty expertise, they gained in the sense of shared intellectual engagement. The benefits of teaching in this course were immense. I gradually developed ways to comment constructively on students' papers and to keep a discussion lively but coherent. I deepened my knowledge of American society and culture in areas I had never formally studied. I conversed with visiting lecturers at the cutting edge of their fields, such as John Hope Franklin, Arthur Goldberg, and Perry Miller.

Impressed by the version of American Studies practiced at Amherst, I accepted offices in both the New England and national organizations. At Amherst and elsewhere American Studies faced charges of chauvinism and of not being a true discipline. The controversy stirred my interest in two developments that played into my research: the emergence of new disciplines and the division of colleges into departments.

The Hopkins ethos had strengthened my longstanding urge to be a writer of books. At Amherst I spent most of my spare time extending my dissertation, my enthusiasm for the subject now enhanced by reading Frederick Rudolph's book on Williams College as well as Richard Hofstadter and Walter P. Metzger's on academic freedom.[4] Because of its tradition and also the quality of the carefully-selected students, teaching at Amherst was demanding; still, the college recognized and supported research.

Like a good mentor, Barker stayed in touch through supportive letters, notably one that urged me to compete for the new Moses Coit Tyler Prize for a "first book, in the field of intellectual history." With this challenge, I worked even harder on the manuscript, but simply couldn't get it ready for submission in 1958. Luckily for me, the referees declined to award the prize and it was offered a second year.

With this second chance, I met the deadline, sending off a manuscript of some thousand pages. Although Barker chaired the prize committee, he assured me that he would abstain from voting in my case. Only later did I learn that the other two judges had backgrounds that made my opus of particular interest. John Higham had been an undergraduate at Hopkins, and Frederick Rudolph was already at work on his broad history of American higher education.[5]

If not the happiest of my life, the day I opened Barker's letter telling me I had won the prize ranks among the most memorable. He declared himself "pleased as a peacock." The oddity that Cornell University Press, which had funded the prize, would publish a work treating a different university appealed to me. At the behest of the Press, Rudolph advised me on revisions. His comments and my visit with him in Williamstown helped immensely in pointing up the book's theme: the innovations possible in a new university not bound by tradition. Central among those innovations: choosing highly specialized and productive professors, acquiring graduate students through fellowships, emphasizing research above teaching, and granting more liberty to undergraduates.[6]

There is no denying the satisfaction of receiving the award from the hand of Allan Nevins at the American Historical Association annual meeting and then shaking hands with Adlai Stevenson. Still, having observed the ease with which authors vegetate in the glow of a first book, I determined to keep writing. I took advantage of Amherst's generous policy of research leaves for younger faculty and in addition applied for a John Simon Guggenheim fellowship with a proposal for a comparative study of late-nineteenth-century university presidents. It took nothing away from the pleasure of winning the Guggenheim to learn that two senior Amherst colleagues, Henry Commager and Leo Marx, had won this fellowship the same year.

I bestirred myself to find an apartment near Harvard Yard, knowing that the vast Charles W. Eliot Papers were freshly opened. That year in Cambridge, 1961–62, proved more significant for my work than I could have foreseen. Just living in the Harvard milieu and reading the *Crimson* broadened me, and three regular luncheon companions, Tilden Edelstein, Arthur Kaledin, and Richard Sewell, stretched me in many ways. Edelstein and Sewell were both working in anti-slavery history, and because of their influence I later designed a new segment for the Amherst American Studies course and edited a relevant volume in the Problems series.[7] Kaledin, researching an earlier period of Harvard history, helped me gain perspective on Eliot's role.

One of these friends mentioned having met a Harvard tutor who seemed to have written on exactly the subject I had proposed. This was the first I had heard of Laurence Veysey. I telephoned him, met him, and read his dissertation, forerunner of the landmark *The Emergence of the American University*.[8] His friendliness prevented any intimidation from his acute intelligence and wide knowledge. I gave him a list of (quite minor) mistakes in his dissertation and he gave me new insights into the generation of educators I intended to study.

Recognizing that his book would accomplish much that I had imagined doing, and impressed by the richness of the Eliot papers, I decided to limit my book to this Harvard president's achievement. Veysey and I agreed that Eliot was the most articulate and effective of the early university builders. Another important friendship began when I visited the University of Chicago Archives and met Richard J. Storr, whose *Beginnings of Graduate Education in America*[9] had answered many questions for me. In my Chicago hotel room, I read the manuscript of his soon to be published *Harper's University*.[10]

Meanwhile, the *Harvard Educational Review* asked me to review Richard Hofstadter and Wilson Smith's two-volume *American Higher Education: A Documentary History*.[11] I took this task very seriously, learning a great deal myself and hoping in a long review to explain the book's special merits. The University of Chicago Press liked the review enough to reprint it in a small pamphlet version.

My book on Eliot took longer than planned. The social ferment of the times often seemed more pressing than scholarship. Influenced by Barker, who with his wife Louise was a strong peace advocate, I participated in establishing the Conference on Peace Research in History (since renamed Peace History Society) and arranging one of its early conferences. Far more of my time went into the civil rights movement and an increasing engagement with African American history. In a minor corrective to the standard view, I had published a short article showing that Edward Jones, a black student from South Carolina, had won his Amherst degree a bit earlier than John Russwurm, usually named as the nation's "first Negro college graduate."[12]

Drawing on my graduate field with Woodward, the first course I introduced at Amherst, in 1958, was in Southern history, including considerable portions on racial questions. That same year, for the American Studies course, I prepared a set of readings that focused on Booker T. Washington and the then little studied W. E. B. Du Bois. The collection appeared in 1962 as *Booker T. Washington and His Critics: The Problem of Negro Leadership.*[13] The second edition, twelve years later, retitled *Booker T. Washington and His Critics: Black Leadership in Crisis*, with new selections on black nationalism, testified to the deepening awareness in academic circles of the complexity of African American history.

Through this project I came to know Rayford Logan, who lectured in the Amherst course, and August Meier, a portion of whose work appeared in the anthology. I supported an early group of concerned students at Amherst, called Students for Racial Equality, and in March, 1965, urged by the college chaplain and a student friend, I flew to Selma after the Pettus Bridge atrocity and shortly before the march to Montgomery. After this life-changing experience, I joined with a group of students to participate in a summer voter registration program, sponsored by the Southern Christian Leadership Conference, with training sessions in Atlanta and residence in Williamston, North Carolina. There we worked with a regional group of black activists.

Personal Favorites

Roger Geiger, ed., *The American College in the Nineteenth Century* (Nashville: Vanderbilt University Press, 2000).

David B. Potts, *Wesleyan University, 1831–1910: Collegiate Enterprise in New England* (New Haven: Yale University Press, 1992).

Jon H. Roberts and James Turner, *The Sacred and the Secular University* (Princeton: Princeton University Press, 2000).

These experiences encouraged my interest in the educational history of African Americans, already part of my concern with Washington and Du Bois. I found fresh material to use in my educational history seminar, launched in 1961, such as the writings of Horace Mann Bond. Pluralist that I am, I also tried to include Catholic education, but found little appropriate material then available. Given the special challenges to an educational history course in a liberal arts setting, I later chose to deposit the syllabi of this constantly-changing course with my papers in the Amherst College Archives.

The seminar remained small. Some students enrolled with the idea of using it toward certification as public school teachers, something that could be done during the undergraduate years at Amherst only with great difficulty. Other students enrolled out of interest in the origins and development of Amherst itself. Notable among these, George Peterson developed his interest into an honors thesis, published shortly after his graduation as *The New England College in the Age of the University.*[14] Countering the neglect of post-Civil War colleges, his book won a warm review from Frederick Rudolph and frequent citation by academic historians.

Although I eventually reworked the course as a seminar in social and intellectual history, education topics always appeared. The last time I taught the course, the fall of 2000, students reported on how 1960s radicalism affected various universities, and one student chose high school militancy as the subject of his research paper. One assignment required using manuscript sources from the college's archives, with several students making good use of the Marshall Bloom Collection, which is richly provided with underground and fugitive publications preserved by the Liberation News Service.

I had rather dreaded being mistaken for an educationist, since I knew the low repute of education courses. Although widespread, this view was intensified by my early reading of Jacques Barzun's *Teacher in America.*[15] This prejudice left me ill-prepared in large areas of the subject I was claiming to teach. In trying to broaden my knowledge of the lower schools, I turned again and again to the work of Lawrence Cremin, welcoming each new publication. Large portions of his *The Transformation of the School*[16] entered the syllabus for my seminar. Through his scholarship, I could see Elwood P. Cubberley, not as an outdated source, but as a milestone in the study of public education. I associate Cremin also with the creation of the History of Education Society, whose meetings, along with the *History of Education Quarterly,* grew increasingly important in my scholarly life.

Between Harvard and America: The Educational Leadership of Charles W. Eliot appeared in 1972.[17] The book was not intended as a biography, and I tried to give some sense of Harvard before and after the Eliot presidency. Despite the book's focus on higher education, I hoped that the chapter "Reform in the Lower Schools" could make me less of an outsider in the general field of educational history. In that chapter, I drew on the currently lively issues surrounding the Committee of Ten, which I had used fruitfully in my seminar.

With a second book completed, I was more willing than ever to devote time to the internal affairs of the college. During the 1970s, a period of reconstruction at Amherst College, I served actively on a range of task forces and committees. With Harold Wade, a black student, I co-chaired an ad hoc committee that stimulated both stronger efforts to admit minority students and the creation of a Black Studies department.

After the gradual abolition of virtually all Amherst's course requirements, the college created a committee to study the curriculum in depth. The group's intense investigation led to the report *Education at Amherst Reconsidered: The Liberal Studies Program,*[18] for which I wrote a historical introduction. Minimal changes followed, chiefly required freshman seminars, but the case the report made for electivism stands in interesting contrast to the rising pressures favoring a required core curriculum, where I found myself in friendly disagreement with Frederick Rudolph.

Although eager to experience teaching abroad, I delayed applying for a Fulbright until completion of the Eliot book. Then, in 1973–74, I happily found myself assigned to Goettingen, where American pioneers of university study in Germany, like George Ticknor and Edward Everett, had studied. Since my courses were in the *Paedigogische Hochschule*, where I regularly attended department meetings, I learned a good deal about the complexities of the German educational system. I had intended a broad study of American students in Germany, drawing on their letters back to German professors. Travelling to other university towns, I found material in a half dozen archives. Luckily for me, Goettingen had full files of letters from two American biologists, one of whom had taught at Amherst, and I focused on them in the single article that emerged from my German research.[19]

Barker once commented to me that book reviewing was a chore performed for the good of the profession. He didn't mention the additional satisfaction of seeing one's name and judgments in print. Except for the review of Hofstadter and Smith's documentary collection, perhaps none gave me greater satisfaction than my reviews of two path-breaking studies of discrimination in college admission.[20] With the long reviews encouraged in *Reviews in American History*, I was able to explore in depth the contributions made by one of Jurgen Herbst's many works, *From Crisis to Crisis: American College Government, 1636–1819* and by Mary Ann Dzuback's *Robert M. Hutchins: Portrait of an Educator.*[21]

A look at the record shows that my earliest articles were parts of in-process books, whereas later ones grew out of conference papers and invited lectures, and these tended to treat liberal arts colleges, not universities. Papers first presented at a meeting of the History of Education Society by James Axtell, David Potts, and myself became something of a landmark in righting past misrepresentations of the post-Civil War colleges.[22] An article on liberal education in *Change* resulted from a talk to visiting Japanese educators.[23]

Hoping to make a methodological contribution as well as forecast my book on the educational associations, I once imposed my reflections on categorization on a History of Education Society audience. To my surprise the editor of the *History of Higher Education Annual* asked to publish it and retained my turgid title.[24] Later this annual, especially under the leadership of Roget Geiger, became the chief outlet for my briefer writings. Appropriately, he has changed the name to *Perspectives on the History of Higher Education.*

Two chapters for anthologies based on papers at conferences sponsored by the American Academy of Arts and Sciences in Cambridge met diverse fates. The collection *Controversies and Decisions: The Social Sciences and Public Policy*[25] was slow to appear, and my section on the ideal of objectivity drew no responses, though I profited from the opportunity to see leading lights like Talcott Parsons and Daniel Bell up close. More useful to scholars, it turned out, has been my chapter in *The Organization of Knowledge in Modern America, 1860–1920.*[26] "University Identity: The Teaching and Research Functions" treated a persisting tension in academic life and one with personal resonance for me.

Hoping to get a good start on a third book and at the same time observe an important university, I sent inquiries to the University of California at Berkeley. Positive responses came from Geraldine Clifford and Martin Trow, granting me status at both the Graduate School of Education and the Center for Studies in Higher Education. As matters worked out, I had office space and presented papers at both. Along with other visitors at the Center, I profited from the generous welcome of Sheldon Rothblatt and Janet Ruyle. Ambitious to write a broad history of American higher education in the twentieth century, I used one of the Center's evening seminars to discuss my draft plan and met an encouraging response.

At nearby Santa Cruz, where I presented a paper treating student radicals in historical perspective, Veysey showed me the intricacies of that innovative branch of the university. All in all, I learned a great deal about the California version of American culture. Among the Berkeley historians, I recall with particular pleasure my talks with Henry F. May, whose books in intellectual history I had admired since graduate school. Later I had the satisfaction of writing a review suggesting the exceptional qualities of his autobiography.[27]

Back in Amherst, I realized that my style of writing and research did not suit the broader volume I had undertaken. I sought counsel from Richard Freeland, whom I had known since his student days at Amherst. He had recently begun work on his study which appeared in 1992 as *Academia's Golden Age.*[28] Given our related projects, we began to correspond and meet. I showed him my table of contents and asked where he thought I should concentrate. He pointed to the section on national institutional associations, noting the almost total lack of relevant secondary literature. I liked the idea of doing something path-breaking rather than trying to synthesize secondary works by others; besides, much of my research at Berkeley had been in the records of these "presidential" associations.

In addition to the published minutes of association meetings, unusually complete and frank in their early years, I examined records in presidential papers at selected universities. In Washington, D. C., I explored various associations' archives. Those of the American Council on Education, an umbrella organization, proved to be voluminous, with much material on member groups. The quite significant archives of another association, it turned out, were stored under the stairs behind the vacuum sweeper. Back at Berkeley's Center for Studies in Higher Education in 1982–83, I concentrated on my modified project and benefitted from interviews with two former association leaders, Clark Kerr and T. R. McConnell.

There being little inherent drama in my chosen subject, I tried to enliven the text by including six "interludes," giving a narrative treatment of one association meeting every ten years, with attention to mood and even verbal exchanges. It helped to find in the record the wittiness of a president like Indiana University's Herman B (no period, he insisted, since it stood for nothing) Wells. Dreading the necessary use of initialisms, I included at the beginning a light-hearted "Apology for Acronyms."[29]

The book showed how higher education, like much of industrial society, moved beyond associations of persons to associations of established institutions. Here I utilized "the organizational synthesis," an approach I associated with Kenneth Boulding and admired especially in the writings of Louis Galambos, but which I knew to be under attack as a conservative distortion. Surprised to find myself to the right of center, I had to admit that most of my scholarship had dealt with "dead white men." Historians I respected were effectively using class-oriented theory. I think for instance of Ronald Story's *The Forging of an Aristocracy,*[30] whose take on the Boston elite contrasts sharply with my largely positive appraisal of Eliot and his career.

Perhaps my early interest in race in America gives me some claim to being an anti-Establishment historian. Besides its prominence in the Amherst series anthologies I edited, race was the topic of a seminar I introduced at Amherst and of the course I offered at the University of Hamburg in 1993 during a second

Fulbright fellowship. And I like to reflect that the chapter "The Uninvited" in my Johns Hopkins history treats the university's barriers against blacks, and women as well.

Not much of a risk-taker and eager to avoid mistakes, I have for the most part eschewed generalization and synthesis. I had, however, grown somewhat bolder by the 1990s, when I wrote two broadly interpretive articles, "The University,"[31] and "The Making of the Liberal Arts College Identity."[32] The two pieces eased my regret about never having produced the big book proposed at Berkeley. Since both include recent times, they let me draw on my observations as a participant-observer in such matters, for instance, as faculty-administration relations.

After full retirement in 2000, still interested in writing about the past but less eager to work through manuscript archives, I decided to use my surprisingly vivid recollections of childhood in Kansas and Oklahoma to write a family memoir.[33] Though hoping the story I told was intrinsically interesting, I intended to provide raw material for social historians. For instance, the portions of *Railwayman's Son* that treat schooling reveal something of the spirit of 1930s classrooms and playgrounds. A few passages speculate on why certain incidents had stayed with me. Here I drew on the seminar on memory that I had co-taught with colleagues from other departments.

Happily, Texas Tech University Press could fit the book into its planned series on Great Plains history, procuring a valuable introduction by H. Roger Grant. Although the memoir stops in 1941, when I was twelve, I have written an article (yet to be published) about my first semester at college in 1946, "Off to College with the GI's."

Looking back on my writings, I conclude that I have tried in the tradition of the profession to "make a contribution." Beyond that, I hope I have enlivened the field of academic history, long degraded by company histories and amateurish work. My early interest in creative writing, which led to one fugitive published short story, one unpublished novel, and one unproduced play, left me with a persisting desire to give my readers pleasure and do more than offer clear information.

I would like to count myself among those making the history of colleges and universities a respected part of the historiographical corpus, especially by showing that the shared ideas within an institution, its ethos, can be identified and described. Presumably, members of the academy can gain perspective from writings like mine that offer historical context for their present experience. Like the work of other historians of my generation, mine has, hopefully, demonstrated that careful attention to sources need not prevent fluid, attractive prose. And my academic histories stand as places where one can check for specifics about significant persons and institutions. In fact, given memory's limitations, I sometimes find myself using them in just that way.

Realizing how much my Hopkins book had been an internal history, I designed *Between Harvard and America* to relate the university to broader social life. With the associations, I considered how groups of presidents and deans tried to demonstrate their institutions' importance to the non-academic world, as in the chapter "When is a Lobby Not a Lobby?" Perhaps because of the palpable threats to universities when I began my researches, I have tended to see higher education as needing defense against, or at least in tension with, certain social tendencies, and in the Eliot book I specifically cited democracy, religion, and utilitarianism. While useful in organizing a book, these categories are of course inadequate to an immensely complex interplay of institutions and society at large.

The sub-field to which I committed myself as a graduate student has flourished in the last half-century. New scholarship has shown how importantly religious motivation contributed to the development of universities, an influence underestimated in my studies of Quaker-inspired Johns Hopkins and Unitarian-dominated Harvard. Both books would have benefitted from works such as Louise Stevenson's exploration of evangelicals at Yale.[34]

Although concentrating on research universities and liberal arts colleges, I have happily observed how many other institutions of post-secondary education have now received serious attention. Among the many historians responsible for this broadening, I think particularly of Roger Geiger, Jurgen Herbst, and Philip Gleason.[35] Colleagueship with others working in the field ranks, in fact, among my life's chief pleasures.

NOTES

[1] Respectively: *Piety and Intellect at Amherst College 1865–1912* (New York: Columbia University Press, 1946), *Andrew D. White and the Modern University* (Ithaca, N. Y.: Cornell University Press, 1942).

[2] Copy available in Hugh Hawkins Papers, Amherst College Archives.

[3] Some of this research appeared in George Boas and Harvey Wheeler, eds., *Lattimore the Scholar* (Baltimore: n. p., 1953).

[4] Frederick Rudolph, *Mark Hopkins and the Log: Williams College, 1836–1872* (New Haven: Yale University Press, 1956); Richard Hofstadter and Walter P. Metzger, *The Development of Academic Freedom in the United States* (New York: Columbia University Press, 1955).

[5] Frederick Rudolph, *The American College and University: A History* (New York: Knopf, 1962).

[6] Hugh Hawkins, *Pioneer: A History of the Johns Hopkins University, 1874–1889* (Ithaca, N.Y.: Cornell University Press, 1960).

[7] Hugh Hawkins, ed., *The Abolitionists: Immediatism and the Question of Means* (Boston: D. C. Heath, 1964).

[8] Laurence R. Veysey, *The Emergence of the American University* (Chicago: University of Chicago Press, 1965).

[9] Richard J. Storr, *The Beginnings of Graduate Education in America* (Chicago: University of Chicago Press, 1953).

[10] Richard J. Storr, *Harper's University: The Beginnings: A History of the University of Chicago* (Chicago: University of Chicago Press, 1966).

[11] Hugh Hawkins, review of Richard Hofstadter and Wilson Smith, eds., *American Higher Education: A Documentary History* (Chicago: University of Chicago Press, 1961), in *Harvard Educational Review* 32 (Summer, 1962): 350–53.

[12] Hugh Hawkins, "Edward Jones, First American Negro College Graduate?" *School and Society* 89 (Nov. 4, 1961): 375–76. Later I published a much fuller account: "Edward Jones, Marginal Man," in *Black Apostles: Afro-Americans and the Christian Mission from Revolution to Reconstruction*, eds. David Wells and Richard Newman (Boston: G. K. Hall, 1982), 243–53.

[13] Hugh Hawkins, *Booker T. Washington and His Critics: The Problem of Negro Leadership* (Boston: D. C. Heath, 1962).

[14] George E. Peterson, *The New England College in the Age of the University* (Amherst, MA.: Amherst College Press, 1964).

[15] Jacques Barzun, *Teacher in America* (Boston: Little, Brown, 1945).

[16] Lawrence A. Cremin, *The Transformation of the School: Progressivism in American Education, 1876–1957* (New York: Knopf, 1961).

[17] Hugh Hawkins, *Between Harvard and America: The Educational Leadership of Charles W. Eliot* (New York: Oxford University Press, 1972).

[18] Lawrence A. Babb, et al., *Education at Amherst Reconsidered: The Liberal Studies Program* (Amherst, MA.: Amherst College Press, 1978).

[19] Hugh Hawkins, "Transatlantic Discipleship: Two American Biologists and Their German Mentor," *Isis* 71, no. 257 (1980): 197–210.

[20] Hugh Hawkins, reviews of respectively, Harold S. Wechsler, *The Qualified Student: A History of Selective College Admission in America, 1870–1970* (New York: John Wiley, 1977), in *Teachers College Record* 78 (Fall, 1979): 549–51; Marcia Graham Synnott, The *Half-Opened Door: Discrimination and Admissions at Harvard, Yale and Princeton, 1900–1970* (Westport, CT: Greenwood Press, 1979), in *American Historical Review* 85 (April, 1980): 475–76.

[21] Respectively, Hugh Hawkins, "Foundations of Academic Pluralism," *Reviews in American History* 10 (Sept., 1982): 341–45; Hugh Hawkins, "The Higher Learning at Chicago," *Reviews in American History* 20 (Sep., 1992): 378–85.

[22] Hugh Hawkins, "University Builders Observe the Colleges," *History of Education Quarterly* 11 (Winter, 1971): 353–62.

[23] Hugh Hawkins, "Liberal Education and American Society: A History of Creative Tension," *Change* 15 (Oct., 1983): 34–37.

[24] Hugh Hawkins, "Problems in Categorization and Generalization in the History of American Higher Education: An Approach through the Institutional Associations," *History of Higher Education Annual* 5 (1985): 43–55.

[25] Hugh Hawkins, "The Ideal of Objectivity among American Social Scientists in the Era of Professionalization, 1876–1916," in Charles Frankel, ed., *Controversies and Decisions: The Social Sciences and Public Policy* (New York: Russell Sage Foundation, 1976).

[26] Hugh Hawkins, "University Identity: The Teaching and Research Functions," in Alexandra Oleson and John Voss, eds., *The Organization of Knowledge in Modern America, 1860–1920* (Baltimore: Johns Hopkins University Press, 1979), 285–312.

[27] Hugh Hawkins, review of Henry F. May, *Coming to Terms: A Study in Memory and History* (Berkeley: University of California Press: 1987), *American Historical Review*, 94 (Feb., 1989): 228–29.

[28] Richard M. Freeland, *Academia's Golden Age: Universities in Massachusetts, 1945–1970* (New York: Oxford University Press, 1992).

[29] *Banding Together: The Rise of National Associations in American Higher Education, 1887–1950* (Baltimore: Johns Hopkins University Press, 1992).

[30] Ronald Story, *The Forging of an Aristocracy: Harvard and the Boston Upper Class, 1800–1870* (Middletown, CT: Wesleyan University Press, 1980).

[31] Hugh Hawkins, "The University," *Encyclopedia of the United States in the Twentieth Century* (New York: Scribner's, 1996), vol. 4, 1819–1839.

[32] Hugh Hawkins, "The Making of the Liberal Arts College Identity," *Daedalus* 128 (Winter, 1999): 1–25.

[33] Hugh Hawkins, *Railwayman's Son: A Plains Family Memoir* (Lubbock, TX: Texas Tech University Press, 2006).

[34] Louise Stevenson, *Scholarly Means to Evangelical Ends: The New Haven Scholars and the Transformation of Higher Learning in America, 1830–1890* (Baltimore: Johns Hopkins University Press, 1986).

[35] Among works by these and other authors: Roger Geiger, ed., *The American College in the Nineteenth Century* (Nashville: Vanderbilt University Press, 2000), Jurgen Herbst, *And Sadly Teach:*

Teacher Education and Professionalization in American Culture (Madison: University of Wisconsin Press, 1989), Phillip Gleason, *Contending with Modernity: Catholic Higher Education in the Twentieth Century* (New York: Oxford University Press, 1995).

JURGEN HERBST

SOLDIER-SCHOLAR

OVERVIEW

So my colleagues classify me as an historian of education, say that I spent my
professional life under that flag. I suppose they are right. But as a child and young
adult I saw myself as both a soldier and a scholar; a soldier, because my father and
some of my teachers had told us about their World War I experiences and, as I
have described it in my *Requiem for a German Past: A Boyhood Among the Nazis*,[1]
we youngsters came to know war at first hand during the bombing raids on our
towns and villages; a scholar, because from my earliest days I had been driven by
curiosity, asking questions, wanting to know. It didn't matter much what I was
wondering about and what answers I received. I followed my own star. I later
learned that it was Nietzsche who had sketched out that approach to learning in *The
Joyful Scholarship*,[2] describing the kind of joyfulness that makes learning an
adventure and turns scholarship into art.

My formal education had begun in elementary school but after three years there,
my parents transferred me to a German *gymnasium*. They had noticed that my
questions were no longer answered in school and that I was forced to memorize. In
the *gymnasium* my education continued with an intensive exposure to the liberal arts
and was accompanied outside its walls by Hitler Youth training for a soldierly career.

As an officer's candidate in the German army's elite division *Grossdeutschland*
I survived mortar and artillery fire during the last months of the war, was promoted
to private first class, and then returned to my hometown's *gymnasium* and to
university studies in Göttingen, Nebraska, and Minnesota. These years led me back
to my quest for answers that now, with the experience of war and holocaust behind
me, were more urgent than ever. My return to Germany then was followed by two
years of work experience in cultural affairs with the American consulate in
Hannover and the German Education Ministry of the State of Lower Saxony. Once
back in the United States and enrolled in Harvard's History of American Civilization
program and subsequently as faculty member at Wesleyan University and the
University of Wisconsin I was privileged to be able to devote my life of teaching
and research to the Joyful Scholarship that Nietzsche had praised.

LIBERAL ARTS AND UNIVERSITY STUDIES

Our teachers at the Wolfenbüttel *Grosse Schule* made the liberal arts for us a
memorable experience. Some of them subtly, and others not so subtly, sabotaged
the officially prescribed Nazi indoctrination, and some of them had to pay for it

W. J. Urban, Leaders in the Historical Study of American Education, 143–152.

through dismissal or transfer. But as there were others who followed the party line we students had to find our own way through these conflicting directions. We were immeasurably helped in this by the education we received in the liberal arts. As I described it in my *Requiem,* we soon learned to distinguish courage and conviction from the mouthing of party slogans. Nobody had to tell us that in so many words. For us the liberal arts were exemplified in word and action, and we secretly cheered along our teachers who lived what they taught. Their instructional lessons, too, told us what the liberal arts were all about. For examinations we were given essay questions instead of test papers. I remember my shock when, receiving back such an essay in which I had discussed at great detail the arguments for and against its topic, I found an "F" staring me in the face. My teacher, noting my distress, smiled at me and said: "Yes, quite well written, but I learned nothing new. You never told me and argued for what you thought about the subject." We learned early that education was not a matter of just memorizing facts, but of learning to use facts to help us shape and defend convictions and live by them.

And that education also helped us as leaders of the *Jungvolk,* the junior branch of the Hitler Youth. For us it meant playing soccer, going on scavenger hunts and training to be brave soldiers who were to fight their country's battles. We, as students of the *gymnasium,* had been urged by teachers and parents to take on that task, and we did so with enthusiasm. These were *our* boys. In my *Requiem* I described how Etzel, a fellow *gymnasium* student whose aunt, in whose house he lived, was Jewish, had read to us one hundred boys the chapter in *Huckleberry Finn* where Huck and Jim float down the Mississippi on their raft. Etzel was supposed to have given a lecture on Nazi race doctrine.

Favorites

From Crisis to Crisis: American College Government, 1636-1819 (Cambridge: Harvard University Press, 1982).

And Sadly Teach: Teacher Education and Professionalization in American Culture (Madison: University of Wisconsin Press, 1996).

The Once and Future School: Three Hundred and Fifty Years of American Secondary Education (New York: Routledge, 1996).

My secondary education was interrupted by basic military training and combat duty and then continued for another semester in my hometown. Again, this was no ordinary schooling, but a coming to terms with the catastrophic national and personal experiences of Nazism, war, and holocaust. Here it was the superb and compassionate guidance of Dr. Friedrich Kammerer that led me on the way to recovery. He introduced me to the Religious Society of Friends, the Quakers, and to Rilke's poetry, especially his *The Song of Love and Death of the Cornet Christoph Rilke.*[3]

A second, quite accidental but also shaping, encounter came when a geography instructor at the Braunschweig teacher training college hired me as his assistant. I shall never forget how he led me to a large world map that hung on his office wall, pointed to Germany, asked me to look at the rest of the world, and then added: How could anybody ever have thought that Germany could have won the war?

Then followed years of university study at Göttingen, Nebraska, and Minnesota. At Göttingen we were hungry and starved both physically and mentally. We were fed one meal a day in the student mensa, sat in ice-cold lecture rooms with no electricity; took notes on the torn-off white edges of old newspapers, and at night struggled with bed-bugs and rain and snow that drifted through the broken roofs of student dormitories on our sleeping bags. Though a geography student I attended also the lectures of world-famous professors like the philosopher Nicolai Hartmann and the historian Hermann Heimpel. These men, themselves hungry and cold, knew that we hung on their every word, that we listened desperately to hear of a different world, that we craved guidance to find our way into a future that to us seemed distant and incomprehensible. Existentialism to us was not a term of abstract philosophy. It was all-engulfing, lived reality.

As a foreign student brought to the United States by the American Friends Service Committee I found a welcoming home in the Geography Department at the University of Nebraska. For the first time I experienced what I thought was the life a student should enjoy under normal circumstances. But here, too, what mattered most did not take place in the classroom. It was the student Cosmopolitan Club that became my real home. Not only did I find my wife at its meetings, but I also met my fellow veterans from England, France, Italy, Norway, not to mention all those others from places far away in Africa and Asia. Here, in the heart of America, we former soldiers proudly wrote Winston Churchill that we had discovered our common European heritage, and as if to seal our newly found union my fellow club members elected me, the German, as their president.

My academic studies at Nebraska and at Minnesota began to focus on American literature, history and political science and prepared me well for the job I found upon my return to Germany in 1952. I served as Education Adviser to the American cultural officer in Hannover and, in cooperation with German education officials, helped arrange American Studies conferences for German teachers. In Hannover, too, began my life-long interest in and work with teachers and university scholars around the world. I participated in many of the teacher education conferences at the International Working Group Sonnenberg in the Harz Mountains. But I also knew that my quest for learning had not been stilled, and in 1954 I decided to return to the United States as an immigrant and to enroll in the Ph. D. program in the History of Americn Civilization at Harvard University.

HARVARD AND NIETZSCHE'S JOYFUL SCHOLARSHIP

At Harvard my real education began. Everything that went before had been prologue. I was struck to realize that Nietzsche's experience resembled my own. He described Joyful Scholarship as convalescence, "the saturnalia of a spirit," he wrote, "who patiently resisted a terrible, long pressure – patiently, severely, coldly, without submitting, but also without hope – and who is now all at once attacked by hope, the hope for health, and the *intoxication* of convalescence." That's exactly the way I felt when I stepped into the yard, looked up to the clock tower, and then, in the four years that followed, found what I had been yearning for all along:

Teachers who answered my questions; teachers who showed me what teaching, research, and scholarship could mean; teachers who, as Nietzsche put it, knew and showed in their lectures and seminars that scholarship required joyfulness to become art; teachers who no longer believed, again in Nietzsche's words, "that truth remains truth when its veil has been torn off. We have lived too much to believe this."

My first assignment upon arrival was to decide upon a field of concentration within the History of American Civilization; a field in which I would write my doctoral dissertation. My advisors for that task were Howard Mumford Jones and Bernard Bailyn, the one an illustrious professor of literature, the other a young scholar who was to make his mark as one of the foremost experts of American colonial and revolutionary history. I could not have had more supporting and more demanding advisors and I shall forever be grateful for the pains they took on my behalf. Knowing of my work in Hannover as education advisor Professor Jones had suggested that I look into the history of education, a major that at that time no one else had chosen. Professor Bailyn, who was then at work on his book, *Education in the Forming of American Society*,[4] readily agreed. Thus my life's professional labors began and eventually resulted in my first book, *The German Historical School in American Scholarship: A Study in the Transfer of Culture*.[5] For me it was as much a first exploration of research scholarship with all that it entailed in learning to struggle with sources and to compose a readable manuscript as an investigation into my own history as a budding historian of German descent.

Professor Jones also had asked me to serve as his research assistant. My job was to write precis of essays and small books that would aid him in deciding whether or not to read them himself. One morning, as I was sitting in his study at Widener Library 115 and working on my assignment, he came in and asked me how I was doing. "Oh, Professor Jones," I said, "this is wonderful. I really love this work. I could do it all my life." "What!" he shouted at me so loudly that it could be heard all through Widener Library. "You don't know what you are talking about. This is the dullest hack work there is. It is necessary, yes, but this is not what you are here for. You are here to find the treasures in our world of learning, to bring them out, to polish them, make them sparkle, and then teach to inspire yourself and your students with the love of learning!" With that he turned on his heels, banged the door shut, and left me with a message I have never forgotten. Research is worthless unless its results appear in print or in the lecture or seminar room, presented with enthusiasm and with concern for those who read or hear it. Jones echoed Nietzsche who had insisted that the veil be placed over the naked truth, that art in writing and lecturing make the truth presentable.

Bernard Bailyn conveyed a similar message in his teaching and advising. Quite fittingly, the headline placed on the Fifty Years of Teaching *Festschrift* we presented to him in 2000 was *Sometimes an Art*. And I had introduced an essay I had entitled "The New Life of Captain John Smith" with a small poem, *Behold the Captain,/ braggadocian, vain,/ morose in turn.// His faults persist,/ his virtues obtrude/ a world to span.// A salted kiss,/ Pocohanta's gift/ burns in his heart.//*

Receive him well./ As he loved and hurt/ he gave us life.[6] Needless to say, academic editors have no patience with poetry. The little verse did not appear in print.

What I took with me as a bequest from both my four years as a student at Harvard and the following eight years as a young instructor at Wesleyan University in Middletown, Connecticut, was a lifelong commitment to scholarship as research and teaching. It was a gift I had received from my mentors, Howard Mumford Jones and Bernard Bailyn. I should add to their names that of Carl Joachim Friedrich whose lectures and seminar talks on the history of political theory left a lasting impression for their trenchant analyses and moving presentation. Friedrich was another scholar whose lectures in the tradition of Nietzsche fused intellectual brilliance with concern for the students and came across as inspiring works of art. The same can be said of Carl Schorske and Norman O. Brown, better known as "Nobby" Brown, two colleagues of mine at Wesleyan University. Schorske's *Fin-de-Siècle Vienna: Politics and Culture*[7] and Brown's *Life Against Death: The Psychoanalytic Meaning of History*[8] demonstrate to perfection how historical works of scholarship, each in their quite different ways, can illuminate for their student readers an understanding of past and present.

My own work at Wesleyan took me from an appointment as instructor in the Master of Arts in Teaching Program and in the history department to an associate professorship. In 1963–1964 I served as president of the New England American Studies Association. The articles I published at that time dealt chiefly with the history of educational thought and theory and then current criticism of teaching in American secondary schools.[9] I also served as Visiting Lecturer at Yale University and received a Fulbright grant to lecture in Germany at the Sonnenberg and in Berlin, Heidelberg, Frankfurt, and Trier.

THE WISCONSIN YEARS

The twenty-eight years of my teaching in the Educational Policy Studies Department of the University of Wisconsin were years of joy and fulfillment. I could not possibly have found a more supportive group of colleagues and of enthusiastic students, both undergraduates in my lecture courses and graduate students in my seminars. Enthusiasm for and commitment to the study of history moved me and was shared by my fellow historians, Carl Kaestle in American history and Sterling Fishman in European history. We carried out our work in the tradition of Bernard Bailyn, viewing history as our discipline and education our field of interest. [10]

My first major research undertaking involved in 1977 a three-months International Research Exchanges Board fellowship to the German Democratic Republic. I had planned to investigate the beginnings of American higher education from the founding of Harvard in 1636 to the precedent-setting Dartmouth College case of 1819 in the United States Supreme Court. As this was going to be in large measure a study in the legal and constitutional history of higher education I felt I needed familiarity with the European background of university history. And this I found in good measure in the State Archives in Merseburg and in the library of the Humboldt University in East Berlin. As I upon entering the library every day confronted Karl Marx's words on the wall, "The philosophers desire to interpret the world; the point, however, is to change it," I could not help but think of him sitting in the British Museum, surrounded by books and documents, as I then shared that experience in Berlin, the center of "real existing socialism." Back in Madison and after seeing my work in print,[11] I turned to investigate the history of teacher education and the history of American secondary schooling. In *And Sadly Teach*,[12] I chided teacher educators for neglecting the training of elementary school teachers in favor of turning out school administrators, normal school instructors, adult educators and educational researchers. In *The Once and Future School*, I referred to what was known in the nineteenth century as "the people's college," a then extraordinarily effective high school. In the book I expressed the hope that after progressive education and life adjustment had run their course and popular dissatisfaction with secondary education could no longer be ignored we should be ready to restructure our educational system that it could keep pace with our fast-developing technology. The high school, I suggested, "will have to share the educational task with many other institutions within a framework that allows room for choice and banishes custodial compulsion. Education, in order to be effective," I wrote, "can take place only in an atmosphere of freedom."[13]

It is unavoidable and necessary, I admit reluctantly, that a university professor's duties include service to his colleagues, students, community, and the wider profession. I had my share of it. I served three times as Educational Policy Studies department chair, one term as president of the History of Education Society, eight years as member of the Executive Committee of the International Standing Conference for the History of Education (ISCHE), and from 1988 to 1991 as its chair. In 1980 I was elected a member of the National Academy of Education, and in 1983–1984 I sat on the Presidential Commission for the German-American Tricentennial. In 1978 Madison's mayor appointed me to the city's Ethics Board, which I then chaired from 1981 to 1994.

But it was teaching and my involvement with ISCHE that roused my enthusiasm and made me cherish the joyful scholarship. In Madison I had introduced an undergraduate seminar on issues in education that was broadcast over the radio and drew in listeners from all over the state. I opened up the subject with a ten minute talk on its historical background, and then it was up to my students to answer the questions that kept pouring in over the phone. It was a marvelous experience for

Influential Works
John I. Goodlad, *Teachers for Our Nation's Schools* (San Francisco: Jossey-Bass, 1990).
Carl E. Kaestle, *Pillars of the Republic: Common Schools and American Society, 1780-1860* (New York: Hill and Wang, 1983).
Deborah Meier, *The Power of Their Ideas: Lessons from a Small School in Harlem* (Boston: Beacon Press, 1995).
David Potts, *Liberal Education for a Land of Colleges: Yale's Reports of 1828* (New York: Palgrave Macmillan, 2010).
Diane Ravitch, *The Death and Life of the Great American School System* (New York: Basic Books, 2010).

both students and listeners, one that few participants will forget. My involvement with ISCHE had begun in 1979 at its first annual meeting in Leuven. For me it was a happy rebirth of the Sonnenberg spirit of my Hannover days in the early fifties. ISCHE-related conferences took me all over Europe from Joensuu in the north to Parma in the south, from Warsaw in the east to Dublin in the west, and to Israel, Australia, Canada, and Japan as well. And I am grateful for the honorary membership and the laudatio I received at ISCHE's 2008 meeting in Newark.[14]

But I cannot close these remarks on my Wisconsin experience without mentioning the wonderful, life-long friendships that made my years there so rewarding and fulfilling. There was Felix Pollak, Viennese-born Jewish poet, whose bilingual poetry and whose prose are scintillating little masterpieces.[15] It was he who more than anyone else urged me to put my memories down on paper. And there is Ted Hamerow, my colleague in the history department, who wrote so compellingly in his many books on World War II, the holocaust and on German resistance to Hitler. For me it is his autobiography that told me more than any other testimony about our common destinies in our varied worlds in which we lived.[16]

RETIREMENT

When in 1994 I left my teaching duties in Wisconsin Sue and I joined our daughter Stephanie and granddaughter Sheyanne in Durango, Colorado. I had no idea then that in the La Plata and San Juan mountains a new life would open for me, a life that would bring back to me the dream of my childhood to spend my days as both scholar and soldier. In the spring of 1995 I was invited to serve as a Visiting Associate at the Center for Studies in Higher Education at the University of California at Berkeley. Other invitations followed to lecture at the University of Hawaii and at the International Christian University at Mitaka, Tokyo. My remarks at Mitaka were there published in a small volume, *Research and Teaching: Personal Reflections and The University in the United States: Tradition and Reform.*[17] The next year I returned to Wolfenbüttel, my hometown, and delivered the commencement address in the presence of the survivors of my own graduating class of 1946. By the spring of 1998 I again was lured abroad, this time to serve as guest professor at the Institute for Interdisciplinary Research at the University of Vienna.

In Durango I was appointed in 1999 as a Professional Associate at Fort Lewis College. The Professional Associates members were retired professionals, men and women who had been active as physicians, economists, businessmen, professors, artists, school superintendents, and CEOs of various corporations and foundations. Our job is to assist the college, its students and faculty, in any way we can. I taught an honors undergraduate seminar on the Liberal Arts and still participate as lecturer in an annual Life Long Learning Program which the Associates inaugurated. As part of left-over work from Wisconsin I completed and published my research on a study of school choice in both the United States and Germany.[18] I also brought to completion my memoirs of growing up in Nazi Germany, the *Requiem* I mentioned at the beginning. Its publication in 1999 brought many invitations to speak in

Colorado and to this day has put me on the "availability list" for discussions in history classes at Fort Lewis College.

It is my signing up as a member of La Plata County Search and Rescue that has brought back to me the dream and now the reality of a return to a soldierly life. Of course, Search and Rescue is not the army, and we are not soldiers. But our commitment, our ever- readiness to serve, our training in rope rescues on land, water and snow and in stretcher and helicopter evacuations, not to mention the actual rescue operations at day or night, create the comradeship of men and women who face danger in the execution of their assignments that resembles that of the bonds that soldiers have come to cherish. Alas, age and health do not permit me today to participate in those activities that inspired me when I first enrolled. I help direct each rescue by telephone and radio from the safety of my home and now serve the group as its treasurer.

And there has also been a direct relation between Colorado and my work as a scholar. My latest book, *Women Pioneers of Public Education: How Culture Came to the Wild West*,[19] was inspired in part by my exposure to the mountainous wilderness surrounding Silverton, the small old mining town fifty miles north of Durango. It occurred to me that we have many histories of schools and education of the East and Midwest but few of the West. We have praised male school reformers like Horace Mann and Henry Barnard but know little or nothing of the role women played in the West, and we have seen the German influence on American education as a thing of the past. *Women Pioneers* will disabuse you of these notions. Silverton today practices Expeditionary Learning-Outward Bound, an approach to education that goes back to Kurt Hahn's co-educational boarding school at *Schloss Salem* on Lake Constance. And finally I am at work on a manuscript that will narrate my experiences and impressions of my three-months stay in communist East Germany in 1977.

CONCLUDING REMARKS

When I look back on my "experiences in education," as I like to see my exposure to and in that field, I am struck above all by the fact that education to me has meant and still means liberal learning. And liberal learning means personal growth in understanding myself and the world around me and through this understanding becoming able to contribute to its welfare and enrichment. This approach to learning manifests itself in the two sides of scholarship: Research and teaching – research as the royal road to understanding; teaching as the scholar's way to enrich his or her students' lives.

There are many ways in which we can enter upon this experience and many fields in which we can practice it. For me it has been history. History because it allows us to broaden and deepen our view beyond the confines of the world we live in today. It permits us, if only we have the determination and staying power to do so, to probe into every corner of mankind's past and draw from it lessons that can aid us shape the future.

What about the history of education? you will ask. Isn't that the field in which you worked? Yes, but as you look back on what I described above you will note that that choice was purely accidental. It wasn't even a choice. It was the job as education advisor I was offered in Hannover when I returned from the United States in 1952, and it was the suggestion of Professor Jones when there had not been any other student who had chosen the history of education as field of concentration, that prompted me to apply my interest and training to history to education.

And thus, if you ask me, what advice do I have for our new colleagues in the history of education, I will say, first and foremost, see yourself and practice your scholarship as an historian. Practice history of education as a liberal profession that will enrich your and your students' lives. You can safely leave the intricate details of the fields of education, from curriculum studies to classroom management, to our colleagues in the education departments. History of education will not teach you techniques of teaching but it will make you aware where and how education fits in the course of human events. And when it comes to advice as I just have given you, keep in mind what Nietzsche wrote in his Joyful Scholarship, this little poem: *Vademecum – Vadetecum:*

> Lured by my style and tendency,
> you follow and come after me?
> Follow your own self faithfully –
> take time! – and thus you follow me.

NOTES

[1] Jurgen Herbst, *Requiem for a German Past: A Boyhood Among the Nazis* (Madison: The University of Wisconsin Press, 1999).

[2] Friedrich Nietzsche. *Die Frohliche Wissenschaft* (Ditzingen: Reclam, 2000); published inappropriately translated as *The Gay Science*, Bernard Williams, ed., (Cambridge University Press, 2001).

[3] Rainer Maria Rilke, *Die Weise von Liebe und Tod des Cornets Christoph Rilke* (Leipzig: Insel Verlag, no date). Translated by Fritz Gibbon, *The Manner of Loving and Dying of the Cornet Christoph Rilke* (London: Wingate, 1958).

[4] Bernard Bailyn, *Education in the Forming of American Society* (Chapel Hill: University of North Carolina Press, 1960).

[5] Jurgen Herbst, *The German Historical School in American Scholarship* (Ithaca: Cornell University Press, 1965).

[6] *Sometimes an Art: A Symposium in Celebration of Bernard Bailyn- Fifty Years of Teaching and Beyond* (Harvard University, May 13, 2000) My essay was published as Jurgen Herbst, "The New Life of Captain John Smith," *Historical Magazine of the Protestant Episcopal Church* 44 (March 1975): 47–68.

[7] Carl Schorske, *Fin de Siecle Vienna. Politics and Culture* (New York: Alfred A. Knopf, 1980)

[8] Norman O. Brown, *Life Against Death: The Psychoanalytic Meaning of History* (Middletown, CT: Wesleyan University Press, 1959).

[9] Jurgen Herbst, "The Anti-School: Some Reflections on Teaching," *Educational Theory* 18 (Winter 1968): 13–22.

[10] My essay in the Bailyn *Festschrift*, mentioned above, was reprinted in slightly altered form as "Nineteenth-Century Schools Between Community and State: The Cases of Prussia and the United States," *History of Education Quarterly* 42 (Fall 2002): 327–341.

[11] Jurgen Herbst, *From Crisis to Crisis: American College Government 1636–1819* (Cambridge: Harvard University Press, 1982).

[12] Jurgen Herbst, *And Sadly Teach* (Madison: University of Wisconsin Press, 1989).

[13] Jurgen Herbst, *The Once and Future School: Three Hundred and Fifty Years of American Secondary Education* (New York: Routledge, 1996), 213.

[14] For the laudatio see http://www.inrp.fr/she/ische/index.htm

[15] Felix Pollak, *Benefits of Doubt* (1988) and *Lebenszeichen: Aphorismen und Marginalien* (1992).

[16] Theodore Hamerow, *Remembering a Vanished World: A Jewish Childhood in Interwar Poland* (New York: Berghahn Books, 2001).

[17] Jurgen Herbst, *Research and Teaching: Personal Reflections and The University in the United States: Tradition and Reform*, International Christian University, Faculty Development Series, No. 1

[18] Jurgen Herbst, *School Choice and School Governance: A Historical Study of the United States and Germany* (New York: Palgrave, 2006).

[19] Jurgen Herbst, *Women Pioneers of Public Education: How Culture Came to the West* (New York: Palgrave, 2008).

CARL F. KAESTLE

HISTORY OF EDUCATION

My Entry and My Odyssey

MY ORIGINS:

My father was born in Paris, Tennessee, a little town northeast of Memphis. His father was a railroad conductor, born in Tennessee in the year of his German parents' arrival, 1870. My grandmother's people were all Dutch. A certified teacher, she schooled her two sons at home until the family moved to Memphis, where the boys went to high-school. A teacher encouraged my dad to go to Georgia Tech to study engineering. In his senior year there a professor suggested that he apply to the Sheffield Scientific School at Yale to study for a master's degree.

At Yale my father's liberal education blossomed. He did his engineering, but most of all he loved courses like Lull's organic evolution and a sociology course taught by William Graham Sumner's protégé, Albert Keller. He met my mother on a blind date in New Haven. She was studying at Albany State Teachers College (now SUNY-Albany), commuting by trolley from her hometown, Schenectady. She was Regina Perreault, born of French immigrant parents. Her father, a painting contractor, used English in his business, but the language of their home was French, and my mother learned English in kindergarten. She became a high school French teacher and taught in nearby Amsterdam, New York.

Frank Kaestle followed his fiancée to Schenectady, landing an internship at General Electric. Both of their jobs remained secure during the Depression, allowing them to help out some of their friends. My father became an expert in designing the electrical systems required for large-scale chemical and petroleum operations, like oil pipelines and aluminum factories. During World War II he worked on the Manhattan Project. My mother ceased teaching after children came; she became very active in community work on schools, parks, a mental health clinic for teen-agers, and other causes.

MY EDUCATION:

We lived in Scotia, New York, a town of middle-class professionals and working-class industrial workers across the Mohawk River from Schenectady. My high school was not prestigious and not generally rigorous, but it had a superb Department of Music (one of my lifelong passions) and some very good teachers sprinkled around. Among them was Mrs. Shaw, whose biology class was so wonderful that I decided to become a doctor. When I went to college in 1958, some

W. J. Urban, Leaders in the Historical Study of American Education, 153–164.

medical schools were saying that applicants could major in humanities if they took the requisite science classes, so I signed up to major in English and added freshman chemistry, secure in the knowledge of my future.

However, I struggled with the chemistry and then with botany and zoology in sophomore year. I had little aptitude for science. Tossing out the doctor idea, I turned with great relish to my English courses and electives, and singing activities, which included the Glee Club and the Whiffenpoofs. Yale's English Department was very influential at this time. Some leading lights of The "New Criticism" were there. According to their theory, students should not read works of criticism (even theirs) nor worry much about the historical context of a work of art. Instead we should cut right to the "meaning "of the work as we each saw it. New Criticism as literary theory has since been debunked, but at the time it invigorated the place. We took Paul Weiss's philosophy course on aesthetics, totally in line with the New Criticism, and in our English courses we wrote essay after essay. I liked that, and it proved to be good training far beyond the guild of literary criticism. Among my notable professors (some New Critics, some not) were Robert Penn Warren and R. W. B. Lewis in recent U.S. prose, Maynard Mack in Shakespeare, Alexander Witherspoon for Milton, and Gordon Haight on the 19th-Century English novel.

In my junior year I thought I should give more thought to a career, and I gravitated toward some role in public education. My mother had been deeply involved in school issues in Scotia, and after dinner we would talk for hours about education policy. Still, my choice was unusual for a Yale student. Yale had abolished its School of Education in the early 1950s. Its President, Whitney Griswold, declared that there was no such thing as pedagogy, only subject matter. One course in education survived this purge. The chair of the Psychology Department, Claude Buxton, offered a fine seminar on education, in which he encouraged us to pursue our education interests through any discipline we wished to use. I wrote a philosophy paper on democracy and education.

Thinking about teacher preparation, I went to see Ed Gordon, director of Yale's highly-regarded Master of Arts in Teaching program (not to be confused with Edmund Gordon, the psychologist, later a Yale professor and now a dear friend). Gordon asked me what my career goal was. I said that I wanted to start by becoming the best English teacher I could be and teach for at least five or six years and then see if school administration looked interesting. He said, "Then we don't want you." He was only interested in candidates who would devote their lives to teaching. "You should go to Harvard." Everyone there, he assured me disdainfully, would teach for a few years and then go into something else higher up the organizational chart.

Ed Gordon was not a man to be messed with, so I applied to the Harvard M.A.T. program. (Gordon's daughter Ann Gordon, an anti-War activist at Wisconsin and later an editor of the Elizabeth Cady Stanton and Susan B. Anthony Papers, was my first doctoral advisee when I joined the Wisconsin faculty, so Ed Gordon did bring something wonderful into my life after all). The Harvard M.A.T. was headed at that time by Ted Sizer, later the dean of the Education School and ultimately the nation's best-known and beloved school reformer, founder of the Coalition for

Essential Schools. Sizer had cooked up a "Plan C" option for the M.A.T., which required two full years instead of one. What did I care--I was young, immortal, and had a National Defense Education loan.

Plan C began with a two-week crash seminar on how to write a decent lesson plan, then full-time teaching, accompanied by frequent observations and coaching by two master teachers. I had chosen Newton, Massachusetts for my internship. Newton had a strong general reputation and a particularly fine English Department. My main mentor was Henry Bissex, a god to us Harvard interns. Henry was full of high standards, nifty pedagogical ideas, and calm friendliness. I learned a lot about teaching, still totally uncertain of how my career would go. Like most first-year English teachers, I was focused on surviving the year with some semblance of self-respect and trying not to drown in the flood of writing I assigned to my students.

In addition to Henry Bissex's tutoring, I gained daily sustenance in the "Blue Grotto," a big basement room where English Department colleagues hung out during free periods, talking mostly about students and pedagogy. ('Can anyone tell me about how to connect with Esther Cranston? She seems so sad,' 'Has anyone got a good lesson plan on relative and non-relative clauses?') Newton was not a perfect school (tracking students into seven levels of English instruction, for example), but it was a great place to learn how good teachers behave from day to day.

In the second year of the M.A.T. program I took courses at Harvard, including Walter Jackson Bate on the English romantic poets; Perry Miller's new course on romanticism in American literature; Israel Scheffler on philosophy of education; and, by transfer to MIT, Noam Chomsky, whose brilliant transformational grammar was taking the English linguistics field by storm. It was rich fare. I'm glad it was, because the English methods and curriculum course was awful, not just useless but irritating.

In late fall, however, the teaching assistant in that English methods course took me out for coffee. He had heard that I was interested in school administration and asked if I would be interested in becoming the principal of the American School of Warsaw the following year. "Well, I'm not qualified," I said. My TA said he knew the current principal, who also had a Harvard M.A.T. He said the school was a small operation, about 100 students, and the board preferred to do appointments through friends they knew.

The school sounded so interesting, and the prospect of living abroad in Europe for two years so attractive, that I suspended my belief that school administrators should teach at least five years before trying to direct a school. I had already decided to propose to my girl friend, so now I proposed both marriage and living in Warsaw for two years, which would involve her taking a lengthy break from her nursing program at Columbia to start our life together in Europe. She said yes, I applied, got the job, changed two of my second-semester courses to elementary school work, and we left for Warsaw in August.

INTERLUDE IN POLAND:

I loved living in Poland, and I loved the school. It was like a laboratory, in a way, small (grades K-6), with wonderfully supportive parents. In my second year there we implemented an innovation I had studied at Harvard, the non-graded elementary school. It seemed particularly relevant to this school, which often presented us with students entering at mid-semester and who were just learning English. Thus a student who was of the proper age for fourth grade might be reading in English at first-grade level and doing math at the eighth-grade level. We decided to group kids by ability in language arts and math, moving individual students whenever they were ready to move to the next level. In contrast, we grouped kids by age for social studies, science, and physical education, to avoid undue emphasis on ability grouping. We also substituted narrative reports for letter grades, and we developed a partner relationship with the Lexington, Massachusetts public schools. Its superintendent, Rudy Fobert, came to visit our school, as did Robert Anderson from Harvard, one of the co-founders of the non-graded elementary school concept. Having these wise heads around was a great boost for the twenty-four-year-old principal.

As with biology and medicine, however, I had miscalculated again. I thought that principals were like philosophers on wheels. In fact they need not only to be instructional leaders but savvy personnel people, shrewd in the politics of school-keeping, and principals need to have other skills that I lacked. Therefore, during my second year in Warsaw (1965–66), I sent off for several diverse books about education. One of them was Lawrence Cremin's *Transformation of the School*, a history of the Progressive education movement. I loved it, wrote to him, and showed up at Teachers College the next July. Cremin welcomed me, said he would see me in the fall, and sent me home to read *The New England Mind* by Perry Miller. Finally, as it turns out, I had calculated correctly.

BACK TO SCHOOL:

Cremin was already highly visible in his field, having won the Bancroft Prize. He was becoming a young sage in the education research community, well-known in foundations like Carnegie and Spencer. Along with Bernard Bailyn of Harvard, he promoted the view that history of education must pull away from its roots in a celebratory history of the American public school and see education as a larger process of cultural transmission. Cremin had attracted an interesting group of graduate students, who, in European fashion, remained in his seminar from year-to-year. Thus I immediately came into contact with students who were seasoned and could help me realize what I had got myself into, a new discipline. ('Who is Richard Hofstadter?' I would say. 'Hmm,' they would reply, 'here are four or five titles you should start with.')

Among other influences on my initial training as a historian that year were Robert Cross in the History Department, who offered a year-long seminar in history and the social sciences, and Lawrence Stone, who had been inveigled by the Columbia Sociology Department to come up from Princeton to teach a course on the causes of the English Revolution. Cross was a sweet and wise man who had caught on to the swirling currents connecting the social sciences and history at this time (1966). He insisted that seminar members conduct the discussions. From Cross and my fellow seminarians I learned that history, like education, is an interdisciplinary field. Stone was a piercing intellect, and his lectures were elegant. I watched in awe, during this course and later, as he expanded outward from political and religious history into the history of the family, quantitative methods, and psychohistory. My research paper was close to Stone's interests, a quantitative study of the English aristocracy and the universities before and after the Civil War. He became a strong friend and mentor in my early career.

During this first year at Teachers College, Cremin proposed that I become the first student in a possible joint program in the history of education between Teachers College and Harvard. In practical terms, he said, there was no chance of getting an actual program approved so quickly, so he had in mind that I would simply apply to Harvard to study with Bernard Bailyn, and make up the program as I went along. I thought hard about it. Cremin's graduate students were happy. They were excited about being at Teachers College studying with him. Was that an environment I should abandon?

> **Some Works that Have Influenced Me:**
>
> Bernard Bailyn, *Ideological Origins of the American Revolution* (Cambridge: Harvard University Press, 1967).
>
> Lawrence A. Cremin, *The Transformation of the School: Progressivism in American Education, 1876–1957* (New York: Alfred A. Knopf, 1964).
>
> Richard Kluger, *Simple Justice: The History of Brown v. Board of Education and Black America's Struggle for Equality* (New York: Alfred A. Knopf, 1976).
>
> Janice Radway, *A Feeling for Books: The Book-of-the-Month Club, Literary Taste, and Middle-Class Desire* (Chapel Hill: University of North Carolina Press, 1997).

But I traveled up to Cambridge, met Bailyn, and he asked me to show him some work. All I had at that point (mid-year) was a term paper from Cremin's research seminar, on the influence of Francis Bacon in seventeenth-century America (there was virtually none). Bailyn thought it wasn't bad, and I was hooked. Ted Sizer, by now the Dean at Harvard's Education School (but fortunately for me, also a historian of education) would be on my committee, as well as Bob Church, the Ed School's historian of education at that time. I enrolled in the Ph.D. in Education program, administered by the Graduate School, because it offered maximum flexibility and was a good way to bridge the History Department and the School of Education.

That bridge was anchored by two activities: serving on the student editorial board of the *Harvard Education Review* and serving as a Teaching Fellow in the History Department. The *HER* stint came at a dramatic time. The year before I joined it, the board had accepted the controversial Arthur Jensen article, with its claims about race, IQ and education policy.[1] It hit the streets just as I became one of two editors in charge of the office, so I fully experienced the turbulence surrounding that event, at Harvard and beyond. I quickly learned some things about statistics, psychometrics, and the politics of research.

My service as a tutor in History came in my last year there. I had fun with my eight juniors until mid-spring of 1970 when the Harvard campus exploded in protests against the bombing of Cambodia, effectively ending the semester. The Vietnam War had been at its terrible worst during the entire three years I spent at Harvard in the Ph.D. program. That involved a lot of marching, talking to students, and poll-watching for Gene McCarthy's campaign. In addition my wife and I had decided to have a baby, and Frederika arrived on Christmas morning, 1969. And, yes, there was the matter of a thesis.

BERNARD BAILYN AND MY DISSERTATION:

For most readers of this book it hardly needs restating that Bernard Bailyn is a powerful and creative historian, the most influential historian of British colonial America of his generation, perhaps ever. It is also well-known that he was a superb advisor, nurturing many distinguished colonial historians and several historians of American education. Obviously, his capacity as an advisor was to some extent a function of his brilliance as a historian. He has an unsurpassed ability to be simultaneously capacious and incisive.

> **Some Works that Have Influenced Me (continued):**
>
> Theodore Sizer, *Horace's Compromise: the Dilemma of the American High School* (Boston: Houghton-Mifflin, 1984).
>
> Lawrence Stone, *The Crisis of the Aristocracy* (Oxford: Clarendon Press, 1965).
>
> David B. Tyack, *The One Best System: A History of American Urban Education* (Cambridge: Harvard University Press, 1974).
>
> Raymond Williams, *The Long Revolution* (London: Hazzell, Watson & Viney Ltd., 1961).

But how did he interact with his big flock of advisees, on a one-on-one basis? My experience was very comfortable. Once he took me on, he had confidence in me. Thus he could critique my work strenuously and not knock me off my pins. He was available as often as I wished to see him, and for as long as it took, as long as we stuck to business. His orientation was intellectual and scholarly. Conversations were rarely personal, though I remember well some touching words of condolence upon the death of my father in 1969. As graduation approached, each of his doctoral students had the pleasure of a dinner with Bailyn and his wife. Thereafter, Bailyn and I were on a first-name basis, and he has supported my career in many ways, including many stimulating lunches at the Harvard Faculty Club over the years.

I had initially planned to study the evolution of education in three New York towns (Schenectady, something in rural Duchess County, and New York City)— but most of the relevant records for the upstate towns had been lost in a huge archival fire in 1911. So I took Bailyn's advice and focused on New York City.

The records for the city were voluminous and intact at the New York Historical Society and the City Archives.

While I worked on this thesis, Michael Katz published his innovative and influential *Irony of Early School Reform*, but I steered myself around that work, and set out to make my own interpretation, New York City being a quite different place from Beverly or the state of Massachusetts. What emerged was a story both of imposition and of bureaucratic development that served various groups' purposes, for better or for worse. On the one hand, I emphasized the reformers' central focus on moral education and their pathological view of the urban poor. There was also a lot of Catholic-Protestant conflict, with the economically poorer Catholics getting the worst of it. On the other hand, I also emphasized the willing consolidation of a set of charity schools from diverse Protestant groups, becoming a set of Lancasterian free schools which, by 1850, had evolved into the publicly governed school system of New York. I sent the manuscript off to Harvard Press with the provisional title, *The Perfect System*, a phrase from one of the self-congratulatory reformers. I thought that the phrase would be understood by modern readers as a touch of irony. The only reader that counted, however---Harvard Press's outside reader—thought it was a terrible title, so the book gained its mundane label, *The Evolution of an Urban School System.*[2]

After the thesis was finished, Barbara Brenzel, a fellow historian of education, invited me to lunch with Sam Bowles and Herb Gintis, authors of the Marxist analysis *Schooling in Capitalist America*, at her apartment in Cambridge. I was excited. Bowles had read through the manuscript, and he made a comment that rattled around in my brain for years: "You had all the evidence for a radical interpretation. Why didn't you make it?" This of course raises a provocative point about the impact of a historian's ideology, theories, and politics in interpreting the development of an imperfect, unequal social system or any other complex historical puzzle. With just a slight shift in the selection of evidence and social theories to draw upon, a radical historian, a left-liberal historian, and a conservative historian can make different interpretations of the same narrative and evidence. I do not think that the relationship between all these influences upon the historian can be settled in any clear-cut or dogmatic way. But I have made my way in the history writing business by striving (as I am sure Professor Bowles has) for the interpretation that seems to best fit the largest bulk of the evidence. While I have not eschewed theory, I have been more an eclectic than a comprehensive practitioner of it.

ON TO WISCONSIN:

Harvard Press accepted the book, Wisconsin offered me a job, and my wife and I headed for Madison with our six-month-old new friend, Rika, in the fall of 1970. We arrived five days after the bombing of Sterling Hall, a math research building blown up by antiwar Wisconsin students. The blast killed a graduate assistant and cast a pall over the antiwar movement in Madison. Still, the divide among students and among colleagues remained deep and the war itself remained a daily horror, so the balancing act continued between pursuing an academic career, having a family life, and being riveted on politics. My wife taught nursing about half-time, eventually returning to graduate school for a Masters in Social Work, which led her into full-time work as a team leader in an HMO run by the state teachers association. I was an Assistant Professor of Educational Policy Studies and History. The active joint appointment was a rare privilege for a person in the subfield of the history of education, and I enjoyed it. Wisconsin had a large complement of historians of education. Jurgen Herbst, Sterling Fishman, Ed Krug, Herb Kliebard, and Bob Koehl, soon joined by Michael Fultz, all pursued historical work in the Department of Educational Policy Studies. Others, including Michael Olneck and Michael Apple, also did substantial historical work. Friendly allies in the History Department included Paul Boyer, John Cooper, Linda Gordon, Gerda Lerner and others.

MY ACADEMIC WORK, BEYOND THE DISSERTATION:

While I was putting the finishing touches on the dissertation book, I cooked up my next project and proposed it for Larry Cremin's series of "Classics in Education." I had been introduced thoroughly to the English reformer Joseph Lancaster in my work on New York City, and I thought that he deserved a place on the roster of "classics," since he was the most influential education reformer of the first two decades of the nineteenth century. The Lancaster materials at Teachers College and especially at the American Antiquarian Society in Worcester were rich and relatively unexplored. This edited volume became quite a large and enjoyable research project. I had done some work comparing English and American school reform, and Lancaster was active in both, starting schools and writing reform tracts on both sides of the Atlantic. He had dreamed up a system by which hundreds of poor children could be instructed by a single master, by using a rigidly prescribed curriculum, with older students teaching the younger students. Lancaster was an eccentric self-promoter. He opposed all physical punishment but invented bizarre shaming punishments instead. Nonetheless, his nondenominational, efficient, charity school system took hold in many cities, indeed, in many countries. In the United States the monitorial schools provided the nucleus for later public school systems in New York, Philadelphia, Schenectady and elsewhere.[3]

Here are Some Stand-alone Articles that I Still LIke and are Not Related to My Books:

"The Public Reaction to John Dickinson's *Farmer's Letters*," *Proceedings*, American Antiquarian Society (October 1968): 323–359.

"Moral Education and Common Schools in America: A Historian's View" *Journal of Moral Education* 13 (May 1984): 101–111.

"Public Schools and the Public Mood" *American Heritage* (February 1990): 66–81.

Standards of Evidence in Educational Research: How Do We Know When We Know?" *History of Education Quarterly* 32 (Fall 1992): 361–366.

"The Awful Reputation of Education Research" *Educational Researcher* 22 (January-February 1993): 23–31.

In my third year at Wisconsin a young historian named Maris Vinovskis showed up on my hallway in the History Department. Another student of Bernard Bailyn, Vinovskis is a historical demographer, and in the 1970s he was interested in the new uses of statistics in social history. He was evangelical about the methods, and his enthusiasm was infectious. I had devised a project to study the development of public schooling in Massachusetts. Being drawn to the statistical techniques for which he was already expert, I asked Maris to join the project as a consultant. Soon we became collaborators on a book called *Education and Social Change in Nineteenth-Century Massachusetts*. Many people assumed that Maris did most of the statistical work and that I did most of the writing. On the contrary, the split was about half-and-half. I had taken a course on statistics for historians at Wisconsin while I was a faculty member, and I had a patch quilt of shaky knowledge of statistics, with Maris there to tutor me. He drafted about half the chapters and I did the final stylistic sweep for the volume. I learned a lot about social history, about multivariate analysis, and about the politics of quantitative work. Numbers don't bring more certitude, though I think the chief contribution of that book may lie in its empirical excavation of school attendance and other variables involving school reform in mid-nineteenth-century Massachusetts.[4]

Beyond that contribution, the book received stern criticisms from some radical historians of school reform. These reminded me of an essay written by Robert Berkhofer, arguing that there were two social histories going on in the 1970s, one in which there was a fairly simple answer, and it was oppression, another in which there was complexity and that seemed to be the main point. One was a moral tale, the other an assertion of empiricism.[5] These dialogues were worth having, but they seem now to be lost in the mists of time.

My next project reached more people than the previous three. *Pillars of the Republic* is a synthetic work with a lot of research behind it, mostly from published primary sources. The subject is the creation of state-sponsored free school systems in the United States; the unit of analysis is states, with examples principally coming from a selection of eight or ten states. It dips down to depict conditions at the grassroots occasionally, for example, the enrollment patterns of New York City in the 1790s, and life in one-room schoolhouses in the ante-bellum Midwest. Its approach is structuralist. After a few chapters on schooling before 1820, in which I emphasized the stark differences between rural and urban modes of schooling at the time, I embarked on a depiction of the economic, ethnic, and religious relations in the society from the 1820s to the 1850s, then to the reigning ideology through which reformers made sense of the structural circumstances they were in, then to the institutional changes that were wrought, then to oppositional forces and their fate. The theme that emerged from this interpretive strategy was the hotly contested but dominant effect of the ideology that wove republicanism, capitalism and Protestantism together in the service of an activist state.[6]

For the next six or seven years I refreshed my brain by moving away from the history of schooling, turning to the history of literacy and reading. That resulted in a book entitled *Literacy in the United States: Readers and Reading Since 1880*, co-authored with four graduate assistants. The book is a set of essays on the nature and extent of literate activity in America from 1880 to the present. My emphasis was on the expansion of literacy and its inevitable but often overlooked association with ideology. All literacy is embedded in a social context.[7]

This interest carried over into a new collaboration on the history of the book, which I pursued while I also returned to a long-standing interest in federal education policy. Thus, for the past fifteen years, I have juggled two projects, one a volume in the five-volume *History of the Book in America*, the other a book on the history of the federal role in education since World War II. My co-editor in the history of the book project was Janice Radway, long at Duke University, now at Northwestern. This was a great stroke of luck for me. Jan became a good friend, and we complemented each other well for the task at hand. She is a cultural theorist focusing on such popular culture topics as romance novels and the Book of the Month Club. She is more theoretically minded than I, and I have more grounding in U.S. social history and its historiography. Both of us have learned a huge amount about the history of print culture. Although the book is an anthology, we did a lot of writing within the volume, developing a fairly coherent narrative, and then attempting to engage our authors in this framework. The book explores what happened when forces for cultural consolidation met equally potent forces for diversification, new participants, and dissent. While working on this book, I got another chance to think hard about social change, race and religious relations in the U.S., as well as the worlds of publishing and reading.[8]

With that project finished, I am concentrating on my history of the federal role in education. I am dealing with two phenomena: first, the incremental and episodic factors that have bumped the federal role in education upward; second, in contrast, the strangely durable appeal of localism and state control that make the United States one of the most decentralized of all education governance systems in the developed world, even in the days of standards-based education. We shall see how that plays out, in my book and in the real world of schools.

COMINGS AND GOINGS:

While I was working on these projects over the past forty years, my professional development was of course influenced by teaching, advising, and moving to different institutions. I was principal advisor for fifteen Ph.D. students, many of whom have been friends ever since. I turn to them often for advice, sympathy, and laughs. The challenges and rewards of teaching the basic lecture course in the field, at Wisconsin and at Brown, never wore thin. It was my only lecture course, all the others being seminar style and quite student-directed. Those smaller courses also required constant revision and new methods, as well as new content, as I learned more about how to construct such courses.

The University of Wisconsin is one of the major centers for graduate training in our field and was for me a very rich and supportive intellectual environment for twenty-five-years. In 1997 I left Wisconsin in the wake of a divorce and then falling in love with Liz Hollander, a city planner who had been Commissioner of

Here are Some Stand-alone Articles that I Still Like and are Not Related to My Books: (continued)

"Literate America: High-level Adult Literacy as a National Goal," in Diane Ravitch and Maris Vinovskis, eds., *Historical Perspectives on the Current Education Reforms* (Baltimore: Johns Hopkins University Press, 1995), 329–354.

"Toward a Political Economy of Citizenship: Historical Perspectives on the Purposes of Common Schools," in Lorraine M. McDonnell, Michael Timpane, and Roger Benjamin, eds., *Rediscovering the Democratic Purposes of Education* (Lawrence: University Press of Kansas, 2000), 47–72.

"Clio at the Table: Historical Perspectives and Policymaking in the Field of Education," in Kenneth Wong and Robert Rothman, eds., *Clio at the Table: Using History to Inform and Improve Education Policy* (New York: Peter Lang 2009), 283–294.

Planning for Mayor Harold Washington in Chicago. Liz was reinventing herself as director of a center for urban outreach activities at DePaul University. We commuted up and down Interstate 90 to see each other on weekends for three years, and then I got a position at the University of Chicago. When the University, in its infinite wisdom, abolished the Department of Education two years later, we moved to Providence, where I became University Professor of Education, History, and Public Policy at Brown and Liz became the Executive Director of Campus Compact, the national organization that advocates for student community service and service learning.

Because my main commitment at Brown was to the Education Department, and that department was mainly engaged in undergraduate instruction, I satisfied my desire to mentor young scholars by becoming director of a postdoctoral program funded by the Spencer and the Hewlett Foundations, around the theme of my research: federal and national strategies of school reform. Ten young scholars, most of them college teachers, became a well-knit and committed group. The program was non-residential, but the Fellows came twice a year for four days to Providence. Between meetings we devised many other ways—electronic and face to face—to relate to each other and to their Brown faculty mentors. That was a lovely experience, watching them grow as individuals, watching them mentor each other, and having great fun talking about education reform. In a nice way, my work on the federal role got absorbed into the program, as I interacted with the Fellows' work and wrote a long chapter for the book that we produced together, *To Educate a Nation: Federal and National Strategies of School Reform*. What was nominally a three-year experience has continued to this day.[9]

CONCLUDING REMARKS:

Both of my daughters have gone into academic life. Rika is a molecular anthropologist at Indiana University-Bloomington. She teaches methods of physical anthropology and courses on the evolution and migration of the human species. Her research utilizes DNA analysis of ancient bones. Christine took her Ph. D. in public health and teaches at Virginia Tech in the Human Development Department.

She studies risk-taking behavior of adolescent women, in sexual behavior, smoking, and other areas. Among her courses is one on sexuality and another on quantitative methods for studying human development.

Once, when she was in high school, Christine said "Dad, it seems that your field, education, has rather low status in the academic world." She said she never would have known it from me, since I seemed to be so enthusiastic about it. So, she asked, "Is that right?" "Yes," I said. And she continued, "Has that ever bothered you?" "No," I said.

This field is full of opportunities. Most of us are in multi-disciplinary departments, and sometimes we get the challenge and rewards of doing genuinely interdisciplinary work, both in teaching and research. Also, history of education is closely related to policy and practice, so there is a sense of ongoing reality to our work. The importance of the work makes it all the more worthwhile.

Finally, this subfield has an abundance of caring, considerate, and collegial people in it, both the old walruses and the pups. The walrus metaphor comes from a meeting I attended a few decades ago, chaired by Patricia Graham. Pat jokingly referred to herself as a "walrus," meaning someone who has been around for awhile. Frank Keppel, the former Commissioner of Education, spoke up from the back of the room. "Pat, I'm a walrus, maybe Doc Howe is a walrus, but you ain't no walrus." Like me, many of my valued friends have now achieved unambiguous walrus status. No one is wiser and kinder than David Tyack, no one is more savvy and supportive than Pat Graham, no one is a better dinner partner than Wayne Urban, and that's just the short list. Wonderfully, the young pups keep coming to the field: smart, sensitive, and enthusiastic.

NOTES

1 Arthur R. Jensen, "How Much Can We Boost IQ and Scholastic Achievement?" *Harvard Educational Review* 39:1 (Winter, 1969):1—123.

2 Carl F. Kaestle, *The Evolution of an Urban School System: New York City, 1750–1850* (Cambridge: Harvard University Press, 1973)

3 *Joseph Lancaster and the Monitorial School System: A Documentary History* (New York: Teachers College Press, 1973)

4 Carl F. Kaestle and Maris A. Vinovskis, *Education and Social Change in Nineteenth-Century Massachusetts* (New York: Cambridge University Press, 1980, paperback edition, 2009)

5 Robert Berkhofer Jr., "The Two New Histories: Competing Paradigms for Intrpreting the American Past," *OAH Newsletter* 11 (May, 1983): 9–11.

6 Carl F. Kaestle, *Pillars of the Republic: Common Schools and American Society, 1780–1860* (New York: Hill & Wang, 1983.

7 Carl F. Kaestle, Helen Damon-Moore, Lawrence C. Stedman, Katherine Tinsley, and William Vance Trollinger, Jr., *Literacy in the United States: Readers and Reading since* 1880 (New Haven: Yale University Press, 1991)

8 *Print in Motion: The Expansion of Publication and Reading in he United States, 1880–1940*, ed. Carl F. Kaestle and Janice A. Radway (Chapel Hill: University of North Carolina Press, Volume 4 of A History of the Book in America, 2008)

9 Carl F. Kaestle, and Alyssa A. Lodewick, eds., *To Educate a Nation: Federal and National Strategies of School Reform* (Lawrence: University Press of Kansas, 2007)

HARVEY KANTOR

ON BECOMING A HISTORIAN OF AMERICAN EDUCATION

When I was in high school and college, it never occurred to me that I would become a historian of education. But I am not, in retrospect, entirely surprised that this is the path I have followed. As far back as I can remember in my adult life, I have been especially interested in American history and politics. That interest could, of course, have taken me in a number of different directions and sometimes did. But, over time, I came to believe that the study of education offered a compelling way for me to combine my interest in history and my interest in politics in a socially relevant fashion.

I

I grew up in the 1950s and 1960s in Newton, Massachusetts, a suburb outside Boston. Both of my parents were college graduates and stressed to me and my sister and brother the importance of education, or at least the importance of doing well in school (which are not, of course, self-evidently the same thing). Neither my sister nor my brother ever took my parents' admonitions to heart. Nor was school necessarily at the top of my own list of priorities either, at least not initially. When I was in elementary school by far my most fervent wish was to play third base for the Boston Red Sox. But fortunately (since I subsequently discovered that it is harder to hit a curve ball than it first appears) it also became important to me to do well in school, and at my parents' urging I worked relatively hard at it. I am not entirely sure why except that I always liked to read. In elementary school, when I was not practicing batting and fielding grounders, I think I read nearly every book in the Landmark series on the history of the United States, which inspired my interest in U.S. history but also taught me lessons about our nation's past that I have spent the rest of my life unlearning.

Newton in the 1950s and early 1960s was one of those places that James Bryant Conant labeled a "lighthouse" school district for its commitment to educational reform and academic excellence. It eagerly embraced curricular innovations like UICSM (Illinois math), SMSG, PSSC physics, and other NSF-sponsored curriculum projects in biology, chemistry, and social studies (including MACOS). Newton High School (NHS), where I graduated in 1966, was also cited by Conant in *An American High School Today* as a model comprehensive high school.[1]But more than anything else, I suspect that what earned Newton the recognition that Conant accorded it was the large number of students from Jewish and professional

W. J. Urban, *Leaders in the Historical Study of American Education, 165–177.*
© 2011 Sense Publishers. All rights reserved.

families–including more than its fair share of sons and daughters of Harvard and MIT professors–who populated NHS's many Advanced Placement classes and nearly all of whom subsequently went on to Ivy League universities and selective liberal arts colleges.

Favorites of My Own:

Harvey Kantor, David B. Tyack, eds. *Youth, Work, and Schooling: Historical Perspectives On Vocationalism in American Education* (Stanford: Stanford University Press, 1982).

Harvey Kantor, *Learning to Earn: Work, School and Vocational Reform in California* (Madison: University of Wisconsin Press, 1988).

Harvey Kantor and Barbara Brenzel. "Urban Education and the 'Truly Disadvantaged': The Roots of the Contemporary Crisis." In Michael B. Katz, ed. *The "Underclass" Debate: Views From History* (Princeton: Princeton University Press, 1993). 366–402.

Harvey Kantor and Robert Lowe. "Class, Race, and the Emergence of Federal Education Policy: From the New Deal to the Great Society," *Educational Researcher* 24 (May 1995): 4–11, 21.

Harvey Kantor and Robert Lowe. "Bureaucracy Left and Right," In Larry Cuban and Dorothy Shipps, eds., *Reconstructing the Common Good in Education: Coping With Intractable American Dilemmas* (Stanford: Stanford University Press, 2000), 130–47.

Harvey Kantor and Robert Lowe. "From New Deal to No Deal: No Child Left Behind and the Devolution of Responsibility for Equal Opportunity," *Harvard Educational Review* 76 (Winter 2006): 474–502.

Comparing notes much later with my good friend and collaborator Bob Lowe, I realized that the academic environment I experienced at Newton High was not the norm for American secondary schools, even in other suburban schools. At the time, however, I didn't think much about it. I remember observing to myself that many of the Irish and Italian kids I had come to be friendly with in junior high school were no longer in the same classes I was. But, for the most part, I was too busy trying to make the varsity basketball team and trying to keep up with my academically precocious classmates to worry much about why that might be the case (or to notice the absence of African American and Latino faces in my classes either). History was the only subject I excelled in, and the only one that I found truly engaging, largely because I had three excellent history teachers whom I still remember. But I managed to do well enough in the rest to be accepted at Brown at a time when the Ivy League had begun to abandon its quota on Jewish students, though I realize now, after reading Jerome Karabel's *The Chosen*, that I must surely also have benefited from the preference that all the Ivy League institutions continue to this day to accord children of alumni in admissions.[2]

It was while I was at Brown in the late 1960s that I began to develop an interest in studying education and to think more critically about it, though this had less to do with anything I was learning in the classes I enrolled in than with other things going on around me while I was there. Most important was the publication of several popular accounts, mostly by teachers in urban schools, detailing the systematic failure of American education, particularly in cities, to educate low-income, African

American and Puerto Rican children–indeed to actively mis-educate them: *Death at an Early Age* by Jonathan Kozol, *36 Children* by Herbert Kohl, *The Way It's Spozed to Be* by James Herndon, *The Lives of Children* by George Dennison, *Our Children are Dying* by Nat Hentoff, *Why Children Fail* by John Holt, and *Village School Downtown* by Peter Schrag. One of my roommates and I read and talked about them all, and I still have all of them on my bookshelf along with others, including Kozol's *Free Schools* and Herndon's *How to Survive in Your Native Land,* that were published a little later.[3]

In retrospect, I'm not entirely certain why I found these books so compelling. I'm sure it was partly due to the power of the writing and the evocative stories they told–so different from my own school experience, in some cases literally just a few miles away from where I had grown up. It probably also traced to the sense of social betrayal I felt reading about the seemingly willful failure of the one institution I had assumed still embodied the best hope of American democracy, at a time when the egalitarian promise of so many other institutions appeared to me to be transparently false. Whatever the reason, this reading marked the beginning of what became a life-long engagement first as a student, teacher, and organizer and later as a scholar with questions about the social, political, and economic functions of education and specifically with the possibilities and limits of liberal social and educational reform. At that time, however, I did not yet have a well-developed framework for making sense of what I was reading about and doubt I would have discussed it in terms of the limits of reform.

But my burgeoning interest in education as a field of future work and study was not due solely to the impact of what I discovered from reading Kozol, Kohl, Dennison, and the others about promises betrayed in urban schools. Ironically, it also grew out of concerns closer to home–discontent over my own formal education.

Brown had many outstanding (and some not so outstanding) professors. At the time, however, it did not seem to me that my college course-work had much to say about what I felt I needed to learn about, or at least I did not very often perceive any connection. Although I had some excellent classes–again, mostly in history, with people like John Thomas, William McLoughlin, and Barry Karl in U.S. history and Tom Gleason in Russian history–I spent the majority of my time studying on my own and talking with my friends, mostly trying to learn more about the imperialist roots of American foreign policy, racial inequality in education, and the political significance of the counter-culture and the New Left–topics that were not typically covered in class.

This preference for independent study prompted my involvement in a group independent study project on higher education that ultimately led to the transformation of the undergraduate curriculum at Brown. Based on the assumption that learning occurred best when it was self-motivated, the "New Curriculum" (as it was referred to for several years afterwards) eliminated letter grades, ended distribution requirements, organized first year course work around inter-disciplinary "modes of thought" courses, and provided the option for a self-defined course of study as an alternative to the standard subject matter major. I have since come to realize that some students might not always know what it is they need to find out about without more structured curricular guidance than the "New Curriculum" offered, something Tom Gleason tried to convince me of at the time. But this experience instilled in me a healthy skepticism for the traditional conventions of institutional learning even as it deepened my engagement with the idea of education as a field of study in a way that eventually led to my decision to apply to the doctoral program in the history of education at Stanford.

The path from Brown to Stanford went through Cambridge, Cheyenne, Wyoming, and Somerville, Massachusetts. During my senior year at Brown (1970), I applied to the Master's of Education program in the Graduate School of Education at Harvard, partly because I wanted to read more about the politics of education but also because I had no idea about what else to do. While I was at the HGSE, Marvin Lazerson and David Cohen offered a course in the history of education. But I did not then see the relevance of history to the kinds of questions I was interested in exploring and did not enroll in the course. Instead, I spent most of my year at Harvard reading about democratic theory in an effort to understand the challenge that the rise of Black Power, the conflict in Ocean-Hill Brownsville, and the idea of community control posed to liberal notions of individualism, equal educational opportunity, and cultural pluralism, and what difference that might make to my own political commitments.

Only later did I begin to see that history might actually have a good deal to say about those things. When I completed my Master's degree, however, I was not much thinking about studying history or anything else. Although I think I knew all along that I would one day return to school, my experiences in college and my reading in graduate school convinced me that it was more important to me to try to construct alternatives to the existing school system. The result was that for the next four years I worked as a teacher and organizer in two "alternative" high schools, first–and most memorably–in Cheyenne, Wyoming, and after that back in Somerville, Massachusetts.

Though I never would have imagined moving there, I lived and worked in Cheyenne with my partner (and future spouse) for two and a half years. What attracted us there was a desire to leave Cambridge and a notice that had been placed in an alternative education paper by the Cheyenne Community Action Agency for two teacher/organizers to run a Street Academy for poor and working class teenagers who had dropped out of high school. Inspired by the "free" school movement that was taking place all around us, we hoped to put into practice the ideas about self-directed learning we had been reading and talking about. Perhaps naively, we also thought that in a small way we could create an alternative model that would put pressure on the local school system to change. Both, of course, turned out to be much more difficult than we anticipated. But, during our time in Cheyenne, we managed to manipulate funding from Richard Nixon's juvenile delinquency prevention program to transform the Street Academy into an alternative high school that was eventually adopted by the public school system and continues to exist today as an option for marginalized students within the public system. We still debate whether that constitutes meaningful educational change or is a good example of what in the 1960s we used to call "cooptation."

My work in Cheyenne also led in a serendipitous way to my desire to study the history of education. For reasons I do not remember, in the summer of 1973 during a lull in the Senate Watergate hearings, I picked up a copy of *The Irony of Early School Reform* by Michael Katz.[4] At the time, Janet and I were trying to figure out why the Street Academy kids were so alienated from school as well as why the Cheyenne school system seemed so skeptical about and resistant to our efforts despite its own failure to educate so many of them and what we might do about it. *Irony* was not much help in thinking through the latter question. What it offered, however, was a compelling account of the role class interest played in the founding of public school systems that both revised how I thought about the institutional obstacles we were encountering every day in our work–illustrating that those obstacles were not simply the unintended consequences of otherwise well-meaning reform. Just as important, it also demonstrated to me how history could inform the study and practice of education in a politically relevant way that I had not seriously considered before.

When I left Cheyenne, I returned to Somerville, Massachusetts. I worked for a while at the Old Corner Bookstore in Boston (which, apart from its name, no longer bore the slightest degree of resemblance to the place where Hawthorne, Emerson and other nineteenth century New England intellectual luminaries used to gather), joined a Marxist study group, and worked as a teacher and fund raiser in an alternative high school in Somerville similar to the one Janet and I had started in Cheyenne. By then, however, I knew that I wanted to study the history of education, and, largely on the advice of Barbara Brenzel, a former student of Michael Katz's whom I knew from the time I lived in Cambridge and who was completing her own doctoral work in the history of education at Harvard, I applied to Stanford. While I was teaching in Somerville, I read *The One Best System*, but, other than what Barbara had told me, that was all I knew about the Stanford School of Education or David Tyack when I arrived in Palo Alto in the fall of 1976.[5]

II

I have no idea what I was thinking, but I arrived at Stanford without any clue about how I was going to pay tuition. I had managed to put a little bit away in savings, but obviously not nearly enough to cover what Stanford charged for graduate work. Fortunately, soon after I arrived, David arranged a research assistantship for me with Norman Drachler, a former superintendent of schools in Detroit, who was at Stanford doing research on big city schools and urban school administrators. Subsequently, I worked regularly as a teaching assistant for David in the course on the history of American education he offered each quarter primarily for undergraduates and for David and Michael Kirst in a course they taught together on history and contemporary education policy. These jobs covered the cost of tuition and provided a living stipend. Without them (and Janet's financial support), I'm not sure what I would have done.

When I began at Stanford, there were only a small number of students studying the history of education. Guadalupe San Miguel (who is now a member of the history department at the University of Houston) was finishing his dissertation around that time and one or two others had completed most of their course work. I was the only one in my cohort in what was then called the Social Sciences in Education program who was studying history; the other students entering that year were in sociology, economics, anthropology, and philosophy. My future collaborator Bob Lowe did not enter the program until I was in my third year; Ted Mitchell who at the time was a Stanford undergraduate and later became President of Occidental College entered at about the same time, as did Tom James (now provost at Teachers College). Others who also came to study with David, including Reuben Donato (now a professor of education at the University of Colorado) and Dan Perlstein (who now teaches history of education at UC Berkeley), who arrived later.

By design, my first year of course work included a number of courses that offered a critical perspective on the social sciences, including a course in the economics of education with Hank Levin that examined the shortcomings of human capital theory and a course on education, philosophy, and social theory with Arturo Pacheco, which was my first formal introduction to the Frankfurt School and western Marxism. Nearly all of the rest of my formal course work was in the history department where I took a seminar on nineteenth century social history with Carl Degler and worked with Al Camarillo and Barton Bernstein on U.S. social and political history in the twentieth century. I also took a year-long seminar with Ronald Schatz that began with a comparison of nineteenth century British and U.S. labor history and concluded with the rise of the CIO in the U.S. in the 1930s. In none of these classes did I experience any of the status politics that historically has characterized the relationship between the liberal arts and schools of education in many universities.

Because there were only a few of us in history, David only offered two courses for graduate students in the history of education—one on historiography, the other on the history of urban education. They were my formal introduction to the history of education. The highlight of these courses was my introduction to Horace Mann Bond's *Negro Education in Alabama*, which was the first class analysis of African American education in the South that I had read.[6] But most of what I know about the history of education did not come from these courses. My real education in the history of education came through my work as a TA in the history of education course and the regular meetings I had with David who solicited my reactions to whatever he was writing and willingly shared with all of us his seemingly encyclopedic knowledge of the history of education. We did not always agree. (Bob Lowe and I were always trying to push him more to the left). But, through his example, I learned (or at least tried to learn) the importance of being open to listening to criticism of one's work that might be difficult to hear.

It was as a result of one of these regular conversations that I began to focus my early research on the origins of vocational education. In the late 1970s, during one conversation when we were talking about Samuel Bowles and Herbert Gintis's *Schooling in Capitalist America*[7] and I was trying to articulate the importance of class analysis in the history of education, David said to me that if I really wanted to know more about the way class mattered in education, I might consider doing my dissertation research on the origins of vocational education. I had not thought too much about the history of vocational education at the time, but for a number of reasons, his suggestion resonated with me. From my reading with Schatz and Bernstein, I knew that the early twentieth century marked a key moment in the evolution of capitalism and class relations in the U.S. At the same time, no Tyack student could be unaware of the significance of the early twentieth century to the history of educational reform. A study of vocational education thus seemed to be a good way to bring together my interest in the history of class relations with my interest in educational reform at a key moment in the history of both.

What ultimately defined my initial interest in the history of vocational education, however, was the reading and research I had been doing on the history of work. Most important was Harry Braverman's book *Labor and Monopoly Capital*.[8] The central theme of this book was the de-skilling of craft labor in the early twentieth century, precisely the moment at which school reformers were arguing for the addition of instruction in technical skills to the school curriculum through vocational education. Having read enough to know the mixed results of most vocational training on employment and wages, I became convinced that trying to un-ravel the apparent paradox Braverman's book suggested–the historical conjunction of the determined de-skilling of working class labor at work with the introduction of skill training for working class students in school–would make for a compelling dissertation. Any lingering doubts I might have had were dispelled by my many conversations with Marvin Lazerson, who, of course, had already done considerable research on the history of vocationalism in American education.[9]

My initial approach to thinking about this topic was shaped by a number of revisionist studies that made vocational education central to their critique of progressivism in public education–specifically that far from equalizing educational opportunity, vocational education was intended to function as a form of social control.[10] As my research progressed, however, I did not think that the social control framework adequately accounted for the wide range of seemingly contradictory interests that coalesced around the demand for vocational training in school. Consequently, what I wound up trying to explain is why so many sought to displace the crisis of skill that Braverman described onto the schools when this did not seem to be a self-evidently educational problem and how this ultimately shaped ideas about the relationship between school, work, and the organization of the labor market. This theme runs throughout the essays in the collection that David and I edited, *Youth, Work, and Schooling: Historical Perspectives on Vocationalism in American Education*, and my dissertation which was subsequently revised and published as *Learning to Earn: Work, Youth, and Schooling in California, 1880–1930*.[11]

In retrospect, I think the greatest accomplishment of this work was to paint a more dynamic, more variegated picture of the labor market and of vocational education in practice than was commonly acknowledged at the time while still highlighting its role in the reproduction of inequality. Most revisionist studies of vocational education, for example, focused mainly on industrial education, which they portrayed largely as a top-down reform. But *Learning to Earn* emphasized that the vocational revolution was also a product of student aspirations, even as it ultimately limited and constrained them in unequal ways. This was particularly the case with young women who seized on commercial education as a route into clerical work, as subsequent research by Jane Powers, Miriam Cohen, and John Rury also pointed out.[12] But partly because I did not fully escape the social control framework that juxtaposed academic to vocational education, I still tended to treat vocational education in too monolithic a fashion. One result was that none of my writing on vocational education at this time considered sufficiently why certain industrial education classes excluded African American youth–indeed, why southeastern European immigrant youth often vocally and sometimes physically defended vocational schools against Black entry. Focused on industrial labor, neither did I think much about why white southerners might promote instruction in scientific agriculture for white youth, while denying it to Blacks, relegating them instead to classes that did little but teach the virtues of hard work and menial manual labor.

Much of the historical interest in vocational education that generated my initial research has since waned. Apart from an occasional essay, the only significant research on the history of vocational education I can think of since Cohen, Powers, Rury, and I published our research is Herbert Kliebard's 1999 volume, *Schooled to Work*.[13] I suspect this is because vocational education has all but disappeared from high schools in the wake of the publication of *A Nation at Risk* in 1983; today, most vocational training and education is concentrated in public community colleges and proprietary technical schools. Yet it remains striking to me that what piqued my interest in writing about the history of vocational education in the first place– namely, the idea that better skill training in school can smooth the transition to new forms of work without disturbing the unequal social relations on which they are based is as resilient as, if not more resilient than, ever. Now, however, the focus is on academic study rather than specifically vocational courses. If I were to return to the study of vocational education now, I would do more to try to break down the academic/vocational binary, examine differentiation and stratification within vocational education itself, and think more deeply about the historical processes through which academic education has now become the dominant form of vocational education.

III

After Stanford, I came to the University of Utah. If I could not have imagined going to Cheyenne, Wyoming, neither could I ever have imagined that I would spend the next twenty-five years in Salt Lake City. But at the urging of a colleague from Stanford who had taken a job at Utah in the philosophy of education the year before, I applied successfully for an opening in the history of education in what was then the Department of Educational Studies. I have been in Salt Lake ever since. Equally surprising, since I have often counseled others against it, I am currently serving my seventh year as chair of what now is the Department of

Education, Culture, and Society, which is one of the few remaining social foundations of education departments in the country.

Since I have been at Utah, much of my scholarly work has been done in collaboration with Bob Lowe. Our collaboration began while we were both at Stanford. It developed slowly at first. But through our discussions with each other in the informal history of education lunch group that met semi-regularly outside Cubberley Hall, we discovered that we had complementary though not identical interests and compatible politics that provided a strong basis for collaboration. Perhaps most importantly, we also discovered that we shared a similar approach to reading history and its implications for education policy based on a skepticism of much that passed for conventional wisdom in history and education, not just on the right but among many self-identified progressives as well.

Works that have influenced me:

Samuel Bowles and Herbert Gintis, *Schooling in Capitalist America: Educational Reform and the Contradictions of Economic Life* (New York: Basic Books, 1976).

Harry Braverman, *Labor and Monopoly Capital: The Degradation of Work in the Twentieth Century* (New York: Monthly Review Press, 1974).

Michael B. Katz, *The Irony of Early School Reform: Educational Innovation in Mid-Nineteenth Century Massachusetts* (Cambridge: Harvard University Press, 1968).

Ira Katznelson and Margaret Weir, *Schooling for All: Class, Race, and the Decline of the American Ideal* (New York: Basic Books, 1985).

David B. Tyack, *The One Best System: A History of American Urban Education* (Cambridge: Harvard University Press, 1974).

Our subsequent work together has built upon and continued to address many of the themes about the connections between class and racial inequality, economic change, and the political functions of liberal reform that initially animated my interest in studying the origins of vocational education—particularly the way social policy has functioned over time to displace political and economic conflicts onto the schools. But it has attempted more self-consciously to develop an historically grounded understanding of the reliance on school reform as a solution to racial and economic inequities as a way to think more expansively about the place that education has come to occupy in American social policymaking and to question many of the school-centric assumptions that have informed much recent writing about social policy and the possibilities of educational policymaking and reform. The end result has been a somewhat eclectic body of work but one that taken together we think offers a way of seeing that differs from standard narrative histories of the development of education policy, on the one hand, and conventional policy studies, on the other.

The core of this project has been our work on the history of race, poverty, and the politics of federal education policy that grew out of work Bob had done on education in the New Deal and work that I had begun after completing *Learning to Earn* on education and social policy in the Great Society.[14] At the time we began this work, we had both been thinking about how we might do more to historicize the idea that education has always been seen as a solution to social problems when we made a simple observation–that whereas education had been central to the Great Society, and the anti-poverty program nestled within it, it had been marginal to New Deal reform. Based on that observation, we set out to explore the social and political processes that pushed education to the forefront of domestic policymaking in the Great Society when it had not been in the New Deal. In doing so, we hoped to understand better why the belief in educational policymaking has been so resilient despite its limits and how this preoccupation with education at the expense of other social policies has shaped the life chances of different classes and ethnic and racial groups.

In thinking about these issues, we built on other historical studies of the evolution of federal education policy. But since most of these studies tended to take the place of education in social policy as unproblematic, they did not help us understand the processes by which social policy came to privilege education. Accordingly, as we proceeded, we sought to reach beyond them to situate the development of education policy more firmly within the history of American social and economic provision, particularly the development of the welfare state.[15] Though the historiographies of these developments have traveled along separate trajectories, bringing them together gave us a way to think about how conflicts in the broader political and institutional context–particularly the struggles between different classes and racial groups over how to balance public and private responsibility for social provision and economic security–worked to propel education to the forefront of post-World War II federal social policy (and sustain it even as political support for other more expansive forms of direct public social provision has continued to erode) that we felt could not be accounted for by focusing on the history of federal education policy alone.[16]

Our collaboration has over the years also produced several more topical essays in which we have sought to use history to question a number of taken for granted assumptions that have informed contemporary debates over education policy. In these essays, we have been especially concerned with charting an alternative to the conservative attack on public education and to what we believe has been the often knee-jerk liberal response to it without abandoning our own understanding of schools as political institutions that tend strongly to reproduce class and racial inequalities. Most notable among these have been our essays about the educational left's response to the right's recent appropriation of the revisionist critique of school bureaucracy and about what the history of education has to tell us about the provision and distribution of what is commonly referred to as "quality" schooling.[17]

Our goal in this work has not been to generate tidy lists of "lessons" from history to guide the formation of education or social policy today. I do not think history can do that–or, at least it can't do that very well. Indeed, I think a strong argument can be made that the lessons of the past are for the most part too time-bound and context specific to provide definitive answers to questions about what policies will necessarily work best today or in the future. Rather, by situating the current moment within the long term trajectory of educational policymaking, what we have endeavored to do in these essays is to de-bunk overly simple analogies from the past that have been used to justify particular policies and to demonstrate how historical knowledge can deepen our understanding of the constraints and possibilities policymakers confront in education today. However, I have come to think that how we choose to act on that understanding and the policies we choose to embrace as a result of it are as much a question of our ideological and political commitments as of our knowledge of the history of education.

IV

In 1993, I co-authored an essay with Barbara Brenzel on the post-war transformation of metropolitan space, labor markets, and urban education that appeared as a chapter in *The Underclass Debate* edited by Michael Katz.[18] Drawing on Ira Katznelson and Margaret Weir's book *Schooling for All,*[19] the essay examined how the confluence of changes in the geographic redistribution of the American population between cites and suburbs after WW II, the spatial patterning of class and race that accompanied it, and the bifurcation of post-war urban labor markets conspired to erode the capacity of city schools to redistribute educational opportunity. Our goal in this essay was to demonstrate how the class and racial differentiation of metropolitan space fused with suburban political autonomy to undermine the promise of *Brown v. Board of Education* and limit the possibilities for reform in urban education.

Implicit in this essay was the assumption that the politics of school reform have been shaped by the social relations between different groups and classes whose interests are tied to particular geographic spaces. But, at the time we wrote, Barbara and I were unable to illustrate how this dynamic worked in practice. Thanks to a fellowship I received from the College of Education at Utah, however, recently I have been studying what these spatial politics look like on the ground through an examination of a conflict that erupted in Salt Lake in 1987 over the closure of one of the city's four high schools and the subsequent realignment of its secondary school boundaries to balance enrollment in the three other high schools by race, class, and educational achievement. The most divisive educational conflict in the city's recent history, it illustrates how suburbanization intensified class and racial conflict in the city at the same time that it complicates Katznelson and Weir's claim about the possibilities of common schooling in class and ethnically diverse cities by revealing the persistence of social divisions embedded deeply within the spatial organization of the city itself.

Apart from the theoretical challenges it presents, what has most excited me about this project is that it has pushed me to use sources (real estate records, city planning and land use reports, zoning ordinances) and to use methodologies–especially oral history–I have not employed before. But this has also made me more cognizant of the partiality of historical knowledge–not just because of the gaps and silences in written sources I am not familiar with (which, of course, is something historians have to deal with all the time) but also because my interviews have made me aware that many of the people I have talked with possess a depth of local knowledge that I know I can only approximate. Anthropologists, of course, deal with this and other similar dilemmas in their research all the time, but as a historian this is the first time I have encountered it in such an immediate way.

Although one of my first publications in graduate school was a defense of revisionist scholarship,[20] I suppose that the path I have followed in this and the rest of my work would be characterized as post-revisionist. Notwithstanding the inspiration I initially drew from *Irony*, I have come to see that aspects of the revisionist argument were overstated. Not only did it tend to blur the distinction between socialization and social control, but it assumed that school systems were impervious to community influence. I now have, as do many of my colleagues, a greater appreciation of the dynamics of school reform–including the liberalizing possibilities of schooling and the struggles of women, working class organizations, and people of color to realize them. But in developing a more nuanced view of the contradictory role of education in the past, I also worry that much of our recent work in the history of education has tended to surrender the strong critique of educational institutions that informed the revisionist project and that motivated my desire to study the history of education in the first place. As Bob Lowe and I wrote in our essay "Bureaucracy Left and Right,"[21] the challenge that defines our work now is how to retain our understanding of schools as institutions that reproduce inequality without discounting the struggles–sometimes successful, other times less so of those who have tried to change them,

NOTES

1 James Bryant Conant, *The American High School Today: A First Report to Citizens* (New York: McGraw-Hill, 1959).

2 Jerome Karabel, *The Chosen: The Hidden History of Admission and Exclusion at Harvard, Yale, and Princeton* (New York: Houghton Mifflin, 2005).

3 Jonathan Kozol, *Death at an Early Age* (Boston: Houghton Mifflin, 1967); Herbert Kohl, *36 Children* (New York: Signet Books, 1967); James Herndon, *The Way It's Spozed to Be* (New York: Simon and Schuster, 1968); George Dennison, *The Lives of Children* (New York: Vintage Books, 1969); Nat Hentoff, *Our Children Are Dying* (New York: Viking Books, 1966); John Holt, *How Children Fail* (New York: Dell Publishing, 1964); Peter Schrag, *Village School Downtown* (Boston: Beacon Press, 1967); Jonathan Kozol, *Free Schools* (New York: Houghton Mifflin, 1972); James Herndon, *How to Survive in Your Native Land* (New York: Simon and Schuster, 1971).

4 Michael B. Katz, *The Irony of Early School Reform: Educational Innovation in Mid-Nineteenth Century Massachusetts* (Cambridge: Harvard University Press, 1968).

5 David B. Tyack, *The One Best System: A History of American Urban Education* (Cambridge: Harvard University Press, 1974). For my retrospective assessment, Harvey Kantor, "In Retrospect: David Tyack's The One Best System," *Reviews in American History* 29 (2001): 319–27.

6 Horace Mann Bond, *Negro Education in Alabama: A Study in Cotton and Steel* (New York: Atheneum, 1969; orig. published 1939).

7 Samuel Bowles and Herbert Gintis, *Schooling in Capitalist America: Education and the Contradictions of Economic Life* (New York: Basic Books, 1976).

8 Harry Braverman, *Labor and Monopoly Capital: The Degradation of Work in the Twentieth Century* (New York: Monthly Review Press, 1974).

9 W. Norton Grubb and Marvin Lazerson, *American Education and Industrialism: Documents in Vocational Education, 1870–1970* (New York: Teachers College Press, 1974).

10 On revisionist interpretations of vocational education, see Paul Violas, *The Training of the Urban Working Class: A History of Twentieth Century American Education* (Chicago: Rand McNally, 1978).

11 Harvey Kantor and David Tyack, eds., *Youth, Work, and Schooling: Historical Perspectives on Vocationalism in American Education* (Stanford: Stanford University Press, 1982); Harvey A. Kantor, *Learning to Earn: School, Work, and Vocational Reform in California, 1880–1930* (Madison: University of Wisconsin Press, 1988).

12 Jane Bernard Powers, *The "Girl Question" in Education: Vocational Education for Young Women in the Progressive Era* (London: Falmer, 1992); Miriam Cohen, *From Workshop to Office: Two Generations of Italian Women in New York City, 1900–1950* (Ithaca: Cornell University Press, 1993); John Rury, *Education and Women's Work: Female Schooling and the Division of Labor in Urban American, 1870–1930* (Albany: SUNY Press, 1991).

13 Herbert Kliebard, *Schooled to Work: Vocationalism and the American Curriculum* (New York: Teachers College Press, 1999).

14 See David Tyack, Robert Lowe, and Elisabeth Hansot, *Public Schools in Hard Times: The Great Depression and Recent Years* (Cambridge: Harvard University Press); Harvey Kantor, "Education, Social Reform, and the State: ESEA and Federal Education Policy in the 1960s," *American Journal of Education* 100 (November 1991): 47–83.

15 Among the many works on the history of race, class, and the welfare state that have informed this work are Richard Cloward and Frances Fox Piven, *The Politics of Turmoil: Poverty, Race, and the Urban Crisis* (New York: Vintage Books, 1975); Margaret Weir, Ann Shola Orloff, and Theda Skocpol, eds., *The Politics of Social Policy in the United States* (Princeton: Princeton University Press, 1988); Michael Brown, *Race, Money, and the American Welfare State* (Ithaca: Cornell University Press, 1999); Michael B. Katz, *The Price of Citizenship: Redefining the American Welfare State* (New York: Henry Holt, 2001); Jacob Hacker, *The Divided Welfare State: The Battle Over Public and Private Benefits in the United States* (Cambridge: Cambridge University Press, 2002); Jennifer Klein, *For All These Rights: Business, Labor, and the Shaping of America's Public-Private Welfare State* (Princeton: Princeton University Press, 2003); James Gilbert, *The Transformation of the Welfare State: The Silent Surrender of Public Responsbility* (Oxford: Oxford University Press, 2002).

16 The argument is developed in Kantor, "Education, Social Reform, and the State"; Harvey Kantor and Robert Lowe, "Class, Race and the Emergence of Federal Education Policy: From the New Deal to the Great Society," *Educational Researcher* 24 (May 1995); 4–11, 21; Harvey Kantor and Robert Lowe, "From New Deal to No Deal: No Child Left Behind and the Devolution of Responsibility for Equal Opportunity," *Harvard Educational Review* 76 (Winter 2006): 474–502.

17 Harvey Kantor and Robert Lowe, "Bureaucracy Left and Right," in Larry Cuban and Dorothy Shipps, eds., *Reconstructing the Common Good in Education: Coping With Intractable American Dilemmas* (Stanford: Stanford University Press, 2000), 130–47; Harvey Kantor and Robert Lowe, "Reflections on History and Quality Education," *Educational Researcher* 33 (June/July 2004): 6–10.

18 Harvey Kantor and Barbara Brenzel, "Urban Education and the 'Truly Disadvantaged': The Historical Roots of the Contemporary Crisis, 1945–1990" in Michael B. Katz, ed., *The "Underclass" Debate: Views From History* (Princeton: Princeton University Press, 1993), 366–402.

19 Ira Katznelson and Margaret Weir, *Schooling For All: Class, Race, and the Decline of the Democratic Ideal* (New York: Basic Books, 1985).

20 Walter Feinberg, Harvey Kantor, Michael Katz, and Paul Violas, *Revisionists Respond to Ravitch* (Washington, D.C.: National Academy of Education, 1980).

21 See note 17.

MICHAEL B. KATZ

AN ACCIDENTAL HISTORIAN

Serendipity in the Making of a Career[*]

In 1961, I intended to study for a doctorate in American intellectual history. A senior majoring in history and literature at Harvard, I wanted to go to Berkeley to work with Henry May. At Harvard, the two great intellectual influences on me had been Perry Miller and Oscar Handlin. Miller dominated American history and literature. His majestic work not only rescued the New England Puritans from the charge of anti-intellectual bigotry, it pointed toward a coherent intellectual tradition throughout American history. Through its passion and brilliance it also conveyed the excitement of ideas in history. For me, Miller shone most brightly not in his written work but in his course on American Romanticism, offered (for the only time, I believe) during my senior year and never adequately represented in his writing. Handlin also influenced me most through a course, his year-long survey of American social history, although *Boston's Immigrants* and *The Uprooted* were among the most important books I read as an undergraduate.[1] My senior thesis, a social analysis of Boston's reaction to the Mexican war, reflected Handlin's empirical approach more than Miller's outlook, but in history and literature circles, Miller clearly had greater glamour, and I wanted to study ideas.

The fellowship Berkeley offered me wasn't large enough to bring my family (wife, two children) across the continent and support us in California. Graduate school, at least for the time, appeared out of the question. The alternative was making money. From my experience as an encyclopedia salesman, my major form of financial aid, I knew I could sell. So, depressed, unshaven, I went one afternoon to Lamont Library to look through books of corporate job listings. Would I do better selling soap or advertising it?

My friend, Dan Fox, a graduate student in history, happened to come by the reading room. I told him my dilemma. He asked if I had heard about the Master of Arts in Teaching Program at the Harvard Graduate School of Education. The School of Education? Teaching? No, I had not heard of the program or ever thought of the School of Education as a possibility. Dan explained that the program allowed students to take half their courses in a discipline, was looking for graduates of Ivy League schools with good grades, and had a lot of money for financial support in the form of internships as well as fellowships. One could enroll, take a number of history courses, then enter a Ph.D. program in history the following year.

W. J. Urban, Leaders in the Historical Study of American Education, 179–192.
© *2011 Sense Publishers. All rights reserved.*

The idea seemed worth at least looking into. Even a school of education held more appeal than Procter and Gamble or J. Walter Thomson. Walking for the first time in my four years at Harvard into Lawrence Hall, then the home of the School of Education, I found the admissions office and asked for literature on the M.A.T. program. To my shock, a secretary showed me into the office of the assistant dean, Frank Duhay, who started to interview me. Why, he asked, did I want to go into high school teaching? Because the idea had not occurred to me more than an hour earlier, answering him required some invention. Uncomfortable with the plausible tale I had begun to spin, I stopped in the middle. I told him I wanted to go to graduate school and needed money. Could he help? He wanted to know my grades. I told him and he asked how much I needed.

Harvard's Graduate School of Education (HGSE) proved an extraordinary place. The M.A.T. year began with an intense summer program. Four of us with two master teachers were to teach the history of the world (defined as Europe since 1789) to Newton junior high school students in six weeks. We taught in the morning, criticized each other and planned the next day's lesson in the early afternoon, staggered back for classes at Harvard a few days a week, and prepared at night. In retrospect, the arrogance with which I started was appalling. Luckily, it didn't survive very long.

Teaching, I imagined, should be easy to learn because I knew a lot of history. How difficult could it be to tell kids about it? As it turned out, teaching, my critics drove home, was very hard, harder than anything I'd ever done, and the master teachers, high school teachers during the regular academic year, knew a lot more history than I did, and they

---

My Main Books (in chronological order)

The Irony of Early School Reform (Cambridge: Harvard University Press, 1968, reissued with new introduction, 2001).

Class, Bureaucracy and Schools (New York: Praeger, 1971 [1975]).

The People of Hamilton, Canada West (Cambridge: Harvard University Press, 1975).

The Social Origin of Early Industrial Capitalism [with Michael J. Doucet and Mark J. Stern], (Cambridge: Harvard University Press, 1982).

Poverty and Policy in American History (New York: Academic Press, 1983).

In the Shadow of the Poorhouse (New York: Basic Books, 1986, [1996]).

Reconstructing American Education (Cambridge: Harvard University Press, 1987).

The Undeserving Poor (New York: Pamtheon Books, 1989).

Improving Poor People (Princeton: Princeton University Press, 1995).

The Price of Citizenship (New York: Metropolitan Books, 2001 [2008]).

One Nation Divisble (With Mark J. Stern) (New York: Russell Sage Foundation, 2006).

knew, as well, how to convey it to adolescents. By the end of the summer, I'd been hooked. What career line I would follow wasn't clear, but it wouldn't be as a conventional historian.

The M.A.T. program left me confused about my career path. The easiest route would be to stay in graduate school and do something connected with education. But what? Fortunately, the award of a traveling fellowship to England allowed me to postpone the decision for a year. I had thought I would study how social studies was taught in British schools, but in the summer of 1962 one of the accidents that shape the process through which careers are formed intervened.

Nearing the completion of my internship teaching history in Winchester High school, I had to find a summer job to sustain my family in the months before we left for England. On the bulletin board in the School of Education was a notice that the Cambridge Neighborhood House was looking for a playschool director. For some reason, possibly because I always liked working with little children, the job intrigued me. Located in a dismal area of the city, not far from MIT, the 'Hood, which claimed to be the oldest settlement house in the United States, occupied the only large house remaining in the neighborhood. Aside from a secretary, its full-time permanent staff consisted of its director, Elsa Baldwin, who, in turn, was looked after by an enormous, forbidding mutt named Max. It was rumored that Elsa had an apartment somewhere; I always found her at the 'Hood. She was, I thought, the last link between the founders of the settlement movement and the present, as close as I ever would come to Jane Addams.

The neighborhood was not especially safe, although by the standards of today's inner cities it appears, in retrospect, comparatively tame. Most of the residents were white, with only a few African Americans scattered throughout the projects. The main trouble came from the knots of teenage men (*gang* is too formal a term) hanging around, unemployed, bored, and sullen. (In those days, because I smoked a large, J-shaped pipe, they nicknamed me "Sherlock.") As I parked my car in front of the 'Hood for the first time, they watched with a mixture of suspicion and curiosity as I pounded on the impenetrable metal door that always was locked after hours. In the course of the evening, as my interview with Elsa progressed, they would take my car for a joyride and bang it up. My relatively calm reaction, I think, more than my degrees or ideas, won me an instant job offer.

Elsa wanted to start a summer program that combined daytime activities for local children with evening activities for and home visiting with their parents. The program would be virtually free of charge. (This was before Operation Headstart, which her ideas anticipated.) She expected the director, who she clearly preferred not to have formal training in social work, to plan the program, hire and train the staff, recruit the children, teach, work with parents, and spend most weekdays and evenings at the 'Hood. For this she offered sixty dollars a week.

I wanted the job, but it seemed an indulgence. I had a family and needed money. Even as an undergraduate working part-time selling encyclopedias, I had averaged a good deal more than sixty dollars a week. Conflicted, I went for advice to my former senior tutor at Harvard, William R. Taylor. He told me to take the job. I'd spent a lot of time, he said, doing things I didn't like; I was entitled to this one.

The summer proved magical. Somehow I recruited a dedicated, talented, energetic staff. We drummed up enough children to fill an old yellow school bus, which defined our capacity. We alternated activities in the 'Hood, on its hot asphalt playground, with trips to playgrounds, amusement parks, places to swim or walk in the woods. We brought in physicians to examine the children, visited their parents, listened to their problems, and invited them to programs at the 'Hood. The children and their parents, mostly warm, open, and generous, became our friends.

We could do little, if anything, about their real problems, we all soon realized. This was the frustration of the job. They struggled to survive on inadequate welfare payments, lived in badly maintained public housing, sent their children to ineffective schools, lacked opportunities or training for jobs, could not afford medical or dental care, and were buffeted by social service, educational, and law enforcement bureaucracies over which they had no influence. This was a course not taught at Harvard: what it took to survive poverty. Whatever I did as a career, I knew, should be in some way relevant to the experience of my new friends at the 'Hood.

This transformative experience working with poor children and their parents in a settlement house altered my plans and, in important ways, my life. I now wanted to study relations between education and the working class, to focus on the links between cities, poverty, and children. So I changed the focus of my year in England, reading extensively in government reports, working class history, and the literature linking poverty and education. Maurice Kogan, then at the Ministry of Education, served as my tutor. I followed up readings by trying to interview authors and visited many different types of schools.

Books Which Have Influenced Me
Bernard Bailyn, *Education in the Forming of American Society* (Chapel Hill: University of North Carolina Press, 1960).
Harry Braverman, *Labor and Monopoly Capital* (New York: Monthly Review Press, 1975).
Daniel Calhoun, *The Intelligence of a People* (Princeton: Princeton University Press, 1973).
Lawrence Cremin, *The Transformation of the School* (New York: Knopf, 1961).
Mike Davis, *City of Quartz* (New York: Verso, 1990).
John Dewey, *Democracy and Education* (New York: Macmillan, 1916).
Oscar Handlin, *Boston's Immigrants* (Cambridge: Harvard University Press, 1941).
Jane Jacobs, *The Death and Life of Great American Cities* (1961).

I returned from England admitted to the doctoral program in HGSE but unable to decide what my focus there should be. One evening in early September, shortly before classes were to start, I walked home with the dean, Theodore Sizer, who was my adviser. Ted had a doctorate in history and had taught a seminar in the history of education that I had taken during my M.A.T. year. He said (I am paraphrasing), "Why don't you go into the history of education? You have the background; you know how to do historical research. History gives you great flexibility. People seem to like to hire historians as administrators." I took his advice.

Based in a school of education, my graduate training took a very different form than it would have had I been in the history department. I read less political and diplomatic history, for one thing. At the same time, an array of instructive experiences taught me about matters other than history: supervising student teachers; studying philosophy of education with Israel Scheffler and working as one of his assistants when he chaired a committee that wrote a comprehensive report on the future of HGSE[2]; serving on the editorial board of the *Harvard Educational Review* and as an assistant to Robert Dreeben when he was writing his important book, *On What Is Learned in School*, which has influenced the way I have thought about schools in the past well as the present[3]; and simply talking every day with the teaching fellows who shared office cubicles on the top floor of Longfellow Hall (where the School of Education had moved), only one of whom, as I recall, also was a historian.

In Daniel Calhoun I found a superb mentor who pushed me toward analytic social history and forced me to use a computer in historical analysis years before quantification had become more common among conventional historians. In the fall of 1963 Calhoun taught the only seminar in the history of education to a small band of students with a serious interest in the field. He announced that computers would become significant tools in historical research and all of us were to use a computer in our seminar papers. Because he was just learning computer-based analysis himself, however, he could not help us; we would have to learn on our own.

As someone who thought history was a way to avoid math, I was terrified and completely at sea. Searching rather aimlessly in the library stacks, I came across a 1911 book by Alexander James Inglis on the origins of high schools in Massachusetts.[4] In 1827, Massachusetts had passed a law that mandated high schools in towns above a certain size. In the next decades, only a portion of the eligible towns complied with the law---Inglis provided a useful list. I thought it would be interesting to examine the differences between the towns that did and did not establish high schools. Censuses would provide the data. The problem was how to carry out the analysis. As a teaching fellow, I had a small office on the top floor of Longfellow Hall. In the next office was Allan Ellis, another teaching fellow and a statistical expert. I begged for help, and he proved generous, instructing me step-by-step. I supplemented the statistical analysis with other primary sources and tried to work out the reasons high schools attracted support.

In the spring of 1964, a Master of Arts in Teaching student I was supervising, who lived in Beverly, Massachusetts, told me of an interesting discovery he had made. He was taking a course with David Riesman and working on a paper on the history of education in Beverly. In the town hall he had stumbled across a ledger that reported a vote to abolish the high school in 1860 and recorded the name and vote of every voter.

I hurried out to Beverly to check his report and inspect the amazing – and as far as I know unique – document he had found. What, I wanted to know, accounted for the divided opinion? The way to start, it seemed, was to see if any systematic differences separated high school supporters and opponents, whom I traced through manuscript census and tax assessment rolls.

By late spring 1964, I had determined to continue with the same line of research by writing a dissertation on the links between the origins of public education in Massachusetts and the state's urban-industrial transformation. Without a clear plan, I viewed the task as a series of probes and hoped that a coherent intellectual frame and interpretation would emerge from the empirical research.

In early winter 1965 I handed Ted Sizer and Dan Calhoun an absurdly long version consisting of several case studies linked together only by a common focus on time and place. They summoned me to Ted's office, where they told me that although each of the case studies was interesting, the dissertation had no theme or argument. I should decide what it said, rewrite, and then return.

For some months I read rather aimlessly, wandered around a lot, and worried. Sensing I was moving nowhere fast, Dan Calhoun sat me down one morning and handed me a list of items. This, he said, is what I think you are saying. With minor revisions and some rewording, he was right, and in a few weeks I rewrote the dissertation, which became *The Irony of Early School Reform*, published in 1968 and reissued with a new introduction in 2001. What Dan had showed me was that, without realizing it, I had written about the links between past and present, that I was using history to interpret contemporary educational reform.

With considerable hubris, I sent the unrevised thesis to Harvard University Press, which farmed it out to a reader. The reader's report proved both complimentary and useful – full of good suggestions for revision. I asked if the reader would be willing to meet. He turned out to be Stephan Thernstrom, and his comments helped direct me to see the needed additions and revisions.

Books Which Have Influenced Me (continued)

Jane Jacobs, *The Death and Life of Great American Cities* (New York: Random House,1961).

Ira Katznelson, *City Trenches* (Chicago: University of Chicago Press, 1981).

Peter Laslett, *The World We Have Lost* (London: Methuen, 1965).

Karl Mannheim, *Ideology and Utopia* (New York: Harcourt Brace and Company, 1936).

Perry Miller, *Errand into the Wilderness* (Cambridge: Belknap Press of Harvard University Press, 1956).

Stanislaw Ossowski, *Class Structure in the Social Consciousness* (New York: Free Press, 1963).

Mike Rose, *Possible Lives: The Promise of Public Education in America* (Boston: Houghton Mifflin,1995).

There is a special thrill to seeing a first book in print. And, for academics, first books serve specific purposes. One hopes they will lead to tenure and a solid place in the profession. Those were the limits of my aspirations. I did not expect the book to have a major impact on the field or a role in debates about current-day school reform. But in book publication timing often proves crucial. Appearing in 1968, with radical school reform very much in the air, *Irony* to my surprise found an audience beyond historians. The great lesson for me was that history really does matter, a lesson painfully reinforced several years later when the so-called "revisionists" came under attack.[5]

When I finished my dissertation in 1966, I thought of myself as a serious professional historian. Nonetheless, my ambivalence remained far from resolved, and when Dan Fox, now director of field operations for the Appalachian volunteers in Berea, Kentucky, invited me down to talk about a job, I went eagerly. For a number of reasons, I chose, in the end, an academic career, although not one completely in the mainstream. I went to a new institution, the Ontario Institute for Studies in Education, affiliated with the University of Toronto, then in its second year, where I could write and teach the history of education, help pioneer the study of modern social history in English-speaking Canada, and contribute to the building of an interdisciplinary social science setting for the study of education. In Toronto, I continued work on the history of urban education. *The Irony of Early School Reform* had examined the origins of urban public education using social structure as its primary lens. Now I decided to substitute organizations as the main lens. This led me to re-imagine the origins of public education as a competition among organizational forms and to analyze its subsequent institutionalization as a classic case of bureaucratization. (The essays exploring these perspectives appear in *Class, Bureaucracy, and Schools* and, in revised form, in *Reconstructing American Education*.)[6]

While working on urban education, I also began a long-term project reconstructing the population of a Canadian city (Hamilton, Ontario) during its early industrialization. The Canadian city project started as an attempt to remedy a weakness in my earlier work on education, the failure to provide an empirical foundation for the assertions about class and social structure on which a number of my interpretations had rested. With quantitative data from one city (later compared to Buffalo, New York), the project reconstructed the intricate relations among occupation, wealth, gender, age, ethnicity, property ownership, social mobility, family organization, and the life course during the emergence of industrial capitalism. (Its primary results appear in *The People of Hamilton, Canada West* and *The Social Organization of Early Industrial Capitalism*, written with my two close collaborators in the research, Michael Doucet and Mark Stern).[7] Nonetheless, trying to build a rigorous, engaged social history proved a task full of irony. With what always has seemed to me a shallow, mistaken disdain, many historians on the political Left rejected quantification as an inherently bourgeois, anti-humanistic tool diverting history from its proper focus on the lives and struggles of ordinary people or the political power that circumscribed their opportunities. In reality, quantification permitted historians to recover, describe, and interpret the lives of common folk, to write history from the bottom up with unprecedented detail, accuracy, and scope. It enabled them, as well, to describe the emergence of class structures and the powerful, persisting influence of class, gender, and race on social relations and opportunity structures. Quantitative data also rendered unmistakable the contextual, socially constructed aspects of family forms and phases in the life course, such as adolescence. My failure to help build wide and sturdy bridges between historians with similar intellectual projects but different methods remains one of my greatest professional disappointments, and one that has diminished the quality of scholarship in both camps.

By the mid-1970s, I began to think about new research directions. I wanted to combine my earlier interest in the history of institutions with the quantitative study of populations represented in the Canadian city project. The analysis of institutional demography seemed the answer. Histories of asylums, reformatories, and prisons for the most part concentrated on the ideas of reformers and administrators, on legislation, and on administrative practices. Almost no one had written about inmates: who they were, what led them to incarceration, what influence they exerted on institutions. Did the sources exist for a history of institutions from the bottom up? To answer the question, I spent a summer wandering around some of the archives in New York State and found more than enough material for a lifetime of work.

Selecting a sample of the available records, I secured funding from the National Institute for Mental Health for a project reconstructing institutional demography, using poorhouse registers, pauper surveys, and census material. As the work progressed, my focus broadened from demography to the issue of dependence in America's past, which historians had not treated adequately. How had dependence been defined? What were its sources? Why were some people unable to care for themselves? How had they been treated by public policy and private charity? Did similar assumptions guide ideas and policy for different categories of dependent people? In *Poverty and Policy in American History*, I explored answers to these questions.[8]

Books Which Have Influenced Me (continued)

Lillian Rubin, *Worlds of Pain* (New York: Basic Books, 1976).

Gareth Stedman-Jones, *Outcast London* (London: Oxford University Press, 1971).

Stephan Thernstrom, *Poverty and Progress* (Cambridge: Harvard University Press, 1964).

David Tyack and Elizabeth Hansot, *Learning Together* (New Haven: Yale University Press, 1990).

Research for the book had turned up wonderful primary sources illustrating ideas about poverty and welfare in the nineteenth century. With two colleagues, Susan Davis and Mark Stern, I proposed to Steve Fraser at Basic Books a little volume illustrating the continuity and parallels in ideas about these issues between past and present. Although he liked the idea, Steve said that authored books about a topic carry more impact than edited collections and suggested we write a social history of American welfare. Not realizing the size of the task, we agreed; the result became *In the Shadow of the Poorhouse* (for a variety of reasons, with me as the author).[9]

The ten years after the book's publication, 1986–1996, proved eventful ones in welfare state history, and I thought that *Shadow* needed updating. The publisher, Basic Books, agreed. I spent the first part of a summer systematically gathering information on events during the decade. Although I amassed a large pile of information, finding the threads to bind it together proved elusive. Frustrated, one afternoon in the mountains of Western Maine, where I spend summers, I went for a long bike ride. Suddenly, the theme hit me: what held the story together was the simultaneous influence of three forces driving change in the same direction. I called these dependence, devolution, and markets. With this framework, I was able to write the new chapter easily. When done, though, I was left with a mass of material that could not be included in the new edition and a coherent framework with which to encompass it. The only thing seemed to be to spin it off into a book by itself. The book that resulted, *The Price of Citizenship*, turned out to be much longer than either the publisher or I had anticipated.[10] It had the misfortune to appear just after 9/11, when the welfare state suddenly dropped off the map as a public issue. As with *Shadow*, the years following *The Price of Citizenship*'s publication proved significant for the American welfare state – not pushing aside the forces that had been driving its history but moving them at an accelerated rate along similar tracks, cementing even more solidly the distinction between first and second class citizenship in America. Once again, I wrote a new chapter encompassing recent history, this time starting with an account of how the response to Hurricane Katrina highlighted the weaknesses of the American welfare state. The updated edition appeared in November 2008, just before the full force of the economic crash and the election of Barack Obama, events that mark a new chapter in welfare state history and, perhaps, in the history of education as well.

One challenge that remains is linking the history of education to the history of the welfare state. I explored the connection in a lecture delivered and revised a number of times, steps on the way to an article, "Public Education as Welfare," published in *Dissent* magazine in the summer of 2010. Both histories should be incorporated into the broader history of the American state, itself subject to revision in exciting recent work in the inter-disciplinary field known as American Political Development (APD). Welfare historians have joined the APD conversation; with only a few exceptions, historians of education have not.[11]

Throughout the years of working on the first two books on poverty and welfare, I was waiting impatiently to turn to an extraordinary collection, case histories from the New York Charity Organization Society, which would be the basis for a detailed exploration of the experience of poverty in the late-nineteenth and early-twentieth centuries. In the course of talking with Andre Schiffrin and Sara Bershtel of Pantheon Books about the project, they described a new series on the politics of knowledge and invited me to write a short book for it on poverty. The opportunity seemed too intriguing to pass up. Again, underestimating the job, I agreed. Within a couple of years, though, I had become depressed about the project. The literature seemed stale; authors repackaged the same ideas over and over again. I could produce my own version, but it hardly seemed worth the effort. One day, suddenly, I realized that the tired, repetitive quality of the literature itself signified the problem that needed a history. The question became how to identify and account for the core ideas running throughout two centuries of comment on poverty and welfare, how to explain the inability to move thinking out of worn and unproductive grooves. With this realization, a new plan for the book that became *The Undeserving Poor* took shape.[12]

I planned to get back to the Charity Organization Society project.[13] I had been putting it off in the interests of work on more contemporary issues, which seemed to me to merit priority. But one day a letter arrived from the Russell Sage Foundation inviting about two dozen social scientists to bid on a project to write a book intended to locate the year 2000 census in the perspective of social and intellectual trends in the twentieth-century – and do so in a manner accessible to a non-specialist audience. The foundation offered generous support. The project intrigued me for a variety of reasons – the sheer intellectual challenge, the potential importance of the book, and, it must be said, the chance to do a quantitative project in the age of the microcomputer: no more raising money for computer time, lugging around boxes of cards or reels of tape, waiting for a computer center to spit out results. My friend and long time research collaborator, Mark Stern, was equally intrigued. Together, we wrote a proposal, which the foundation accepted – we were one of two teams funded to do essentially the same book. The story of the book is too long for this essay. It did prove daunting to an extent we had not anticipated. In ways it nearly killed us. But we did finish, and in the process of researching and writing *One Nation Divisible: What America Was and What It Is Becoming* learned an enormous amount about how inequality has worked in American history.[14]

Writing *One Nation Divisible* drove home for me the relative abandonment of political economy by historians. As Americans, we were experiencing the most severe increase in economic inequality in a century. Yet, historians were proving remarkably slow to interrogate its sources, impact, and implications. Historians of education were no different; they largely had abandoned the concern with inequality and bureaucracy that had revitalized the field in the late 1960s and 1970s.[15]

Working on *One Nation Divisible* forced me to look carefully at immigration, past and present. Coming to terms with massive, recent immigration clearly is a national project of immense importance and urgency and one that historians are just beginning to illuminate. Public discussions of immigration are notable more for their heat than light. Again, a hot, urgent issue pushed me in an unanticipated direction with the result that immigration has become a major focus of my current research and teaching.

Remaining strictly within the boundaries of the academy always has made me uneasy. Decades as an academic have not wholly tamed my activist streak. The trick has been to discover ways to use history to contribute to on-going debates about public issues. I have been fortunate to have found instances where this was possible. Five stand out. It would take me far over the word limit of this essay to discuss even one in detail. So I mention them briefly to illustrate the unexpected places to which a little historical hubris, or *chutzpa*, can lead and the variety of pathways through which opportunities open.

The first did not take me outside the university, but it did point me in a different, more policy-related direction. In the early 1980s, the position of director of Penn's Urban Studies program opened up. At the time, I was dividing my efforts between

the Graduate School of Education and the History Department. For some reason –
I'm still not sure exactly why – I was drawn to the position, which required
reviving a dying program with minimal resources and no institutional power. Its
basic design was sound and its goal was linking theory with practice. It was the
only Penn program at the time that offered an internship for academic credit. I
spent 13 years as the program's director or co-director; on leaving the position, I
founded a graduate certificate program in Urban Studies. Urban Studies is a
thriving, wonderful program, now led by Mark Stern and Elaine Simon. Teaching
in the program unexpectedly led to a deep academic engagement with cities that
has shaped much of my subsequent research and writing.

Another instance began unexpectedly when, late in 1992, Pennsylvania Governor
Robert Casey appointed me to a task force to suggest ways of reducing welfare
dependency. To my surprise, the politically and institutionally diverse members
agreed on a moderately progressive report. Everyone disliked welfare, albeit for
different reasons, and everyone could see the disincentives and perverse provisions
built into the current system, dysfunctional relics that needed to be stripped away
before any plan for a fundamental overhaul could be debated.

An earlier example is the Social Science Research Council's Committee on
the Urban Underclass. In 1987, the Rockefeller Foundation asked the SSRC to
consider creating a committee on the urban underclass (a term I have spent a
considerable amount of time attacking). SSRC committees usually combine a
program of scholarships and fellowships with setting a research agenda. One of the
committee's staff asked if I would attend an initial meeting of researchers to
discuss the foundation's request. At the time, I was thinking and writing a little
about the triangular relations among academics, foundations, and policy in
America. In the 1960s and 1970s, these relations, I knew, had influenced the War
on Poverty and Great Society, but their inner workings remained relatively
undocumented. I sensed in the SSRC committee a new round whose documentation
would leave a record of how big social science worked in the late twentieth-
century. I proposed to the SSRC staff that the new committee include from its
outset an archivist, who would gather and preserve documents and interview key
players as the work progressed. Staff, committee members, and the foundation all
approved, and I served as both ex-officio member and archivist during the
committee's five year existence. The archive of interviews and documents resides
in the Minnesota Social Welfare History Archives. The committee also gave me the
money and administrative support with which to edit a volume of commissioned
essays shining a historical perspective on urban poverty. The book that resulted,
The "Underclass Debate": The View From History, brought an unprecedented
concentration of historical research to bear on urban poverty and, in the process,
undermined some of the premises on which the SSRC committee had built its
work.[16]

A fourth example began in November 1989 when I was in Chicago for the first
major conference sponsored by the SSRC committee. Before going to bed one
night, I turned on the late television news in my room in the dingy Holiday Inn
near the lake on the city's south side. A local newscaster reported the inauguration

of elected councils of parents, community members, and teachers to govern each of the city's nearly six hundred schools. Their election had resulted from a new school-reform law implementing radical decentralization. How could this have happened? Why had those of us outside Chicago heard so little about it? Why had the national press paid it so little attention? As a historian of education, I realized immediately that Chicago had undertaken the swiftest, most dramatic structural reform of any urban school system in a century. I wanted to know many things about the reform's origins and to watch how it played out. When I returned to the Russell Sage Foundation in New York, my base for the year, I contacted two colleagues, Michelle Fine, a social psychologist deeply involved with educational reform in Philadelphia, and Elaine Simon, an urban anthropologist and specialist in qualitative evaluation of educational programs, who shared my excitement. To finance an exploration of Chicago school reform, we turned to the Spencer Foundation and its president, the late Lawrence Cremin, dean of American educational historians. Cremin speedily gave us an initial grant, which his successor, Patricia Graham, also a historian, renewed. For about six years we traveled back and forth to Chicago, interviewing representatives of all the constituencies concerned with the reform, gathering documents, and visiting schools. I learned an immense amount about school reform, Chicago, and the limits of historical research. Each person we interviewed told us a slightly different story about reform's origins. Were I writing the history of reform 50 or 100 years from now with the usual sources, I might well get it significantly wrong. I published one article on my own, "Chicago School Reform as History," as well as one with Fine and Simon, "Poking Around: Outsiders View Chicago School Reform."[17] We also wrote op-eds for the *Chicago Tribune* and memos for the reform community.

More recently, as I mentioned already, my book with Mark Stern for the Russell Sage Foundation awakened a deep interest in current-day immigration. With a group sponsored by the Penn Institute for Urban Research, I undertook to build a database of immigration to metropolitan Philadelphia, primarily from 1970 forward, and to analyze trends. A year or so after our work was well underway, a group of Philadelphia foundations engaged the Brookings Institution to prepare a report on immigration to metropolitan Philadelphia. Learning of our work, the foundations put us in touch with Brookings, and we decided to collaborate. The principal researcher from Brookings was Audrey Singer, its leading expert on immigration. Working for a client – the local foundations – which wanted to be kept informed of findings and to help shape the project - was a new experience for those of us inside the university, though not for Audrey. The collaboration proved a happy one, where, as with the other "real world" experiences, I learned a great deal about both the topic and the pleasures and frustrations of applied scholarship. Our report, *Recent Immigration to Philadelphia: Regional Change in a Re-Emerging Gateway,* was launched in November 2008 at a packed auditorium in the Philadelphia Free Library's Central Branch and discussed in the local media.[18] But for reasons that are not clear the foundations so far have not followed the report's major recommendations, which they have endorsed. There is another lesson here, although I am not sure exactly what it is.

What is next? There is work I want to do, or sponsor, on immigration. I have ideas for a few books and essays. Which ones will get done, and in what order, is hard to say, although I am well into one on cities, race, and inequality. I've reached age 71 with an intellectual agenda long enough for another career. So, what happens next is partly a matter of luck, but that's the way it has been since the day in 1961 when Dan Fox steered me to the admissions office at Harvard's Graduate School of Education. Most of that luck has been good. I was, after all, part of that fortunate generation too young for Korea and too old for Vietnam who came on the job market as higher education institutions were expanding. Demography may not be destiny, but being on its right side sure helps. Every time I've made plans for future work, every time it has seemed that I was on track moving in one direction, something has happened to derail the train, or, more accurately, to open a switch and send it off in another direction. I've gone along, mostly unresisting; the results often have been surprising, but never dull.

NOTES

*   For permission to adapt material from my books, *Improving Poor People: The Welfare State, The "Underclass"* and *Urban Schools as History* (Princeton: Princeton University Press, 1995) and *The Irony of Early School Reform: Educational Innovation in Mid-Nineteenth Century Massachusetts*, reissued with a new introduction (New York: Teachers College Press, 2001) I would like to thank the respective presses.

1   Oscar Handlin, *Boston's Immigrants, 1790–1865: A Study in Acculturation* (Cambridge: Harvard University Press, 1941 [reprinted several times]); Oscar Handlin, *The Uprooted* (New York: Grosset and Dunlap, 1951 [also, later editions; republished most recently by University of Pennsylvania Press]).

2   The committee's report was published as Harvard University. Committee on the Graduate Study of Education, *The Graduate Study of Education* (Cambridge: Distributed for the Graduate School of Education by Harvard University Press, 1965).

3   Robert Dreeben, *On What Is Learned in School* (Reading, MA: Addison-Wesley Publishing, 1968).

4   Alexander James Inglis, *Rise of the High School in Massachusetts* (New York: Teachers College, 1911).

5   For an account of the episode see my book, *Reconstructing American Education* (Cambridge: Harvard University Press, 1987), 144–152.

6   The piece on bureaucratization was first published in long form as a two-part article: "The Emergence of Bureaucracy in Urban Education: The Boston Case, 1875–1884, Part 1," *History of Education Quarterly* 8 (Summer 1968), and "The Emergence of Bureaucracy in Urban Education: The Boston Case, 1875–1884, Part 2," *History of Education Quarterly* 8 (Fall 1968).

7   Michael B. Katz, *The People of Hamilton, Canada West: Family and Class in a Mid-Nineteenth Century City* (Cambridge: Harvard University Press, 1975); Michael B. Katz, Michael J. Doucet, and Mark J. Stern, *The Social Organization of Early Industrial Capitalism* (Cambridge: Harvard University Press, 1982).

8   Michael B. Katz, *Poverty and Policy in American History* (New York: Academic Press, 1983).

9   Michael B. Katz, *In the Shadow of the Poorhouse: A Social History of Welfare in America* (New York: Basic Books, 1986; expanded 10th anniversary edition, 1996).

10 Michael B. Katz, *The Price of Citizenship: Redefining the American Welfare State* (New York: Metropolitan Books, 2001; expanded edition, University of Pennsylvania Press, 2008).

11 The major exception among historians of education is Patrick J. McGuinn, *No Child Left Behind and the Transformation of Federal Education Policy, 1965–2005* (Lawrence: University Press of Kansas, 2006).

12 Michael B. Katz, *The Undeserving Poor: From the War on Poverty to the War on Welfare* (New York: Pantheon, 1989).

13 I have written some essays based on the project. See "Improving Poor People," and "Devotion and Ambiguity in the Struggles of a Poor Mother and Her Family: New York City, 1918–1919," in Larry Cuban and Dorothy Shipps, eds., *Reconstructing the Common Good in Education: Coping with Intractable Dilemmas* (Stanford: Stanford University Press, 2000).

14 Michael B. Katz and Mark J. Stern, *One Nation Divisible: What America Was and What It Is Becoming* (New York: Russell Sage Foundation, 2006; paperback edition 2008).

15 Perhaps the most famous example of the 1960s and 1970s concern with educational inequality in history was Samuel Bowles and Herbert Gintis, *Schooling in Capitalism America: Education and the Contradictions of American Life* (New York: Basic Books, 1975).

16 Michael B. Katz, editor, *The "Underclass" Debate: Views from History* (Princeton: Princeton University Press, 2005).

17 Michael B. Katz, "Chicago School Reform as History," *Teachers College Record* 94,1 (Fall, 1992): 56–72; adapted as chapter 3 in Katz, *Improving Poor People*; Michael B. Katz, Michelle Fine, and Elaine Simon, "Poking Around: Outsiders View Chicago School Reform," *Teachers College Record* 99,1 (Fall 1997): 117–157.

18 Audrey Singer, Domenic Vitiello, Michael Katz, David Park, *Recent Immigration to Philadelphia: Regional Change in a Re-Emerging Gateway* (Metropolitan Policy Program, Brookings Institution, November 2008).

DAVID F. LABAREE

ADVENTURES IN SCHOLARSHIP

Instead of writing an autobiographical sketch for this volume, I thought it would be more useful to write about the process of scholarship, using my own case as a cautionary tale. The idea is to help emerging scholars in the field to think about how scholars develop a line of research across a career, both with the hope of disabusing them of misconceptions and showing them how scholarship can unfold as a scary but exhilarating adventure in intellectual development. The brief story I tell here has three interlocking themes: You need to study things that resonate with your own experience; you need to take risks and plan to make a lot of mistakes; and you need to rely on friends and colleagues to tell you when you're going wrong. Let me explore each of these points.

STUDY WHAT RESONATES WITH EXPERIENCE

First, a little about the nature of the issues I explore in my scholarship and then some thoughts about the source of my interest in these issues. My work focuses on the historical sociology of the American system of education and on the thick vein of irony that runs through it. This system has long presented itself as a model of equal opportunity and open accessibility, and there is a lot of evidence to support these claims. In comparison with Europe, this upward expansion of access to education came earlier, moved faster, and extended to more people. Today, virtually anyone can go to some form of postsecondary education in the U.S., and more than two-thirds do. But what students find when they enter the educational system at any level is that they are gaining equal access to a sharply unequal array of educational experiences. Why? Because the system balances open access with radical stratification. Everyone can go to high school, but quality of education varies radically across schools. Almost everyone can go to college, but the institutions that are most accessible (community colleges) provide the smallest boost to a student's life chances, whereas the ones that offer the surest entrée into the best jobs (major research universities) are highly selective. This extreme mixture of equality and inequality, of accessibility and stratification, is a striking and fascinating characteristic of American education, which I have explored in some form or another in all my work.

Another prominent irony in the story of American education is that this system, which was set up to instill learning, actually undercuts learning because of a strong tendency toward formalism. Educational consumers (students and their parents) quickly learn that the greatest rewards of the system go to those who attain its highest levels (measured by years of schooling, academic track, and institutional

W. J. Urban, Leaders in the Historical Study of American Education, 193–204.
© *2011 Sense Publishers. All rights reserved.*

prestige), where credentials are highly scarce and thus the most valuable. This vertically-skewed incentive structure strongly encourages consumers to game the system by seeking to accumulate the largest number of tokens of attainment – grades, credits, and degrees – in the most prestigious programs at the most selective schools. However, nothing in this reward structure encourages learning, since the payoff comes from the scarcity of the tokens and not the volume of knowledge accumulated in the process of acquiring these tokens. At best, learning is a side effect of this kind of credential-driven system. At worst, it is a casualty of the system, since the structure fosters consumerism among students, who naturally seek to gain the most credentials for the least investment in time and effort. Thus the logic of the used-car lot takes hold in the halls of learning.

In exploring these two issues of stratification and formalism, I tend to focus on one particular mechanism that helps explain both kinds of educational consequences, and that is the market. Education in the U.S., I argue, has increasingly become a commodity, which is offered and purchased through market processes in much the same way as other consumer goods. Educational institutions have to be sensitive to consumers, by providing the mix of educational products that the various sectors of the market demand. This promotes stratification in education, because consumers want educational credentials that will distinguish them from the pack in their pursuit of social advantage. It also promotes formalism, because markets operate based on the exchange value of a commodity (what it can be exchanged for) rather than its use value (what it can be used for). Educational consumerism preserves and increases social inequality, undermines knowledge acquisition, and promotes the dysfunctional overinvestment of public and private resources in an endless race for degrees of advantage. The result is that education has increasingly come to be seen primarily as a private good, whose benefits accrue only to the owner of the educational credential, rather than a public good, whose benefits are shared by all members of the community even if they don't have a degree or a child in school. In many ways, the aim of my work has been to figure out why the American vision of education over the years made this shift from public to private.

This is what my work has focused on in the last 30 years, but why focus on these issues? Why this obsessive interest in formalism, markets, stratification, and education as arbiter of status competition? Simple. These were the concerns I grew up with.

George Orwell once described his family's social location as the lower upper middle class, and this captures the situation of my own family. In *The Road to Wigan Pier*, his meditation on class relations in England, he talks about his family as being both culture rich and money poor.[1] Likewise for mine. Both of my grandfathers were ministers. On my father's side the string of clergy went back four generations in the U.S. On my mother's side, not only was her father a minister but so was her mother's father, who was in turn the heir to a long clerical lineage in Scotland. All of these ministers were Presbyterians, whose clergy has long had a distinctive history of being highly educated cultural leaders who were poor as church mice. The last is a bit of an exaggeration, but the point is that their prestige and authority came from learning and not from wealth. So they tended to value education and disdain grubbing for money. My father was an engineer who managed to support his family in a modest but comfortable middle-class lifestyle. He and my mother plowed all of their resources into the education of their three sons, sending all of them to a private high school in Philadelphia (Germantown Academy) and to private colleges (Lehigh, Drexel, Wooster, and Harvard). Both of my parents were educated at elite schools (Princeton and Wilson) – on ministerial scholarships – and they wanted to do the same for their own children.

What this meant is that we grew up taking great pride in our cultural heritage and educational accomplishments and adopting a condescending attitude to those who simply engaged in trade for a living. Coupled with this condescension was a distinct tinge of envy for the nice clothes, well decorated houses, new cars, and fancy trips that the families of our friends experienced. I thought of my family as a kind of frayed nobility, raising the flag of culture in a materialistic society while wearing hand-me-down clothes. From this background, it was only natural for me to study education as the central social institution, and to focus in particular on the way education had been corrupted by the consumerism and status-competition of a market society. In doing so I was merely entering the family business. Someone out there needed to stand up for substantive over formalistic learning and for the public good over the private good, while at the same time calling attention to the dangers of a social hierarchy based on material status. So I launched my scholarship from a platform of snobbish populism – a hankering for a lost world where position was grounded on the cultural authority of true learning and where mere credentialism could not hold sway.

EXPECT TO GET THINGS WRONG

Becoming a scholar is not easy under the best of circumstances, and we may make it even harder by trying to imbue emerging scholars with a dedication for getting things right.[2] In doctoral programs and tenure reviews, we stress the importance of rigorous research methods and study design, scrupulous attribution of ideas, methodical accumulation of data, and cautious validation of claims. Being careful to stand on firm ground methodologically in itself is not a bad thing for scholars, but trying to be right all the time can easily make us overly cautious, encouraging us to keep so close to our data and so far from controversy that we end up saying nothing that's really interesting. A close look at how scholars actually carry out their craft reveals that they generally thrive on frustration. Or at least that has been my experience. When I look back at my own work over the years, I find that the most consistent element is a tendency for getting it wrong. Time after time I have had to admit failure in the pursuit of my intended goal, abandon an idea that I had once warmly embraced, or backtrack to correct a major error. In the short run these missteps were disturbing, but in the long run they have proven fruitful.

Maybe I'm just rationalizing, but it seems that getting it wrong is an integral part of scholarship. For one thing, it's central to the process of writing. Ideas often sound good in our heads and resonate nicely in the classroom, but the real test is whether they work on paper.[3] Only there can we figure out the details of the argument, assess the quality of the logic, and weigh the salience of the evidence. And whenever we try to translate a promising idea into a written text, we inevitably encounter problems that weren't apparent when we were happily playing with the idea over lunch. This is part of what makes writing so scary and so exciting: It's a high wire act, in which failure threatens us with every step forward. Can we get past each of these apparently insuperable problems? We don't really know until we get to the end.

This means that if there's little risk in writing a paper there's also little potential reward. If all we're doing is putting a fully developed idea down on paper, then this isn't writing; it's transcribing. Scholarly writing is most productive when authors are learning from the process, and this happens only if the writing helps us figure out something we didn't really know (or only sensed), helps us solve an intellectual problem we weren't sure was solvable, or makes us turn a corner we didn't know was there. Learning is one of the main things that makes the actual process of writing (as opposed to the final published product) worthwhile for the writer. And if we aren't learning something from our own writing, then there's little reason to think that future readers will learn from it either. But these kinds of learning can only occur if a successful outcome for a paper is not obvious at the outset, which means that the possibility of failure is

---

Influential Works

David K. Cohen, "Teaching Practice: Plus Ça Change," in Philip W. Jackson, ed., *Contributing to Educational Change: Perspectives on Research and Practice*, (Berkeley, CA: McCutchan, 1988), 27–84.

Randall Collins, *The Credential Society: An Historical Sociology of Education and Stratification*. (New York: Academic Press, 1979).

Emile Durkheim, *The Evolution of Educational Thought: Lectures on the Formation and Development of Secondary Education in France* (Boston: Routledge and Kegan Paul, 1938 [1969]).

Michel D. Foucault, *Discipline and Punish: The Birth of the Prison*, trans. by Alan Sheridan (New York: Pantheon, 1977).

Albert O. Hirschman, *Exit, Voice, and Loyalty* (Cambridge: Harvard University Press, 1970).

Carl F. Kaestle, *Pillars of the Public: Common Schools and American Society, 1780–1860* (New York: Hill and Wang, 1983).

Michael B. Katz, *The Irony of Early School Reform: Educational Innovation in Mid-Nineteenth Century Massachusetts* (Cambridge: Harvard University Press, 1968).

Karl Marx, "The Fetishism of Commodities and the Secret Thereof," in *Capital*, vol. 1, (New York: International Publishers, 1867/1967), 71–83.

---

critically important to the pursuit of scholarship. Getting it wrong is also functional for scholarship because it can force us to give up a cherished idea in the face of the kinds of arguments and evidence that accumulate during the course of research. Like everyone else, scholars are prone to confirmation bias. We look for evidence to support the analysis we prefer and overlook evidence that supports other interpretations. So when we collide with something in our research or writing that deflects us from the path toward our preferred destination, we tend to experience this deflection as failure. However, although these experiences are not pleasant, they can be quite productive. Not only do they prompt us to learn things we don't want to know, they can also introduce arguments into the literature that people don't want to hear. A colleague at the University of Michigan, David Angus, had both of these benefits in mind when he used to pose the following challenge to every candidate for a faculty position in the School of Education: "Tell me about some point when your research forced you to give up an idea you really cared about."

I have experienced all of these forms of getting it wrong. Books never worked out the way they were supposed to, because of changes forced on me by the need to come up with remedies for ailing arguments. The analysis often turned in a direction that meant giving up something I wanted to keep and embracing something I preferred to avoid. And nothing ever stayed finished. Just when I thought I had a good analytical hammer and started using it to pound everything in sight, it would shatter into pieces and I would be forced to start over. This story of misdirection and misplaced intentions starts, as does every academic story, with a dissertation.

MARX GIVES WAY TO WEBER

My dissertation topic fell into my lap one day during the final course in my doctoral program in sociology at the University of Pennsylvania, when I mentioned to Michael Katz that I had done a brief study of Philadelphia's Central High School for an earlier class. He had a new grant for studying the history of education in Philadelphia and Central was the lead school. He needed someone to study the school, and I needed a topic, advisor, and funding; by happy accident, it all came together in 15 minutes. I had first become interested in education as an object of study as an undergraduate at Harvard in the late 1960s, where I majored in Students for a Democratic Society and minored in sociology. In my last year or two there, I worked on a Marxist analysis of Harvard as an institution of social privilege (is there a better case?), which whet my appetite for educational research.

For the dissertation, I wanted to apply the same kind of Marxist approach to Central High School, which seemed to beg for it. Founded in 1838, it was the first high school in the city and one of the first in the county, and it later developed into the elite academic high school for boys in the city. It looked like the Harvard of public high schools. I had a model for this kind of analysis, Katz's study of Beverly High School, in which he explained how this high school, shortly after its founding, came to be seen by many citizens as an institution that primarily served the upper classes, thus prompting the town meeting to abolish the school in 1861.[4] I was planning to do this kind of study about Central, and there seemed to be plenty of evidence to support such an interpretation, including its heavily upper-middle-class student body, its aristocratic reputation in the press, and its later history as the city's elite high school.

That was the intent, but my plan quickly ran into two big problems in the data I was gathering. First, a statistical analysis of student attainment and achievement at the school over its first 80 years showed a consistent pattern: only one-quarter of the students managed to graduate, which meant it was highly selective; but grades and not class determined who made it and who didn't, which meant it was – surprise – highly meritocratic. Attrition in modern high schools is strongly correlated with class, but this was not true in the early years at Central. Middle class students were more likely to enroll in the first place, but they were no more likely to succeed than working class students. The second problem was that the high school's role in the Philadelphia school system didn't fit the Marxist story of top-down control that I was trying to tell. In the first 50 years of the high school, there was a total absence of bureaucratic authority over the Philadelphia school system. The high school was an attractive good in the local educational market, offering elevated education in a grand building at a collegiate level (it granted bachelor's degrees) and at no cost. Grammar school students competed for access to this commodity by passing an entrance exam, and grammar school masters competed to get the most students into Central by teaching to the test. The power that the high school exerted over the system was considerable but informal, arising from consumer demand from below rather than bureaucratic dictate from above.

> **Influential Works, (continued)**
>
> John W. Meyer & Brian Rowan, "The Structure of Educational Organizations," in John W. Meyer & William R. Scott, eds., *Organizational Environments: Ritual and Rationality* (Beverly Hills, CA: Sage, 1983), 71–97.
>
> James Scott, *Seeing Like a State* (New Haven: Yale University Press, 1999).
>
> Martin Trow, "American Higher Education: Past, Present, and Future," *Educational Researcher* 17 (March, 1988): 13–23.
>
> Ralph Turner, "Sponsored and Contest Mobility and the School System," *American Sociological Review* 25 (1960): 855–67.
>
> Willard Waller, *The Sociology of Teaching* (New York: Wiley, 1932 [1965]).
>
> Max Weber, "Science as a Vocation," in H. H. Gerth & C. Wright Mills, *From Max Weber* (New York: Oxford University Press, 1958), 129–56.

Thus my plans to tell a story of class privilege and social control fell apart at the very outset of my dissertation; in its place, I found a story about markets and stratification: Marx gives way to Weber. The establishment of Central High School in the nation's second largest city created a desirable commodity with instant scarcity, and this consumer-based market power not only gave the high school control over the school system but also gave it enough autonomy to establish a working meritocracy. The high school promoted inequality: it served a largely middle class constituency and established an extreme form of educational stratification. But it imposed a tough meritocratic regime equally on the children of the middle class and working class, with both groups failing most of the time.

CALL ON YOUR FRIENDS FOR HELP

In the story I'm telling here, the bad news is that scholarship is a terrain that naturally lures you into repeatedly getting it wrong. The good news is that help is available if you look for it, which can turn scholarly wrong-headedness into a fruitful learning experience. Just ask your friends and colleagues. The things you most don't want to hear may be just the things that will save you from intellectual confusion and professional oblivion. Let me continue with the story, showing how colleagues repeatedly saved my bacon.

MARKETS GIVE GROUND TO POLITICS

Once I completed the dissertation, I gradually settled into being a Weberian, a process that took a while because of the disdain that Marxists hold for Weber.[5] I finally decided I had a good story to tell about markets and schools, even if it wasn't the one I had wanted to tell, so I used this story in rewriting the dissertation as a book. When I had what I thought was a final draft ready to send to the publisher, I showed it to my colleague at Michigan State, David Cohen, who had generously offered to give it a reading. His comments were extraordinarily helpful and quite devastating. In the book, he said, I was interpreting the evolution of the high school and the school system as a result of the impact of the market, but the story I was really telling was about an ongoing tension for control of schools between markets and politics.[6] The latter element was there in the text, but I had failed to recognize it and make it explicit in the analysis. In short, he explained to me the point of my own book; so I had to rewrite the entire manuscript in order to bring out this implicit argument.

Framing this case in the history of American education as a tension between politics and markets allowed me to tap into the larger pattern of tensions that always exist in a liberal democracy: the democratic urge to promote equality of power and access and outcomes, and the liberal urge to preserve individual liberty, promote free markets, and tolerate inequality. The story of Central High School spoke to both these elements. It showed a system that provided equal opportunity and unequal outcomes. Democratic politics pressed for expanding access to high school for all citizens, whereas markets pressed for restricting access to high school credentials through attrition and tracking. Central see-sawed back and forth between these poles, finally settling on the grand compromise that has come to characterize American education ever since: open access to a stratified school system. Using both politics and markets in the analysis also introduced me to the problem of formalism, since political goals for education (preparing competent citizens) value learning, whereas market goals (education for social advantage) value credentialing.

DISAGGREGATING MARKETS

The book came out in 1988 with the title, *The Making of an American High School.*[7] With politics and markets as my new hammer, everything looked like a nail. So I wrote a series of papers in which I applied the idea to a wide variety of educational institutions and reform efforts, including the evolution of high school teaching as work, the history of social promotion, the history of the community college, the rhetorics of educational reform, and the emergence of the education school.

Midway through this flurry of papers, however, I ran into another big problem. I sent a draft of my community college paper to David Hogan, a friend and former member of my dissertation committee at Penn, and his critique stopped me cold. He pointed out that I was using the idea of educational markets to refer to two things that were quite different, both in concept and in practice. One was the actions of educational consumers, the students who want education to provide the credentials they needed in order to get ahead; the other was the actions of educational providers, the taxpayers and employers who want education to produce the human capital that society needs in order to function. The consumer sought education's exchange value, providing selective benefits for the individual who owns the credential; the producer sought education's use value, providing collective benefits to everyone in society, even those not in school.

This forced me to reconstruct the argument from the ground up, abandoning the politics and markets angle and constructing in its place a tension among three goals that competed for primacy in shaping the history of American education. "Democratic equality" referred to the goal of using education to prepare capable citizens; "social efficiency" referred to the goal of using education to prepare productive workers; and "social mobility" referred to the goal of using education to enable individuals to get ahead in society. The first was a stand-in for educational politics, the second and third were a disaggregation of educational markets.

ABANDONING THE GOOD, THE BAD, AND THE UGLY

Once formulated, the idea of the three goals became a mainstay in my teaching, and for a while it framed everything I wrote. I finished the string of papers I mentioned earlier, energized by the analytical possibilities inherent in the new tool. But by the mid-1990s, I began to be afraid that its magic power would start to fade on me soon, as had happened with earlier enthusiasms like Marxism and politics-and-markets. Most ideas have a relatively short shelf life, as metaphors quickly reach their limits and big ideas start to shrink upon close examination. That doesn't mean these images and concepts are worthless, only that they are bounded, both conceptually and temporally. So scholars need to strike while the iron is hot. Michael Katz once made this point to me with the Delphic advice, "Write your first book first." In other words, if you have an idea worth injecting into the conversation, you should do so now, since it will eventually evolve into something else, leaving the first idea unexpressed. Since the evolution of an idea is never finished, holding off publication until the idea is done is a formula for never publishing.

So it seemed like the right time to put together a collection of my three-goals papers into a book, and I had to act quickly before they started to turn sour. With a contract for the book and a sabbatical providing time to put it together, I now had to face the problem of framing the opening chapter. In early 1996 I completed a draft and submitted it to *American Educational Research Journal*. The reviews knocked me back on my heels. They were supportive but highly critical. One in particular, which I later found out was written by Norton Grubb, forced me to rethink the entire scheme of competing goals. He pointed out something I had completely missed in my enthusiasm for the tool-of-the-moment. In practice my analytical scheme with three goals turned into a normative scheme with two: a Manichean vision of light and darkness, with Democratic Equality as the Good, and with Social Mobility and Social Efficiency as the Bad and the Ugly. This ideologically colored representation didn't hold up under close scrutiny. Grubb pointed out that social efficiency is not as ugly as I was suggesting. Like democratic equality and unlike social mobility, it promotes learning, since it has a stake in the skills of the workforce. Also, like democratic equality, it views education as a public good, whose benefits accrue to everyone and not just (as with social mobility) to the credential holder.

This trenchant critique forced me to start over, putting a different spin on the whole idea of competing goals, abandoning the binary vision of good and evil, reluctantly embracing the idea of balance, and removing the last vestige of my original bumper-sticker Marxism. As I reconstructed the argument, I put forward the idea that all three of these goals emerge naturally from the nature of a liberal democracy, and that all three are necessary.[8] There is no resolution to the tension among educational goals, just as there is no resolution to the problem of being both liberal and democratic. We need an educational system that makes capable citizens and productive workers while also enabling individuals to pursue their own aspirations. And we all act out our support for each of these goals according to which social role is most salient to us at the moment. As citizens, we want graduates who can vote intelligently; as taxpayers and employers, we want graduates who will increase economic productivity; and as parents, we want an educational system that offers our children social opportunity. The problem is the imbalance in the current mix of goals, as the growing primacy of social mobility over the other two goals privileges private over public interests, stratification over equality, and credentials over learning.

EXAMINING LIFE AT THE BOTTOM OF THE SYSTEM

With this reconstruction of the story, I was able to finish my second book, published in 1997, and get it out the door before any other major problems could threaten its viability.[9] One such problem was already coming into view. In comments on my *AERJ* goals paper, John Rury (the editor) pointed out that my argument relied on a status competition model of social organization – students fighting for scarce credentials in order to move up or stay up – that did not really apply to the lower levels of the system. Students in the lower tracks in high school and in the open-access realms of higher education (community colleges and regional state universities) lived in a different world from the one I was talking about. They were affected by the credentials race, but they weren't really in the race themselves. For them, the incentives to compete were minimal, the rewards remote, and the primary imperative was not success but survival.

Fortunately, however, there was one place at the bottom of the educational hierarchy I did know pretty well, and that was the poor beleaguered education school. From 1985 to 2003, while I was teaching in the College of Education at Michigan State University, I received a rich education in the subject. I had already started a book about ed schools, but it wasn't until the book was half completed that I realized it was forcing me to rethink my whole thesis about the educational status game. Here was an educational institution that was the antithesis of the Harvards and Central High Schools that I had been writing about thus far. Residing at the very bottom of the educational hierarchy, the ed school was disdained by academics, avoided by the best students, ignored by policymakers, and discounted by its own graduates. It was the perfect case to use in answering a question I had been avoiding: What happens to education when credentials carry no exchange value and the status game is already lost?

What I found is that life at the bottom has some advantages, but they are outweighed by disadvantages. On the positive side, the education school's low status frees it to focus efforts on learning rather than on credentials, on the use value rather than exchange value of education; in this sense, it is liberated from the race for credentials that consumes the more prestigious realms of higher education. On the negative side, however, the ed school's low status means that it has none of the autonomy that prestigious institutions (like Central High School) generate for themselves, which leaves it vulnerable to kibitzing from the outside. This institutional weakness also has made the ed school meekly responsive to its environment, so that over the years it obediently produced large numbers of teachers at low cost and with modest professional preparation, as requested.

When I had completed a draft of the book, I asked for comments from two colleagues at Michigan State, Lynn Fendler and Tom Bird, who promptly pointed out several big problems with the text. One had to do with the argument in the last few chapters, where I was trying to make two contradictory points: ed schools were weak in shaping schools but effective in promoting progressive ideology. The other problem had to do with the book's tone: as an insider taking a critical position about ed schools, I sounded like I was trying to enhance my own status at the expense of colleagues. Fortunately, they were able to show me a way out of both predicaments. On the first issue, they helped me see that ed schools were more committed to progressivism as a rhetorical stance than as a mode of educational practice. In our work as teacher educators, we have to prepare teachers to function within an educational system that is hostile to progressive practices. On the second issue, they suggested that I shift from the third person to the first person. By announcing clearly both my membership in the community under examination and my participation in the problems I was critiquing, I could change the tone from accusatory to confessional. With these important changes in place, *The Trouble with Ed Schools* was published in 2004.[10]

ENABLING LIMITATIONS

In this essay I have been telling a story about grounding research in an unlovely but fertile mindset, getting it wrong repeatedly, and then trying to fix it with the help of friends. However, I don't want to leave the impression that I think any of these fixes really resolved the problems. The story is more about filling potholes than about re-engineering the road. It's also about some fundamental limitations in my approach to the historical sociology of American education, which I have been unwilling and unable to fix since they lie at the core of my way of seeing things. Intellectual frameworks define, shape, and enable the work of scholars. Such frameworks can be helpful by allowing us to cut a slice through the data and reveal interesting patterns that are not apparent from other angles, but they can only do so if they maintain a sharp leading edge. As an analytical instrument, a razor works better than a baseball bat, and a beach ball doesn't work at all. The sharp edge, however, comes at a cost, since it necessarily narrows the analytical scope and commits a scholar to one slice through a problem at the expense of others. I'm all too aware of the limitations that arise from my own cut at things.

One problem is that I tend to write a history without actors. Taking a macro-sociological approach to history, I am drawn to explore general patterns and central tendencies in the school-society relationship rather than the peculiarities of individual cases. In the stories I tell, people don't act. Instead, social forces contend, social institutions evolve in response to social pressures, and collective outcomes ensue. My focus is on general processes and structures rather than on the variations within categories. What is largely missing from my account of American education is the radical diversity of traits and behaviors that characterizes educational actors and organizations. I plead guilty to these charges. However, my aim has been not to write a tightly textured history of the particular but to explore some of the broad socially structured patters that shape the main outlines of American educational life. My sense is that this kind of work serves a useful purpose—especially in a field such as education, whose dominant perspectives have been psychological and presentist rather than sociological and historical; and in a sub-field like history of education, which can be prone to the narrow monograph with little attention to the big picture; and in a country like the United States, which is highly individualistic in orientation and tends to discount the significance of the collective and the categorical.

Another characteristic of my work is that I tend to stretch arguments well beyond the supporting evidence. As anyone can see in reading my books, I am not in the business of building an edifice of data and planting a cautious empirical generalization on the roof. My first book masqueraded as a social history of an early high school, but it was actually an essay on the political and market forces shaping the evolution of American education in general—a big leap to make from historical data about a single, atypical school. Likewise my second book is a series of speculations about credentialing and consumerism that rests on a modest and eclectic empirical foundation. My third book involves minimal data on education in education schools and maximal rumination about the nature of "the education school." In short, validating claims has not been my strong suit. I think the field of educational research is sufficiently broad and rich that it can afford to have some scholars who focus on constructing credible empirical arguments about education and others who focus on exploring ways of thinking about the subject.

The moral of this story, therefore, may be that scholarship is less a monologue than a conversation. In education, as in other areas, our field is so expansive that we can't cover more than a small portion, and it's so complex that we can't even gain mastery over our own tiny piece of the terrain. But that's ok. As participants in the scholarly conversation, our responsibility is not to get things right but to keep things interesting, while we rely on discomfiting interactions with our data and with our colleagues to provide the correctives we need to make our scholarship more durable.

NOTES

1   George Orwell, *The Road to Wigan Pier* (New York: Harcourt, Brace, 1958).
2   I am grateful to Lynn Fendler and Tom Bird for comments on an earlier draft of this portion of the essay. As they have done before, they saved me from some embarrassing mistakes. I presented an earlier version of this analysis in a colloquium at the Stanford School of Education in 2002 and in the Division F Mentoring Seminar at the American Educational Research Association annual meeting in New Orleans later the same year. A later version was published as the introduction to *Education, Markets, and the Public Good: The Selected Works of David F. Labaree* (London: Routledge Falmer, 2007). Reprinted with the kind permission of Taylor and Francis.
3   That doesn't mean it's necessarily the best way to start developing an idea. For me, teaching has always served better as a medium for stimulating creative thought. It's a chance for me to engage with ideas from texts about a particular topic, develop a story about these ideas, and see how it sounds when I tell it in class and listen to student responses. The classroom has a wonderful mix of traits for these purposes: by forcing discipline and structure on the creative process while allowing space for improvisation and offering the chance to reconstruct everything the next time around. After my first book, most of my writing had its origins in this pedagogical process. But at a certain point I find that I have to test these ideas in print.
4   Michael B. Katz, *The Irony of Early School Reform: Educational Innovation in Mid-Nineteenth Century Massachusetts* (Cambridge: Harvard University Press, 1968).
5   Marx's message is rousing and it can fit on a bumper sticker: Workers of the world, unite! But Weber's message is more complicated, pessimistic, and off-putting: The iron cage of rationalization has come to dominate the structure of thought and social action, but we can't stop it or even escape from it.
6   He also pointed out, in passing, that my chapter on the attainment system at the high school – which incorporated 17 tables in the book (30 in the dissertation), and which took me two years to develop by collecting, coding, keying, and statistically analyzing data from 2,000 student records – was essentially one big footnote in support of the statement, "Central High School was meritocratic." Depressing but true.
7   David F. Labaree, *The Making of an American High School: The Credentials Market and the Central High School of Philadelphia, 1838–1939* (New Haven: Yale University Press, 1988).
8   David F. Labaree, "Public Goods, Private Goods: The American Struggle over Educational Goals," *American Educational Research Journal* 34:1 (Spring, 1998): 39–81.
9   David F. Labaree, *How to Succeed in School Without Really Learning: The Credentials Race in American Education* (New Haven, Yale University Press, 1997).
10 David F. Labaree, *The Trouble with Ed Schools* (New Haven: Yale University Press, 2004).

ELLEN CONDLIFFE LAGEMANN

A PROGRESSIVE EDUCATION

A Career in the History of Education

I have always been interested in history, and the history of education, defined in an expansive cultural sense, has enabled me to have a wonderfully varied, tremendously satisfying career. How did that happen? Where has it taken me? In the pages that follow, I shall try to explain, in the process extolling the pleasures of exploring a wide range of topics and professional roles.

EARLY EDUCATION

The story begins with my family and childhood. I was born in New York City and grew up in a small tight-knit community in Riverdale, NY. My father, who owned a travel business, was born in New Zealand and educated in England; my mother, a lifelong New Yorker, was the child of well-established, totally assimilated German Jews. My three brothers and I went to independent schools in New York and then to boarding schools in New England, in my case, to Concord Academy. In all the subtle ways families socialize, shape, and teach, my family brought me up to be self-conscious about matters of gender, committed to progressive social values, and oriented toward history as an integral part of one's daily experience.

My mother and closest aunt, both graduates of women's colleges, talked often of returning to school. Both eventually got master's degrees in social work. My great aunt Maddie, a proud graduate of Bryn Mawr, handed me a copy *The Feminine Mystique* as soon as it was published. My paternal grandmother gave me Beatrice Webb's biography and other books about women Fabians. My maternal grandmother died when I was six, but I always knew she had "done things," including work at the Henry Street Settlement House and participation in the NAACP. In these ways, among others, my female relatives made me aware that along with being a wife and mother, non-domestic accomplishments mattered.

My father loved music, theater, ballet, and travel. He seemed to know a lot about the history of all the places he visited. He kept a world map in our basement and showed us slides he took of sites he had visited. He was a wonderful storyteller. I especially remember the tales he spun about English monarchs and Maori gods.

My parents had attended progressive schools, my father a school called Abbotsholm in England and my mother the Lincoln School, which was part of Teachers College, Columbia University (TC), in New York City. Following in that

W. J. Urban, Leaders in the Historical Study of American Education, 205–216.

mold, they sent me initially to the Fieldston Lower School, where the curriculum was built around a social studies core. It was there that history really came alive for me. When we studied Native Americans (whom we called "Indians") or Vikings, we did so by learning some of their languages, by sewing clothes they might have worn, and cooking food of the kind they might have eaten. After school, I played with my papoose or practiced writing the Viking alphabet. If that made me a historian long before I formally joined the historians' guild, it also left me with an intuitive affinity for progressive educational theory.

Subsequently, after a brief stint at the Riverdale Country School, I went off to Concord Academy, then known as the most progressive of traditional New England girls' schools and the most traditional of the ones that were progressive. We lived in colonial houses and canoed to the bridge leading to the Concord battlefield. We spent weekends exploring the Alcott and Hawthorne homes. I even learned to smoke sitting on Ralph Waldo Emerson's grave. Living in the town of Concord, immersed in a culture that was so proud of its place in American history and literature, profoundly reinforced my interest in history. Beyond that, chapels talks given by Elizabeth Hall, our charismatic, powerful Headmistress, got me to thinking about my obligations in the world. Primed for this by my family, I became head of the current events club and the student charity organization, which raised money for a neighborhood house in the Roxbury neighborhood of Boston.

From Concord, I went off to Smith College in Northampton, MA. During my first two years, Smith seemed like just another girls' school. I was bored and almost dropped out. Then, toward the end of my sophomore year, I decided to "honor" in history. I wanted to write a senior thesis. That marked a significant turning point for me. From then on, I became seriously academic.

After many conversations with my advisor, I decided for my thesis to write a biography of Vida D. Scudder, a Christian Socialist, who had been a professor of English literature at Wellesley and one of the founders of the College Settlement Association. Her diaries were in the Sophia Smith Collection and I found working with original documents tremendously exciting. I also went to tea with Josephine Starr, a niece of Ellen Gates Starr, who had founded Hull House with Jane Addams. Along with Scudder, she had been a member of the Society of the Companions of the Holy Cross and gave me a copy of the prayer book the Society had used. Though I never could figure out how praying to the Holy Ghost could foment revolution, working on my thesis hooked me on the writing of history. I loved unraveling the mysteries of a life and mind, piecing together patterns of influence, and reading secondary literature that now, as context for my subject, came alive with new relevance.

Even though my world had come to revolve around Smith's wonderful Nielson Library, my friends and I were not indifferent to events happening around us. I contemplated, but did not go to Mississippi in the summer of 64. I met Marion Wright (not yet Edelman), who was then a student at Yale Law School. She came to Smith to recruit a small group of us to raise money for poor children in the Mississippi Delta. The fact that children there did not have shoes shocked me. Then, of course, there was also the War in Vietnam. I remember many late night discussions about how much we hated the war, while also feeling guilty because our brothers and male friends were being drafted and we were not being asked to serve.

BECOMING AN HISTORIAN OF EDUCATION

As my four years at Smith were coming to an end, I was torn between enrolling in a doctoral program in history and becoming a high school teacher. I chose teaching largely as a result of the experience I had had as a teaching intern at Phillips Exeter Academy in Exeter, NH. I taught, advised, and lived with summer school students recruited from inner-city neighborhoods. Each week, there had been an outside speaker brought to lecture to the interns; Jonathan Kozol was the one who most impressed me. The excitement I had found working with those students and meeting our speakers, combined with reading books like *Up the Down Staircase* by Bel Kaufman, set my direction.[1]

In search of a license, I enrolled in an MA program in social studies at TC. I did so for two reasons. I had read about student teaching placements at Benjamin Franklin High School in Harlem. The possibility of working there resonated with my idealism and interest in civil rights. In addition, while at Smith, I had found *The Transformation of the School* by Lawrence A. Cremin and had read it cover to cover, in one sitting. It encompassed everything I wanted to study.[2] I still have my original copy of that book, with three lines scribbled on the first page: "robber barons, the settlement movement, and progressive education." Since Cremin was a professor at TC, that also drew me there.

Neither of my original hopes for TC panned out. The supervisor of the internship program in which I was enrolled assigned me to Roslyn, NY, for my student teaching and would not consider my pleas to be sent to Harlem. He wanted me to work with Joseph Katz, a renowned master teacher. Joe had done his graduate work with Richard Hofstadter and was both a serious historian and an inspired social studies teacher. As soon as I met him, though I still wanted to go to Harlem, I signed on to work with him. Joe Katz was the best teacher I have ever known. Our daily conversations about history and how to teach it were inspiring. Watching him totally energize a classroom of kids was exhilarating. When he picked me from among a group of six interns to stay on as a regular teacher, I was thrilled. Even though Roslyn, a wealthy North Shore Long Island suburb, was worlds away from where I wanted to be, Joe taught me how difficult, important, and rewarding teaching can be. He and I remained very close friends until his death in early 2009.

My wish to study with Lawrence Cremin was also initially diverted. All the students in the social studies program were required to enroll in Cremin's large history of education class. He was just finishing the first volume of his trilogy, *American Education*, and announced to the class that he would be happy to meet with us during his office hours, but that we should see the teaching assistants about routine questions.[3] I found that off-putting and, as a result, spent the entire class sitting in the back row, passing notes with a friend. For a term paper, I handed in a re-written version of a paper I had originally written at Smith. That I would become a historian of education and Larry one of my closest friends and colleagues would have been hard to predict in the fall of 1967.

That spring, Columbia was swept up in student protests, triggered by plans to build a gym in Morningside Park. Because I was student teaching, I was less directly involved than I might otherwise have been, but those protests planted lots of questions in my mind. To whom did the Park and even the University belong? Were the black students right to insist that only blacks could occupy Hamilton Hall? Questions of power and politics that had previously seemed distant now became real and relevant. Putting those aside for now, however, I finished my MA and got on with my life.

Between June 1968 and January 1974, when I became a doctoral student in the history of education, I taught at Roslyn High School and in a street academy run by the Urban League on the Lower East Side of New York; I produced a talk show on WMCA Radio and helped run an ombudsman service named "Call for Action" that dealt with housing, health, and immigration problems; and I worked as the assistant to the director of the Bank Street School for Children. Kord Lagemann and I had also gotten married in 1969. Our brothers had been friends at the Fieldston School and we had always known each other, though distantly, until Kord finished his military service and became a law student at NYU. When our son, Nick, was born in November of 1972, I had planned to stay home fulltime, but I took one course and quickly realized that, having earlier chosen teaching over graduate school, I was now ready to turn back toward the academic aspirations I had begun to develop at Smith.

As a doctoral student at TC, I was lucky enough to work almost exclusively with Larry Cremin. I earned my tuition by serving as his teaching and research assistant. Except for one seminar I took with Douglas Sloan and another with Hope Jensen Leichter, I earned all the credits I needed in independent study with Cremin. I worked extremely hard, getting up at five am every morning and working till I fell asleep at night, and also sitting down at my desk whenever Nick took a nap or was happily occupied. But being able to devote all my time to writing research memoranda for the second volume of Cremin's *American Education*, reading for my doctoral exams, and working on my dissertation meant that I was able to complete my degree in only four and a half years.[4]

When I began my doctoral work I knew that I wanted to write a dissertation that would be continuous with my Smith thesis. My dissertation, *A Generation of Women: Education in the Lives of Progressive Reformers*, which also became my first book,[5] grew out of a section of my undergraduate thesis in which I compared Vida Scudder to Jane Addams and Lillian Wald. Larry tried to convince me go in a different direction. He wanted me to write about "museums as educators," but he quickly recognized that I would not be persuaded. I was intent on pursuing my curiosity about women and social reform and wanted to return to the writing of biographies.

Even though I was not willing to pursue the topic Larry preferred, I did adopt his concept of "educational biography." This made it possible to move beyond simplistic equations between education and formal institutions of schooling. During that early stage in the revival of women's history it seemed important to step outside templates built around the experience of men. In consequence, finding a way to derive significant educational patterns from the life experiences of actual women made sense.

TEACHERS COLLEGE, COLUMBIA UNIVERSITY, 1978–1994

When I finished my doctorate, there were no jobs for historians of education in the New York metropolitan region. My husband had finished law school and a federal clerkship and was doing well at a law firm in NYC, so I was not mobile. I was offered a teaching job in the education program at Yale, but the commute was too long and I did not want to begin my career in a small teacher education program. At the time, Larry Cremin was finishing the second volume of *American Education* and wanted me to continue helping him with the research and writing of that book. Without other good options, I agreed to do that for a year and soon thereafter joined the faculty at Teachers College, initially as an adjunct and then as a full member of the Department of Philosophy and the Social Sciences (and later also as a member of the Columbia University Department of History).

During those years, Larry and I met frequently to discuss his research and writing or mine and, since he had become President of Teachers College in 1974, we also often talked about College business. Increasingly during that year and the ones that followed, our conversations ranged over all sorts of topics – everything from how one should write about, say, the nineteenth century common-school movement, to whether TC should run a deficit or lay off faculty, to more personal matters concerning our friends, families, ambitions, hopes, and disappointments. Because we talked so often, about so many things, it is difficult to isolate exactly what I learned from Larry – though his influence on me was profound.

Larry revered the scholarship of education, conceived more as a social science than as a body of technical, professional knowledge, and he certainly passed that on to me. Watching him work his way toward and through many difficult decisions taught me a great deal about the importance of reflection. Larry was a person of definite tastes and exactingly high standards. But he was also generous in his approach to other people and extremely loyal. Much that he believed was embodied in simple, yet deeply wise statements like "they're doing the best they can" and "keep your eye on the long run." *"Scribere est agir"* [to write is to act] was one of his favorite phrases. I included it when I dedicated my most recent book, *An Elusive Science: The Troubling History of Education Research*, to him.[6] I think it aptly captures the belief he instilled in me that research and writing can embody and advance one's social convictions differently, but no less importantly than more direct action.

Before becoming President of TC in 1974, Larry had chaired the TC Department of Philosophy and the Social Sciences. I was the third woman to become a full member of "THE Department," as we called it, the other two having been Donna Shalala (who had resigned by the time I joined) and Maxine Greene, who remained a close, much beloved colleague for many years. There had been and were still a few other women who served as adjunct members, but "THE Department" was a very masculine place. Maxine and I often lamented that fact during our frequent conversations in the Ladies Room, but its predominantly masculine membership and tone were integral to its historic place at Teachers College.

Even though TC had always had women on its faculty, its leading intellectual figures had always been male. Many of them had been gathered together in earlier incarnations of our department, where, as historians, philosophers, economists, sociologists, and anthropologists, they had studied education "broadly conceived." Although that orientation has become most closely associated with Cremin's writing, it actually derived from perspectives developed by George Counts, John Childs, and others of "the Frontier Scholars" of the 1930s. The radicalism of the Depression era had been lost over the years, but there was a sense among us of standing for the belief that education policy and practice should be grounded in an understanding of culture and society.

Because the department was oriented toward general questions of politics and culture, it was a very congenial home for me. Following the rather prescient road map I had scribbled on the first page of *The Transformation of the School*, I had moved on from studying women and social reform to the history of philanthropy. If fitting in terms of long-established interests, this turn was nonetheless precipitated by coincidence and luck. Alan Pifer, then president of the Carnegie Corporation and the Carnegie Foundation for the Advancement of Teaching (CFAT), was looking for someone to write a 75th anniversary history of the CFAT. Having hoped to get Merle Curti, and then Larry Cremin, on Larry's suggestion, he settled for me. In consequence I wrote, first, *Private Power for the Public Good: A History of the Carnegie Foundation for the Advancement of Teaching*, and then a second book, which was published as *The Politics of Knowledge: Carnegie Corporation, Philanthropy, and Public Policy*.[7]

Writing those books turned out to be important in my professional development. I learned a lot about topics I had never explored before. For example, because the CFAT was primarily interested in advancing professional education, I read a great deal about the history and sociology of the professions – medicine, law, nursing, engineering, and education, central among them. At the time, the sociology of the professions was a lively topic with Marxists challenging the functionalists and important links being forged between sociologists and political scientists interested in the growth of "the state."

Beyond that, there was very little good critical writing about philanthropy, which made it both necessary and possible for me to choose whichever context I thought made sense as the interpretative background for the people and events I was investigating. In both cases, the Carnegie foundations had been engaged in many admirable activities – for example, creating TIAA-CREF and supporting the writing and publication of Gunnar Myrdal's *An American Dilemma*.[8] In both cases, too, there were examples of ill-considered activities or ones that had had unanticipated negative consequences. To give just one example, the *Flexner Report on Medical Education*, sponsored by the Carnegie Foundation, forced the closing of almost all medical colleges open to African Americans.[9]

As I wrote the two books on Carnegie philanthropy, I found I was much less interested in what the two foundations had done than in the implications of their capacity to exercise great influence with relatively little public accountability. Doing so was certainly legal, but was it legitimate in terms of democratic theory for one person to amass as much wealth and power as Andrew Carnegie had held? Should a private organization be allowed to take actions that have profound public consequences, as for example, the Carnegie Corporation did when it facilitated the establishment of the Educational Testing Service? More generally, could "private power" be in "the public interest"? Those questions led me to political philosophy. I especially liked Michael Waltzer's *Radical Principles*, Sheldon Wolin's *Politics and Vision*, Peter Bachrach's *The Theory of Democratic Elitism*, and, most of all, John Dewey's *Liberalism and Social Action* and *The Public and Its Problems*.

Around the time *The Politics of Knowledge* was published, I was asked to become editor of the *Teachers College Record*. I said yes because I was eager to try my hand at less formal scholarly writing. As editor, one could write an introductory column called "For the Record." Most of my predecessors had not done that on a regular basis, but I was eager to learn to write in less detached, more accessible and engaged ways. In consequence, for the next five years, I not only wrote quarterly columns on topics of current interest in education, I also had to read or at least scan most books and journals published in the area. Editing the *Record* enabled me to continue broadening my engagement in all sorts of current questions related to education.

My teaching had also taken me beyond the history of education. As soon as I joined the faculty, Larry asked me to co-teach his large lecture class in the history of education and thereafter we developed a sequel course that dealt with policy questions. In addition, from 1982–87, I was director of the Program for Entry into the Educating Professions (PEEP), a doctoral program for people who wanted to work in education outside of schools, creating programs for educational television stations, developing educational materials for museums, or offering training courses within large corporations.

As Director of PEEP, I taught core courses on organizational theory, the economics of non-profit organizations, and the sociology of culture. More important, since the PEEP program required internships, I worked with students placed in a wide variety of social and cultural agencies. As a result of a grant to work in Newark, New Jersey, I spent a good deal of time there and even helped found a still-operating independent school. I had never made it to Harlem, but the children we served in Newark were just as severely in need of effective schooling as those in northern Manhattan. Working for equal opportunity still mattered a great deal to me, but it did not impress my senior colleagues at TC. Not long before I was to come up for promotion to full professor, they made it clear that working in the field would not count for much in our department. Finishing the book I was working on would count a great deal more. Returning to 120th Street with more than a little reluctance, I began to question the detached orientation of the department of which, to this point, I had been such a proud member. What was it about TC or about education generally that had created such a gulf between theory and practice?

Spurred on by that question, I finished *The Politics of Knowledge*, got promoted, and began the work that would culminate later in *An Elusive Science*. Then, in September of 1990, Larry Cremin died suddenly of heart arrhythmia. His untimely death at the age of sixty-four was a staggering loss to people all over the country and especially to those of us at TC who were closest to him and his family. It was as if the lights had gone out on the 2nd floor of Main Hall, where his totally on-pitch whistling had so often filled the halls. All his teaching responsibilities fell to me. That made sense since we had taught so many classes together, but the load – seven classes and more doctoral dissertations than I can remember – was staggering. I was very glad when the year came to an end. I had long been slated to spend the 1991–92 academic year as a Fellow at the Center for Advanced Study in the Behavioral Sciences (CASBS) and was extremely grateful when it came time to head to the West.

At the Center, I began to read in the history of philosophy, psychology, and curriculum studies. I immersed myself in the histories of various "ed schools." The more I read, the more *elusive*, quite literally, writing a history of educational scholarship seemed. After all, education is neither a discipline, nor even a clearly bounded field. That made framing the book I was writing extremely difficult.

Despite that, I loved my year at the Center. Everything about it -- the sun, the view over the hills from my study, the conversations at lunch, during walks, and over wine, the birding and seal watching, and our many trips to restaurants in San Francisco – was restorative. I missed my family, though Kord and I managed to be on the same coast about every other week. But many of my "fellow fellows" were also living alone for the year and we often ate dinner together and went walking and biking during the weekends. Beyond that, the intellectual camaraderie was stimulating, fun, and thought provoking. I got to know how people in many different disciplines ask questions and marshall evidence. Our conversation made me think hard about my own sense of craft. I became aware that for me writing history was more instrumental and engaged and, in a sense, less strictly scholarly than it was for many of my peers. Writing history had helped me think about how women could make a difference in the world; it had helped me explore questions about power and politics. Now I hoped it could help me understand the historical circumstances that had nurtured such respect for theory and disinterest in practice among my TC departmental colleagues.

MOVING ON: NYU, SPENCER, HARVARD, AND BARD

I returned to TC in September 1992. As always, I had wonderful doctoral students, working on all sorts of interesting topics, and I was glad to be back with them. But in comparison to the intellectual excitement I had found at the Center, TC seemed like a dreary place. Having once expected to spend my entire career there, I now found myself intrigued by some of the job offers I received. The most appealing one came from NYU, where the dean of education, Ann Marcus, seemed especially smart and strategic. In September 1994, I therefore began taking the subway downtown rather than uptown.

NYU was, and is, a very lively place. I spent most of my time in the School of Education, though many of my students were in the History Department in Arts and Sciences. Ann Marcus allowed me to begin building an outstanding faculty in the history of education and then an entirely new department of Humanities and the Social Sciences. My hope was to capture the broad social and humanistic focus that had characterized the TC department, but to orient it more directly to serving students in more-practice oriented departments within the School of Education. At the same time, Ann allowed me the leave time I needed to finish *An Elusive Science*. Having always in the past had my next book project in mind as I finished the current one, I came to the end of that one without a concrete idea for a follow on book. Then fate intervened with opportunities to test my thinking about education as a field of scholarship, first, as President of the Spencer Foundation, and, then, as Dean of the Harvard Graduate School of Education.

When I arrived at Spencer, it was encumbered with too many long-term grant commitments and more staff than the work demanded. After addressing those matters, I was able to turn to the more interesting challenge of program. Dissatisfied with the grant proposals that had been coming in, the Board enthusiastically endorsed developing a more targeted approach to grant making. Our new vice president, Paul Goren, and I decided we should do something about the "usability" of education research. We wanted to begin supporting the translation of research findings into the texts, tests, and toys that practitioners could use and the charts, formulas, and theories of action that policy makers rely upon.

The work at Spencer was engrossing and I was not at all enticed when, in the beginning of my second year there, I began to get calls from Harvard about the deanship of the Graduate School of Education. Then, Larry Summers, the new president, got on my calendar to check other names. I had a good list for him. Within minutes, he interrupted my recommendations and asked why I did not want the job. As I gave him my reasons, he demolished each one and ended by saying: "If you really care about American education, you can do more from Harvard than Spencer." The extraordinary power of his mind was appealing as was his keen interest in education. What is more, the previous year, I had been asked to lead an ad hoc committee to provide advice about future directions for the Ed School – so I knew there was interest at Harvard in developing a new model. In the end, however, it was not the opportunities the Ed School offered so much as personal considerations that led me to accept the deanship. My husband had not been able to move to Chicago and we found the joys of a commuting marriage dubious, to say the least. Having vacillated for months, I finally accepted the Harvard job when he decided he could move to Cambridge.

At the Harvard Ed School, there was a strong group among my new senior colleagues who shared my enthusiasm for moving the school toward a more professional focus on matters of policy and practice. They took the lead in developing new core courses, built around the case method, and in building collaborations with other faculties. My job was to raise the necessary money, while also retiring an accumulated deficit of over $10 million dollars and addressing the school's longstanding structural debt.

Even though there was much at Harvard I enjoyed, it quickly became clear to me that being a dean there at that particular moment in its history was not something I wanted to do for very long. Despite the president's interest in education, people in Massachusetts Hall, the administrative center of Harvard, had little respect for the Ed School. I was constantly pressed to develop initiatives in which other faculties might take the lead. I was not eager to design projects that would increasingly marginalize the faculty I led, and that caused conflict. I could easily have turned the situation into a media circus. During those years, controversies stirred up by the President meant that all of us at Harvard were under the constant eye of the press. Unlike some of my faculty colleagues, however, who relished talking to reporters, I did not feel that publicity was in anyone's best interest. Ed Schools were and are fragile institutions. I think they need to be strengthened by becoming more focused and professionally oriented, but I do not believe, as many people do, that they should be eliminated. Airing grievances in public might have strengthened the hand of those who still agreed with former Harvard President Lowell that the Ed School was like a kitten that should be drowned. Toward the end of my third year as dean, I therefore simply announced that I was planning to resign at the end of the year in order to return to teaching and writing.

In truth, I did not then know what I wanted to do next. Having worked my way through the list I had compiled on the first page of *The Transformation of the School*, I still did not have a book in mind. Colleagues in the History Department in Arts and Sciences asked me to teach there, but doing so created tensions with the Ed School, even though there was not much interest there in the history of education. Since the early 1990s, my husband and I had spent a lot of time in Ghent, a town in Columbia County, NY, two hours north of New York City. In conversation with various friends, the possibility of moving there and teaching at Bard College emerged. Kord had always wanted to live in Ghent fulltime and I found great appeal in the prospect of leaving behind the territorial wars inevitable in a university where the faculty of each school is a distinct world unto itself. After a two-year visiting appointment, I therefore resigned from Harvard to join the faculty at Bard.

Harvard and Bard are about as different as two institutions of higher education can be. One is a large, sprawling multiversity, deeply divided among its various faculties and endowments; the other is a small liberal arts college, closely knit around shared democratic values. At Harvard, many faculty members regard teaching as something to be avoided whenever possible; at Bard, teaching is what we do. Harvard is deeply conservative in its avoidance of risk (except in the investment of its endowments); Bard is daring in pursuit of its mission. At Bard, I have found much more interesting ways to unite my longstanding interest in social problems, especially those related to civil rights, with my experience as a teacher and a historian of education than I could possibly have found at Harvard.

The Bard Prison Initiative (BPI) has been central in this. Soon after I arrived at Bard, I met Max Kenner, a charismatic, tremendously engaging young Bard alum, who has directed BPI for the last ten years. At the end of our first conversation, Max asked me if I would be willing to teach in BPI. Inspired by the challenge, I said yes, and soon thereafter found myself being escorted down the long concrete halls of a maximum security prison, into a classroom with a dozen men, most of them African American or Hispanic, all serving long sentences for serious, mostly violent crimes. Over the next ten weeks, I taught a class on educational history, using biographies as a medium to learn about both American history and education. The students were bright, curious, willing to work very hard, and eager to learn. Since then, I have spent most of my time teaching and advising students in the five prisons in which BPI gives AA or BA degrees and, now, leading a study of our students, their experience, and what is gained by offering them a rigorous liberal arts education. The work I am doing does not fit within the confines of the history of education as traditionally defined, but it is all about matters of power, politics, race, equity, education, and opportunity, which are all matters that have been central to my writings as a historian of education.

Having reached the point in this story where past meets present, I would like to close with one observation about the history of education as a field of scholarship. I admire the History of Education Society and the *History of Education Quarterly* and cherish being a member of such a lively community of scholars. At the same time, I have also gained immensely from association with scholars outside of our field, in other areas of education, other sub-fields of history, other social sciences, and across the humanities. Many of the boards and committees on which I have served have allowed me to work not only with a wide range of scholars, but also with lawyers, politicians, finance people, and journalists. Just as I believe it is important to translate the findings of our work into formats of use to practitioners and policy makers, so, too, do I believe it is important for historians of education to interact with people who do not belong to our guild. Doing so is challenging: it often takes one beyond one's comfort zone. But doing so is vital, if one believes the history of education can be of value to people thinking about current as well as past problems and opportunities. Defined as the study of culture and its transmission through time, the history of education can open for study an almost limitless range of topics and can help one move through many different positions in academe and outside. If, as has been the case for me, one's hope for one's professional life is to have it be centered in continuing learning, then a career in the history of education is a winning ticket. I am tremendously grateful for the doors it has opened for me.

NOTES

1   Bel Kaufman, *Up the Down Stair Case* (New York: Prentice Hall, 1964).
2   Lawrence A. Cremin, *The Transformation of the School* (New York: Knopf, 1961).
3   Lawrence A. Cremin, *American Education: The Colonial Experience, 1607–1783* (New York: Harper & Row, 1972).
4   Lawrence A. Cremin, *American Education: The National Experience, 1783–1896* (New York: Harper & Row, 1980).
5   Ellen Condliffe Lagemann, *A Generation of Women: Education in the Lives of Progressive Reformers* (Cambridge: Harvard University Press, 1979).

6 Ellen Condliffe Lagemann, *An Elusive Science: The Troubling History of Education Research* (Chicago: University of Chicago Press, 2000).

7 Ellen Condliffe Lagemann, *Private Power for the Public Good: A History of the Carnegie Foundation for the Advancement of Teaching* (Middletown, CT: Wesleyan University Press, 1983) and Ellen Condliffe Lagemann, *The Politics of Knowledge: The Carnegie Corporation, Philanthropy, and Public Policy* (Chicago: University of Chicago Press, 1989).

8 Gunnar Myrdal, *An American Dilemma: The Negro Problem and Modern Democracy* (New York: Harper & Row, 1944).

9 Abraham Flexner, *Medical Education in the United States and Canada*, Carnegie Foundation Bulletin #10, (1910).

JEFFREY E. MIREL

THREE TEACHERS

I grew up in Beachwood, Ohio one of the hastily built suburbs that proliferated around America's great industrial cities in the decades immediately following World War II. My life in suburban Cleveland was something of an American idyll filled with seemingly endless numbers of children, back yard swing sets, bikes with baseball gloves hanging from the handle bars, Saturday afternoon movies, and lots of television.

My educational world in those years did not revolve around school. My mother and father were the educators who mattered most. Both my parents were children of immigrants. My mother was only a high school graduate, but like my dad she had attended one of the finest high schools in Cleveland at a time when the city's public schools were among the best in the country. She graduated with a solid liberal arts education, and she was determined to pass as much of it as was possible on to me. At some early point in my life, she decided that I needed to spend at least part of my day learning something more valuable than the words to the theme song of the "Mickey Mouse Club." So, every afternoon in summers, she would make me lunch and, while we sat around a bright yellow Formica kitchen table, she would read to me (and eventually we would read together) the Classic Comics version of books she thought that I should know. Long before E. D. Hirsch, Jr. popularized the idea of cultural literacy,[1] my mother recognized the importance of familiarity with the works of such writers as James Fenimore Cooper, Charles Dickens, Alexander Dumas, Victor Hugo, Walter Scott, Jules Verne, and H.G. Wells. When I finally got around to reading the actual books and much later when I taught some of them to my middle school and junior high school students (e.g., *A Tale of Two Cities*, *The Time Machine*), I felt like I had arrived at a reunion with a wonderful group of old friends. My mother did something more important than teach me to read. She taught me to love to read and to appreciate great stories.

My father's influence was subtler. He read widely and often, coming home after work to a pile of books borrowed from the public library that he would quickly move through. At the age of 95, he is still at it. When I visited him several months after the 2008 election, he was deep into Barack Obama's *Dreams from My Father*. For the most part, he influenced me by example. He rarely talked about what he read and he seemed not to notice what I read, or so I thought. In my early adolescent years, I was totally consumed by science fiction. Once evening my father came into my bedroom with a copy of George Orwell's *1984* explaining that it was kind of like a science fiction novel but with more to offer than the junk I was reading. He added that if I liked it, I might try Aldous Huxley's *Brave New World* as well.

W. J. Urban, Leaders in the Historical Study of American Education, 217–229.
© *2011 Sense Publishers. All rights reserved.*

I read both books. They were a revelation. I realized that there was more going on in these novels than just engaging stories. Indeed, I recognized that their stories were largely vehicles for expressing a point of view on a wide range of political and social issues. This realization could not have come at a better time. John Kennedy's election, which I had followed closely, had made politics and history exciting and interesting. Given the nudge by my father, there was suddenly a whole new genre of novels to read and a world of non-fiction books about such topics as the Russian Revolution, World War II, and the Cold War. My reading was undisciplined and scattered, but in looking back, I'm surprised at the quality of at least some of the books I read including *The Communist Manifesto*, *Animal Farm*, C. Wright Mills's *Listen Yankee* on the Cuban revolution, Arthur Koestler's *Darkness at Noon*, and the powerful collection of anti-Communist essays in the book *The God that Failed*.

Without the educational foundation that my parents provided, I would never have been open to the ideas and the influence of the three teachers—Robert Dober, Bernard Mehl, and David Angus—who most directly and powerfully shaped my life and career.

***

The problem with all the reading was that I had no one to talk to about it. School was worthless in this regard. No teachers ever mentioned the books I was reading and no one seemed to care about the arguments these authors raised. By the time I got to senior high school I was a good student, but an indifferent one. Like most teenagers then and now, I believed that my high school existed mainly to provide a place where I could see my friends on a daily basis. But as far as learning things in class that engaged me intellectually my high school was pretty dismal until tenth grade. Then I met Bob Dober.

Without trying, Mr. Dober taught me that teaching could be a noble and exciting enterprise and that a great teacher can change your life. He was an English teacher from a working class, Polish family and was an amazingly gifted educator. I knew him by reputation only and his reputation was, to put it diplomatically, strange. He gave his students writing assignments on such topics as "Love is a turtle" or "Hate is a rhinoceros" (the latter I later discovered was "borrowed" from the absurdist playwright Eugène Ionesco). He sometimes lectured while standing on his desk. When he wasn't teaching you could often find him walking the halls with a group of students, a group of really smart students,

---

Favorites from My Work

Patriotic Pluralism: Americanization Education and European Immigrants (Cambridge: Harvard University Press, 2010).

The Failed Promise of the American High School, 1890-1995 [co-authored with David Angus] (New York: Teachers College Press, 1999).

The Rise and Fall of an Urban School System: Detroit, 1907-81 (Ann Arbor: University of Michigan Press, 1993 [second edition, 1999]).

arguing passionately about literature and philosophy. This was unusual to say the least.

One day, Dober showed up at a study hall that I was in, walked over to my desk and asked if I had some time to go for a walk. I had no idea that he knew who I was and could not fathom why he would want to talk to me. But anything was better than study hall, so somewhat nervously I said, "Sure." Most of what I did in study hall was write satirical stories making fun of teachers and students in the school, stories that I thought were hilarious, a judgment in which my friends generally concurred (unless, of course, I was writing about them). Occasionally, I tried my hand at something serious, and much to my surprise as we walked Dober took out of his pocket one of these missives, a short essay entitled "Life is Like a Mountain Road." He told me that one of my friends had given it to him and he liked it.

In retrospect, I have no idea why he liked it. It was embarrassing. In it I cleverly compared human life to the process of going up a mountain road defeating or eluding all sorts of trials and tribulations (youth), and then going down the mountain losing strength and battles (aging), and ending finally in the valley of DEATH (yes, it had all caps). For some reason, Dober thought this masterpiece showed promise and he asked me if I would like to join a special class that he was teaching at the same time as my study hall. There were only about ten other students in the class (all of whom were intellectually intimidating) and Dober was guiding them through a study of some of the great works of existentialism. I had never heard of existentialism, but again nervously I said, "Sure." With that my life changed.

For the rest of the semester, we read and discussed things like Sartre's "No Exit," and Camus's *The Stranger*, selections from Martin Buber's *I and Thou*, and when the French existentialist philosopher, Gabriel Marcel spoke at nearby John Carroll University, Dober arranged for all of us to go and hear him. It was my first visit to a college campus. With Bob Dober I finally met someone who cared passionately about books, ideas, and teaching and who could help me understand the kinds of things I had been reading and thinking about. While I rarely contributed to class discussions, I read and listened intensely.

The following year, I changed "tracks" and moved into Mr. Dober's honors English class. He taught a traditional English and American literature curriculum but taught it so unconventionally that it was stunning in its impact. Like Mr. Keating, the Robin Williams character in "Dead Poets Society," Dober had two qualities that contribute to great teaching. First, he had an actor's sense of the theatricality of great literature. He got us to see that great literature was great because of its engaging and powerful stories. He told stories well, read and explained poetry in ways that made it accessible to even the most un-poetic student, and he had an actor's gift for dialogue. When we were reading *Macbeth* he gave the most memorable presentation of the drunken gatekeeper scene that I have ever seen— funny, bawdy, and absolutely riveting.

Second, he shared John Dewey's vision that "the curriculum" is a vast storehouse of human knowledge, the responses to genuine, lasting human problems.[2] In a similar vein, great literature, for Dober, addressed universal questions: What is a good life? What is friendship? What is love? Do the ends ever justify the means? Why do people use and abuse others? Dober's genius was that he recognized that these were not abstract, academic questions for high school students. Rather, they are precisely the questions that teenagers think about *all the time* as they try to negotiate the shifting and often painful nature of relationships, which are at the core of teenage life.

Favorites from My Work (continued)

Book Chapters

"Educating Citizens: Social Problems Meet Progressive Education in Detroit, 1930-52" [co-authored with Anne-Lise Halvorsen] in Robert Rothman and Kenneth Wong, eds., *Clio at the Table: Using History to Inform and Improve Educational Policy* (New York: Peter Lang, 2009), 9–36.

"There Is Still a Long Road to Travel, and Success Is Far From Assured': Politics and School Reform in Detroit, 1994-2002" in J. Henig and W. Rich, eds., *Mayors in the Middle: Politics, Race, and Mayoral Control of Urban Schools* (Princeton: Princeton University Press, 2004), 120–58.

"Mathematics Enrollments and the Development of the American High School in the Twentieth Century' [co-authored with David Angus] in George Stanic and Jeremy Kilpatrick, eds., *A History of School Mathematics* (Reston, VA: National Council of Teachers of Mathematics, Inc., 2003), 441–89.

"A History of Urban Public Education in the Twentieth Century: The View from Detroit" in Diane Ravitch. ed., *Brookings Papers on Educational Policy 1999* (Washington, DC: Brookings Institution Press, 1999), 9–66.

While Dober rarely commented on current events or the dramatic changes that were gripping American society in the mid-1960s, he provided his students with the tools to judge and evaluate them. William Blake was one of his favorite poets, and by the time I graduated from Beachwood High School in 1966, it was increasingly clear to me that the "dark Satanic mills" that Blake described in nineteenth century London, were only a literary stone's throw from the factories in the Flats along Cleveland's Cuyahoga River which were spewing out the same problems of materialism, greed, exploitation, and inequality that this country was wrestling with at this time.

In all, Bob Dober did for me what Jack McFarland did for Mike Rose. In Rose's wonderfully apt phrase Dober gave me the knowledge and the confidence necessary for "entering the conversation," the rich and unending conversation about important questions in literature, philosophy, and eventually history, where I would stake my claim.[3]

***

In 1968, I came to the Ohio State University (OSU) after two forgettable years at Northwestern University. I was an English major particularly enamored with two groups of writers, the English romantic poets of the early nineteenth century—Byron, Keats and Shelley—and American novelists from the 1920s and 1930s—especially Hemingway and Fitzgerald. I was attracted to these writers in part because their works challenged and critiqued the artistic, political, and social order of their eras, much as I saw my generation doing in our opposition to the war in Viet Nam, and in our support of the Civil Rights movement, and later the women's movement.

Unlike Berkeley, Columbia, or Michigan, OSU was *not* a hotbed of student radicalism in these years (although massive student protests against the shootings at Kent State completely shut down the university in May 1970). Despite being on the periphery of the national debates, the same kinds of arguments about how to facilitate political and social change that were defining university life elsewhere were increasingly becoming part of many humanities and social science classes at OSU. Perhaps more importantly, these arguments shaped the free-wheeling conversations that many of us engaged in night after night. In my three years in Columbus, no one became more central to these arguments than the second profoundly important teacher in my life, Bernie Mehl.

As other contributors to this volume have noted, serendipity often seems to play as big a role in shaping people's lives as design. My first encounter with Bernie was wholly serendipitous. A high school friend came in from Wisconsin and mentioned that his older sister had taken an amazing course from an education professor at OSU and he'd like to see the guy teach. It turned out that Bernie had an evening class that day and off we went. The scene we came upon was, on the one hand, quite typical, a large lecture hall with the professor up on a dais teaching well over a hundred students. But that was all that was typical. Bernie *was* lecturing but in a way that I had never seen before or since. He had no notes, no books to refer to or quote from, and he never filled the blackboard with names or dates or important ideas that were going to be on the test. His lectures depended on nothing more than his charisma, astonishing range of knowledge, breathtaking intellectual agility, and, as importantly, his comedic talents that easily gave Lenny Bruce a run for his money. Moreover, unlike other lecture classes his were highly interactive, with students frequently challenging and questioning him, which in turn usually led to long and at times heated exchanges about the great issues of the day—race relations, the war in Viet Nam, the youth counter-culture. I was hooked. I attended the class for the rest of the quarter without registering and then signed up for it in the next term.

I quickly realized "taking" the class once did not insure that I would know what it was about the second time. There was a syllabus, which described the class as an exploration of the Social Foundations of Education, but the relationship between that document and what happened on any given day was tenuous at best. In an approach to teaching that was more akin to jazz than playing music with a score, Bernie came to class with a theme in mind, which he would develop and riff on as his lecture progressed. The themes were as eclectic as the books he required, which included at one time or another, *Catcher in the Rye*, *Huckleberry Finn*, *The Education of Henry Adams*, *The Autobiography of Malcolm X*, Edgar Z. Friedenberg's *The Vanishing Adolescent*, Paul Goodman's *Growing Up Absurd*, B. F. Skinner's *Walden II*, and Jaques Ellul's *The Technological Society*.

Perhaps the most notable quality of his lectures was how provocative they were. Bernie used seemingly outrageous statements to get students to interact with him.

He was trained as an historian of education at the University of Illinois and he studied with people committed to the progressive belief that teachers had to make their subjects relevant for their students. He was amazingly adept at doing this with history, but in ways that pushed the edge of the "relevance" envelope.

For example, my colleague Bob Bain (who I met at Ohio State because of Bernie and who has been my closest friend ever since), recalls how Bernie began one of his classes with the pronouncement that hippies were the Puritans of the late twentieth century. The outcry from the students, most of whom were sporting long hair, tie-dyed t-shirts, granny glasses and beads, was immediate and angry.

Favorites from My Work (continued)

Articles in Refereed Journals

"Camping at the Great Divide: What History Teachers Need to Know," (with Robert Bain), *Journal of Teacher Education* 57 (May/June 2006): 212–19.

"Old Educational Ideas, New American Schools: Progressivism and the Rhetoric of Educational Revolution," *Paedagogica Historica* 39 (August, 2003): 477–97.

"Civic Education and Changing Definitions of American Identity, 1900-1950," *Educational Review* 54 (June 2002): 143–52.

While many (probably most) knew little about Puritanism – and even more could care less – the claim that they were allied to anything "puritanical" was a clear attack on their sense of self and their stance in the world. As soon as they reacted, Bernie had them exactly where he wanted them. In the course of responding to their outcry, he worked his way through the history of Puritanism, its role in shaping American ideas about education and society, and its doctrine of the elect and damned. He then returned—like the brilliant jazz artist that he was – to the opening riff showing how the overwhelmingly middle class members of the counter culture shared similar beliefs about good and evil, and a willingness to accept the benefits of their own half-way covenant with the American cultural mainstream, which they criticized from the safety of election.

This approach to teaching enabled all of us—from undergraduates to Ph.D. students—to engage in the dialogue and assess the critiques and counter-critiques. As a consequence, these ideas and arguments frequently continued outside of class as we rehashed the issues being debated, and turned to learn more about the references (ranging from Montaigne to Big Mama Thornton) that Bernie made to further his case. I came to realize that these dialogues were becoming a key element in my intellectual growth. It did not matter whether the dialogues were external in lectures, discussions, or arguments with friends or internal as I wrestled with contending ideas on my own, what Bernie taught me was that academic debates when looked at in the right perspective were anything but academic. Like Bob Dober before him, Bernie made great ideas real and meaningful for the here and now.

Because of what I experienced in his classes, I decided not to pursue a master's degree in English, but instead asked Bernie if he would be my advisor for an MA in Education. He agreed and soon after I began hanging around with the students who met almost daily in his office and often at his home in the evening where the conversations and arguments seemed to go on forever. I am not sure whether I learned more in these unstructured and unpredictable get-togethers than I did from his equally unpredictable classes. His office – decorated with dozens of photographs that Bernie had shot, piles of books, and an over-worked coffee machine—was a vibrant salon that attracted some of the most interesting, thoughtful and thought-provoking people on the OSU campus. Discussions of ideas, politics and culture were on-going but were always mixed with humor, and occasionally spiked by vociferous arguments. Initially I just listened but Bernie never allowed people to just sit around trying to absorb what was going on by osmosis. He was always asking questions and to survive in that environment you had to quickly get up to speed not just on educational history and philosophy, but also on such novelists as Ken Kesey, Philip Roth, or Isaac Bashevis Singer, such social commentators as Lenny Bruce, great photographers, jazz musicians and Billie Holiday, as well as places to shop for good ethnic food. At the core of this education was a new understanding of the power of history to deepen our understanding of the context within which we live and act. Few periods in my life were more intellectually and culturally rich than the two years that I spent as an undergraduate and then master's student working with Bernie and immersed in the community that surrounded him. It ultimately led to my career as a historian of education.

Was there a clear Mehl school of thought that his students came away with? I'm not sure. But at least one theme reoccurred often enough in his lectures and conversations to be noteworthy. Bernie was more of a rebel than a revolutionary with a stance toward teaching, learning, and doing that was more Erasmus than Luther, Camus than Sartre. I am certain that many people at OSU in these years saw Bernie as a dangerous radical—his struggles with his colleagues and the administration also became part of our understanding of the academy. But what he taught and what he influenced his students to internalize belied radicalism in a fundamental way. He appreciated the value of long-standing institutions and he recognized that their destruction was a process fraught with peril. This is not to say that he believed all institutions were equally worthy of protection—he routinely argued that slavery and Jim Crow were so odious they had to be destroyed. But in regards to other institutions, most notably public schools, he deplored people such as Ivan Illich who garnered great attention in this era with his call for "deschooling society." Similarly, Bernie rejected the burgeoning revisionist trend in educational history seeing it as an attack on the moral and political foundations of a flawed but nevertheless valuable institution. I have no doubt that he would have opposed vouchers and been quite skeptical of charter schools as well.

Bernie also transformed my understanding of the role that teachers and scholars can and must play from *within* the institutions in which we work. He demanded that we recognize our responsibility to try and live these ideals themselves. These points have become key elements in how I approach my teaching and my research. I do not know whether other historians of education who studied with Bernie—Bob Bain, Wayne J. Urban, Joe Watras, and Alan Wieder—see these as important aspects of Bernie's intellectual legacy. We should probably sit down over drinks and hash that out. But I do believe that this was, in large part, how David Angus, another of Bernie's students, thought of him.

***

Favorites from Other People's Work

James Anderson, *The Education of Blacks in the South, 1860-1935* (Chapel Hill: University of North Carolina Press, 1988).

Carl Kaestle, *Pillars of the Republic: Common Schools and American Society, 1780-1860* (New York: Hill and Wang, 1983).

Herbert Kliebard, *The Struggle for the American Curriculum, 1893-1958* (New York: Routledge, 1995).

Edward A. Krug, *The Shaping of the American High School*, Vols. 1 & 2 (Madison: University of Wisconsin Press, 1969, 1972).

David F. Labaree, *The Making of an American High School: The Credentials Market and the Central High School of Philadelphia, 1838-1939* (New Haven: Yale University Press, 1988).

Meeting, studying, and working with David did not occur until about eight years after I left Columbus. During that time I returned to my love of literature, expanded my interests to history, and learned how to teach. While doing my master's work at OSU, I took all the required course work including student teaching to get certified in English on the secondary level. In the fall of 1971, I began my career as a middle school/junior high school teacher. My first job was in a large suburban middle school in upstate New York, which had adopted the educational fad of the moment and had most of its interior walls torn down to encourage innovative teaching (it didn't). I moved and then taught at an orthodox Jewish day school located in the Little Havana section of Miami, Florida; and finally, in 1975, I came back to Cleveland to teach at Roxboro Junior High School in Cleveland Heights. I got the Roxboro job in part because I had added history to my Ohio teaching certificate (having taken a series of American history courses in the evenings and summers at Florida International University), thus enabling me to cover eighth grade American history classes as well as various English classes for ninth graders.

Roxboro was a marvelous junior high school. It was one of the most racially and economically diverse schools in Cuyahoga County; the students were interested, even enthusiastic about learning; and, I worked in a program that allowed faculty enormous latitude in what they taught. Roxboro enabled me to draw on all the things that I had learned from Bob Dober and Bernie Mehl and to try them out in my own classroom. With them as my models, I sought to bring my students "into the conversation," to introduce them to and get them excited about as wide an array of questions, ideas, and authors as possible. In doing this, what surprised me most was how increasingly important history was becoming to all of my teaching. I actually enjoyed teaching American history to eighth graders, and I found when teaching literature to my ninth graders that I needed to present a great deal of historical context before we plunged into the texts (e.g., Richard Wright's *Black Boy*, Eli Wiesel's *Night*, and Jeanne Wakatsuki Houston's *Farewell to Manzanar*).

I also continued my practice of taking history courses in evenings and summers, first at Cleveland State and then at Case Western Reserve University (CWRU).

In 1977, I applied to and was accepted into the Ph.D. program in American history at CWRU. I figured I could do the degree part time while I taught at Roxboro. Here, once again, serendipity entered the picture. On a summer evening not long after I had heard from CWRU, I was hanging out with Bob Bain (who then was teaching history at Beachwood High School and who I talked with almost every night about what we were doing in our classrooms) when Alan Wieder, a new Ph.D. student of Bernie's, stopped by. We talked late into the night and at one point I mentioned the CWRU program. Alan suggested that before I got too committed to CWRU, I should call David Angus at the University of Michigan (UM) and talk with him about the possibility of doing a Ph.D. there in the history of education.

Even before I called David, I recognized that UM had some clear advantages over CWRU, especially the prospect of paying for my Ph.D., either through scholarships or teaching assistantships, neither of which were likely at CWRU. Even as my wife, Barbara, and I tried to maintain our counter-cultural disdain for materialism, with two toddlers and another child on the way, financial support was a powerful incentive to go to UM. With that in mind, I called David and made arrangements to meet him in Ann Arbor several weeks later.

By the time I left his office, David had convinced me to apply and suggested that we all should come up for the Summer session in 1978 to see if this was really what I wanted to do. We pretty much followed that plan. I took my first history of education course with Dave in that summer session, loved it, and knew that this was what I wanted to study. At the end of the summer, Barbara and I and our three kids went back to Cleveland for one more school year and in June 1979 we packed our things and moved to Michigan. Barbara also had applied to graduate school and began her work a year after we moved. In looking back on our five years in Ann Arbor with both of us in graduate school and three little kids at home we now recognize that we were totally insane. But it worked, in no small part because of David who made us a part of his family and who became an integral part of ours.

David was the best of all possible mentors. I started working with him when the debate between revisionist historians and their critics was at high tide. Perhaps because we both had studied with Bernie and found Bernie's vision of public schools compelling, we gravitated towards the "liberal" rather than revisionist position. Both of us, for example, were great admirers of Diane Ravitch's historical scholarship and critical stance in the field. Dave loved nothing better than a good scholarly dust-up and he brought to this controversy insight, passion, and energy. But the most important aspect of his approach to history of education generally and the revisionist/anti-revisionist controversy specifically was his skepticism. He was first and foremost driven by data rather than theory and never by ideology. The question he routinely asked people giving job talks at UM was whether they could provide an example of something in their research that had forced them to scrap one of their basic theoretical assumptions. People who responded "no" to that question more often than not saw flashes of his legendary temper. This was not a stance that David reserved for visiting job seekers alone. He was equally as demanding of his own work and that of his graduate students.

Favorites from Other People's Work (continued)
Diane Ravitch, *Left Back: A Century of Failed School Reforms* (New York: Simon & Schuster, 2000).
Diane Ravitch, *The Great School Wars: A History of the New York City Public Schools* (Baltimore: Johns Hopkins University Press, 2000 [third edition]).
William J. Reese, *America's Public Schools: From the Common Schools to "No Child Left Behind"* (Baltimore: Johns Hopkins University Press, 2006).
David Tyack, *The One Best System: A History of American Urban Education* (Cambridge: Harvard University Press, 1974).
Maris Vinovskis, *From a Nation at Risk to No Child Left Behind* (New York: Teachers College Press, 2009).
Jonathan Zimmerman, *Whose America? Culture Wars in the Public Schools* (Cambridge: Harvard University Press, 2002).

In addition to his skepticism, David brought two other approaches to doing historical work that have strongly shaped my thinking. First, he had little patience for historical studies that were long on grand pronouncements and short on "down and dirty" research. Second, he was wary of studies, even those that *were* well researched, that concentrated on what people *said* about changes in policy and practice rather than on evidence that clearly demonstrated these changes. While David had dozens of examples of both of these problems, there was only one book that he regularly pointed to that he believed successfully avoided them both—David Labaree's *The Making of an American High School: The Credentials Market and the Central High School of Philadelphia, 1838–1939*. [4] Labaree's book became the model that he used with his students to show them how educational history should be done.

Like Bob Dober and Bernie Mehl, David coaxed me into new and fascinating intellectual conversations. I left his classes my head buzzing with ideas he had introduced, new books to read, and articles to track down. He also urged me to take courses in the History Department, especially those offered by Maris Vinoskis, who became a member of my dissertation committee and is now a great colleague and close friend. As I became more interested in Detroit, I also worked with Sidney Fine, who was a brilliant scholar, teacher, and critic. But above all, David was committed to having me write and present papers at conferences almost from the first day I arrived in Ann Arbor. The most important thing about this process was that it was not "sink or swim." During the five years that I studied with him at Michigan and for the next fifteen years until his death in 1999, he read and critiqued virtually everything I wrote. And, while I read and commented on his scholarship as well, I clearly got the better of this deal.

Even before I reached candidacy, I became interested in education in the 1930s in large part because it was so under-researched and because almost all of the extant scholarship on this period fit David's "grand pronouncements" category. Overwhelmingly these grand pronouncements declared that nothing of lasting importance educationally took place in the Depression decade (except possibly the ideas of the social reconstructionists). But based on his scholarship and research, David was sure that due to the massive increase in high school enrollments in the 1930s, something profound had to have been going on in these schools. Two years later, when I finished my dissertation on the Detroit Public Schools in the Great Depression, I corroborated David's hunch about dramatic changes in high schools, at least in Detroit, but I also found a great deal more particularly about the politics of education on the state and local level.

The problem with my dissertation, as Barbara Finklestein pointed out at a memorable lunch with David and me, was whether what I found in Detroit in the 1930s was something new or just the continuation of earlier trends. History is after all the study of change over time and I had only a vague sense of what the Detroit schools were like before the 1930s and what they were like after the Depression ended. In other words, my dissertation could not stand as a book on its own. That realization was simultaneously exciting and disheartening. Clearly if I was going to understand the meaning of what happened in the Detroit schools in the 1930s, I would have to do a lot more research on the Progressive era and follow the story through the World War II and post war years. I assumed that doing this would take a lot more time for research but I badly underestimated how much more.

With a clear research agenda set, I started my first academic job at Northern Illinois University (NIU) in August 1984. I finished the last draft of *The Rise and Fall of an Urban School System: Detroit, 1907–81* nine years later.[5] I was supported in this effort by numerous summer research grants from the NIU graduate school and two substantial grants that bought me out of teaching nearly for two years. The other crucial factor was David. Since much of my research still had to be done in Detroit, over those nine year I regularly came to Ann Arbor and often stayed with David. In the evenings over numerous glasses of single malt scotch he helped me think through every section of every chapter, showed me the holes in my arguments, and he helped me see how to address those problems. The book would not have seen the light of day were it not for his support.

As I was finishing *Rise and Fall*, David and I talked about working together on a new book on the history of the American high school. We had co-authored a number of articles on high schools that questioned some of the traditional interpretations and we thought this was a topic worth pursuing. If my early work on education in the 1930s was inspired by David's disdain for grand pronouncements based on scanty research, our high school book was a response to his second concern about educational history, the tendency to assume that changes in policy talk actually relate to changes in practice. In regards to the history of secondary education in the U.S., even such studies as Edward Krug's magnificent two-volume study *The Shaping of the American High School* rested largely on that assumption.[6] We sought to bring new data on student course taking nationally, in the state of Michigan, and in Grand Rapids and Detroit, to test traditional interpretations.

Writing this book was difficult not because of problems in doing the research or the writing. Rather, during most of the six years that we worked on *The Failed Promise of the American High School, 1890–1995*,[7] David was struggling with cancer. He persevered though all the treatments and, overall, he seemed to be doing well. In 1998, I moved to Emory University in Atlanta, which made getting together with him more difficult. Nevertheless in late 1998 we sent off the completed manuscript of the book. We met in Montreal in March of the following year to hawk the book at the American Educational Research Association conference. We had a grand, celebratory dinner at a chic French restaurant with Bob Bain (who by this time was a faculty member at UM), and Maris Vinovskis. The future looked promising. But in July, David's condition suddenly worsened. He died in August. For twenty years we had had a dialogue that nurtured and utterly shaped my intellectual life and, I believe I enlivened his also, and we had a friendship that was rich beyond measure.

****

In January 2001, I came to the University of Michigan in essence filling David's position as the K-12 historian in the School of Education. Being in the School of Education Building with my office one door away from what had been his office, the site of literally thousands of hours of our conversations, is bitter sweet. I love the sense of continuity. I miss him terribly.

Since the mid-1990s, I began working on issues of civic education in Eastern Europe and the former Soviet Union. I did so perhaps unconsciously because civic education was a topic and Eastern Europe was a part of the world that David had little interest in. For me, however, given my family's background in that region, it was fascinating and meaningful work. From my experiences there, I began to see the outlines of a new research project on Americanization education, a project that has been central to my years at UM. My latest book, *Patriotic Pluralism: Americanization Education and European Immigrants*, is the first major study that I have worked on without any guidance or involvement from David.[8]

As I researched and wrote *Patriotic Pluralism*, I was aided and encouraged by some wonderful friends and colleagues particularly Bob and Maris who continue to influence and inspire me. Since I have come to UM, Bob and I have co-authored some articles on teaching history and I look forward to doing more. Maris and I are thinking about a book that links our interests in history and policy. In addition, my good friends Mary Ann Dzuback, David Labaree, Diane Ravitch, Bill Reese, John Rury, Alan Wieder, and Jon Zimmerman continue to make working in this field an intellectual and social joy.

I look back with a profound sense of gratitude for the teachers whose voices and ideas I have assimilated into internal dialogues and who opened the doors that have led me here. I have been extremely lucky to have friends, teachers, and students who continue to stimulate my curiosity and interests and who keep me honest, skeptical, and quietly rebellious.

NOTES

1   E. D. Hirsch, Jr., *Cultural Literacy: What Every American Needs to Know* (New York: Houghton Mifflin, 1987)

2   John Dewey, *The Child and the Curriculum* in Martin S. Dworkin (ed) *Dewey on Education* (New York: Teachers College Press, 1959), 97.

3   Mike Rose, *Lives on the Boundary* (New York: Penguin Books, 1989), 32–39

4   David F. Labaree, *The Making of an American High School: The Credentials Market and the Central High School of Philadelphia, 1838–1939* (New Haven: Yale University Press, 1988).

5   Jeffrey Mirel, *The Rise and Fall of an Urban School System: Detroit, 1907–81* (Ann Arbor: University of Michigan Press, 1993).

6   Edward A. Krug, *The Shaping of the American High School, 1880–1920* (Madison: University of Wisconsin Press, 1969); Edward A. Krug, *The Shaping of the American High School, 1921–1941* (Madison: University of Wisconsin Press, 1972).

7   David L. Angus and Jeffrey Mirel, *The Failed Promise of the American High School, 1890–1995* (New York: Teachers College Press, 1999).

8   Jeffrey E. Mirel, *Patriotic Pluralism: Americanization Education and European Immigrants* (Cambridge: Harvard University Press, 2010).

DIANE RAVITCH

"OH, THE PLACES YOU'LL GO!" AND OTHER GOOD THINGS ABOUT BEING A HISTORIAN OF EDUCATION

When I was growing up in Houston in the 1940s and 1950s, I knew what I wanted to be. I wanted to be a reporter. I wanted to write. I started writing for a local community newspaper when I was in junior high school, then edited the high school yearbook. In college, I was editor of the *Wellesley College News*. I firmly believed that if I had a career (and, given how few professional women I had met, I was not sure that I would), it would be in journalism. It never occurred to me that I might one day be a professor, an academic, a historian of education.

I had to laugh when I read Geraldine Joncich Clifford's reference to my family in her delightful essay about her own professional journey. She assumed that I was "a Jew from an intellectually and culturally distinguished family, product of an expensive eastern women's college." She is right that I am Jewish and that I graduated from Wellesley College, but my family was not intellectually or culturally distinguished. I was third of eight children, with five brothers and two sisters. My mother, an immigrant from Bessarabia, arrived in the United States in 1917; she was a proud graduate of the Houston public schools. Her father was a tailor; her mother never learned to speak English, despite living in Texas for half a century. My father, born in Savannah, Georgia, never finished high school; his fondest wish was to be a vaudevillian, and he would occasionally break into one of his soft-shoe routines and crack corny jokes. My parents owned mom-and-pop liquor stores, where they worked long hours, six days a week. One of my dad's friends gave him a 1929 Rolls-Royce (considered a white elephant at the time), and he liked to pile all his children into it and drive around town, blaring his old-fashioned horn (A-ruugga! A-ruugga!) at passersby. My parents put a high priority on our going to school, but there was neither intellectual nor cultural distinction in our household. It was not opera we listened to, but Al Jolson, Eddie Cantor, Milton Berle, Bing Crosby, and Beatrice Kay. The usual description for our family was "zany," "crazy," or "wild," but never "distinguished."

Of the eight children, some attended college, some did not. My older sister attended the University of Alabama for two years and quit when she got married (her purpose in going to college was to find a husband and she succeeded). My younger sister eloped in high school and did not go to college.

As an adolescent, I loved sports. I was a tomboy. I loved to play baseball, volleyball, and basketball, to bowl and ride horseback. But there was one thing I loved even more than sports: reading. In junior high school, I devoured the John

W. J. Urban, Leaders in the Historical Study of American Education, 231–240.

Tunis novels about sports. In high school, I joined a subscription book club and read classic novels. My favorite teacher taught English literature. Life at San Jacinto High School was very much like the schools James Coleman described in *The Adolescent Society*.[1] What mattered most to my peers were cars, looks, dating, clothing, and being popular. What mattered least was doing well in school. Since I did well in school and often spoke up in class, I was often referred to as a "brain," which was not a good thing to be. No one took school seriously, cheating was rampant, and our real life began when school was over. I excelled, for example, at drag racing and had three automobile accidents before I was sixteen. It was important to prove that I was not just a brain.

Although I was not religious, my rabbi took an interest in my intellectual development and recommended books for me to read. His wife had graduated from Wellesley, and she encouraged me to apply. I took her advice. I desperately wanted to get away from what I perceived as a deeply anti-intellectual climate and see the world beyond Texas. My parents were not pleased that I wanted to go to an eastern college, but I was relentless and eventually persuaded them to let me go if I were accepted.

> **Some of My Own Favorites:**
>
> *The Great School Wars: New York City, 1805–1973* (New York: Basic Books, 1974).
>
> *The Troubled Crusade: American Education, 1945–1980* (New York: Basic Books, 1983)
>
> "Tot Sociology: Or What Happened to History in the Grade Schools," *The American Scholar* 56, 3 (Summer 1987): 343–354.
>
> "Multiculturalism: E Pluribus Plures," *The American Scholar* 59, 3, (Summer 1990): 337–354.
>
> "Adventures in Wonderland," *The American Scholar* 64, 4, (Fall 1995): 497–516.

I loved my four years at Wellesley. It was everything that my schooling in Houston had not been. Almost every student was a "brain," and I was far from the top of the class. Educational values were preeminent, and for the first time in my life I was academically challenged. I majored in political science, with a minor in history; my first term paper was an analysis of the struggle between political moderates and right-wing extremists for control of the Houston public school board, perhaps a precursor of my later professional interest in education.

Three weeks after my graduation from college in 1960, I married. I met my future spouse while holding a summer job at the *Washington Post* as a copyboy. In the fall of 1960, I began looking for a job, hoping to find something in journalism or publishing. No luck. Everyone wanted a "gal Friday," no one wanted to hire an aspiring and inexperienced journalist. Then one day I read in the *New York Times* about the death of Sol Levitas, the founder of the *New Leader* magazine. He had been a Menshevik, and it was a democratic socialist magazine of ideas. This sounded like a good place for me. I called to ask if I could work for them. The receptionist said, "We are in chaos here, come on in and talk to Mike Kolatch, the new editor." I did and was hired as an editorial assistant for a token amount.

Kolatch didn't ask, so I didn't tell him that I had never met a Menshevik and knew next to nothing about democratic socialism.

Over the next few years, I worked on and off at the *New Leader*, earning what I later considered an informal, hands-on master's degree in modern political thought. I learned firsthand about the political debates of the day from some of the nation's greatest thinkers. I met remarkable writers—Daniel Bell, Nathan Glazer, John Simon, Stanley Edgar Hyman, Irving Kristol—and proof-read hand-typed manuscripts from authors such as Michael Harrington, Sidney Hook, Erich Fromm, Theodore Draper, Ralph Ellison, Paul Samuelson, and Hans Morgenthau. I wrote a few book reviews and was satisfied that at last I had a chance to get published. I had no field of expertise, however, and Myron Kolatch, the editor, advised me to find something I cared about and make myself an authority. I listened respectfully and filed away his advice. Since I was just starting my family, it was not a propitious time to turn myself into an expert. My first child was born in 1962, the second in 1964.

Then tragedy struck, and my life changed. My younger son was diagnosed with leukemia and died in 1966. I immediately got pregnant and had another son, born in 1967. And I began to look for part-time work. A friend recommended me to a program officer at the Carnegie Corporation, who hired me to do research and writing (for $5 an hour). One of my assignments was to report on the demonstration school districts funded by the Ford Foundation in three impoverished communities in New York City; Ford had asked Carnegie to join in supporting them. I spent time at I.S. 201 in Harlem and Ocean Hill-Brownsville in Brooklyn. The leaders wanted decentralization and community control. I watched with fascination as the confrontation between the districts and the teachers' union grew ever more bitter, eventually culminating in a strike that shut down the city's public schools for two months in the fall of 1968.

I wondered why the city school system, enrolling more than one million children, was centralized. It seemed such a strange idea. I went to the New York Public Library, then to the library of the New-York Historical Society, and became absorbed by what I learned. The schools in the late nineteenth century had been decentralized, and reformers demanded centralization to make the schools efficient and rid them of corruption; now reformers wanted decentralization to counter the stasis of the vast bureaucratic system. Wow, this is it, I thought. This is a great story! So I dashed off a letter to an acquaintance, Mitchel Levitas (ironically, the son of Sol Levitas), who was an editor at the *New York Times* magazine, and proposed to write an article about the history of school decentralization. Perhaps because of my complete lack of experience, he laughed off my suggestion, advising me instead to write an article called "I danced with my dentist," which he facetiously promised to publish. I don't know why I remember that jibe after all these years. I guess it was because its condescension jarred me.

Undaunted, I went back to the library and kept reading. I learned that the last history of the New York City public schools had been published in 1905. I decided that this was the project I had been seeking. But I realized I needed some sort of academic training. One day, I took my older son to a birthday party for six-year-olds and met David Rothman, the Columbia University historian, whose child was attending the same party. I told him that I was interested in applying to Columbia to study history, as I wanted to write a history of the New York City public schools. He said that I should not waste my time. He said I had three strikes against me: First, I was a woman and would not feel comfortable in the history department; second, I was too old (I was 32), and it would be a waste of the department's time to train someone my age; and third, I was interested in education, and the Columbia history department was not. He suggested that I go to Teachers College. I spoke to my friends at the Carnegie Corporation, and they provided an introduction to Lawrence A. Cremin, who held a joint appointment at Teachers College and in the history department at Columbia. Cremin was then in the midst of a major Carnegie-sponsored history of American education. We met in January 1968, and I told him what I wanted to do. Larry spent over an hour talking to me, and he jotted down an extensive reading list. He told me that I should forget about writing a book—after all, I had no training and no experience—and suggested that I write a series of essays. I promised to continue my research and get back to him. Six months later, I returned with 125 pages of manuscript. It was not an essay, but the early chapters of a book. He encouraged me to keep going. He also told me that I should not bother to get an advanced degree, because our society is too degree-conscious, and I didn't need one.

Some of My Own Favorites (continued):

"What If Research Really Mattered?" *Education Week*, (December 16, 1998).

Left Back: A Century of Failed School Reforms (New York: Simon & Schuster, 2000).

The Language Police: How Pressure Groups Restrict What Students Learn (New York: Knopf, 2003).

"The Fall of the Standard-Bearers," *The Chronicle of Higher Education*, (March 10, 2006).

The Death and Life of the Great American School System: How Testing and Choice Are Undermining Education (New York: Basic Books, 2010).

Over the next few years, I would meet periodically with Larry, show him new chapters, and get his comments. He always had a new reading list for me, but was careful, as he said, "not to put his thumbs on my writing," that is, to let me say what I wanted to say in my words, not his. Then one fall, he returned from his regular summer sojourn at the Center for Behavioral Sciences at Stanford, and told me that he had discussed my situation with Bruno Bettelheim while they were relaxing together in a swimming pool. Bettelheim had read an article that I wrote in *Commentary*,[2] and saw that I was a research associate at Teachers College. He asked Larry if I was studying for a doctorate, and Larry told him that he had advised against it. Bettelheim said, according to Larry, "Tell the young woman that I disagree with you. Tell her that she will hit a glass ceiling. Tell her to get her doctorate."

When Cremin told me this, I was almost finished with the book, but quickly concluded that Bettelheim was right. I enrolled as a doctoral student, took a statistics course, took whatever other courses I needed, and completed all the requirements for the degree (even though I never had received a master's degree). My book was published in 1974, before I earned my degree. Cremin was adamant that I could not use the book as my doctoral dissertation, because it had not been written in a seminar. For a time, I took his advice, then learned from Patricia Graham (who was then on the faculty at Teachers College) that several people (including Daniel Bell) had submitted a published work as their dissertation at Columbia. But it had never been done at Teachers College. So, having surmounted other obstacles, I began the process of applying to submit my published work as my dissertation, initially against the wishes of Cremin. Eventually, he relented, but warned me that the vote on the dissertation committee would be "up or down," because there was no possibility of revision. I said I was willing to take my chances.

The committee consisted of Cremin, Kenneth Jackson (representing the history department at Columbia), Donna Shalala (then at Teachers College in political science), and Douglas Sloan (also at Teachers College in history). The doctorate was a Columbia Ph.D., not a Teachers College Ed.D. The committee questioned me, I presumably answered satisfactorily, and I won my doctorate. Even better, my book—*The Great School Wars: New York City, 1805–1973*—received favorable reviews in the scholarly journals and popular press.[3]

I settled in as an adjunct assistant professor at Teachers College, teaching one course a year. I had time to write opinion pieces, which satisfied my need to publish and do research, and had many opportunities for informal conversations with Cremin, who continued to be my mentor.

One day in 1975, Larry approached me about a new writing project. He asked if I might be willing to undertake a critique of the self-described revisionist historians of education, who were regularly pummeling him and other "consensus" historians; they claimed that the public schools were not engines of opportunity, but had been devised as a means by which the elites could control the lives of children of the poor and working classes. Since I shared his negative view of their bleak assessment of the role of public schools in American history, I readily assented. I wrote a lengthy review of their work for the National Academy of Education; as I wrote each chapter, Cremin read and enthusiastically approved it. Erwin Glikes, the publisher at Basic Books, asked me to turn the Academy pamphlet into a book, which became *The Revisionists Revised: A Critique of the Radical Attack on the Schools*.[4] I was not surprised when some of the radical professors wrote slashing attacks on me, but was disappointed that no one came to my defense, not even Cremin. A few years after I wrote the book, I sat in the audience at a meeting where he praised the revisionist historians whom he had enlisted me to criticize. I suppose that is what it means to be a consensus historian.

In the 1980s, I wrote *The Troubled Crusade: American Education, 1945–1980*, and became deeply interested in political and ideological battles over the curriculum, even participating in such battles myself.[5] In 1983, when the New York State Department of Education proposed to replace chronological history with unrelated themes, I wrote a critical commentary that was published as a guest column in Albert Shanker's weekly space in *The New York Times*.[6] Chester E. Finn

Jr. and I received a grant from the National Endowment for the Humanities to work with the National Assessment of Educational Progress to develop the first assessments of history and literature; the results appeared in a book called *What Do Our 17-Year-Olds Know?*[7] Right before the book's publication, we got into a major contretemps with Lynne V. Cheney, then chairman of the NEH. She scooped our results for a pamphlet of her own, without attribution and was accused by ABC's Sam Donaldson on national television of having "plagiarized" our work.[8] In retribution, staff lawyers at the NEH pored through the financial records of the project, seeking some grounds by which to harass us (they found nothing).

I found myself increasingly engaged in advocacy for history education, which intensified after I received an invitation in 1985 from Bill Honig, the state superintendent of instruction in California, to help write the state's new K–12 history-social science framework. For nearly two years, I commuted monthly to California to meet with the framework committee of scholars and teachers. It was an exhilarating and edifying experience, as I got a firsthand view of ethnic politics and the politics of curriculum-making. The framework that our committee developed was history-centered and paid due recognition to the nation's diverse cultural heritage as well as to its common democratic ideals; it united the arts and social sciences, encouraged history in the elementary grades, increased the study of world history from one to three years, and became a model for other states. The eventual framework was adopted by the State Board of Education in 1987 and, with only minor revisions, has been in place since then.[9]

About the same time, I helped assemble the membership and funding for the Bradley Commission on History in the Schools, which brought together a number of the nation's leading historians as advocates for improving history instruction (the Bradley Commission later evolved into the National Council on History Education, on which I was a founding member). I simultaneously got drawn into a bruising battle over multiculturalism in New York State's social studies curriculum. The controversy is too complex to explain in this short space, but suffice it to say that I challenged the ethnocentrism of a report by a state panel that sought to use the curriculum to raise ethnic self-esteem.[10] For my efforts, I was denounced as a racist. Arthur Schlesinger Jr. and I wrote a joint statement—co-signed by a group of eminent historians—holding that the history taught in schools "must meet the highest standards of accuracy and integrity" and warning that the schools should not be used "to promote the division of our people into antagonistic racial groups."[11] Arthur subsequently wrote a book, and I wrote several articles. None of my articles, however, described the hate mail, the death threats, and the vilification I received after I criticized ethnic extremism.[12]

Then came a new turn of events. In 1991, I was invited by Lamar Alexander, the new Secretary of Education, to become Assistant Secretary of Education in charge of the Office of Educational Research and Improvement and to serve as his counselor. Initially, I was not interested. I was a lifelong Democrat, and I enjoyed research and writing. (If Cremin had been alive—he died suddenly in 1990--I would certainly have rejected the offer, because Cremin always discouraged me from leaving academe for any policymaking role). When Alexander told me of his interest in promoting voluntary national curriculum standards, I readily agreed to join him. For the last eighteen months of the George H. W. Bush administration, I oversaw the underfunded federal research agenda and encouraged the allocation of about $10 million in discretionary funds to support voluntary national standards in history, science, the arts, economics, civics, geography, foreign languages, physical education, and English. After Bill Clinton was elected to the presidency, I was invited to be a senior fellow at the Brookings Institution, where I spent eighteen months and wrote a book about national standards.[13] Just about the same time, the whole effort to develop national curriculum standards blew up in a major controversy, when Lynne V. Cheney lambasted the history standards as unacceptably leftist and politically biased.[14] The ensuing media firestorm put an end to all discussion of national standards for the next fifteen years.

Favorites by Other Authors:

William C. Bagley, *Education and Emergent Man: A Theory of Education with Particular Application to Public Education in the United States* (New York: Nelson, 1934).

Arthur Bestor, *Educational Wastelands: The Retreat from Learning in Our Public Schools* (Urbana: University of Illinois Press, 1953).

Raymond E. Callahan, *Education and the Cult of Efficiency: A Study of the Social Forces That Have Shaped the Administration of the Public Schools* (Chicago: University of Chicago Press, 1962).

Jeanne Chall, *Learning to Read: The Great Debate* (New York: McGraw Hill, 1967).

Lawrence A. Cremin, *The Transformation of the Schools: Progressivism In American Education, 1876-1957* (New York: Knopf, 1961).

In 1995, I returned to New York City. I expected to return to Teachers College, where I had been an adjunct faculty member since 1975. During my three years in Washington, while I worked in the federal government and at Brookings, my office at the college had remained intact, along with my files and books. But the new president of Teachers College bluntly informed me that my colleagues did not want me back. Apparently the act of serving in a Republican administration, along with my contrarian views, had made me persona non grata. Fortunately I was offered an adjunct position at New York University and settled there in the fall of 1995.

I resumed work on a book that I had started in the mid-1980s, which was intended to be a history of the curriculum. After my immersion in the Beltway world of policymaking, it was not easy to return to scholarship, but I was determined to finish the book. Now that I was once again the owner of my time and my voice, I enjoyed nothing better than long hours in the library, reading dusty documents and books that had not been checked out for decades. *Left Back: A Century of Failed School Reforms* was published in 2000.[15] The title was imposed on me by the editor, who wanted to market the book as yet another tale of the failure of our schools, but I hated the subtitle and changed it when the book was issued in paperback; the subtitle became *A Century of Battles Over School Reform*, which more accurately reflected what the book was about.

While renewing my scholarly pursuits, I kept a hand in the policymaking world. In 1997, President Clinton appointed me to serve as a member of the National Assessment Governing Board, which oversees the National Assessment of Educational Progress (NAEP). I was reappointed for a second term by Secretary Richard Riley and served on that board for seven years. This was a very important learning experience for me, as I gained insight into the construction of large-scale assessments. I also learned about bias and sensitivity reviewing and wrote *The Language Police: How Pressure Groups Restrict What Students Learn* in 2003.[16] That book provided more pleasure for me than any previous book; it was alternately funny and appalling to discover how censored and sanitized the mass-produced textbooks and tests are. I appeared on many radio and television programs. The most exciting was when I was interviewed by Jon Stewart on the "Daily Show." When the interview was scheduled, I had no idea who he was. I watched the night before I went on, and Caroline Kennedy was the guest. I realized that his audience was young, cool, and hip, which I am not. I was really nervous when I waited to go on, and one of Stewart's assistants literally pushed me onto the stage. When Stewart announced my name, the youthful audience began clapping, and then he said, "education historian," and the clapping suddenly died. I laugh now when I remember that moment.

In the decade after I worked in the first Bush administration, I had become identified as a conservative in policy circles. Not only had I worked in a Republican administration, but I supported testing, accountability, choice, and merit pay. And I frequently wrote opinion pieces in the *New York Times*, the *Washington Post*, and the *Wall Street Journal* in support of these policies.

Thus, it was yet another interesting turn of events in my life and in my evolution as someone who thinks about education policy, when I concluded that I was wrong. I am an avid consumer of research, and I began to realize that the policies I had been promoting were not likely to improve education and were in fact likely to inflict damage. First, I turned against the No Child Left Behind law, after concluding that it was narrowing the curriculum, turning schools into testing factories, and having little impact on achievement. Worse, it was imposing an unrealistic goal on the schools and then punishing them for not meeting that goal, which fed a spreading sense of despair about the public schools. Then I began surveying the evidence on accountability and choice and realized that they too were having negative effects. Similarly, much of the research on teacher evaluation, I discovered, was deeply flawed. Its conclusions, if translated into policy, would likely make teaching a very unattractive profession as teachers would be judged largely by their students' scores on very limited tests of basic skills. The charter school movement, which I had once admired, was turning into a privatization juggernaut, supported by Republicans and Democrats alike.

Armed with evidence and concerned about the future of public education, I wrote *The Death and Life of the Great American School System: How Testing and Choice Are Undermining Education.*[17] I expect this is my last book about education. I have occasionally dreamed about writing a memoir—don't we all?—but I think

Favorites by Other Authors: (continued)
John Dewey, *Experience and Education* (New York: Macmillan, 1963, first published by Kappa Delta Pi, 1938).
Richard Hofstadter, *Anti-Intellectualism in American Life* (New York: Knopf, 1961).
Isaac L. Kandel, *The Cult of Uncertainty* (New York: Macmillan, 1943).

I am ready to leave the battle of ideas to others. I have had a very full and satisfying career, one that has given me much intellectual excitement and many opportunities to wrestle with important issues of the day. Being a historian of education provides an excellent starting point to interpret and reflect on all kinds of debates. It offers the opportunity to explain how the past informs our decisions and discussions.

I continue to be deeply concerned about the future of history as a field of study. I have always wished that everyone might be educated enough to have a historical context for debating issues. Yet I fear that knowing about history has become as specialized as knowing about robotics or metallurgy: It is something left to experts and gifted amateurs, but not for the general public. It has always been my hope and conviction that knowledge of history would be so widely dispersed that we might all be able to talk about Abraham Lincoln, Frederick Douglass, Thomas Jefferson, Emma Goldman, the Alien and Sedition Acts, the Wobblies, the Red Scare, Manifest Destiny, the *Plessy* decision, the *Brown* Decision, the Great Depression, the Dust Bowl, and other significant individuals and events in American life as part of our normal public discourse. Instead, the public is inundated with the latest exploits and personal problems of entertainers and athletes. I also care about literature and wish that we could hold on to the best of the past while reading the best of the present; that is why I edited anthologies of classic American and English literature, trying to save the things I loved from oblivion.[18]

Thinking about a world in which public education is privatized, in which history is relegated to specialists and literature is replaced by electronic trivia and confessions, thinking about the need to make education better, to make it really matter, gets my juices flowing. Maybe I have one more book to write!

NOTES

[1] James S. Coleman, *The Adolescent Society: The Social Life of the Teenager and Its Impact on Education* (New York: Free Press, 1961).

[2] Diane Ravitch, "Community Control Revisited," *Commentary* (February 1972).

[3] Diane Ravitch, *The Great School Wars: New York City, 1805–1973* (New York: Basic Books, 1973.)

[4] Diane Ravitch, *The Revisionists Revised: A Critique of the Radical Attack on the Schools* (New York: Basic Books, 1978).

[5] Diane Ravitch, *The Troubled Crusade: American Education, 1945–1980* (New York: Basic Books, 1983)

[6] Diane Ravitch, "How to Make a Mishmash of History," *The New York Times*, guest columnist for Albert Shanker, (May 15, 1983).

[7] Diane Ravitch and Chester E. Finn, *What Do Our 17 Year-Olds Know?; A Report on the First National Asse3ssmemnt of History and Literature* (New York: Harper & Row, 1987).

[8] Edward B. Fiske, "Schools Criticized on the Humanities; Dispute Over Use of Data," *New York Times* (September 8, 1987).

[9] History-Social Science Framework for California Public Schools, Kindergarten Through Grade Twelve, developed by the History-Social Science Commission Framework and Criteria Committee, adopted by the California State Board of Education, July 1987.

[10] Diane Ravitch "A Phony Case of Classroom Bias," *New York Daily News* (January 23, 1990).

[11] Diane Ravitch and Arthur M. Schlesinger Jr., "Text of Statement by 'Scholars in Defense of History,'" *Education Week* (August 1, 1990): 38. The statement was signed by Thomas Bender, John Morton Blum, Jerome Bruner, James MacGregor Burns, Robert Caro, Kenneth B. Clark, Henry Steele Commager, Marcus Cunliffe, David Herbert Donald, Frances Fitzgerald, David Garrow, Henry Graff, Akira Iriye, Michael Kammen, Stanley N. Katz, William Leuchtenberg, Arthur S. Link, William Manchester, William H. McNeill, Stuart Prall, Richard Sennett, Hans Trefousse, Richard Wade, and C. Vann Woodward.

[12] Arthur M. Schlesinger Jr., *The Disuniting of America: Reflections on a Multicultural Society* (Knoxville, TN.: Whittle Direct Books, 1991); Diane Ravitch, "Multiculturalism: E Pluribus Plures," *American Scholar* 59, No. 3 (Summer 1990):. 337–354; Ravitch, "Multiculturalism, Yes; Particularism, No," *Chronicle of Higher Education* (October 24, 1990); "History and the Perils of Pride," *Perspectives* (March 1991); Diane Ravitch and Arthur M. Schlesinger Jr., "The New, Improved History Standards," *Wall Street Journal* (April 3, 1996).

[13] Diane Ravitch, *National Standards in American Education: A Citizen's Guide* (Washington, D.C.: Brookings Institution Press, 1995).

[14] Lynne V. Cheney, "The End of History," *Wall Street Journal* (October 20, 1994).

[15] Diane Ravitch, *Left Back: A Century of Failed School Reforms* (New York: Simon & Schuster, 2000).

[16] Diane Ravitch, *The Language Police: How Pressure Groups Restrict What Students Learn* (New York: Knopf, 2003)

[17]. Diane Ravitch, *The Death and Life of the Great American School System: How Testing and Choice Are Undermining Education* (New York: Basic Books, 2010).

[18] *The American Reader: Words That Moved a Nation* (New York: Harper Collins, 1990); *The English Reader: What Every Literate Person Needs to Know* (with Michael Ravitch) [New York: Oxford University Press, 2006].

WILLIAM J. REESE

STORY TELLING AND HISTORY

I am looking at a digital image of a photograph shot on November 22, 1958 at the American Legion Post 585, in Duryea, Pennsylvania. I was then six years old, and I have no memory of this particular photograph. But similar ones, capturing the same event, later appeared in the *Pittston Dispatch*, a weekly newspaper. I remember those quite well, and the blow ups they caused at home. Pittston was the biggest town between Wilkes-Barre and Scranton in the anthracite region of northeastern Pennsylvania. It had a movie theater and a few stores and restaurants downtown, though like every nearby community it never recovered from the collapse of the mining industry. With a population of a few thousand, Duryea did not have its own newspaper, or library, or many amenities. All but a few of its people were working-class. There was one lawyer, one dentist, one doctor. But, like in wealthier communities, people lived and died, married, went to ball games and funerals, and sometimes got their names and faces in the Sunday paper. The *Dispatch* dutifully published gossip and news for many area towns and featured pictures of graduation ceremonies and reunions, bowling league and Little League champions, church picnics, the Fourth of July Parade, and other local doings.

My discovery of the 1958 image a few years ago brought to life in my mind the world I grew up in and that shaped my sensibilities, as a person and as an historian. For many years close friends have heard my stories about growing up in Duryea and most have now seen the image. Before I saw it, I often thought of the fierce arguments that occurred every year between my mother, who was embarrassed by the event in question, and my father, who put on his best clothes and took some pleasure in seeing his picture in the paper. Even when I was in high school, I did not really understand what all the fuss was about. My mother, a high school graduate, would complain, "You are setting a poor example for the boys. I want them to go to college." My father would shrug off the criticism. Recognizing the dim prospects for the uneducated, he also wanted us to go to college. The noisy dispute would end, then revive a year later. Only with seeing the old image did I realize that this argument had ensued for many years, longer than I realized.

What was the fighting all about? A little more context. According to family lore shared by my father and grandfather, dad was expelled from high school. The story was essentially this. My father said that he was clowning around in the back of the classroom, and a teacher came from behind and hit him on the head with a book. My father turned around quickly, punched him, and got expelled. He had a chance to return to high school, my grandfather told me, if he apologized to the teacher; grandpa Reese said, there were no hard feelings with the superintendent of schools, who came to the house in person to make the offer. I don't know if my father had

W. J. Urban, Leaders in the Historical Study of American Education, 241–254.
© *2011 Sense Publishers. All rights reserved.*

much say in the matter, since my grandfather doubted whether a high school diploma would do his son any good. Better to work at some job and help the family. And so my father never graduated, fought in France, returned home, worked at a slaughter house, and began a family.

Personal Favorites of My Own

Power and the Promise of School Reform: Grassroots Movements during the Progressive Era (Boston: Routledge & Kegan Paul, 1986).

The Origins of the American High School (New Haven: Yale University Press, 1995).

America's Public Schools: From the Common School to 'No Child Left Behind' (Baltimore: The Johns Hopkins University Press, 2005).

The image in question was shot at the American Legion hall on Main Street. There are thirty-nine men in the photograph. All but one wear a coat and tie. They epitomize working-class respectability (a term I learned in graduate school). Many of the men also wear a smile, some wry and mischievous. My father (later a textile worker), my grandfather (a retired miner), and two uncles are present. In the front of the three rows of men are two banners. The smaller one, left of center, announces that this is the "NON-GRADUATES' REUNION." In the center, the larger banner reads, in bigger capital letters and in bold, "DIDN'T MAKE IT STILL TRYING," and beneath it in smaller letters, "CLASS OF ????" Hanging above the group are streamers suspended from a metal coat hanger attached to a heating vent in the ceiling. All of the men are holding fake diplomas, their way of thumbing their noses at the world.

I have no idea who concocted this annual event, or if any of the men ever considered getting a G.E.D. That would not have helped them much. But the reunion is a revealing send-up of that familiar American event: a high school reunion. A parody only works if it mocks convention. These men left school to work, to fight for their country, or both. It's a patriotic group. On the Legion wall are the opening lines to the "Preamble to the Constitution." My father was, like quite a few of the men, a World War II veteran. Since they met year after year, they must have enjoyed themselves. They don't seem embarrassed at all. When I became aware in the late 1960s of the nature of the reunions, I didn't give them much thought. I remember thinking that the guys were having fun. I never asked my father, who died young, why he attended. As I thought about it over the years, I tried to analyze it more and simply concluded that they were skewering pretensions and asserting their manliness (another word from graduate school) and working-class pride. Whoever suggested the fake diplomas was a genius.

Moments captured long ago in black and white film like this one, one of the most vivid in my youth, live with me still. While schools certainly played an essential role in my becoming an historian and educator, such memories of family and working-class life and the story telling so basic to daily existence were far more important. After all, stories are basic to history. The ones I heard, and told, were how I came to understand America and became curious about the world beyond my doorstep. Stories can do many things: they can entertain, connect past and present, and teach lessons and morals. Without them we are rudderless. In a world where no one, I mean no one, outside of school, ever asked me about or told me anything about a book, talking, speaking, listening, and hearing stories helped me make sense of everything. Stories substituted for the best sellers.

My next door neighbor Freddy Greco, who was Italian, was a great story teller. He owned a grocery store and I worked for him through high school. He imported cheese and canned tomatoes and spices in huge quantities, all stored in a big garage on his property. He sold them to dozens of restaurants, pizzerias, and bars all over northeastern Pennsylvania. We delivered everything in an old green Jeep, which I drove before I was 16. A natural salesman, Freddy had the gift of gab and he introduced me to everyone we'd meet on the road. Many of the people liked to talk and joke and some told bawdy tales.

Of all my neighbors, Freddy could spin a yarn: mostly about mob hits he heard about, dramatic tales that took forever to tell but always ended up with bodies dumped somewhere in New Jersey. Like everyone else in Duryea, he never forgot that he was ethnic. He beamed when an Italian-American, one Judge John Sirica, helped nail Nixon in Watergate. While I was in junior high school, one of Freddy's "business associates," a real mobster who later died in prison, gave me $20 in an envelope for hand delivering some goods to him outside the grocery store. That was a lot of money then, and the man, who smoked cigars and had a chauffeur-driven limousine, told me, "Here, sonny, for college." Most people only see such things in the movies. Freddy, wearing a blood covered apron since he was butchering some meat, watched this unfold from a short distance and was laughing heartily as I returned to the store. I pocketed the money and never told my parents. Working-class kids were expected to turn over everything they earned; this was mine.

History is about large-scale social forces, big ideas and movements, and change over time, yet it always comes to life through biographies, collective or individual. Observing people and listening to their stories, more than reading books, taught me how individuals make choices, often under difficult circumstances not of their making. School–at least studying and doing well there–took second place in my education and mattered more when I was an adult. Until then, I was surrounded by people for whom school was relatively unimportant. More than once, Freddy told me that he quit school in fifth grade; it was his way, I think, of affirming how well he did despite this, but also to contrast his life with mine. He didn't think his was the path to follow.

Telling stories was obviously around before anyone wrote or read books, and Freddy was always sharing them, delicately weaving what I later learned were called narratives. They all had a beginning, middle, and an end, with a dramatic punch line, and sometimes a laugh, to release the tension. Explaining how and why the bad guys or snitches were rubbed out by the mob took a lot of talent: all the parts of the story had to be stitched together seamlessly and made believable. The stories, probably told second and third hand, seemed to come out of nowhere, occurring at some indeterminate time and place in the past. It didn't matter if any of it was true. I heard that Freddy briefly went to jail during World War II for selling my grandparents too much sugar, but whenever I asked him or family members about it they only laughed. The joke was on me. Freddy also regaled me with stories about the hypocrisy of every priest he knew; they drove beautiful black Cadillacs and stole pennies from the poor. He'd cite chapter and verse to prove his point that priests were the biggest shake-down artists in town. Then he'd laugh. I quit as an altar boy before serving a single mass, and he didn't disapprove.

Because Freddy was Italian and anti-clerical in a town filled with devout, or at least church-going, Catholics, he was always a bit exotic and an outsider in my neighborhood. That helps explain why he is not in the photo of the non-graduates' reunion. There were Italians in Duryea, but not many of them; he was from Old Forge, a town away, with many more Italians. While the Reese clan came from Wales, most of the other men in the 1958 photo were of Slavic descent, from eastern or central Europe, like my maternal grandparents.

Freddy told me to take school seriously and get as far away from Duryea as possible. He was especially proud of a sister who taught at a local Catholic college. It set her apart. As a student in the local public schools, however, I was never quite sure what all the learning was for, exactly, though it seemed like a possible ticket out of town. It's not easy to explain working-class attitudes toward school to people whose parents went to college or to graduate school and expected their children to rise to the top of the class. Working-class parents knew education had economic value but could not know what going to college actually meant, apart from getting a job as a teacher or a nurse, the usual aspiration. These were soft, clean, secure, safe jobs, hard to argue with. School, they knew, was a hedge against the abyss awaiting the next generation of non-graduates. Northeastern Pennsylvania was the land of pot holes, abandoned mines, strip mines galore, and numerous factories that were soon shuttered.

The men in the 1958 photo were not radicals protesting against the economic system, and most working-class adults I knew had ways to share their sense of ambivalence about schools to young people. My relatives believed that too much learning made you ill equipped for anything practical, such as moving refrigerators, fixing a car, or laying concrete for a new sidewalk. They sneered at successful people in positions of power, those "big shots," the put-down liberally applied to politicians who dispensed patronage. There were no big shots on either side of the family; my parents and aunts and uncles mostly worked in factories and that was about it. Anyone who stood out invited ridicule; "all nails get hammered down," I often heard. Even attending college could backfire. Adults emphasized that it did not make you morally superior, and the Catholics all around me, on both sides of the family, warned that it could destroy your faith and ties to family and to place. Going could make you "big headed." Working-class parents wanted their sons (and often their daughters) to get ahead, and that usually meant joining the military or more schooling, for better or worse. But school was not an unalloyed good.

The men I knew in the photo were proud of who they were. It was a badge of honor that they made their way through life without much formal education. By making fun of schools, however, they revealed their conflicted feelings. Every year another round of pictures of graduating classes and reunions appeared in the *Dispatch*, reminding them of what they had not achieved. Mocking the rituals and hoopla surrounding graduation–the banners and streamers, the diplomas and regalia–they affirmed the rising importance of succeeding at school. The world was passing them by.

Even before I knew anything about the "Non-Graduates' Reunion," I absorbed their mixed feelings about school. I still divide the world into people who attend high school reunions and those who do not; I can't imagine attending one. Recently I found a picture of my kindergarten graduation, Class of 1956, which I attended at my neighborhood public elementary school, named for Woodrow Wilson. The boys are standing on the left, the girls on the right. With black cap and gown, I am standing in the front row, on the steps of the Sacred Heart Church (not in front of the Wilson School, for some reason). I am helping to hold a banner which reads, "BE KIND." Incongruously, I have a frown on my face. Maybe Wordsworth would have understood as I felt the shades of the prison house being drawn.

School was not something one thought about but what one did, year after year. It was where children were from September through early June. After my kindergarten graduation, I was back at Wilson elementary for a few more years. Mostly I remember a few friends, recess, milk breaks, and the wooden building, a fire trap. It was a big ugly box and all the teachers were, as far as I knew, unmarried women, most with Irish surnames: Miss McHale, Miss McLaughlin, and Miss Gilhooley come to mind. By junior high school, Duryea had consolidated with several adjacent school districts. Now formal tracking (another word I learned in graduate school) separated the sheep and the goats. Those destined for the hardest classes were slotted into 7–1, those for less challenging pursuits sank to 7–4 on down. How decisions were made was a mystery, but there I was in 7–2, then 8–1, and then I must have regressed in someone's eyes since I dropped to 9–2. Some friendships crossed these divides, but the college bound mostly formed their own cliques, and cliques within cliques, and separated themselves from the academically marginal.

While in high school, our school system consolidated with Pittston to form an even larger district. No one noticed any improvement in quality. Without telling my parents, in tenth grade I shifted from "college prep" to "voc ed," since I concluded for some unknown reason that I would not go to college. I was even elected President of the class and earned straight A's with ease, given the low expectations. My parents only learned of my voluntary transfer when I brought my first report card home showing the change in status. They forced me to attend summer school to take Algebra II and Spanish II to get back into college prep. Most of my classmates that summer were from that track but had failed. Being with failures and those often deemed uneducable was in retrospect a godsend, reminding me of the diversity of people and cruelties of institutions. That frown at kindergarten reflected my ambivalence about schools, a feeling that never went away and was reinforced often. The snobbery of some of the college bound, who often had nothing to be snobbish about, was clear to those not of the elect. Watching and observing all this was for me time better spent than reading, since there would be time enough for that later in life.

Out-of-school experiences remained fundamental to shaping my world view, which no doubt crept into every class I've taught or word I've written. I continued to work after school and in the summers for Freddy. I also picked up quite a few other jobs including a stint on the town garbage truck. I was a "topper," standing on the top of the heap as other high school students and the regular crew threw the cans and bags of refuse at my feet; I arranged everything to maximize the use of space, seeing how high I could go. Jobs at fast food joints also gave me spending money thanks to a small allowance. On the garbage truck or at fast food restaurants, as in most menial jobs, workers tell stories, mostly jokes at each other's expense, to make the day bearable.

> **Books that Greatly Influenced Me, in Chronological Order.**
>
> Merle Curti, *The Social Ideas of American Educators* (New York: C. Scribner's Sons, 1935).
>
> Lawrence A. Cremin, *The Transformation of the School: Progressivism in American Education, 1876-1958* (New York: Alfred A. Knopf, 1961).
>
> Michael B. Katz, *The Irony of Early School Reform: Educational Innovation in Mid-Nineteenth Century Massachusetts* (Cambridge: Harvard University Press, 1968).
>
> David P. Thelen, *The New Citizenship: Origins of Progressivism in Wisconsin, 1885-1900* (Columbia: The University of Missouri Press, 1972).

I learned over and over how many people did essential work, day in day out, without much pay or glory. For many people, the working world, like the schools, had many dead ends. One of the regulars on the garbage truck wore three watches, and greenhorns like myself were always asked by his co-workers to ask him for the time. None of the watches worked. He didn't laugh as he rolled up his sleeve. Everyone else laughed. I'm not sure he was in on the joke, exactly. This man had installed speakers under the hood of his Rambler; at the flip of a switch he would blast his music on Main Street, his own version of the Bronx Cheer, I suppose. It was amusing and annoyed a lot of people–but more laughs.

While in high school, I earned some money and, more importantly, got to skip classes, by playing taps at funerals for veterans. Learning to play the trumpet had its advantages. With my friend Robert Proietto, mispronounced by most teachers as Pryetta, we would take turns, one of us playing the sad notes somewhere near the grave site, while the other would position himself further away to provide an echo. Our trigonometry teacher knew a scam when he saw one and nicknamed us "Toots and Return." The VFW and American Legion members who called our principal to request our services seemed satisfied, since they kept inviting us back. Most of the funerals were for old men (meaning anyone old enough to be our parents). By the late 1960s the deceased were sometimes younger, casualties of Vietnam. On one cold day in Scranton, I was playing taps near a grave site when a young bride started crying uncontrollably and ran to embrace the coffin. It was snowing and sleeting, the valves on my trumpet froze, and I resolved to find better ways to skip school.

That unsettling moment was not some epiphany that led me to become an historian. But it made me wonder what, in the deepest existential sense, had placed me at that spot in history. Why were any of us there on that blustery, unhappy day? I sometimes think my fascination with historical origins, of how things come to be, was becoming seared into my consciousness.

While I had no idea that I would ever be an historian or college professor, during my high school years I was fascinated by classmates who actually liked to study and do well. I did not understand their behavior or my fascination. I studied a little, earned B's and A's, and found it odd that the high achievers worried so about their grades. Peer cultures are pretty vicious, and making fun of "brown-nosers" and high achievers, particularly girls who led the pack, was rampant at Pittston Area High School. Oddly enough, given my cynicism and often clownish behavior, I didn't make fun of those who succeeded academically. My friends often did so. Adults, I learned, were equally good at dressing others down. When we took our SATs in our junior year, a guidance counselor interrupted Latin class to deliver our scores. He handed out a slip to one of my friends, which dropped to the floor, and told him, "I hope *you* aren't planning to go to college." I did little better with standardized tests but was not ridiculed for it. I remember that day and similar incidents more than any classes I attended. Instilling a love of learning in pupils where it does not exist is not easy, especially when some adults behave so.

While many social historians of my generation were heavily influenced by the civil rights movement or various 1960s social movements, they played a lesser role in my education. It only influenced me indirectly, as adults railed against most progressive changes. Working-class Pennsylvania was not a hotbed of radicalism but a place defined by ward politics, ethnic rivalries, declining industrial economies, and patriotism. Living there helped teach me about the art of story telling, the importance of humor, and a respect for working people. But for different reasons than 1960s radicals it also made me suspicious of authority and nurtured a life-long, ambivalent view of institutions.

Thanks to television, by high school I was aware of the civil rights movement and anti-war protests. Integration, however, was an abstract issue since everyone in Duryea was white, as were most people in the region outside of Wilkes-Barre and Scranton. Unless you were about to be drafted or knew someone in the service, Vietnam also seemed far removed from the daily concerns of high school. Whenever the subject of Vietnam emerged at school or home, it quickly led adults to condemn hippies and long hairs, though there were few living examples around us. A classmate asked one of our teachers during study period for permission to get a drink of water, and she loudly answered, "Give it up for the boys in Vietnam." I remembered thinking, what is this lady, who never smiled, talking about?

In my eleventh grade English class, Vietnam became the source of nervous conversation in a more personal and bizarre way. We had a male classmate, with us since elementary school, who was more academically challenged than most; in fact, he sat in the corner in the back of the room year after year, never speaking, never making any trouble, never called upon. He just sat there and with the rest of us moved from class to class when the bell rang. One day he disappeared. Someone asked our teacher, Miss Fahey (note the surname and marital status), where he was. Fahey had mastered the short sentence: "He's been drafted." John Williams, sitting behind me, showed better economy, whispering in my ear, "We're screwed." Our former classmate, who was shaving since about fifth grade, was, we learned, twenty-one and by law had to leave school. Later in the year his picture appeared in the *Dispatch*: he was being shipped out to Vietnam, as a cook. I couldn't believe it. He made it home alive. At least two people I knew from Duryea did not.

Adults seemed unreservedly opposed to thinking Vietnam was a mistake. Had any anti-war sentiment emerged at Pittston Area High–which enforced the dress codes and where teachers slapped (on rare occasions punched) any boys out of line–it would have been crushed. Outside school, adults would yell at the handful of shaggy young people standing on the corner on Main Street to get a haircut. Certainly the men at the non-graduates' reunions seemed pretty uniformly Gung Ho. For my Catholic relatives, anti-communism was as much a religious crusade against godless doctrines as anything else. "My country, right or wrong" could have also hung on the Non-Graduates' banners and not been out of place.

I knew in a vague way that other big events were shaping America but mostly felt closeted from them. I thought more about how to extricate myself from my world and move on to something better. High school was suffocating. Everyone worried

---

Books that Greatly Influenced Me, in Chronological Order. (continued)

David B. Tyack, *The One Best System: A History of American Urban Education* (Cambridge: Harvard University Press, 1974.)

Carl F. Kaestle, *Pillars of the Republic: Common Schools and American Society, 1780-1860* (New York: Hill and Wang, 1983).

James D. Anderson, *The Education of Blacks in the South, 1860-1935* (Chapel Hill: The University of North Carolina Press, 1988).

---

about what everyone else thought and expended lots of energy in fear of being ridiculed, in or out of class. There were also genuine over-aged thugs better suited for other institutions who tormented the weakest boys in gym; no one squealed for fear of reprisals. It was better to mind your own business and look the other way when others substituted for punching bags. Parents did not want to hear about boys who could not take care of themselves.

If engagement with the big social issues of the day, of which I was poorly informed, had little direct effect on me during my high school years, neither did books. This did not help when I applied to college, which I gradually realized, after I transferred back to the college prep stream, might be an escape hatch. My academic preparation was pretty poor. At home the family "library" consisted of a dictionary and the *Golden Book Encyclopedia*, purchased weekly, letter by letter from A to Z, at the A & P in Old Forge. Later a traveling salesman brought us a more sophisticated encyclopedia, one with fewer pictures. Except for comic books (including an occasional "Classic Comics"), the textbooks assigned at school, and *Reader's Digest* at the barber shop (and some men's magazines, so called), that was the extent of my literary culture.

Because no one in my family knew exactly what college was about, except a way to avoid low paying factory jobs, I did not know one could apply for admission to more than one at a time. I had a steady girlfriend and only applied to one local college and was rejected. By chance I told a fellow band member about the rejection sometime in winter during my senior year. He asked me what I was going to do after high school and, rejection in hand, I replied, "Find a job." When he asked me why I wasn't going to college (his father was a guidance counselor, so he understood the world differently), I told him I had been rejected by Wilkes College, to which he said: "I know a lot dumber people than you going to college." I could only say, "But they were accepted somewhere." A few days later, my name blared over the intercom in one of my classes, a summons to the principal's office. I assumed I had done something wrong and was about to be disciplined. But the guidance counselor, my acquaintance's father, had his office in the principal's suite. He told me he had arranged for an interview with an admissions officer the next Saturday, concerning my rejection. He told me to be sure to wear a coat and tie, which I found patronizing (though I did not know that word then), but I knew he meant well. One has to play the game.

Everything about my education, and what I observed about life, seemed to have something to do with patronage. Getting into college did not seem different. In Duryea, everyone I knew laughed at the notion that the best man wins, or that merit conquers all. In describing how someone got a job, my parents would say that so-and-so had "pull," or knew someone. I worked for Freddy because I knew him. My teachers (all of them Irish, it seemed) worked in a system where a James Joyce had been the superintendent for many years. Thomas Kelly was the high school principal and John Donovan the vice-principal. The Irish were everywhere. Their resumes must have been special since they frequently rose to the top. Or, as I heard, they had pull. My temporary jobs on the Duryea garbage truck were no doubt due to someone putting in a good word for me, maybe the local councilman, one "Zimbo." Now a friend's father had called the registrar or some official and I was getting a second chance on college admission. All these lessons about how the world worked, its patterns and its capriciousness, helped make me a social historian without my knowing it.

I disliked the Wilkes official I met that Saturday morning. He seemed to the collegiate manor born, decked out with a tweed coat and cigarette holder. Another character from some old movie. I sat in an oversized couch feeling uncomfortable in my coat and tie. Aloof and with almost no eye contact, he blew smoke out an open stained glass window and was obviously annoyed at being there on a chilly Saturday morning. But I was admitted to Wilkes on probation, forced to attend summer school and complete two courses with at least a B to merit full admission and remove the stigma. I swallowed hard and did fine. One of my professors at the end of his course wrote a nasty letter to the admissions official: he berated him for making me attend summer school, when I should have been working trying to earn some money to pay for my tuition in the fall. I was shocked that he showed me the letter. The men obviously had some history between them.

Despite embarrassment at the terms of my admission, Wilkes College, which I entered in 1969, changed my life and gave me the skills necessary to go to graduate school and follow my life's course. I never actually received an admission letter but the tuition bill arrived on time. At Wilkes, my world literature (mostly European and American) classes were eye opening and transformative: we read the classics from Beowulf through the European existentialists, and the latter spoke to me like no other literature since. Required survey courses in Western literature opened my eyes to the past, making me wonder why authors wrote what they did, when they did.

By 1969 and 1970, history was not dead but alive, all around us. Actions by powerful, older people, so called leaders and decision-makers interviewed by Walter Cronkite or quoted in the newspapers, had produced more than one widow in Scranton, spared the world from my trumpeting, and led a classmate to sling hash in some jungle. History was personal, unfolding as it would even in the coal regions. America was at war, my draft number was low, and everything I studied had relevance. As I wondered how and why everything came to be, I became a history major in my junior year. A politically connected friend from Duryea, a clever and kind man known as Dom Dom, helped me land a well paying job in the summer of 1972 removing refuse after Hurricane Agnes flooded the Wyoming Valley, including the lower part of Duryea, helping me afford college. I had recently been fired from my summer job at a fast food chain, told "off the record" that the manager heard I supported unions, which I did. That I was planning to unionize anything was ridiculous. But Dom Dom appeared, like many a patron, to bail me out.

At Wilkes I was fortunate to have fabulous teachers. Two stood out: James Rodechko in American history (where I learned there was something called "social and intellectual history" and read Merle Curti's *Growth of American Thought*),[1] and Joel Berlatsky in English history and early modern Europe (where I first read Rousseau and the romantics). I watched them closely to try to figure out how they knew so much and made learning so challenging but also enjoyable. In college I never had better teachers. Both men also had time for anyone who was eager to learn, and they corrected my lousy prose and encouraged me. I got certified to teach secondary social studies, student teaching at a rural school, Lake-Lehman Junior Senior High School, which was memorable and enjoyable. Initially I did not want to student teach, but my father leaned on me to do something practical, even though I told him I planned to go to graduate school. I'm glad I took his advice. I taught history and social studies to academic and vocational streams of students in the 7th, 9th, and 11th grades. My two supervising teachers quickly gave me control over my classes, which boosted my confidence. The whole experience sealed my love of teaching.

After graduating from Wilkes, I was offered a job at my old high school–for a kickback, the way teaching jobs were often procured–but I wanted to get away. I was offered the job at my college graduation party and politely declined. The scandalous system of paying for jobs still exists in different districts in northeastern Pennsylvania, where quite a few school board members and superintendents have perfected the fine art of nepotism and corruption. Periodically, they go to prison. An FBI sting recently sent the superintendent for Pittston Area, who lived in Duryea, to jail, one in a string of scandals in the region that never seem to end. Years ago, when asked why he planned to run for the school board, I heard a person I admired reply, "Why should those guys get all the gravy!" Historians of education often forget that, among their many functions, schools are always about jobs and, where I grew up, no-bid contracts.

Teaching at my old high school had no appeal to me. Paying for a job was offensive, though it was the way it was. I knew how little I knew about history and hoped that graduate school would lead me away from the open corruption and the always sagging economy. When I graduated in 1973, my professors at Wilkes were not encouraging about job prospects in academe; the market for historians had collapsed. But I thought I had to take the chance. Rodechko had taught at Bowling Green State University in Ohio, and his letter of recommendation no doubt helped me gain admission to its master's program in History complete with funding. Who one knew mattered as much, I again assumed, as what one knew. I was lucky to have the right teachers and mentors. I sometimes tell undergraduates, to get them to think about social class and mobility in America, "choose your parents carefully." And your patrons.

Graduate school prepares students to become specialists, emphasizing expertise over general knowledge. And while I was often fascinated by what went on in schools, and finally discovered a passion for learning at Wilkes, I stumbled into the field of history of education. Majoring in history and becoming a certified teacher may seem to make the choice easy enough to explain, but a variety of mentors at Bowling Green were pivotal in how things turned out. My advisor, David Roller, was a specialist on the Progressive era, and when it was time to think about writing a master's thesis, I was uncertain what to study. I had a research assistantship at the Great Lakes-Northwest Ohio Research Center, whose archivist, Paul Yon, encouraged me to look at the recently acquired records of the Toledo public school system. It included school board minutes and other materials, I was interested in education and in history and ended up writing a master's thesis on the city's schools between the 1890s and World War I. I audited a class taught by Malcolm Campbell, another excellent teacher, in the School of Education, and discovered that there were some exciting books in the field. I read Lawrence Cremin's *Transformation of the School*, Michael Katz's *Irony of Early School Reform*, Joel Spring's *Education and the Rise of the Corporate State,* and Carl Kaestle's *Evolution of an Urban School System*.[2] I was hooked.

In Roller's seminar on the early twentieth century, we read the then-classic works on Progressive reform (some of which I still assign). Among the newer books, David Thelen's on Wisconsin progressivism, *The New Citizenship*, left a major impact on my thinking.[3] I decided to try to study with him at the University of Missouri at Columbia, applied, and was accepted. A charismatic teacher, Thelen underscored for me the importance of state and local history, on which I cut my teeth as a researcher. He not only had a new way of thinking about Progressive reform, but he also wrote quite a lot about schools. Thelen was later a colleague when I taught at Indiana University at Bloomington, and he reminded me that he had been a teaching assistant in history of education classes while a graduate student at Wisconsin. The class had been taught by Merle Borrowman, himself apparently quite a charismatic person.

There was much dissatisfaction among graduate students at Missouri regarding the perennial question of funding, and I grew unhappy with the uncertainty of the situation and decided to transfer. I wrote to Carl Kaestle at Wisconsin, he wrote a kind reply, and I was accepted for graduate work in the Department of Educational Policy Studies.

While historians are trained to seek out historical patterns, we all know that chance–as well as family, contacts, and institutional connections–plays a huge role in our lives. It was my good fortune to study with Carl. He was already a rising star, a model advisor, kind and considerate, and encouraging. In one seminar we explored the comparative history of nineteenth century education and I wrote a research paper on the Owenites in England and America. While the job market was horrific, fellow students such as John Rury and I knew that we were lucky to be at Wisconsin. Carl was an engaging and stimulating teacher but, no fault of his, I found graduate school pretty intimidating. Some of us wondered how we could ever learn how to write and think and speak so well. I was one of Carl's research assistants as he worked on *Pillars of the Republic*.[4] At Wisconsin, I also studied with other important scholars such as Jurgen Herbst, Mike Apple, and Herbert Kliebard. Ed Krug, while retired, was often in the office, ready to talk history, and Herb Kliebard seemed to have all the time in the world even for non-advisees. As I got to know Herb better, I realized there were other people from modest backgrounds who became professors, in his case a very distinguished one.

What impressed me most about doctoral studies at Wisconsin was how my teachers never imposed their views upon us. There was a healthy sense of give and take, honoring the spirit of academic freedom historically associated with it. Kaestle and others let us send up trial balloons and try out new ideas without making us feel foolish. They knew when to allow students to speak their minds and when to direct us along more fruitful lines of inquiry. By the mid-1970s, radical revisionists were turning the liberal interpretations of Lawrence Cremin and others on their head. But no one at Wisconsin ever told me what to think. My teachers knew that every generation, as Carl Becker said, writes its own history. All they demanded was careful research, clear prose, and the ability to defend an argument, in writing and orally.

Building upon my master's thesis and inspired by the new social history, with Thelen's and Kaestle's scholarship to help guide me, I wrote a dissertation on grass roots movements and urban schools during the Progressive era. It was influenced by the new labor history, women's history, and the various ongoing revisionist debates then enlivening the history of education. In the fall of 1979, I applied for a few dozen teaching positions and had one interview, at the University of Delaware, received an offer, and accepted it. I taught in Newark for one year and enjoyed it but applied for a job at the School of Education at Indiana University at Bloomington, where I would teach from 1981 to 1995. There I had the most remarkable colleagues, especially B. Edward McClellan, the epitome of a gentleman and scholar, who spent countless hours helping me understand Indiana's norms and how to cope with life's inevitable adversities. I had courtesy appointments in American Studies and in History and loved the interdisciplinary atmosphere, allowing me to become close friends, for example, with Robert Orsi in Religious Studies and with many other people within and outside the School of Education too numerous to mention.

I revised my dissertation and published it in 1986 and, reflecting contemporary concerns about the state of America's secondary schools, began research on the origins of the high school, which led to a book in 1995.[5] For a number of years at Indiana, I was also editor of the *History of Education Quarterly*, which enabled me to read broadly in the field. Teaching at Indiana was an incomparable experience, since it enabled me to teach across three departments.

In 1995, I moved back to my alma mater, the University of Wisconsin-Madison, where I teach courses on the graduate and undergraduate level in the history of education, all of them cross-listed between Educational Policy Studies and History. I typically teach one course exclusively in the History department, a seminar on reform movements from Populism through the New Deal. I've written other books, and John Rury and I have co-edited a volume to honor Carl Kaestle.[6] So our views and that of many colleagues on the state of the field are easily retrieved by anyone so interested.

Scholars in any academic field are mostly known by the fruits of their labor: their articles or books. I have said little in this essay about what I have written, or why. I've concentrated on what helped make me a historian, as best as I can determine, to reconstruct the unpredictable path that led me to study the history of education.

School was obviously central to providing me with the skills and knowledge to become a teacher, a student of educational policy, and an historian. But Wordsworth was right: the child is father to the man. What I became as a teacher and historian is rooted in the experiences that influenced me before books and school meant that much to me. The home battles over and meaning of the Non-Graduates' Reunion. Freddy's story telling. Memories of who got jobs at the Wilson School and how I was admitted to college after being rejected. My college and university teachers and mentors. While I am grateful for everything schools have done for me, the out-of-school lessons of growing up in northeastern Pennsylvania shaped everything that followed. In many ways I never left home.

NOTES

[1]   Merle Curti, *The Growth of American Thought* (New York: Harper & Brothers, 1943).
[2]   Lawrence A. Cremin, *The Transformation of the School: Progressivism in American Education, 1876–1958* (New York: Alfred A. Knopf, 1961); Michael B. Katz, *The Irony of Early School Reform: Educational Innovation in Mid-Nineteenth Century Massachusetts* (Cambridge: Harvard University Press, 1968); Joel H. Spring, *Education and the Rise of the Corporate State* (Boston: Beacon Press, 1972); and Carl F. Kaestle, *The Evolution of an Urban School System: New York City, 1750–1850* (Cambridge: Harvard University Press, 1973).

[3] David P. Thelen, *The New Citizenship: Origins of Progressivism in Wisconsin, 1885–1900* (Columbia: The University of Missouri Press, 1972).

[4] Carl F. Kaestle, *Pillars of the Republic: Common Schools and American Society, 1780–1860* (New York: Hill and Wang, 1983).

[5] William J. Reese, *Power and the Promise of School Reform: Grassroots Movements during the Progressive Era* (Boston: Routledge & Kegan Paul, 1986) and *The Origins of the American High School* (New Haven: Yale University Press, 1995).

[6] William J. Reese and John R. Rury, eds.. *Rethinking the History of American Education* (New York: Palgrave Macmillan, 2008).

JOHN L. RURY

SEEKING A SOCIAL AND URBAN HISTORY OF EDUCATION

British historian and philosopher R. G. Collingwood once suggested that biography should not be considered a branch of history, largely because he considered it preoccupied with matters of "gossip-value" rather than more important issues in the past. The biographer, he argued, begins from a standpoint of sympathy with a subject, rendering critical judgment difficult—if not impossible—to achieve.[1] If Collingwood was scornful of biography as a genre, we can scarcely imagine how he would describe autobiography, even an exercise as brief and professionally motivated as this. On this cautionary note I undertake the task of outlining the major steps in my own academic experience. While admittedly well-disposed to its subject, if not necessarily flattering, this account dwells on events and circumstances that have affected my development as a historian. Along the way, I describe some of the twists and turns that have characterized a rather peripatetic career. Learning, as Dewey would remind us, is a product of living, and as such is inescapably tied to the conditions encountered in life. Beyond gossip, in that case, the stories in this volume ought to shed light on just how the history of education has been produced from the ideas and experiences of many historians.

NEW YORK AND WISCONSIN: FORMATIVE EXPERIENCES
AND EDUCATION

Growing up in upstate New York, I was intrigued at a distance by large cities. I also saw education as a fundamental human activity of growth and transformation. From an early age, like many of my baby boom peers, I was told that school was important. It was also associated with order and discipline, in contrast to a somewhat jumbled family life, and the promise of fulfilled potential. These interests eventually contributed to an abiding concern with urban education, fueled in part by a budding awareness of social inequality and commitment to equity and democracy as basic principles.

I was fascinated by history as a child, encouraged by my father's interest in military campaigns, and it was always my favorite subject in school. After declaring a history major in college, I was drawn by the egalitarian appeal of the social turn in academic historical research and writing. It seemed intuitive that education was a key feature of collective experience, and hence a worthy topic for the "new" social history. Since I went to college in New York City, links between urban schooling and social inequality were readily evident, especially as I made friends who had

W. J. Urban, Leaders in the Historical Study of American Education, 255–264.
© *2011 Sense Publishers. All rights reserved.*

grown up in various city and suburban neighborhoods. This fueled my curiosity. Even though schooling was rarely touched upon in my undergraduate courses, I began writing class papers on topics in the history of education. This quickly led me to works by Richard Hofstadter, Merle Curti and Lawrence Cremin, among others, and I wondered if indeed it was a field to consider for graduate study.

Works Representative of My Development as a Historian of Education:

John L. Rury, "The New York African Free School, 1827–1836: Conflict over Community Control of Black Education," *Phylon* 44 (3rd Qtr., 1983): 187–197.

John Rury, "Urban Structure and School Participation: Immigrant Women in 1900," *Social Science History* 8 (Summer, 1984): 219–241.

John L. Rury, *Education and Women's Work: Female Schooling and the Division of Labor in Urban America, 1870–1930* (Albany: State University of New York Press, 1991).

John L. Rury and Jeffrey E. Mirel, "The Political Economy of Urban Education," *Review of Research in Education* 22 (1997): 49–110.

John L. Rury, "Democracy's High School? Social Change and American Secondary Education in the Post-Conant Era," *American Educational Research Journal* 39 (Summer, 2002): 307–336.

John L. Rury, "Social Capital and Secondary Schooling: Interurban Differences in American Teenage Enrollment Rates in 1950," *American Journal of Education* 110 (August, 2004): 293–320.

John L. Rury, "The Curious Status of the History of Education: A Parallel Perspective," *History of Education Quarterly* 46 (Winter, 2006): 271–298.

John L. Rury, *Education and Social Change: Contours in the History of American Schooling* (New York and London: Routledge, 2009).

College graduation seemed to come all too quickly, just as things were getting interesting. Ignoring family expectations to study law, I enrolled in a "social foundations of education" masters program at the City University's Convent Ave campus, attending on a part-time basis and driving a cab three or four days a week while figuring out just what to do. The tuition was modest and I encountered a number of thoughtful historians who suggested that an academic career was worth contemplating. I also began to explore the history of American education in greater depth, along with reading widely in social history. Under the guidance of Fredrick Binder and Robert Twombly, I wrote a thesis on black education in ante-bellum New York, a project that opened multiple subfields, including African American and urban history. I also discovered the work of a young historian at the University of Wisconsin who had also completed a thesis (and book) on early schooling in New York—Carl Kaestle.[2] Since Twombly had trained at Wisconsin, both he and Binder encouraged me to consider it for doctoral work. I looked at other programs but left New York in August of 1975 bound for Madison.

It turned out to be a fortuitous decision. I was among the first students to arrive at Wisconsin to study with Kaestle, along with Bill Reese a year later, just as Carl was embracing the social history phase of his own career. Everyone was abuzz about research in the "new" urban history, and I was soon immersed in computer cards and census manuscripts, performing basic statistical studies of school enrollment in nineteenth century cities. This marked the beginning of a graduate course of study that combined work in history, economics, sociology and education. I was especially interested in urban and economic history and the use of quantitative analysis to identify the impact of such factors as ethnicity and social class on schooling. It also was the heyday of "radical revisionism," with Michael Katz, Clarence Karier and the economists Samuel Bowles and Herbert Gintis, among others, turning the field in a decidedly leftward direction.

I also became something of a campus activist, helping to organize protests against the university's investments in companies doing business in South Africa, among other issues. But I was skeptical of the revisionist interpretive framework, as it seemed neither particularly radical (certainly not compared to campus Marxists) nor especially promising with respect to a sustainable research agenda. Instead, I was impressed by the possibilities of a "structural" analysis of underlying economic and social forces that shaped educational development, particularly urbanization and the changing labor market. Carl was completing work on his Massachusetts study with Maris Vinovskis, and a number of other historians were examining similar issues.[3] Consequently, my research focused on links between education and the economy, urban development and the experiences of groups omitted from the prevailing historical narrative. I also wanted to tackle a topic that had been neglected, so my dissertation examined women's schooling and work in the progressive era, with financial support from the short-lived National Institute of Education.

MICHIGAN AND OHIO: LAUNCHING A CAREER

I left Madison after five years, still working on a dissertation about female education, headed for Detroit, where my spouse-to-be, Ellen Kennedy, had taken a job in the public schools. It was there that I eventually completed my degree, while teaching in the history department as an adjunct lecturer at Wayne State. It was a difficult time, filled with uncertainty about the future as the economy plunged into a severe recession, with Michigan getting the worst of it, as usual. But the department kept me on, and I learned a great deal in three years of teaching a variety of courses, before leaving to become an assistant professor of history at Antioch College in Yellow Springs, Ohio. Teaching experience helped, but I was hired at Antioch largely *because* of my specialization in education, a topic of keen interest on that campus given its own historical roots. It was great fun working with the inventive and eager students there, even while commuting weekly from Detroit, where my wife and growing family still resided. I also started to turn dissertation chapters into articles, and collaborated with an older student on a study of the institution's first women collegians and its founding president, Horace Mann. After a rewarding year, however, I accepted a position about an hour away at Ohio State University in Columbus, and entered the next phase of a budding career.

> **Works that Have Influenced My Development as a Historian:**
>
> Carl F. Kaestle, *Evolution of an Urban School System: New York City, 1750–1850* (Cambridge: Harvard University Press, 1973).
>
> Michael B. Katz, "Who Went to School?" *History of Education Quarterly* 12 (Autumn, 1972): 432–454.
>
> Carl F. Kaestle and Maris A Vinovskis, *Education and Social Change in Nineteenth Century Massachusetts* (New York: Cambridge University Press, 1980).
>
> Carl F. Kaestle, *Pillars of the Republic: Common Schools and American Society, 1780–1860* (New York: Hill and Wang, 1983).

Ohio State, of course, was the polar opposite of Antioch. It was a big research institution and my appointment was in the College of Education, a prominent professional school with a strong emphasis on doctoral training. It also had a long tradition in educational history as a field, which I was immediately apprised of. I taught a large section of a history of education course each quarter, along with a seminar on topics ranging from higher education to educational policy and supervised graduate teaching assistants. Suddenly I was a specialist, and even if my graduate training provided a strong foundation for it, much of my prior teaching did not help much. Fortunately I had supportive colleagues who were tolerant of occasional missteps. I also made connections with departments across campus, most notably history, where I found new colleagues and students interested in my work.

There were other challenges too. I was informed in no uncertain terms that publication was a high priority for assistant professors, and set about getting pieces of my dissertation and an assortment of other papers into print. As it turned out, these were fruitful years in that regard and my interest in quantitative and social history continued to evolve. Utilizing city level census data collected for the dissertation and individual-level data (Integrated Public Use Microdata Sample or IPUMS), I explored different facets of school enrollment at the turn of the century in a variety of articles. Building on grad school statistics courses, I learned new techniques and gradually gained confidence in the value of this line of work. I published other papers as well, including the one on Antioch's early history, which gained a bit of notoriety.[4] But historians are supposed to write books, and the big task that remained for my early career was making a publishable manuscript from the work completed for my dissertation. The problem was that additional research was necessary to expand upon its somewhat disparate chapters and bring them together in a coherent, multifaceted narrative. Doing this required time, and dashing between my family still in Detroit and a junior faculty appointment in Columbus left little occasion to get it done.

An answer to this dilemma came in 1985 when Carl Kaestle suggested that I apply for the newly enhanced National Academy of Education Spencer Fellowship program. Fortunately, I was included in the first group of fellows, permitting a year devoted to research and writing for the manuscript that eventually became my first book, *Education and Women's Work*.[5] It also allowed me to reside full time with my family in Detroit, working as a visiting scholar at the University of Michigan and Wayne State. It was an unusually productive period, not least because of the good friends that I made, particularly David Angus and Jeffrey Mirel. We held an informal seminar that year, with David Labaree (then up the road at Michigan State) and Maris Vinovskis (in history at Michigan) also participating. This proved very helpful in the reconceptualization of my work, and widened my thinking about a variety of issues. While the manuscript still was not complete at the end of the year, I had finished the lion's share of new research that it needed. Publication of the book, however, would have to wait for yet another step in a career path that was about to take a curious turn.

CHICAGO: THE URBAN SCENE

Not relishing a return to the long-distance commuting routine following my fellowship year, Ellen and I decided to move west to Chicago. There she could continue her career as a bilingual educator while I taught at DePaul University, where I was offered a job in an alternative program for adults, the School for New Learning (SNL). DePaul was not a research institution and SNL was not a traditional college, so it was another big change. As a private, Catholic, and urban university, DePaul historically had served metropolitan Chicago, and was best known for its professional programs in law, business, music and theater. The School for New Learning was a competency-based college, which offered courses and documented achievement for students aged 24 or older. Most of its clientele was female and worked for corporations or other businesses downtown or in the suburbs. I was among the first full time faculty members in SNL, working from an office in the Loop and occasionally teaching in the suburbs as well.

DePaul's institutional ethos tilted heavily toward instruction, and while the classes in SNL were small, its adult customers demanded considerable attention. I matured as a teacher in those years, learning to respond to students with a wide range of interests, while offering a variety of courses on social history and basic research methods. I became a generalist once again, and learned much from reading widely in connection with my classes. Research productivity was slow, however, and it took several years to finally complete *Education and Women's Work* (with helpful guidance from Barbara Finkelstein). In the meantime, I was engaged as a consulting historian on a study of the Milwaukee Public Schools, funded by a local foundation. This project, which took me back to longstanding interests in urban history and city schools, entailed collaboration between faculty members from a number of disciplines at the University of Wisconsin-Milwaukee. It culminated in the publication of a collection of essays on different facets of the city's educational history, which I co-edited with UWM historian Frank Cassell.[6] The project closed with a conference on the future of the Milwaukee Public Schools, which were gaining national attention as a focal point of reform. It was all very stimulating, and affirmed my belief that urban education was a topic that deserved even more attention from the field.

Works that Have Influenced My Development as a Historian (cont.):
Joel Perlmann, *Ethnic Differences: Schooling and Social Structure among the Irish, Italians, Jews, and Blacks in an American City, 1880–1935* (New York: Cambridge University Press, 1988).
Jeffrey Mirel, *The Rise and Fall of an Urban School System: Detroit, 1907–1981* (Ann Arbor: University of Michigan Press, 1993).
David F. Labaree, "Public Goods, Private Goods: The American Struggle over Educational Goals," *American Educational Research Journal* 34 (Spring, 1997): 39–81
Claudia Goldin and Lawrence F. Katz, "Human Capital and Social Capital: The Rise of Secondary Schooling in America, 1910-1940," *Journal of Interdisciplinary History* 29, Patterns of Social Capital: Stability and Change in Comparative Perspective: Part II (Spring, 1999): 683–723

My scholarly career was taking another turn, however, along with my personal life. In 1992 I was named editor of the Social and Institutional Analysis Section of the *American Educational Research Journal* (AERJ), succeeding Wayne J. Urban in that role. At the same time my marriage came unraveled, and because Ellen and I agreed upon a joint custody arrangement, I also became a part-time single parent. Balancing editorial duties with raising two young boys turned out to be quite time consuming and my research agenda reflected it. I did explore the possibility of collaborating with Jeffrey Mirel and some of his colleagues at Northern Illinois University on a study of the Chicago schools, a project that necessitated even more immersion in the literature on urban education and related issues. Even though the proposed study was never funded, Jeff and I co-authored an extended review essay on the topic, and I prepared a paper on the city's recent educational history that eventually served as a presidential address to the History of Education Society.[7] Jeff, of course, had published his celebrated study of the Detroit schools, along with a number of shorter pieces on urban education, and I learned a good deal from working with him.[8] Both he and his wife Barbara, who became a DePaul colleague, were great help as I coped with the challenges of divorce and fatherhood. Bill Reese also was a good friend, teaching my sons to fish in a magical Indiana pond and sharing bits of Hoosier folklore, along with the sterling example of his own scholarship.

The other major project at this time was a study of DePaul's history, planned to mark its centennial in 1998. This too was a group effort representing a variety of disciplines, and I again served as coeditor, this time with my sociologist colleague Chuck Suchar.[9] The two of us collaborated on the oral history portion of the project and I worked with history graduate students in conducting analyses of the university's yearbooks and student papers. The book that grew out of these efforts was largely intended for alumni, students and staff, but provided an opportunity to further expand my research experience and to renew a connection to higher education history, a subfield that I had followed since taking courses with Jurgen Herbst in Madison.

The Chicago and DePaul projects marked a period of immersion in the city's rich history. I taught courses on urban studies with an emphasis on Chicago, featuring field trips to sites across the city. As a study in urban higher education, the DePaul history shed light on Chicago's multifaceted educational past. I grew familiar with the city's vibrant social science community and became involved with the schools, especially after being elected to the local council of a junior high close to home. By the time I took a position in the university's School of Education, moving from the Loop to its Lincoln Park Campus in 1997, I was prepared to focus my attention on urban schooling. My AERJ editorial term had just ended and I was elected to national offices in both the History of Education Society (HES) and Division F of the American Educational Research Association (AERA), but I looked forward to finally getting back to a sustained program of research and writing. With faculty research grants from DePaul, I started collecting statistical data on urban education in the postwar era, building on the work that I had completed earlier. Back in a conventional academic environment, I returned to teaching the history of education and related topics in the social foundations. I had married a remarkable Chicago attorney, Aida Alaka, and with my sons Aaron and Derek in high school, life seemed to assume a comfortable balance. And then my career took yet another unanticipated turn.

In early 1999 I was in my office—minding my own business—when Patricia Graham called out of the blue, asking me to join the staff of the Spencer Foundation. I quickly discovered that she could be very persuasive and by the summer I had a new position and a three year leave from DePaul. I had become a senior program officer, responsible for managing the review of proposals, similar to my editorial duties at AERJ but on a grander scale. When combined with assorted other tasks this made for a very hectic calendar, but it also was quite invigorating. Needless to say, I learned a great deal in the process, and enjoyed the privilege of participating in innumerable meetings about all sorts of interesting topics. I had the opportunity to interact with many of the world's leading educational and social science researchers, and to work with an exceptionally bright and competent foundation staff. While we managed to fund some projects in the history of education, most of my attention was devoted to other disciplines. I became particularly interested in the sociology of education, reading widely in the field and eventually even joining the American Sociological Association.

When Pat Graham retired in 2001, returning to Harvard to resume writing history, I had the opportunity to work with yet another distinguished historian as president of the foundation, Ellen Lagemann. Pat and Ellen observed a generous policy of permitting program officers to work one day a week on their own scholarship, which I used to write a brief interpretive history of American schooling, *Education and Social Change*. I attempted to infuse a broad social science perspective throughout the book, starting with a discussion of history and social theory. I also managed to produce some additional articles and reviews, but for the most part my time was devoted to assessing other scholars' research ideas and not pursuing my own.[10] When the three year term at Spencer was complete, I gladly returned to the university, although I remained a "senior advisor" to the foundation for another year, just one day a week. My Spencer years had taught me a lot about research and writing, and I was anxious to get back to work. But as had been the case before, another change was in the offing, and this time it would entail relocation to a new part of the country.

KANSAS: RENEWING A SCHOLARLY CAREER

In the spring of 2003, just as my commitment to Spencer was ending, I received an invitation from the University of Kansas to consider serving as chair of a large department in the School of Education. Aaron and Derek were away at college, and to my surprise Aida was willing to consider a move. I had recently become a department chair at DePaul, and the idea of an administrative role at a research institution was intriguing. Aida and I decided to take the plunge, and we put our Chicago home on the market and started packing. By the end of the summer we were ensconced in a different house and learning about our new community. It was a fresh start, but one that would entail a bit of turmoil before we finally settled into a comfortable routine.

It turned out that the situation I encountered at Kansas was not a happy one. The department was internally divided, and the dean that hired me resigned in little more than a year. Shortly thereafter I stepped down as chair and joined the faculty, and when Rick Ginsberg arrived as the new dean in 2005 the department was reorganized into separate units. My administrative tenure at KU was relatively brief, but in the end I was happy to put it behind me. Although I had come to Lawrence to be an administrator, I now found myself a professor at a research university once again, specializing in the history of education.

Of course, my thinking about problems in the field, and urban education in particular, had continued to evolve during my administrative hiatus from research. I had remained somewhat active, publishing occasional articles and a "historical reader" of classic essays on urban education by a variety of authors.[11] But now I had time to explore a number of matters that had proved intriguing for a while. First on the list was the question of secondary education for African Americans in the postwar era, an issue that seemed to repeatedly surface in discussions of the urban educational crisis of the 1960s and beyond. If the principal problems of city schools were linked to matters of race, after all, it made sense to tackle the matter squarely, especially in light of the many changes affecting black youth in that period. Second, my interest in quantitative analysis continued to evolve as I became aware of the potential for the history of education in using IPUMS data, which had become considerably more elaborate and user-friendly in the decades since I first encountered them. And third, I discovered a number of colleagues—many considerably younger than me—who were interested in historical questions, and willing to collaborate on a range of projects.

I set to work on each of these fronts, and started making more connections across campus. A number of colleagues in the history department were (and are) interested in the history of education and I was offered a courtesy appointment. My recently retired colleague Ray Hiner, a longtime faculty member in education and history, had left a helpful legacy in many respects. I also was selected as a "Keeler Intra-University Professor," a competitive award given annually to two Lawrence faculty members, which allowed me a semester "in residence" in the Sociology Department. Freed from teaching obligations, I used this time to sit in on classes and begin collaborating with Shirley Hill, a specialist in black families and women. We drafted a proposal to the Spencer Foundation to study the history of African American secondary education, which eventually was funded. Shirley and I are finishing work on that project.

At about the same time I became a co-conspirator in a clandestine plan to bring together essays from former students and friends of Carl Kaestle to commemorate his retirement. Bill Reese and I co-edited the resulting book, *Rethinking the History of American Education,* which focused on changes in the field since the 1970s.[12] I also began collaborating with KU colleagues in the School of Education, most of them rather inexperienced in historical analysis. These projects took various directions, but most entailed one form or another of statistical analysis, typically with IPUMS data, focusing on changes in secondary education in the post-war era. This enabled me to update a somewhat rusty statistical tool box, and to explore some new dimensions of educational history. In a relatively short time, I had gone from being a largely inactive researcher to one with a full agenda.

Following the commotion of my brief administrative turn, life in Lawrence gradually assumed an agreeable—if still somewhat frenetic—pace. After a period of job searching and part time teaching, Aida took a position in the law school at Washburn University in nearby Topeka. We weighed the prospects of moving to other research institutions and decided to remain in Kansas. Meanwhile, I became involved in efforts to create a multi-university educational research consortium to serve metropolitan Kansas City, which was eventually funded by a local foundation and formally launched in 2009. Since Kansas City is just a short drive from Lawrence, I have continued to focus my attention on urban education and related issues of metropolitan inequality and racial discrimination. A number of talented and energetic graduate students have come to Lawrence to study the history of education and related topics, further enhancing my work as a teacher and scholar. With these developments in view, and the opportunity to work on questions of longstanding interest, I look forward to the years ahead.

SOME CONCLUDING THOUGHTS

Drawing conclusions about a career still underway is inevitably tricky, but a few observations seem pertinent. First, there can be little doubt that the early imprint of Carl Kaestle's social and urban history phase, and particularly its quantitative chapter, has remained evident throughout my work. I remain compelled to address various forms of inequality that are reflected in the education system, and deeply committed to redressing them, values I have held since graduate school. Fortunately, a rather irregular career has permitted me to indulge these predilections, especially the sixteen years I spent in Chicago. Second, I have long been intrigued by the connections—extant and potential—between history and the social sciences, and have enjoyed the freedom that working in education has afforded to utilize insights gained from this. My time as an editor and as a program officer, while hardly fruitful from the standpoint of research productivity, was helpful in fostering a broad interdisciplinary perspective. Even my administrative work helped me to understand the outlook and values of my education colleagues, and the importance of making historical research relevant to their interests.[13] In the end, however, I consider myself a social historian, one particularly concerned with urban education and related questions of democracy and equity. That is likely to remain my particular corner of our field for the foreseeable future, inevitably reflecting the many people, institutions and places encountered in a journey that is hopefully still far from complete.

NOTES

[1]   R.G. Collingwood, *The Principles of History and Other Writings* (Oxford: Oxford University Press, 1999), 69–75.

[2]   Carl F. Kaestle, *Evolution of an Urban School System: New York City, 1750–1850* (Cambridge: Harvard University Press, 1973).

[3]   Carl F. Kaestle and Maris A Vinovskis, *Education and Social Change in Nineteenth Century Massachusetts* (New York: Cambridge University Press, 1981).

[4]   Studies produced in this period included "Gender, Salaries and Career: American Teachers, 1900–1910," *Issues in Education* 4 (Winter, 1986): 215–235, and "The Trouble with Coeducation: Mann and Women at Antioch, 1853–1860," *History of Education Quarterly* 26 (Winter, 1986): 481–503.

[5]   John L. Rury, *Education and Women's Work: Female Schooling and the Division of Labor in Urban America, 1870–1930* (Albany: SUNY Press, 1991).

[6]   John L Rury and Frank A. Cassell, eds. *Seeds of Crisis: Public Schooling in Milwaukee since 1920* (Madison: University of Wisconsin Press, 1993)

[7]   John L. Rury and Jeffrey E. Mirel, The Political Economy of Urban Education," *Review of Research in Education* 22 (1997): 49–110; John L. Rury, "Race, Space and the Politics of Chicago's Public Schools: Benjamin Willis and the Tragedy of Urban Education," *History of Education Quarterly* 39 (Summer, 1999): 117–142.

[8]   Jeffrey E, Mirel, *The Rise and Fall of an Urban School System: Detroit, 1907–81* (Ann Arbor: University of Michigan Press, 1993)

[9]   John L. Rury and Charles Suchar, eds. *DePaul University: Centennial Essays and Images* (Dubuque, IA: Kendall Hunt, 1998).

[10] The latest edition of this work is John L. Rury, *Education and Social Change: Contours in the History of American Schooling* (New York: Routledge, 2009) ; the principal article published during my Spencer years grew out of a project on the history of the comprehensive high school: John L. Rury, "Democracy's High School? Social Change and American Secondary Education During the Post-Conant Era," *American Educational Research Journal* 57 (Summer, 2002): 307–336.

[11] John L. Rury, ed. *Urban Education in the United States: A Historical Reader* (New York: Palgrave Macmillan, 2005).

[12] William J. Reese and John L. Rury, eds. *Rethinking the History of American Education* (New York: Palgrave Macmillan, 2008).

[13] This idea is evident in my essay, "The Curious Status of the History of Education: A Parallel Perspective," *History of Education Quarterly* 46 (Winter, 2006): 271–298.

DAVID TYACK

REMINISCENCES OF A TEACHER

As I look back on my work as an educational historian I have been struck by the ways in which the public events and personal experiences of my lifetime have shaped the choices I have made as teacher and writer. There has been no sharp line between the "real world" and the historical puzzles I wanted to explore.

MYOPIA

Born in 1930, I grew up in Hamilton, a small community in eastern Massachusetts. It was hardly typical of small town America, however. There were two main groups of inhabitants. They talked differently, they attended different schools and colleges, and they hardly ever intermarried. One group lived on hilltops in mansions modeled on those of England's Cotswold; the other lived mostly in small houses in the flatlands. Both of the groups were white, both native born. And most churchgoers were Protestant. Amid such similarities what distinguished them from each other was wealth and social standing. My own family was part of a small group of middle class people in the town.

The signs of class inequality were everywhere. I assumed the divisions between rich and working class were just the way things were. Sometimes my elders needed to teach me the rules of class explicitly. Once I made the mistake of delivering a package to the front door of a mansion; the butler told me "Always go to the back door, David." Another time, while waiting for my mother in the Episcopal Church, I sat in the Bishop's chair and was scolded by the minister. A proper education should teach people to know their place.

Some of the mansions had extensive farms that provided local jobs and taught traditional skills. For four summers I worked on the farm of Standish Bradford alongside two veteran farm hands who taught me how to drive a tractor, clean the barns, milk the cows, and tend the vegetables. When we harvested the hay on muggy August days, I learned how strenuous traditional farming could be.

The mansion-dwellers were likely to belong to the Myopia Hunt Club (yes, that was, and is, the Club's name). Members liked to gallop on horseback through the woods in bright hunting costumes, play polo, and compete in golf and tennis. Ceremonial events in the Club, Church, and mansions reassured the Brahmins that maintaining the Anglophile traditions of the rich mattered, even in hard times. Meanwhile, their servants cared for the horses and hunting dogs and golf greens and children.

W. J. Urban, Leaders in the Historical Study of American Education, 265–273.

In the depths of the Great Depression the schools tried to carry on business as usual. Some federal aid came from time to time. My mother's kindergarten was funded by the WPA. Sometimes she and I delivered coal and food to families who were hungry and cold. Memories of their faces came back when I worked decades later on a book on public schools in the Great Depression.[1]

As I look back at life in Hamilton in those years, the town seemed to be in a time warp. As I noted, during my childhood I took for granted the divide between rich and poor as just the way things were. And like many other scholarship boys I became much more aware of inequality and injustice when I attended Harvard College with a national scholarship.

It is ironic that so many scholarship boys of the time became radicalized, for leaders like James Bryant Conant argued that attending the college would attach them to the existing political and economic system. Influenced more by the left-liberal than by the conservative side of Harvard, I began to ask how inequality and cultural dominance became so imbedded in divisions of class in New England. My first book --*George Ticknor and the Boston Brahmins*-- offered one attempt to answer that question.[2]

WINTER AND SUMMER LEARNING

Tyack Bibliography:

The One Best System: A History of American Urban Education (Cambridge: Harvard University Press, 1974).

(With Elisabeth Hansot) *Managers of Virtue: A History of Leadership in American Public Schools, 1820–1980* (New York: Basic Books, 1982).

(With Robert Lowe and Elisabeth Hansot) *Public Schools in Hard Times: The Great Depression and Recent Years* (Cambridge: Harvard University Press, 1984).

(With Elisabeth Hansot) *Learning Together: A History of Coeducation in American Public Schools* (New Haven: Yale University Press and Russell Sage Foundation, 1990).

(With Larry Cuban) *Tinkering toward Utopia: A Century of Public School Reform* (Cambridge: Harvard University Press, 1995).

The first time I looked at a Harvard catalogue I felt like a fisherman with a license facing a lake full of fish. I knew that I wanted to understand the United States, and there seemed to be no end of teachers and books on every conceivable American subject. How could I possibly choose a major when I needed to know so much? I rejoiced when I discovered the cross-disciplinary field called American History and Literature (even that name was too narrow for my taste, but one could also take philosophy, political science, and many other subjects under its aegis). By my sophomore year my aspirations had become less grandiose but my joy at that lake full of fish was undiminished.

I decided to focus on history, especially on the experience of immigrants. Studying immigrants was somewhat marginal during my undergraduate years (1948–1952), as was black history. Oscar Handlin, my advisor, helped to change this general inattention to the lives of immigrants. He encouraged me in my decision to write my BA thesis on African-American immigrants from the Cape Verde Islands who settled near Cape Cod. In my research on the Cape Verdeans I was able to study concepts like race and ethnicity as they worked out historically and in contemporary communities. In my undergraduate years at Harvard I went from wanting to study everything to studying one group up close.

Summer work helped pay my college bills and it also played a big part in my education as a social historian. Working in different jobs in different places variously illuminated social theory, clarified how institutions work, gave resonance to literature, and gave a sense of the motivation behind unionization and social movements. Winter work was organized as book learning. Both were important.

In the summer of 1948 I worked in a CCC-style project in the back country of Yosemite National Park. Like many New Deal programs for youth, the Blister Rust Corps had varied purposes. One was conservationist, to preserve Sugar Pines by eradicating the gooseberry bush, a host plant that spread the disease. Another was to provide paying jobs in a time of recession. The camp also embodied a New Deal style of active education that Bob Lowe. Elisabeth Hansot and I explored in *Public Schools in Hard Times*.

In the summer of 1949 I worked in a fruit packing plant, in the foothill town of Loomis, California dumping plums on a conveyor belt. In the busiest harvest times we sometimes worked 14 hours a day. The sorters picked out plums that were hard because ripened plums would never make it to Chicago. The hoboes who camped across the railroad tracks ate rejected plums, that is, the tasty ripe ones.

Though the packing house was in a small town, it was part of a vast distribution network of factories in the field. Between harvest times of frenetic activity the vast farms of the Valley seemed to be empty of people. Although the ideology of the family farm was politically potent, the world of the migratory workers resembled *The Grapes of Wrath* more than the traditional farm. Children in migrant families got their education on the run, unlike the children of managers and owners of the enormous farms. Again, education reflected the divisions of the larger society.

In 1950 I found a job on the assembly line in a Chevrolet factory in Flint, Michigan. The new plant was notorious (or renowned) for its speed-up of the line, depending on whether you were a worker or a boss. Some days the factory turned out a car a minute. True, many of these cars lacked parts like fenders or headlights and were sent to a vast lot to be fitted with the missing parts. The new assembly line at Flint, with its young workers, seemed to have been targeted as a good place to challenge the union and co-opt its leaders. Workers had minimal academic education and received practically no training before being placed on the line. There was a very high turnover, but high wages attracted new laborers.

My first job on the main assembly line required that I pick up a headlight, put its wire through a hole in the left fender, and secure the light with seven screws—all done as the assembly line sped by inexorably. In back of my station was a pit where workers crouched as they tightened floor bolts. The man who inserted the other headlight was a young white male from Appalachia who night after night dreamed that he was riveting eyes into a dragon as it was pushing him over a cliff. My second job was on the fender subassembly station fastening rubber gaskets to the baffles with large staples. The machines made a terrific racket. Subassembly lines fed into the main line. One day, cars started rolling off the assembly line with no left fenders. The prospect of thousands of Chevrolets lined up in the parking lot for defective new cars galvanized the Flint management to action. What *was* the matter? The supervisor of the subassembly section turned up, followed by managers of various levels. Finally a man in a three-piece suit arrived. That meant that the situation was serious.

The cause of the fender-free cars proved to be easy to discover and difficult to remedy. That day three of the four workers did not show up for work at the subassembly line. The utility man who filled in for missing workers was absent that day. Feeling pressure from the group of bosses, the foreman went up to the man who was still at work, a skilled and experienced black worker, and said: "why don't you go faster?" The black worker stared at the man in the three-piece suit and said: "Those machines may run you, but Lincoln freed this man" And then he walked away, and the fender-free cars continued to pour out of the model factory. Of all the jobs I have held, the Flint assembly line was the most stressful and most revealing. In reaction to the relentless noise and pace and stress of life on the line workers found various ways to protest and resist being treated as part of the machine. The men who literally dropped wrenches into the line became heroes because they halted the assembly process. Old timers who had taken part in the sit-ins told stories of resistance in bars after the shift. But the system—a mechanical bureaucracy and bureaucratic machine—usually found ways to deflect opposition. Although urban schools are different in significant ways from factories, periodically school reformers have used the factory as a model of efficiency and productivity. But they, too, discovered that it is easier to industrialize humanity than to humanize industry, whether in school or factory floor.

My next summer job was close to home, in Cambridge. I worked as a construction laborer alongside two immigrants from the Cape Verde Islands, Paul and Gus. At noon we would talk in the shade of a sycamore tree about life in the Islands compared with the U.S. We puzzled over the fact that most Americans seemed to believe that there were two kinds of people, black and white. We talked about "race."

Paul and Gus said that in Cape Verde people did make distinctions between each other based on appearance but rejected the "one drop of blood" version of race. In the Islands there was racism but not race--that is, there were differences of class and color that influenced an individual's standing in society but not one arbitrary and punitive division of all people into white and black. Cape Verdeans taught me a lot about alternative cultural conceptions of social difference. The theme of diversity became central to my work in educational history.

When I decided to write my BA thesis on Cape Verdean experiences in America I discovered few written sources in the enormous library collections at Harvard and only a few fugitive records kept by Cape Verdean leaders. I based the thesis largely on oral histories and conversations in churches, clubs, and homes. That was in 1951–52.

When I returned to Roxbury and Dorchester half a century later I found diversity thriving. School teachers were developing Creole bilingual programs, Cape Verdean students were attending college and forming ethnic clubs, communities were collecting school supplies for children in the islands. Community leaders and social groups were eager to preserve Cape Verdean traditions and to win more political influence

CAREER PATHS

Writing about the lives of Cape Verdeans confirmed my desire to be a social historian. The question remained, however, about how to prepare myself for such a career. The blend of winter and summer learning, academic and activist roles, had worked well for me in my undergraduate years, but it was time to focus on an academic union card and a steady job. Because I had a fellowship at Harvard I limited my search to two programs there that appealed to me: a Ph.D. in history and a Ph.D. in Education. Either would have prepared me to teach social history, but which would best combine activism with intellectual challenge?

I chose the Graduate School of Education because it was a lively place undergoing one of its periodic campaigns to reform American schools this time through improving the education of teachers, the quality of curriculum, and the caliber of leaders. Besides pursuing school reform the School of Education appointed scholars thought likely to set new intellectual agendas and link the School of Education with liberal arts departments.

Bernard Bailyn was one such scholar. He wanted to bring the history of education into the mainstream of social and intellectual history by taking a broad view of education and interpreting it as the transmission of culture across generations. He developed that perspective in the path breaking book *Education in the Forming of American Society*.[3] He called for historians to move beyond parochial perspectives and to create a new history of education.

As Bailyn's teaching assistant and advisee I deeply appreciated the opportunity to be an apprentice as he was thinking his way through these new historical questions and interpretations. I was ambivalent, however, about what was sometimes called the new history of education. I agreed that too many histories in the field had become celebratory and narrowly institutional in scope. I agreed that education was far broader than schooling and took place in a variety of familiar institutions like families, churches, and the media. But I was uneasy with the vagueness of the cultural transmission notion and worried about whether it explained too much. As I proceeded in my own research I found Robert Wiebe's organizational approach more useful for the kind of research I wanted to do.

PRAGMATIC REFORM IN PORTLAND

Dick Sullivan and I sat on the steps of Widener Library for two hours speculating about what an education department at Reed College might become. He was president of Reed, and I was a newly-minted Ph.D, a candidate for a Reed job. As we talked, a template emerged (not surprisingly, it borrowed freely from Harvard). The key purpose was to coordinate the resources of a first-rate liberal arts college and of a fine urban school system so that together they could improve the teaching of academic subjects in the high schools. That kind of reform, buttressed by effective teacher education and an up-to-date curriculum, seemed feasible and important. I was itching to get started.

There was a problem, however: not enough time. At Harvard I had taught in education and history and served as Assistant Dean of freshmen, all at the same time. I had a similar set of responsibilities at Reed except that I was the education department and head of the two master's programs. I also taught a course in American intellectual history and squeezed in a seminar in history of education. Research was for sabbaticals.

A ridiculous workload? Yes--I barely kept my head above water, but I did learn a lot about how schools work, and I had a chance to build the education department from the ground up. I didn't have much time to keep up with scholarship in history of education. A story like this is familiar to many professors who work in small and understaffed education departments, and then are vulnerable to criticism when they fail to produce monographs, Cinderella and her sisters live on. To be fair, this overload of work was mostly of my own doing. Initiating reforms is a stimulating but time-consuming business.

Influential Books
Horace Mann Bond, *Negro Education in Alabama; A Study in Cotton and Steel* (Washington, DC:The Associated Publishers, Inc.,1939).
Bernard Bailyn, *Education in the Forming of American Society* (Chapel Hill: University of North Carolina Press, 1960).
Lawrence A.Cremin, *The Transformation of the School: Progressivism in American Education, 1876–1957* (New York, Knopf, 1961).
Carl Kaestle, *Pillars of the Republic: Common Schools and American Society, 1780–1860* (New York: Hill & Wang, 1983).
Michael B. Katz, *The Irony of Early School Reform : Educational Innovation in Mid-Nineteenth Century Massachusetts* (Cambridge: Harvard University Press, 1968).
Patricia Albjerg Graham, *Community and Class in American Education, 1865–1918* (New York: Wiley, 1974).
Diane Ravitch, *The Troubled Crusade : American Education, 1945–1980* (New York: Basic Books, 1983).

The conditions were ripe for reforms in teacher education and in academic curriculum. In the Portland district as in the nation there was a post-Sputnik pressure to raise academic standards; the school board supported the reforms. Reed professors in liberal arts and sciences were experienced in teaching institutes for high school teachers. They wanted well-prepared students. The Ford and Danforth Foundations gave Reed generous grants for the projects.

I collaborated with Portland on three reforms aimed at strengthening the liberal arts in the high schools: Creating an MAT program to train teachers; revising the high school course in American history; and providing free Reed seminars and institutes designed to bring high school teachers up-to-date in their fields. In my decade at Reed I found it satisfying to build programs and to work with teachers, but the most satisfying part of the Reed work for me turned out to be teaching history of education, swapping classes with three high school history teachers, and researching and writing about Oregon public schools.

RETURNING TO HISTORY OF EDUCATION

When I had a sabbatical I came across some historical actors in the archives whom I have continued to track. George Atkinson was an energetic minister who believed that the common school was an agent of the kingdom of God. In a dark corner of the Oregon Historical Society Library I stumbled over a box full of KKK documents bearing on the origins of the *Pierce* Supreme Court case. I wrote an article on the history of reform of the Portland schools at the turn of the twentieth century that led to the main argument of *The One Best System.*[4] And rounding out the cast was Oliver Cromwell Applegate of Medford, a teacher who preserved his students' themes and orations and poems. Each of these discoveries later led to articles; each reminded me of the pleasures of scholarly inquiry.

After a decade of trying to balance demands in administration, teaching, research, and activism in reform I decided to move on to the University of Illinois, a research university where I could concentrate on teaching and scholarship. It was not easy to leave Portland. My family and I had found lasting delight in climbing and skiing in the Cascades, kayaking on the Columbia, and hiking in the desert and seacoast. I had an image of the balanced and rich life resembling a three-legged stool, with one leg representing family and friends, the second standing for work, and the third (for me) enjoyment of wilderness.

For the first time in my life I was able to concentrate on research and teaching in history of education at Illinois. At Harvard and Reed I always had projects to cultivate or programs to run; at Illinois I was able to take time to link research with the development of new courses. My favorite class was one I co-taught with Jim Anderson, who was then a graduate student. In order to increase the number of African-American students the University admitted a large cohort of first-year students who had attended struggling urban schools in cities like East St. Louis. Of this group about one hundred wanted to become teachers, but there were few curricular adaptations for them. On the contrary, as in most universities at the time, first year students attended large lecture classes while graduate students typically enrolled in small classes adapted to their needs. Pedagogical priorities were upside down. If nothing had been done to accommodate the college of education to the students, drop-outs would have soared.

Different faculty adopted different strategies. Jim Anderson and I taught fifteen students in a seminar that gave them half-time credit. The product of the seminar was a plan for the kind of school they would like to teach in, a composite of the papers they had written and presented to each other. I have rarely met students who were so motivated. Almost all of them continued into the sophomore year. They, in turn, motivated Jim and me to learn more about life in city schools.

COLLABORATION

In the mid 1960s I wrote an essay on the history of the Portland Public Schools, focusing on the turn of the twentieth century.[5] I was beginning to see that a history of urban education could not only be fascinating in its own right but also might illuminate policy questions. I discovered that Michael Katz, whose *Irony of Early School Reform* I found path breaking and eloquent, was writing a history of Boston's schools. When we met to discuss our work, I was delighted to discover that we had both settled on the concept of bureaucracy as a key to understanding the pathologies of urban school system. Critics of urban education in the late 1960s and 70s argued that urban schools were no longer the pinnacle and pride of American education but had become grossly unequal, shrouded in red tape, hostile to innovation and out of touch with the families they are supposed to serve. These were not simply organizational problems, we thought, but fissures in the political economy. In *The One Best System* my intent was not to undermine or destroy public education but to improve it radically. In the last two decades, however, conservative critics have used the bureaucratic critique—and the title *The One Best System*—as evidence that public schools are incurable. There is no way of predicting what will happen when books go public and are kidnapped.

I began my book on urban schools in Illinois and made it my main project when I moved to Stanford in 1969. A group of ten students signed up to take my seminar on the history of urban schools. I warned them that I was just beginning to make sense of the piles of statistics and autobiographies and school reports and other primary sources culled from the Ellwood P. Cubberley Library. So rich was the evidence that it seemed that Cubberley had collected it for our own use. Each student in the seminar presented one kind of primary source and raised an interpretive question about the history of urban schools. At the end of the quarter there were many puzzles left to ponder, and as I entered the library I saw a sign on the wall "**Urban School Seminar Lives On.**" The students, their curiosity piqued, had decided to continue the course on their own and invited me to join them. This experience reinforced my desire to treat research and teaching as two sides of the same coin and to regard motivated students as collaborators.

During my thirty years of teaching at Stanford I was often the only historian of education on the faculty. That made collaboration in teaching with TAs and faculty colleagues a necessity as well as a pleasure. Most of the courses I taught had discussion sections taught by graduate students in history of education. I felt blessed to have talented and scholarly advisees who became, over time, colleagues and friends. They sometimes were able to teach courses based on their own research. Typically, the TAs and I met weekly to confer on how the course was going; teaching is a powerful form of learning. I also co-taught courses with faculty colleagues in philosophy, public policy, sociology, political science, economics and curriculum. Some of these collaborations lasted over twenty years and led to common research and co-authoring

Stanford facilitated cross-disciplinary research by faculty by providing space for short-term seminars and long-term centers. The School of Education is itself a mixture of disciplines. I benefited from these many ways of seeing. When I began research on a new subject—coeducation or leadership or the Great Depression, say--there was usually a seminar or center to learn from. The venue for collaborative research was not always an academic building: Larry Cuban and I developed some of the argument in *Tinkering toward Utopia* on weekly bike rides to Skyline in the Santa Cruz Mountains.[6] My wife Elisabeth Hansot and I have sometimes discovered key research ideas out walking on a Pacific beach.

I have tried in various ways to share what I have learned with people who are not specialists in the field but who wanted to know, as one Maine teacher said to me, "how did we ever create the schools we have?" It has been a pleasure to work on the PBS documentary School with Sarah Mondale and Sarah Patton and to help the staff of *Education Week* produce a thoughtful popular history of education.[7] Efforts to reach a general audience may arouse controversy, just as militancy may produce an ideological push-back. But that is to be expected: books are for engagement, not embalming. In a democratic society the public needs to be part of an on-going conversation about the purposes and practices of education. If my work has contributed to that deliberation, I count myself fortunate.

NOTES

1 David B. Tyack, Robert Lowe, and Elisabeth Hansot, *Public Schools in Hard Times: The Great Depression and Recent Years* (Cambridge: Harvard University Press, 1984).

2 David B. Tyack, *George Ticknor and the Boston Brahmins* (Cambridge: Harvard University Press, 1967).

3 Bernard Bailyn, *Education in the Forming of American Society* (Chapel Hill: University of North Carolina Press, 1960).

4 David Tyack, *The One Best System: A History of Urban Education* (Cambridge: Harvard University Press, 1974.

5 David B. Tyack, "Bureaucracy and the Common School: The Example of Portland, Oregon, 1850–1913,"*American Quarterly*, 19 (Fall 1967): 475–498

6 David Tyack and Larry Cuban, *Tinkering Toward Utopia: A Century of School Reform* (Cambridge: Harvard University Press, 1995)

7 Sarah Mondale and Sarah B. Patton, Eds, *School: The Story of American Public Education* (Boston: Beacon Press, 2001

WAYNE J. URBAN

A VIEW FROM THE PROVINCES

I have had one previous experience in doing an autobiography. That essay, "Wayne's World, Growing Up in Cleveland Ohio," was published in 1996.[1] It detailed my family background (third generation Polish American), my early religion (Roman Catholic), and an education through the bachelor's degree spent in public schools and Catholic schools in and around Cleveland, Ohio. I graduated from John Carroll University in suburban Cleveland, one of many Jesuit institutions in big cities in several states, in 1963. I was a commuter student, making for a relatively narrow undergraduate experience; but I was a football player, offering some glimpse of a campus life, though not much.

When I went to college, I had little idea of what professors did and was uninterested in finding out. My goals, though extremely vague, were mainly centered on teaching and coaching in a high school. I did a little of each during my years at JCU. I was a history major, with a secondary education minor, and my history adviser had gotten his doctorate at Ohio State some years earlier. The ominous shadow of the draft was but one of several factors that inclined me to graduate study. Neither intellectual enrichment nor scholarly accomplishments were in the mix. I entered the master's program in history at OSU, but needed a job to help finance my studies. I interviewed for and was granted an assistantship in a program for training residence hall staff. I was responsible for a small residence hall with 200 students. As a result of this assignment, I also had to take two courses per quarter in the areas of education or psychology. I followed the path of least resistance and changed from history to higher education in my second quarter of graduate study. By the beginning of the second year of graduate school, I realized that I had made a mistake. After getting my master's in higher education and working for one year as an academic adviser in the College of Arts and Sciences at OSU, I discovered an area called history of education, that would give me due credit for both my bachelor's and my master's studies. I was sold, especially as I got to know other students in the area of history (and philosophy) of education. The teaching assistantship that I managed to obtain at OSU was financially rewarding, enough money for my wife and me to begin a family while I was in my doctoral program. Those of us in the doctoral program in history and philosophy of education often joked that OSU had the best graduate students money could buy, and there was some truth in that statement.

The history and philosophy of education program at OSU had a rich past, including the work of notable scholars such as Boyd Bode and H. Gordon Hulfish in philosophy of education, and H. G. Good in history of education. By the time I arrived, the faculty were less noticed than their predecessors, though the program

W. J. Urban, Leaders in the Historical Study of American Education, 275–285.
© 2011 Sense Publishers. All rights reserved.

and the College of Education were still prominent. My doctoral adviser at OSU was Bernard Mehl. Bernie Mehl had been a student of Archibald Anderson at the University of Illinois and came to OSU after a few other positions, one at Hampton University in Virginia, a historically black college made famous by its founder Samuel Chapman Armstrong and his student, Booker T. Washington. Bernie was more of an intellectual gadfly than a scholar, though he published moderately.[2] In those days, history of education meant the history of western (European) education as well as the history of American education. The four of us who taught sections of an advanced undergraduate level history of western education class often visited each other's classes. Occasionally an argument would start in one class and be continued in a succeeding class, taught by another teaching assistant. This was before the days of the accountability movement, which surely would have reined in our arguing with each other in front of students. Nevertheless, the arguments were good for us, the graduate students, and not too harmful to our students, I would think.

Favorites in My Own Writings

"Organized Teachers and Educational Reform in the Progressive Era, 1890–1920," *History of Education Quarterly* 16 (Spring, 1976).

"History of Education: A Southern Exposure," *History of Education Quarterly* 21 (Summer, 1981).

Why Teachers Organized (Detroit: Wayne State University Press, 1982).

"Black Subject, White Biographer," in Craig Kridel ed., *Writing Educational Biography: Explorations in Qualitative Research* (New York: Garland Publishing, 1999).

"Liberalism at the Crossroads: Jimmy Carter, Joseph Califano, and Public College Desegregation," in Wayne J. Urban, ed., *Essays in Twentieth-Century Southern Education: Exceptionalism and Its Limits* (New York: Garland Publishing, 1999).

More than Science and Sputnik: The National Defense Education Act of 1958 (Tuscaloosa: The University of Alabama Press, 2010).

Illinois did not seem to influence Bernie Mehl, at least not in any obvious way that I, or others, could see. He was Jewish, in fact he was a New York Jew; he flaunted his Jewishness and his being a New Yorker in the face of the usually docile and non-argumentative Midwesterners he encountered in Columbus. He was not a mentor to his students, in the ways that we want our faculty to mentor graduate students these days, but he cared for us, perversely we often thought. He picked at us in terms of our backgrounds, urged us to see ourselves as we were and to be proud and critical at the same time of where we had come from. He seemed to want us to work within whatever tradition we came from, not to perpetuate it but to understand it critically, but not necessarily negatively. He valued intellectual argument above all else, and as often as not, he alienated most but also attracted some very good students. I hope I was one of those students. I respected Mehl, at times I feared him; but I learned much from him.

OSU in the 1960s, like many other campuses, was a center of political and personal radicalism. Radicals of many stripes gravitated toward Mehl, and those of us who were less radical, at least in our demeanor, often gazed in awe at what we were seeing.[3] I often referred to myself as Bernie Mehl's "straightest student," a term by which I meant much more than heterosexuality. Yet I must say that Mehl was as intellectual as anyone I have ever met. As an adviser he urged his students to take courses from the best people on the OSU campus, whether in history (Robert Bremner), political science (David Spitz), or sociology (John Cuber). Those three fields were the ones in which I studied in addition to history and philosophy of education.

As I mentioned earlier, I was not mentored for scholarly achievement. Graduate students at OSU went to meetings of the regional philosophy of education society and on occasion to national meetings of groups like the National Society of College Teachers of Education, within which was a history of education section that would become the History of Education Society. But we were not urged to read papers at these meetings. We did, however, try and attend presentations by the big names in our field, in those days Larry Cremin, R. Freeman Butts, Maxine Greene, and a few others. And we also attended presentations by those who had preceded us in the OSU doctoral program.

My dissertation compared educational radicalism in the 1960s to its predecessor movement in the 1930s. I favored the earlier movement over the later one, and tried to make my case, using published books and articles for both movements as my major sources. It was an interesting exercise, one that captured my attention for the year it took to complete. Mehl had gone to Hawaii for most of the year I was writing, and Paul Klohr, a professor of curriculum at OSU who was on my committee, saw me through most of the research and writing on the dissertation. He even encouraged my first publication out of the dissertation, in a curriculum journal.[4] I am grateful to Klohr for the guidance he offered, and to Mehl, in spite of the lack of mentoring I received, or perhaps even in part because of it. I finished my doctoral program a much different person from the one who had started. Sensitivity to dissent, to racial issues, and appreciation for both the strengths and weaknesses of my own culture and educational background, were the results of my doctoral education.

*

It turns out that the job market was not good, at least for OSU history and philosophy of education doctorates, in the late 1960s. After considerable effort seeking a position, I managed to get my first job at the University of South Florida in Tampa in fall, 1968, largely because the leader of the social foundations area at USF, Bozidar Muntyan, had been a philosophy of education graduate student at Illinois when Mehl was there as a history student. I started my first quarter teaching no history of education, but three undergraduate social foundations courses. I came to USF the same year as another educational historian, Erwin Johanningmeier, and he was senior to me, in that he had finished his doctorate a year before I did and had been hired by USF a month or so before I was hired. So, he had prior claim to the one history of American education course that existed at USF. I eventually proposed another history course, titled differently but essentially similar to the other one, and taught it twice in my three years at South Florida. My colleagues at USF were congenial, though not particularly academically inclined. I remember Johanningmeier and I going through the catalog (printed in those days) and finding that about half of the faculty had doctorates from the University of Florida or Florida State University. Neither of us was impressed. The teaching load was three courses a quarter and summer work was available, meaning that everyone got about as much teaching as they wanted, but this left little time for meaningful research.

The result of all of this was that the research culture at USF, especially but not exclusively in the College of Education, was close to non-existent. I don't know exactly why I wanted to research and write history of education; but I did. Perhaps it's because few others at USF, with Johanningmeier as an exception, were inclined toward research. I did some digging around in Florida sources, and wound up doing a study of the Florida teacher walkout of 1968. I published one article out of that work, and I still have some of the interview tapes and documents I collected at that time. When I was asked to review a book on the walkout for the *History of Education Quarterly*, recently, I hoped that I would have no reason to hang on to the materials.[5] The book I reviewed is not by an historian, but rather by one of the NEA staffers who worked in Florida during the walkout. It is a workmanlike job, but there is still room for a good scholarly treatise of that event. I'm not sure I've got enough time left in my career, or the inclination, to write that treatise.

Shortly after my arrival at USF, Michael Katz's path-breaking *The Irony of Early School Reform* was published. Though I was interested in critical analysis of that volume, like everything I read, its reliance on quantification for much of its analysis helped me build bridges to at least one educational statistician on the USF faculty. His explanations of Katz's techniques were helpful to my understanding, and later helped me deal with Maris Vinovskis's volume on Beverly, Massachusetts, which reanalyzed Katz's data and reached a very different conclusion about schools and social mobility. Since that time, though I can't say that I have embraced quantitative history, I have never shied away from reading and trying to incorporate it into my own understandings of educational history.[6]

Tampa, Florida was a bit of a culture shock for me and my wife. It was more southern than I thought it would be, though I had no idea what being "southern" really meant. It was relatively unsophisticated culturally, though it had a vibrant Latin area called Ybor City that is still healthy. The rest of Tampa, however, was not intellectually or culturally oriented. In some ways, it made Columbus, Ohio attractive, something I never thought I would believe. Schools in Tampa, as well as elsewhere in the state, were going through a wrenching development as they strived to meet desegregation demands that had been put on the state. I met Rob Sherman, an educational historian and philosopher now retired from the University of Florida, at a conference on desegregation in my first or second year at USF. Rob and I became friends, as well as colleagues, and I would go to Gainesville, Florida to visit him and his colleagues once or twice a year.

On one of those visits I met John Hardin Best, who had recently come to UF from a long tenure at Rutgers where Sherman had earned his doctorate. While I thought Gainesville was a mecca, it had hills, trees, and a decent bookstore, none of which were in Tampa, John was unimpressed. He left Florida after one year and went to become chair of a new Foundations of Education department at Georgia State University, a commuter school in downtown Atlanta that was in the process of becoming more than a business school and an arts and sciences college. A year later there was an opening at Georgia State and I was hired. I was pleased to get the chance to work with John Best,[7] who at the time was a "name" in the history of American education. He also was a gentle person, a good colleague, and sort of a "mentor," something I had not had before then.

I want to pause and say something about my first two jobs. Though I went through an interview process in each case, I am convinced that I got the positions because of connections, of my adviser with the senior professor at South Florida and of myself with John Best at Georgia State. I've never been a huge fan of merit or meritocracies, though as a student I always tested relatively well. Living and working in the Midwest and the South sensitized me to the biases left unaddressed in meritocratic systems, as did reading Michael Young's *The Rise of the Meritocracy*.[8] The moral of this story, if there is one, is to cultivate connections with others in the field. You never know when they will pay off.

**

I went to Georgia State in the fall of 1971, and by that time the History of Education Society had established itself as an independent scholarly society, not attached to some larger group within education. Also, we had established a regional society in Atlanta, the Southern History of Education Society (SHOES), under the leadership of John Best and Erwin Johanningmeier, in 1970. I enjoyed my early HES experiences and enjoyed SHOES even more. SHOES reflected John Best's laid back approach to things. It had no officers, no dues, no discussants of papers, it was informality at its utmost: but it was a success from its beginning. And John, as a department head, was able on occasion to squeeze out enough money to invite a senior scholar from elsewhere to come to SHOES. Paul Nash and Clarence Karier came to SHOES in its early years, and we have continued to try and entice senior scholars and others from outside the region to its meetings. It continues to exist, now under the leadership of Philo Hutcheson of Georgia State University, and it's still my favorite meeting.

Early on at Georgia State, I was talking about teacher unionism in my graduate history of American education class. This was a topic that had interested me during my graduate study and was featured in my dissertation. I grew up in Cleveland, Ohio, a good, blue-collar, labor union town, and I had plenty of relatives who were union members. Teacher unions and associations were prominent, though not dominant, in the state of Ohio when I was a graduate student. Many of my grad student colleagues were, or had been, working teachers who had a variety of attitudes about teacher unions. I came to the conclusion that the unions were basically ok; they served their members as well as they could. I always included unions and unionism in my teaching, especially in the South where they did not have much of a presence, or a good reputation.

A student in my GSU graduate class told me about an old activist from the Atlanta Public School Teachers Association who was then a principal at a local high school and who had some records of the group. I tracked down these records in a closet at Franklin Delano Roosevelt High School (a beautiful building dating to the 1930s that has recently been made into condominiums), and they became the basis for my first real scholarly work in educational history. My development as a scholar was largely through trial and error. Best was good at helping me with locating outlets and dealing with others in the profession, but he was not particularly interested in my own topic of interest, teacher unions. Fortunately, at Georgia State we had a group of labor historians, including Merl Reed and Gary Fink in the history department, and it was from them that I received support for, and criticism of, my work. In addition, we had a Southern Labor History Archives at GSU, then led by David Gracey and later by Les Hough, that further enhanced the importance of labor history at GSU. Through Reed and Fink I was granted the vaunted "joint appointment" in the history department. I eventually managed to get the Atlanta Public School Teachers Association records deposited in the archives, one of my better scholarly accomplishments..

Works that Influenced My Work:

Horace Mann Bond, *Negro Education in Alabama: A Study in Cotton and Steel* (Washington, DC: Associated Publishers, 1939).

Merle Curti, *The Social Ideas of American Educators* (Paterson, NJ: Pageant Books, 1935).

C. Wright Mills, *White Collar: The American Middle Classes* (New York: Oxford University Press, 1951).

David B. Tyack, *The One Best System: A History of American Urban Education* (Cambridge: Harvard University Press, 1974).

Willard Waller, *The Sociology of Teaching* (New York: Russell and Russell, 1961 [1932].

My first published book was a small, co-authored volume with Don Martin and George Overholt, two of my fellow graduate students at Ohio State, called *Accountability in American Education: A Critique.*[9] It was a workmanlike volume of three chapters, one produced by each of us. It disappeared rather quickly, but I was pleased to hear someone at the 2009 History of Education Society meeting say that it was worth reading to gain some insights into the contemporary accountability movement in education that is responsible for things like the No Child Left Behind Act (NCLB).

My early scholarship, however, was mainly on the history of teacher unions. That work culminated in a 1976 article in the *History of Education Quarterly* and a 1982 book published by the Wayne State University Press.[10] In it, I argued that the historical record squared with my earlier view of teacher unions, that is that they worked hard to serve their members. While this work might not please non-teachers or historians studying teachers, it was good work, and it was done consistently. The book is long out of print and the article seems remote, but I got enough attention paid to that work, and my subsequent work on the National Education Association, to think that I had a worthwhile research emphasis, one that I have not abandoned completely, even to this day.

I want to digress here to recount what I remember as the first paper I ever gave at a History of Education Society meeting. It was in the early 1970s, in Chicago, and the topic was the early history of the Atlanta Public School Teachers Association. I recall a small woman in the front row who listened attentively to my paper, and the others presented with it, and proceeded to ask questions of me that were simultaneously probing and supportive, helpful and critical. I introduced myself to her after the session and that was the beginning of a long friendship and colleagueship with Geraldine Clifford. I know that many other junior scholars had similar experiences with Geraldine and I watched her closely at professional meetings for many years after my first encounter with her in Chicago. I try my best at professional meetings now to emulate Geraldine; to attend as many sessions as I can, including Sunday morning sessions, to listen attentively to what is being presented, and to be simultaneously supportive and critical of the work presented.

John Best left Georgia State in 1977 to become a department head at Pennsylvania State University. I was elected to succeed him for a year as chair of the Department of Educational Foundations and then for two more three year terms. In my seven years as a chair, from 1977 to 1984, my greatest accomplishment was the publication of *Why Teachers Organized* in 1982. I happily stepped down from administration in 1984 and began a new chapter in my scholarly life.

I intended from that point on to emphasize research and scholarship over all other emphases in my academic career. I had tried administration and been reasonably successful, but I didn't like the work. While I was department chair, I also had been elected President of the History of Education Society. My presidential address added a regional focus to my other interest in teacher unions, and I indicated why I was content working as an educational historian in the South in that essay, published as "History of Education: A Southern Exposure."[11] In pursuit of the scholarly emphasis I had set for myself, I received a National Endowment for the Humanities fellowship in the late 1980s to work on a biography of the noted black academic, Horace Mann Bond. That volume was published in 1992 by the University of Georgia Press.[12] A biography was a new experience for me, one that I chose in order to expand my scholarly horizons and one that opened me up anew to the relationships between one's own background and one's research.[13] I wanted to study an educational historian and, in Bond, I found one who struggled with the same tension between scholarship and administrative work throughout his career that I had struggled with in my near decade as a department chair while writing my teacher union book.

Shortly after the Bond book was published, I was hired by the Research Division of the National Education Association to write its history, in time for its seventy-fifth anniversary in 1997.[14] While doing research for that volume, I also looked for materials related to a larger history of the NEA, which I published in

2000.[15] I have kept up an intermittent relationship with the NEA, especially its Research Division, since that time. Ron Henderson, director of the Research Division, is a committed scholar with a doctorate in sociology of education from Michigan State University who has chosen to work for a teachers' union. As I watched him conduct his work, I came to appreciate the ways in which scholarship can, and does, intersect with action, giving life to problems often discussed in university hall-ways. My work on the NEA made liberal use of its archives, one of the most valuable collections of documents related to the history of American education that exists. The problem is that one had to navigate the NEA bureaucracy to get access to the archives, and that was not always an easy process. I am happy to note that the Archives are now housed at George Washington University in the special collections division, which also holds the AAUP papers.

***

At the dawn of the twenty-first century, I considered myself to be both fortunate and unfortunate in my career. I had risen through the ranks at Georgia State to become a Regents' Professor, one of only two in the College of Education and less than ten in the entire university. Yet I also understood that scholarship, though rewarded at Georgia State, was not the primary value of the institution. I always was on the lookout for opportunities away from GSU, however, and I took advantage of several, including teaching at the University of Wisconsin-Madison in the summers of 1973, 1974, and 1989 and at Monash University in Australia in 1984. I learned much about historical scholarship from others in these assignments, especially from Edward Krug, Herbert Kliebard, Jurgen Herbst, and Carl Kaestle in Madison, and from Andy Spaull, Richard Selleck, and Martin Sullivan in Australia. I furthered my international involvement by attending meetings of the International Standing Conference for the History of Education (ISCHE), starting in 1995 in Berlin. Building on ISCHE contacts, I received a Fulbright to the Krakow Pedagogical University in 1999, giving me a chance to teach both undergraduate and graduate students in the land of my ancestors, and to develop a friendship with Czeslaw Majorek of the WSP (initials in Polish for the pedagogical university). In 2004, I applied for and received a Fulbright to York University in suburban Toronto, Canada. I had been to Toronto a few times before, serving as an external examiner on the doctoral thesis of Harry Smaller and attending joint meetings of the US History of Education Society with the Canadian History of Education Association (CHEA/ACHE). At York, I team taught a class with noted Canadian historian of education, Paul Axelrod, who was also then dean of the education school. I have great regard for Canadian scholars, and also have come to appreciate the reasons for their suspicion of American academics. More about that in the next paragraph.

I have attended every ISCHE conference since the Berlin meeting in 1995, and have profited immensely from that attendance. I was elected to the ISCHE executive committee at a meeting in Sydney Australia in 1999 and was elected President of ISCHE for three years at the Sao Paolo meeting in 2002. I think that

ISCHE and other international experiences have taught me at least two things. The first is that there are educational historians in many parts of the world who work quite differently from the way that we do in the US. The ISCHE historians, at least the prominent ones, are much more theoretically sophisticated than we are in the US, and the best of them do not let that sophistication get in the way of their research. They use theory to enhance their research, but not to displace it. The second thing I learned is that there is an often unconscious but very real scholarly imperialism practiced in US history of education that makes us suspect in many other parts of the world. We are often disdainful, or perhaps blissfully ignorant, of the work of scholars outside our boundaries, and that is often obvious to non-American scholars when they meet and interact with Americans. This is shortsighted and ignorant on our part, and I am not sure what, other than increased contact, can improve the situation. In a global age, I would think that we cannot afford such narrowness.

Near the end of 2005, I decided to retire from Georgia State, mainly because of a program review which the Provost of our institution used to end one of the doctoral programs in my department and to seriously put the others in jeopardy. As retirement drew near, I decided that I didn't want to stop academic work, so I began to look for another job. I was aware that positions in history of education were scarce and so I widened my search. Fortunately for me, a position was open in the newly re-established Education Policy Center at the University of Alabama. I had several acquaintances on the Alabama faculty and had had contact with the dean doing work related to journal publishing some years earlier. I interviewed for the position, without really knowing the ins and outs of education policy, and accepted the post of Associate Director of the Center. I was to be responsible for the inside duties of the Center, coordinating work with faculty in the College and helping bring relevant outsiders to Tuscaloosa to work with us on policy issues.

I had no intention of abandoning historical research in my new position and I managed to complete a historical study of the National Defense Education Act, a work with obvious federal policy implications.[16] In my six years at Alabama, I have taught history of American education only once, but have managed to conduct some policy seminars with sizable history components. I recently taught a seminar on James Bryant Conant, long-time president of Harvard University, participant in the development of the atomic bomb in World War II, diplomat in Germany after the war, and a giant in the development of mid-twentieth American educational policy. Conant's policy work, which will be the topic of what I am calling an educational biography I plan to publish, pertained mainly to the high school but also related to higher education. I knew of Conant, of course, but he came more directly to my attention as part of my work on the Educational Policies Commission, a creation of the NEA and the American Association of School Administrators. My EPC study was funded by the Spencer Foundation, and I intend to approach them, and other funding agencies if necessary, to support my work on Conant.

One other aspect of my work has been a textbook, written with Jennings Wagoner of the University of Virginia, who was also a graduate student in the same doctoral program I finished at Ohio State. We kept up with each other over the years and, when Jennings had gotten a contract for a textbook, he asked me to join him in the project. Textbooks are not particularly valued in the scholarly world, and history of education is no exception to that rule. While colleagues acknowledge the text, they don't usually say anything substantive about it. Yet our book has gone through four editions and has been read by many more students than have ever read any piece of research I produced.[17] Jennings and I are proud of our textbook, and happy to have done it.

****

As I reread this essay and ponder the circumstances of my career, I want to offer the following conclusions. History of education was an excellent field in which someone like me, with non-prestigious credentials to begin with, could achieve something. Yet it also seems the case that history of education was, and is, not immune to the status hierarchies that plague the academy at large and influence success and failure in it. Second, working in areas like the history of teacher associations and southern educational history were good choices for me, though certainly not in any way trend setting or trend seeking. This conclusion may be another version of the second part of the first conclusion. Following one's interest and not the fashions in one's discipline may be an appropriate choice for scholars who do not start out from institutions holding its highest ranking and have little expectation of attaining that ranking. Finally, one exceptionally good aspect of working in the history of education is that one interacts with colleagues from both the education side, and the history side, and that the interaction is productive, based on achievement, and takes place in a field small enough that one can build lasting relationships with both sets of colleagues.

My Conant project is undertaken to explore the larger relations between arts and sciences and education and the impact those relations have had on the development of high schools and of education faculties in colleges and universities since World War II.[18] Just as in my Bond biography, I am exploring Conant, and also myself. That is, the relations between education and arts and sciences are relations in which I have been enmeshed since graduate school. No one whom I know would characterize these relations as amicable. Exploring Conant's views on them is a way to get at the relations within a set of concrete particulars, that is, one man's views and contacts. But I also want to get some insight into the larger course of those relations since Conant wrote. I don't think it will be a pretty picture.

NOTES

[1] Wayne J. Urban, "Wayne's World: Growing Up in Cleveland Ohio, 1942–1963," *Educational Studies* 26 (Winter, 1995). .

[2] Bernard Mehl, *Classic Educational Ideas from Sumeria to America* (Columbus, OH: Merrill, 1972) and idem., "Education in American History," in George F. Kneller, ed., *Foundations of Education* (New York: John Wiley, 1964).

[3] Mehl was also the advisor for Dave Angus of the University of Michigan and Jack E. Williams, of the University of Wisconsin-Milwaukee, both of whom finished the doctoral program before I did.

[4] Wayne J. Urban, "Militancy and the Profession," *Educational Leadership* 26 (January, 1969).

[5] Don Cameron, *Educational Conflict in the Sunshine State* (Lanham, MD: Rowman and Littlefield, 2008).

[6] Michael B. Katz, *The Irony of Early School Reform: Educational Innovation in Nineteenth Century Massachusetts* (Cambridge: Harvard University Press, 1968) and Maris Vinovskis, *The Origins of Public High Schools: A Reexamination of the Beverly High School Controversy* (Madison: University of Wisconsin Press, 1985). Katz and Vinovskis also conducted a scholarly exchange on their research and contrasting conclusions about Beverly in the Summer, 1987 issue of the *History of Education Quarterly*.

[7] John H. Best, ed., *Benjamin Franklin on Education* (New York: Bureau of Publications, Teachers College, 1962); and Best and Robert T. Sidwell, eds., *The American Legacy of Learning: Readings in the History of Education* (Philadelphia, Lippincott, 1967).

[8] Michael Young, *The Rise of the Meritocracy* (New Brunswick, NJ: Transaction Publishers, 1994 [1958]).

[9] *Accountability in American Education: A Critique* (Princeton, NJ: Princeton Publishing, 1976).

[10] Wayne J. Urban, "Organized Teachers and Educational Reform in the Progressive Era, 1890–1920, *History of Education Quarterly* 16 (Spring, 1976) and idem *Why Teachers Organized* (Detroit: Wayne State University Press, 1982).

[11]. Wayne J. Urban, "History of Education: A Southern Exposure," *History of Education Quarterly* 21 (Summer, 1981). I was delighted to hear Eileen Tamura mention my presidential address in her own presidential address at the HES meeting in Philadelphia in October of 2009. See the published version of Tamura's address, Eileen H. Tamura, "Value Messages Collide with Reality: Joseph Kurihara and the Power of Informal Education," *History of Education Quarterly* 50 (February, 2010).

[12] Wayne J. Urban, *Black Scholar: Horace Mann Bond, 1904–1972* (Athens: University of Georgia Press, 1992).

[13] I wrote about these issues in the Preface to the Bond biography and in an essay published in the volume on educational biography edited by Craig Kridel. See Wayne J. Urban, "Black Subject: White Biographer," in Craig Kridel, ed., *Writing Educational Biography* (New York: Garland, 1998).

[14] Wayne J. Urban, *More than the Facts: The Research Division of the National Education Association, 1922–1997* (Lanham, MD: University Press of America, 1998). Again, connections were important in getting this assignment. Ron Henderson asked James Anderson, noted historian of education at the University of Illinois, if he knew anyone working on the history of teacher associations. Jim gave Ron my name and he contacted me about the assignment, which I happily accepted.

[15] Wayne J. Urban, *Gender, Race, and the National Education Association: Professionalism and Its Limitations* (New York: Routledge/Falmer, 2000).

[16] Wayne J. Urban, *More than Science and Sputnik: The National Defense Education Act of 1958* (Tuscaloosa: The University of Alabama Press, 2010).

[17] Wayne Urban and Jennings Wagoner, *American Education: A History* (New York: McGraw-Hill, 1996, 2000, 2004: Routledge, 2009).

[18] Two of the other contributors to this volume have addressed these issues, see Geraldine J. Clifford and William J. Guthrie, *Ed School: A Brief for Professional Education* (Chicago: University of Chicago Press, 1988) and David F. Labaree, *The Trouble with Ed Schools* (New Haven: Yale University Press, 2004).

MARIS A. VINOVSKIS

FROM RIGA TO ANN ARBOR

Belatedly Pursuing Education History and Policy

Education always played a very important role in my life, but issues relating to education were not a major focus of my scholarly and policy work at first. In part, this reflects the unexpected, but fortuitous events in my academic endeavors that later made education history and policymaking a central part of my academic and policy work.

EARLY EXPERIENCE

I was born in Riga, Latvia in January 1943 during World War II while Latvia was the site of continuous warfare. At that time, my father (Arveds) and mother (Lucija) lived in Riga with their eighteen-month-old daughter (Daila). My father, who grew up in a peasant household, attended the University of Latvia and received his law degree. Before the war, he worked in the Latvian comptroller's office. When the Soviet Union forcibly annexed Latvia in June 1940, my father's future was precarious since he had worked for the previous Latvian government and while at the university had joined a fraternity (most of which were strongly nationalistic). When the Soviets secretly prepared to deport to Siberia a large number of former Latvian government employees and members of the intelligentsia in June 1941, one of his former communist university classmates warned him so that he was able to flee to the forests. After Germany invaded the Soviet Union a week later, their army quickly occupied Latvia. My father returned and worked for the new Latvian government (now controlled by the Germans).

By late 1943 the Soviets regained the military initiative and were expected to reoccupy Latvia soon. Latvian civilians now were sent to Germany to work. Initially our family was assigned to go to Dresden (just prior to the allied bombing attacks), but after the massive bombings there we were rerouted to Czechoslovakia. As the Red army approached, our family fled toward Munich and fortunately ended up in the American zone. We spent the next five years in a displaced person's camp (populated mainly by Latvians). My father, who had legal training and spoke several languages, commuted to nearby Munich and worked for the United Nations Relief and Rehabilitation Commission.

The United States passed special immigration legislation to allow 400,000 displaced persons to enter the country. In 1949 we emigrated to Blair, Nebraska, a small rural town of about 5,000 people. We were welcomed and greatly assisted by

W. J. Urban, Leaders in the Historical Study of American Education, 287–298.

the community. My father worked in the Lutheran Publishing Company and my mother washed dishes at a local restaurant. In the evenings my parents were janitors in an elementary school.

My sister and I were placed into the first grade. Since neither of us knew the English language, we sat through most of the classes without any idea of what was being discussed. Gradually by the second grade we learned the English language. Several teachers provided extra help so that I quickly caught up with my classmates academically.

OMAHA CENTRAL HIGH SCHOOL

My father changed jobs to work as a common laborer at an Omaha packinghouse where the work was much harder, but the pay was better. We moved to Omaha in 1957 and I attended Central High School, an inner-city school attracting a diverse student body, fielding strong sports teams, and providing high quality academic instruction (Central was named by *Newsweek* in the late 1950s as the 38th best high school in the nation). I did well academically and in my senior year took calculus and advanced placement courses in history, English, and physics. I also played varsity football and basketball. Our football team was the state champion and our basketball team reached the state finals.

> ### My Favorite Publications
>
> Carl F. Kaestle and Maris A. Vinovskis, *Education and Social Change in Nineteenth-Century Massachusetts* (Cambridge: Cambridge University Press, 1980).
>
> Maris A. Vinovskis, *Fertility in Massachusetts from the Revolution to the Civil War* (New York: Academic Press, 1981).
>
> Maris A. Vinovskis, *The Origins of Public High Schools: A Re-Examination of the Beverly High school Controversy* (Madison: University of Wisconsin Press, 1985).
>
> Maris A. Vinovskis, *An "Epidemic" of Adolescent Pregnancy? Some Historical and Policy Perspectives* (New York: Oxford University Press, 1988).
>
> Maris A. Vinovskis, ed., *Toward a Social History of the Civil War: Exploratory Essays on the North* (Cambridge: Cambridge University Press, 1990).

The continued economic challenges facing our family aroused my early interest in public policy, especially on how to help low-income families. With a private mortgage from a kind American, my parents purchased a home in Blair; but we were forced to relocate when an elementary school was built there. After going to Omaha, we acquired another home, but soon had to move when our property became part of a freeway project. A few years later, our next home was urban renewed as well. In all of these transactions, my father felt we never received a fair market price for the condemned properties, but he could not afford the lawyer fees and time necessary to contest those decisions. The Cudahy packinghouse, where my father worked for many years, closed unexpectedly. Partly because of his age, my father had great difficulty finding another job (eventually he obtained a minimum-wage job at a local Omaha printing house).

Everyone, including myself, assumed that I would go to college. My academic grades and test scores were strong and my football skills were competitive, a combination that appealed to colleges. I willingly played football and basketball, but my parents only praised academic achievement, seeing sports as a temporary and potentially dangerous diversion. Therefore, I hoped to go to a college where I would not be required to play football.

Many college representatives visited Central High School recruiting potential students. I went to several sessions and was particularly impressed by Wesleyan University, a small liberal arts school that seemed ideal. I applied for early admission and was offered an academic scholarship (though I suspect my football experiences also may have played a role in their decision). My financial circumstances improved later that spring when I received a National Merit Scholarship which made it possible for me to attend college without any financial assistance from my parents (I chose not to play any college football or basketball).

WESLEYAN UNIVERSITY

Wesleyan University turned out to be an ideal place for me. Initially I was home sick and worried about competing with my well-prepared prep school classmates. Over time, however, I managed to do well in my studies and benefited once again from the special help and encouragement provided by my professors. I debated whether to pursue science or history. I became a history major because of my passion for the subject and the realization that I was competent, but not outstanding in science (I also toyed with the idea of sociology, but was discouraged by the limited number of courses available at Wesleyan).

I still had no idea of what career I might pursue, but continued to have strong interest in public policy. During my senior year in 1965, I hitchhiked to Alabama to participate in the march in Selma. I never made it to Selma as I was arrested during a peaceful NAACP demonstration in Montgomery and spent a week in jail on a hunger strike before being bailed out. My parents feared for my safety and wondered what effect that arrest might have on my future. That experience was an important turning point for me in many ways, reinforcing my interest in fostering social justice and helping the disadvantaged.

During my senior year I received several awards at Wesleyan and was selected as the university's representative to a White House student leadership meeting. As an informal part of that trip, I met with John Macy (chair of the Civil Service Commission and a Wesleyan alumnus) who urged me to consider a federal civil service career. At the same time, under the guidance of Richard Buel, I wrote an honors thesis on the nullification crisis in antebellum South Carolina. This was an important experience as it proved to me that I could undertake and enjoy original historical research. Interestingly, despite the importance of teachers and schooling in my own life, it never occurred to me to pursue education history as a possible honors thesis topic.

As I prepared to leave Wesleyan, I only had a vague idea of what I might do next. My interest in entering public service had increased, but others also urged me to continue my education. I briefly considered attending law school, but I really did not know much about American lawyers or law schools. Buel suggested that I apply to three history graduate programs as well as compete for several national fellowships. I received a four-year Danforth graduate fellowship (for someone interested in college teaching) and entered the Harvard History Department in 1965.

HARVARD UNIVERSITY

At Harvard I wanted to study the congressional career of John F. Kennedy (1946–1960), focusing on his relationship with his constituents as well as his Washington policymaking. The Harvard History Department, however, considered the topic to be too close to the present and I switched to working with Bernard Bailyn, a prominent colonialist who was sympathetic to social science research. My interests now shifted to colonial and antebellum demographic and social history. Although Bailyn had written an influential, short monograph on colonial education, we never discussed the possibility that I might pursue a career in education history. Similarly, although my wife (Mary) was a high school science and math teacher we did not spend much time discussing education issues.

My Favorite Publications (continued)

Gerald F. Moran and Maris A. Vinovskis, *Religion, Family, and the Life Course: Explorations in the Social History of Early America* (Ann Arbor: University of Michigan Press, 1992).

Diane Ravitch and Maris A. Vinovskis, eds., *Learning from the Past: What History Teaches Us About School Reform* (Baltimore: Johns Hopkins University Press, 1995).

Maris A. Vinovskis, *History and Educational Policymaking* (New Haven: Yale University Press, 1999).

Maris A. Vinovskis, *The Birth of Head Start: Preschool Education Policies in the Kennedy and Johnson Administrations* (Chicago: University of Chicago Press, 2005).

Maris A. Vinovskis, *From A Nation at Risk to No Child Left Behind: National Education Goals and the Creation of Federal Education Policy* (New York: Teachers College Press, 2009).

Rather than live in Cambridge, where the rents were high and the nearby community populated mainly by Harvard faculty and students, Mary and I decided to live in Somerville, an adjoining working-class, Catholic community notorious for its corrupt municipal politics. I joined the NAACP and became active in the recently formed Somerville Racial Understanding Committee. An unknown Episcopalian minister, S. Lester Ralph, decided to challenge the incumbent Irish mayor in 1969. Although almost no one believed he had any chance of winning in the three-way race, I joined a small number of reformers who organized his campaign. Angry with Somerville cronyism and corruption, the voters handily elected Ralph.

I almost postponed my Harvard graduate studies to accept a full-time Somerville administrative job. Instead, I continued working on my dissertation, received a part-time Somerville Zoning Appeals Board appointment, and spent much of my time working closely with the mayor for the next three years. Most of my involvement was helping him with local, county, and state political activities (including working on Lester Ralph and Paul Tsongas's successful Middlesex county races, Ralph's unsuccessful Massachusetts attorney general election, Senator Henry M. Jackson's [D-WA] unsuccessful Massachusetts presidential primary contest, and Ralph's successful mayoral re-election). Although I was involved in Somerville politics only a short time, it remains one of my most satisfying experiences. Ralph served as mayor for four terms and then was succeeded by another local reformer for four more terms. While the more traditional Somerville politicians continue trying to regain control of the community, they have failed to do so.

My own political orientation at the time was complex. Based upon my background and continued foreign policy interests, I strongly opposed the Soviet Union's policies; but I supported U.S. government programs to help disadvantaged Americans of all races. Like my father, I was a registered Republican; but I spent most of my time in Massachusetts working for Democratic candidates. At Harvard I joined the Ripon Society, the newly created liberal Republican organization and was selected as a Somerville delegate to the 1970 Massachusetts Republican State convention. Mary and I represented the Ripon Society in the 1968 Poor People's March on Washington. While some of my Wesleyan and Harvard classmates joined more radical organizations such as the Students for A Democratic Society (SDS), I disagreed with many of their policies and preferred supporting moderate state and local reform efforts.

My Ph.D. thesis set out to explain the late eighteenth-century and antebellum decrease in Massachusetts birth rates, well before such a sustained decline occurred in most other nations. As I was working on the thesis, I wandered by the newly created Harvard Population Center. I stopped in and encountered by chance Roger Revelle, the center director. After explaining my thesis topic, Revelle provided me with an office and I became one of the few graduate students informally associated with the center.

The Population Center faculty accepted me as a junior colleague and my work benefited greatly from attending their seminars and talks. Even more importantly, Revelle became a close personal mentor and role model. I was fascinated by Revelle, who had served as a science adviser to the U.S. Department of Interior during the Kennedy administration. He combined academic excellence with Washington policymaking, and still managed to find time for aspiring graduate students. When Revelle decided to offer a new undergraduate science course in 1968–69, "Population, Natural Resources, and the Environment," I became one of the course planners and section leaders (Al Gore was a student in one of my sections). With another graduate student, Ashok Khosla, the three of us edited a collection of course readings[1] which provided a more moderate, and we thought a more realistic, assessment than the popular doomsday *Population Bomb* (1968) by Paul Ehrlich.[2]

As I continued on my dissertation, the topic of education emerged. One possible explanation for the antebellum decline in Massachusetts fertility was the increase in the education level of the population due to Horace Mann's common school reforms in the late 1830s and 1840s. Yet Albert Fishlow, an economic historian, used partial state education data to argue provocatively that Mann's reforms actually did not increase Massachusetts school attendance.[3] I re-examined those trends in more depth and found that the percentage of Massachusetts children in school actually declined from 1840 to 1860. The explanation for that decline was that a high percentage of children under age four had enrolled in public and private infant schools in 1840, but by 1860 there were almost no children under age four in Massachusetts schools.[4] In part this change occurred because medical experts argued that premature intellectual stimulation of young children's minds would lead to their subsequent insanity as adolescents.[5]

Influential Publications in My Past
Bernard Bailyn, *Ideological Origins of the American Revolution* (Cambridge: Harvard University Press, 1967).
Ernest Becker, *The Denial of Death* (New York: Free Press, 1973).
Theodore Caplow, *The Academic Marketplace* (New York: Anchor Books, 1965).
Merle Curti, *The Making of an American Community: A Case Study of Democracy in a Frontier County* (Stanford: Stanford University Press, 1959).
Robert William Fogel and Stanley L. Engerman, *Time on the Cross: The Economics of American Negro Slavery* (Boston: Little Brown, 1974), 2 vols.

The unexpected rediscovery of the antebellum infant school movement resulted in several co-authored papers as well as other education articles on trends in Massachusetts education, antebellum female teachers, and an analysis of Horace Mann's ideas about the economic productivity of education.[6] At the same time, however, I spent most of my academic time working on my dissertation. In 1974 I delivered the Bland-Lee Lectures at Clark University on "Demographic History and the World Population Crisis" and wrote several substantive and methodological demographic and family history essays.[7]

UNIVERSITY OF WISCONSIN

After seven years in graduate school, it seemed an appropriate time to start looking for a permanent academic job. While I was making good progress on my dissertation, it wasn't finished and would likely require several years to complete. On the other hand, there was growing interest in quantitative history and a shortage of qualified practitioners. Although I had been advised to complete my dissertation and forego publishing any articles, by 1972 I had published four essays and several others had been accepted for publication. In October 1972 I was invited by the University of Wisconsin to give a job talk in U.S. social history and soon afterwards I was invited to join their faculty. At the same time, Revelle offered me a position at the Harvard Population Center. I was uncertain what I should do, but Bailyn felt strongly that it would be a mistake not to join such a distinguished history program. Mary and I agreed and that led unexpectedly to further work in education history. While I was still finishing my dissertation at Wisconsin, I met Carl Kaestle from the School of Education. Carl had just received a large grant from the National Institute of Education (NIE) to study Massachusetts antebellum education. Initially I was designated as a statistical consultant to his NIE project, but soon the work led to a full collaboration and co-authorship of the report and subsequent book.[8]

Working with Carl on the Massachusetts project was one of the great intellectual and personal joys in my career. Though there were some differences in our interpretations, we never had any difficulty in resolving them. Our orientations and strengths nicely complimented each other and the book was certainly much stronger analytically, better written, and more interesting than if I had ever tried to do such a project by myself. Whereas education history had been just another fascinating, but small academic issue for me, now it became one of my two or three major intellectual pursuits. Over the years, I have co-authored articles or books with about 30 first-rate scholars (about a third of them with my students). My collaboration and continued friendship with Carl still remains among the very best of those experiences.

SELECT COMMITTEE ON POPULATION

Thanks to a generous offer in 1974, I joined the Department of History and the Institute for Social Research (ISR) at the University of Michigan. I completed my dissertation the following year and received tenure in 1977. At Michigan I pursued many different research topics besides my heightened interest in education history. I continued studies of demographic and family history, began a large-scale NIH project on antebellum insane asylums (with Barbara Rosenkrantz), and analyzed the politics of federal abortion funding (working closely with both the pro-choice and pro-life organizations).

My interest in public policy continued during the 1970s. Just after President Richard Nixon's re-election, a Wesleyan classmate working on the White House staff invited me to join him in Washington. I declined since it would have delayed completion of the dissertation and disrupted the start of my academic career. Then the U.S. House of Representatives created a Select Committee on Population in 1977. When Chairman James Scheuer (D-NY) was looking for a professional staff, I was recommended by Revelle as a possible candidate. Although I was a registered Republican, Scheuer offered me the position of Assistant Staff Director and I accepted. The Republicans led by John Erlenborn (R-IL) had difficulty finding their own appropriate social science staffers. By mutual agreement of Scheuer and Erlenborn, I was switched and became the Minority Staff Director of the Select Committee. Under the circumstances, the majority and minority staffs were merged in practice (though still technically separate). This facilitated the bipartisan cooperation of the representatives and staffs in what otherwise might have been a more contentious endeavor.

Working on the Select Committee was a valuable and satisfying personal experience, both in participating in the Washington legislative process as well proving to myself that I could succeed in such an administrative and policy capacity. It also demonstrated my ability and willingness to work with both Republican and Democratic Washington policymakers. I led the Task Force on Adolescent Pregnancy and served as the staff liaison to groups involved with abortion issues. I was promoted to Deputy Staff Director, and later offered the Staff Director's job. Given my other commitments as well as my decision to remain in academia, I returned to the University of Michigan in early 1979.

OFFICE OF ADOLESCENT PREGNANCY PROGRAMS

Upon my return, I continued analyzing federal adolescent pregnancy policy. In early 1981 Marjory Mecklenburg, a pro-life and pro-family planning advocate, was appointed as the Director of the Office of Adolescent Pregnancy Programs (OAPP) in the Reagan Administration. She invited me to spend a few days as a consultant analyzing her new office and offering suggestions for improving its operation. I gladly agreed as it provided me with a unique access to the OAPP records. My brief experiences there led to an invitation to join her staff, but I did not want to return to Washington full-time at that point. Instead, she hired me as a social science consultant. In addition, I helped draft sensitive office memos, with the understanding that I would not share any of the confidential information at that time, but later could use it in my scholarly analyses.

Influential Publications in My Past (continued)

Oscar Handlin, *Boston's Immigrants, 1790–1865: A Study in Acculturation* (Cambridge: Harvard University Press, 1941).

Carl F. Kaestle, *Pillars of the Republic: Common Schools and American Society, 1780–1860* (New York: Hill and Wang, 1983).

Michael B. Katz, *The Irony of Early School Reform: Educational Innovation in Mid-Nineteenth-Century Massachusetts* (Cambridge: Harvard University Press, 1968).

Stephan Thernstrom, *Poverty and Progress: Social Mobility in a Nineteenth-Century City* (Cambridge: Harvard University Press, 1964).

Yasukichi Yasuba, *Birth Rates of the White Population in the United States, 1800–1860: An Economic Study* (Baltimore: Johns Hopkins University Press, 1962).

I commuted regularly to Washington for about five years to work with OAPP as well as the Office of Family Planning Programs (which Mecklenburg soon inherited). Since I have never taken a public stand on abortion policies (because as a scholar I worked with both sides), I was surprised later when Mecklenburg asked me to become the Director of Family Planning Programs. I decided not to pursue that job as I preferred continuing my academic work while simultaneously being a regular Washington consultant involved with domestic policymaking. Drawing upon those experiences, I published a book on adolescent pregnancy.[9]

Many of my 1980s publications focused on issues such as adolescent pregnancy, the decline in fertility, the role of the elderly in the past, death and dying, Puritan religion, Civil War social history, and life-course analysis. But work on education continued as well. My co-authored book with Carl Kaestle on education in nineteenth century Massachusetts appeared in 1980.[10] Five years later, I questioned Michael Katz's classic interpretation of Massachusetts school politics in my book centered on his analysis of the Beverly High School.[11] In addition, I published several articles and essays on colonial and antebellum schools.[12]

OFFICE OF EDUCATIONAL RESEARCH AND IMPROVEMENT

Diane Ravitch, a distinguished education historian, was appointed as the Assistant Secretary of the Office of Educational Research and Improvement (OERI) in the George H.W. Bush administration. In 1992 she invited me to come to Washington as the OERI Research Adviser and I agreed. My primary OERI assignment was assessing the quality of the educational research produced by the 10 regional education laboratories and 25 research and development centers. I also provided advice on a variety of other research-related OERI issues. In addition, as Diane and I are both education historians, we remembered the complaints from our colleagues that education policymakers rarely incorporated an historical perspective into their decision-making. Therefore, OERI commissioned 14 historical essays about the current education reforms. Diane and I co-edited the book which has been adopted in college-level courses and consulted by some policymakers.[13]

My OERI experiences expanded my historical work into analyzing current education policies. Having worked under several different Washington decision-makers, it was a particular privilege and pleasure to work with Diane. She always was supportive and never tried to influence inappropriately my judgment of the quality of the OERI research. Moreover, Diane's continued friendship and intellectual advice over the past 15 years has provided invaluable assistance for my education policy studies.

When Democrats recaptured the presidency in November 1992, there was speculation that I might be encouraged to leave OERI. Although my appointment had not been political, I was hired as a temporary Senior Executive Service employee, a well-paid and highly-desirable position. Moreover, some lab and center directors opposed the release of my forthcoming report because it raised serious questions about the quality of their research during the past five years. A "secret" inquiry was made within the Department of Education whether my report could be suppressed when I returned to the University of Michigan (since the report had already placed in the ERIC government document system, it was deemed public information).

When Sharon Robinson arrived as Diane's replacement, I remained as the OERI Research Adviser. It was fascinating to watch how career employees adjusted to a new administration. I continued working on a variety of research issues, including writing policy briefs on the concept of systemic reform as well as analyzing the earlier Follow Through program. Previously I had promised to return to the University of Michigan in fall 1993 to chair the History Department and did so. OERI then hired me as a consultant for the next two years and I regularly commuted to Washington. I later revised the lab and center report and incorporated its findings into my book on OERI.[14]

INCREASING INVOLVEMENT IN EDUCATION RESEARCH AND POLICY

My participation in contemporary education policy increased substantially after working with OERI. I was commissioned to write agency histories for the National Assessment Governing Board (1998) and the National Education Goals Panel (1998–2001). These opportunities broadened my understanding of the field of education policies as well as provided me with access to their records and personnel. I participated in evaluations for the National English Standards (1994), the National History Standards (1995), the Iowa and Kentucky state education plans (1996), the Even Start Family Literacy program (1997–2003), the Comprehensive Service Centers (1998–9), and the ERIC history program (2004–9). I testified about education before six House and Senate committees (1997–2000) as well as served twice on the congressionally-mandated independent review panels to review Goals 2000 (1995–2001) and No Child Left Behind (2003–8). During this period, several education and policy-related books appeared.[15]

Since my work focused heavily on education policy in the 1990s, there were other opportunities as well. Some of my GOP friends were concerned that I had worked in the Clinton administration, but most policymakers appreciated or at least tolerated my interest and willingness to serve in different administrations. Following the close election of George W. Bush in November 2000, I was appointed to the 31 person education transition team for the new administration (as a group our transition team did not meet or draft any education proposals). Around Christmas I was asked, on behalf of the new administration, whether I would consider becoming the next OERI Assistant Secretary. I was honored by the opportunity, but remained at Michigan in order to complete my various research projects. In 2003 I was reappointed to the congressionally-mandated independent panel to help assess No Child Left Behind.

When the Harris School of Public Policy at the University of Chicago searched for a faculty member with Washington experience in the late 1990s, I was approached and eventually offered the position. Although Mary and I were very tempted by the prospect of being in Chicago, we finally decided to stay in Ann Arbor. I did, however, become a faculty member at the Gerald R. Ford School of Public Policy in addition to my History Department and ISR appointments at the University of Michigan.

My current work includes collaborating with my colleagues in the Education School, Bob Bain and Jeff Mirel, in recruiting undergraduate history majors for K-12 teaching. Gerald Moran, my long-time co-author from the University of Michigan at Dearborn, and I continue to work on our draft book manuscript, "Mass Literacy, Public Schooling, and Gender in America, 1630–1870." My new research projects include studying Head Start in the Richard Nixon, Gerald Ford, and Jimmy Carter administrations as well as analyzing Barack Obama's education policies. Jeff Mirel and I are planning to investigate current and future K-12 education policies from a broad historical perspective. And after almost seven decades since I left Riga, I especially look forward to returning there In May 2010 to deliver the keynote address at the Baltic Association for Teacher Education.

NOTES

1　Roger Revelle, Ashok Khosla, and Maris A. Vinovskis, *The Survival Equation: Man Resources, and his Environment* (Boston: Houghton Mifflin, 1971).

2　Paul R. Ehrlich, *The Population Bomb* (New York: Ballantine, 1968).

3　Albert Fishlow, "The Common School Revival: Fact or Fancy?" in *Industrialization in Two Systems: Essays in Honor of Alexander Gershenkron*, ed. Henry Rosovsky (New York: Wiley, 1968), 40–67.

4　Maris A. Vinovskis, "Trends in Massachusetts Education, 1826–1860," *History of Education Quarterly* 12 (Winter 1972): 501–29.

5　Dean May and Maris A. Vinovskis, "A Ray of Millennial Light," in *Family and Kin in Urban Communities, 1700–1930*, ed. Tamara K. Hareven (New York: New Viewpoints, 1977), 62–99.

6　Maris A. Vinovskis, "Horace Mann on the Economic Productivity of Education," *New England Quarterly* 43 (December 1970): 550–71; Richard M. Bernard and Maris A. Vinovskis, "The Female School Teacher in Antebellum America," *Journal of Social History* 10 (Spring 1977): 332–45.

7　Maris A. Vinovskis, *Demographic History and the World Population Crisis* (Worcester, MA: Clark University Press, 1976). Maris A. Vinovskis, "The 1789 Life Table of Edward Wigglesworth," *Journal of Economic History* 31 (September 1971): 570–90; Richard D. Tabors and Maris A. Vinovskis, "Preferences for Municipal Services of Citizens and Political Leaders: Somerville, Massachusetts, 1971," in Elihu Bergman, et al., eds., *Population Policymaking in the American States: Issues and Processes* (Lexington, MA: D.C. Heath, 1974), 101–34; Maris A. Vinovskis, "The Field of Early American History: A Methodological Critique," *The Family in Historical Perspective* no. 7 (Winter 1974): 2–8; Maris A.Vinoskis and Tamara K. Hareven, "Marital Fertility, Ethnicity, and Occupation in Urban Families," *Journal of Social History* 8 (Spring 1975): 69–93; Maris A. Vinovskis, "Angels' Heads and Weeping Willows: Death in Early America," *Proceedings of the American Antiquarian Society*, 86, part 2 (1976): 273–302; Maris A. Vinovskis, *Fertility in Massachusetts from the Revolution to the Civil War* (New York: Academic Press, 1981).

8　Carl F. Kaestle and Maris A. Vinovskis, *Education and Social Change in Nineteenth-Century Massachusetts* (Cambridge: Cambridge University Press, 1980).

9　Maris A. Vinovskis, *An "Epidemic" of Adolescent Pregnancy? Some Historical and Policy Considerations* (New York: Oxford University Press, 1988).

10　Kaestle and Vinovskis, *Education and Social Change in Nineteenth-Century Massachusetts*.

11　Maris A. Vinovskis, *The Origins of Public High Schools: A Re-Examination of the Beverly High School Controversy* (Madison: University of Wisconsin Press, 1985).

12.　Maris A. Vinovskis, "Quantification and the Analysis of American Ante-Bellum Education," *Journal of Interdisciplinary History* 13 (Spring 1983): 761–86; Gerald F. Moran and Maris A. Vinovskis, "The Great Care of Godly Parents: Early Childhood in Puritan New England," in Alice B. Smuts and John W. Hagen, eds., *History and Research in Child Development, Monographs of the Society for Research in Child Development* vol. 50, nos. 4–5 (1986): 24–37; Maris A. Vinovskis, "Family and Schooling in Colonial and Nineteenth-Century America," *Journal of Family History* 12, nos. 1–3 (1987): 19–37; David Angus, Jeffrey Mirel, and Maris A.Vinovskis, "Historical Development of Age-Stratification in Schooling," *Teachers College Record* 90 (Winter 1988): 211–36.

13　Diane Ravitch and Maris A. Vinovskis, eds., *Learning from the Past: What History Teaches Us About School Reform* (Baltimore: Johns Hopkins University Press, 1995).

14 Maris A. Vinovskis, *Revitalizing Federal Education Research: Improving the Regional Educational Laboratories, the R&D Centers, and the "New" OERI* (Ann Arbor: University of Michigan Press, 2001).

15 Maris A. Vinovskis, *Education, Society, and Economic Opportunity: A Historical Perspective on Persistent Problems* (New Haven: Yale University Press, 1995); Ravitch and Vinovskis, *Learning from the Past*; Maris A. Vinovskis, *History and Educational Policymaking* (New Haven, Yale University Press, 1999); David L. Featherman and Maris A. Vinovskis, eds., *Social Science and Public Policy: A Search for Relevance in the Twentieth Century* (Ann Arbor: University of Michigan Press, 2001); Maris A. Vinovskis, *The Birth of Head Start: Preschool Education Policies in the Kennedy and Johnson Administrations* (Chicago: University of Chicago Press 2005); Maris A. Vinovskis, *From A Nation at Risk to No Child Left Behind: National Education Goals and the Creation of Federal Education Policy* (New York: Teachers College Press, 2009).

DONALD WARREN

SERIATIM

What follows is more meditation (and mediation) than autobiography, although no
less calculated. It intends to reach across boundaries. Several entry points come to
mind, family; working class background in southeast Texas; schools; universities;
teachers; wife of 50+ years and our sons; friends; jobs; students who may have
thought their learning was unilateral; lecture tours, memorably in China, Egypt,
India, and Vietnam; and blends of joys and sorrows. On reflection, none survives
in its chronological order, and all become reconfigured when I dwell on them.
There have been too many surprises to pretend I controlled the flow, much less
planned it. Looking back, I see series, not linear or circular and definitely not
progressive ones, but a shifting confluence of agencies, my own among them.
Almost from the beginning, my background music has been stories, originally from
sources close at hand. Others came later through artistic and scholarly works. They
continue to accumulate, thanks in large part to wife Beverly (a perceptive storyteller),
sons Will and Ben, artists by temperament and training, and friends like Charles
Tesconi, who once proposed that my Texas upbringing made me an ethnic even
though my family name does not end in a vowel. Mine has been an expanding
world, for which I have been occasionally grateful, often belatedly. The chapter
thus mingles personal episodes with developments in the history of education. The
difficulty, as those of us working this ground know well, is that our field, like
others, exhibits a certain indisposition toward restarting contested formative stages.
Where we are now in the process is unclear, which may be a good thing.

As prologue, one place to begin is with Paul Tillich, who constructed education
as travel filled with risk and portent, a connecting primary element in the contents
and methods of what he called the system of knowledge that everyone builds from
the raw materials of existential and prescribed learning. He spent a lifetime
reading, thinking, arguing, and writing about how individuals, groups, even nations
confront and possibly transcend their own ambivalence and nature's ambiguity.
Alienation in its various manifestations, and the many ways it could morph along
continuums of good to evil and vice versa, fascinated him. I read some of his work
as an undergraduate at the University of Texas, encounters that led me to Harvard
where Tillich's systematic theology lectures introduced students to contextualized
readings of intellectual history. Like stalwarts in education history, he blurred
genres and disciplinary specializations with abandon, turning relentlessly to places,
including ideas, where people learned. For him the destination of learning was
unexplored territory and more questions, not the usual stuff at the end of well-trod
paths. Tillich trafficked in irony. It was his way of keeping complex matters where

W. J. Urban, Leaders in the Historical Study of American Education, 299–312.
© *2011 Sense Publishers. All rights reserved.*

they belong and not letting them slide into romanticism or superstition. This sense of comedic drama, timed as not too heavy or too light, can be found in other literatures. Consult Marshall McLuhan, who cautioned that anyone who tried to make a distinction between education and entertainment didn't know the first thing about either.

For Tillich, all history was at once profane and sacred, or could be, and he employed both analytical categories as substantively linked. His key contemporary referent was Nazi Germany, an environment he fled. Do not categorize it, he warned; accept its ordinariness. At the time Harvard and Radcliffe students were lining up to join bus trips to challenge southern racism. You could be making history, he glumly advised in his thick German accent, but all we needed was one affable Hitler, a demagogue catering to ripened fears of change, to nurture the destructive potential of a Nazi-like regime on American soil. As it happened, students returned from their "freedom rides" beaten, jailed, and profoundly shaken. Tillich's warning inserted urgency and the possibility of learning onto the history-making process they endured, dimensions often cleansed from written histories. Largely missing, he complained, was curiosity about the "religious situation," searches for characteristics denoting a special epoch in the past, a period that could qualify as a "fullness of time." Not all eras do. Either way, typically historians can label them only after the fact, a chronological warp leaving inquiry more or less on its own as it probes for clarity about potential ranges of significance.

INSTITUTIONS

> **Personal Favorites**
>
> *To Enforce Education: A History of the Founding Years of the United States Office of Education* (Detroit: Wayne State University Press, 1974).
>
> *History, Education, and Public Policy: Recovering the American Educational Past* (Berkeley, CA: McCutchen Publishing Corporation, 1978) [ed.].
>
> *Pride and Promise: Schools of Excellence for All the People* (Westbury, NY: American Educational Studies Association, 1984) [with Charles A. Tesconi Jr. and Mary Anne Raywid].
>
> "Learning from Experience: History and Teacher Education," *Educational Researcher* 14 (December 1985): 5–12.
>
> *American Teachers: Histories of a Profession at Work* (New York: Macmillan, 1989) [ed.].

That prospect of pregnant time serves to recast the gentlemanly disagreement that erupted between R. Freeman Butts and Lawrence Cremin in the 1960s over the role of public schools in American history. Butts saw them as central and irreplaceable. They have to be defended for the same reasons citizens must struggle to protect their liberties and the tenuous constitutional balances of individual preferences and the common good. Otherwise, the civic fabric could be shredded, as it has been in the past. Taking cues from Bernard Bailyn, Cremin thought the schools' importance could not be assumed. Their historical status became established (or not) in relation to the multiple educational institutions revealed in the past, an approach that explicitly questioned the precise jurisdiction of education history. As Sol Cohen, the acknowledged expert on Cremin's thinking, has observed, Cremin's answers shifted as did interest in his projected comprehensive history of American education broadly defined.[1] At the outset, Richard Storr proposed a methodological exit from the Butts-Cremin conflict, in effect suggesting it should be ignored as distraction from a more promising door to inquiry, but the contribution was largely ignored.[2] Eventually, the institutional concentration, now expanded beyond schools, recovered its footing.[3] Even Cremin adapted it as his encompassing history moved toward the twentieth century, the graceful prose bloated, as Alfred North Whitehead might have put it, by "oceans of facts." A basic historiographical dichotomy remains with us. What is the essential orientation of our field, education policy or the history discipline, scholarship or professional development? By contrast, we could look for escape hatches from binary options that permit broader, even shifting, scopes yet more nuanced emphases, all aimed at understanding education's historical place.

In the vein of repetition and conceptual inertia, consider American common schools. Education historians have returned to them repeatedly, adding details to the analysis but only sometimes fresh perspective. Michael Katz did precisely that in *The Irony of Early School Reform,* a book that quite literally turned our field inside out, at least for awhile.[4] What continues to intrigue me is not its historical impact or critics' quibbles about statistical methods. Nor have I been persuaded by those who wanted him to pay more attention to reform schools and other "alternative" educational arrangements. He accomplished something potentially more important by expanding the field simultaneously on conceptual, methodological, and substantive fronts. The book exhibited a young scholar's brashness, as he observed later (unapologetically). For good or for ill, broadly defined or not, education touched peoples' lives, in practice and theory the places where they learned. Look for it amid profound transitions, not through the filtering screens of definitions or unexamined assumptions. As process or institution, education leaves trails in voting tallies; demography, especially social class divisions, given the effects of emergent capitalism on American society; debates over curriculum; nascent school bureaucracies; and, yes, reformatories, but also in the careers of boys who left them to fight and perish in the Civil War. The irony was not that schools, their adjuncts, or any other institution failed to democratize or even that those who designed, managed, and controlled them rarely entertained such an outcome or expressed understanding of what it would look like. The dysfunction lay deeper in the young republic's coalescing hegemony and the meandering individual and policy choices it coaxed regarding the distribution of wealth and opportunity. In this fluid context (mid-nineteenth century), the idea of education as a liberating force, rather than a social engineering tool in the modernization project, barely survived. None of this developed by some invisible hand or cloudy anti-intellectualism. Consequential decisions were made, a cumulative trajectory that we can see was underway at the point Katz's analysis began. Throughout, he insisted that to reconstruct the multi-layered narratives, we needed hard evidence to replace hopeful, often repeated, rhetoric portraying schools as exemplars of democracy. It has struck me as a telling failure of the history of education that his subsequent explorations into social welfare have been commonly consigned to the periphery of our field, however central they were in American history.

Personal Favorites (continued)

"Passage of Rites: On the History of Educational Reform in the United States." In *The Educational Reform Movement of the 1980s: Perspectives and Cases*, ed., Joseph Murphy, (Berkeley, CA: McCutchen Publishing Corporation, 1990), 57–81.

"Looking for a Teacher, Finding Her Workplaces," *Journal of Curriculum and Supervision* 19, no. 2 (Winter 2004): 150–68.

Civic and Moral Learning in America (New York: Palgrave Macmillan, 2006) [ed. with John J. Patrick].

"Twisted Time: The Educative Chronologies of American Indian History." In *Bridging the Gap Between Theory and Practice in Educational Research: Methods at the Margins*, ed., Rachelle Winkle-Wagner, Cheryl A. Hunter, and Debora Hinderliter-Ortloff, (New York: Palgrave Macmillan, 2009) , 97–110.

"History of Education in a Future Tense." In *Handbook of Research on the Social Foundations of Education*, ed., Steven Tozer, Bernardo P. Gallegos, and Annette M. Henry, (New York: Routledge, 2010).

The possibility that schools of any sort could misfire or that their effects emerged from delimiting premises first occurred to me during jobs I held as a social worker. I entered them for practical if naive reasons. As an undergraduate hoping to avoid another dead-end summer job, I took an internship in New York that placed me on the staffs of settlement houses in East Harlem and the Bronx. The trip perilously stretched my Texas roots. It was a wonder I survived and in significant ways I didn't. The internship had me leading day camp activities for Puerto Rican and African American children. By the end of it, I acquired a nagging skepticism about the value of our planned events. The youngsters enjoyed the organized play and toured previously unseen parts of Manhattan, all of us gawking like the sightseers we were. Benefits resulted, but could they last or lead to something that could? Answers proved to be fleeting. So far as it went, the question posed a legitimate if baffling concern. These children were damaged goods, circumscribed by small, routinely dangerous worlds. After several years of schooling, most had attained barely borderline literacy, whether in English or Spanish. Raw emotions burst to the surface easily. The social services staff who tended them were empathetic and, save for me, trained. I came to think of us as fingers in a dike.

My next stint as social worker occurred in Cambridge, Massachusetts. Needing a job, I scanned bulletin boards at Harvard for opportunities. One struck a nerve. The Cambridge Neighborhood House wanted a staff member for the summer. Instead I got a position that lasted three years. It involved multiple assignments as counselor at summer day camps, sponsor (and watcher) of pre-formed groups of teenagers willing to enlist as in-house clubs (enticements offered a meeting room and field trips), and delegate to streetcorner associations in Cambridge and nearby Somerville that with coaxing might agree to come in from the cold. This time I did homework, my original encounter with educational research literature. Its prescriptions relative to streetcorner societies delivered a consensus: Move these teenagers back to school or, short of that medicine, into the army. Irish lads all, Eddie and the other Jokers (their club name) waved away facile diagnoses. Street smart and articulate, an orphan living with an alcoholic grandmother in an apartment of utter filth, Eddie predictably was a dropout. After my umpteenth suggestion that he return to school, he retorted, "I'd sooner steal cars." He did and spent six months in a state penitentiary for his troubles. This was no middle class quest for meaning but a fight for survival and dignity, to paraphrase his words, a middle finger raised against anonymous indifference. It was not a battle he was prepared for or equipped to win. For him, the defeat proved wasteful and tragic. At a safer distance, it was that for me too, but a question lingered. What was it about schools that alienated young people like Eddie? I had walked the halls of the Jokers' former high school, speaking with teachers, counselors, and principals, my first such encounters since my own pleasantly rewarding school days in Beaumont, Texas. Something was wrong here and maybe there too, even if I had missed it at the time. School personnel seemed listless and defensive. Eddie and his Jokers represented distractions from their mission. If not exactly happy, they were relieved to wave good-bye to troublesome, unmotivated kids, and their choices did not seem strained. Were school personnel acting on their own or representing someone or something else? The question seemed apt to teachers' work and to mine. Later, in the 1960s, a popular literature appeared offering insider peeks into the failed cultures of urban schools that rang true.

By then, I was committed to the history of education, almost literally ambushed by a feeling that behind and above the Cambridge schools and others like them lay diverse narratives to be exposed and explored. As Jonathan Kozol recounted in *Death at an Early Age*, a memoir on teaching in Boston, education of sorts occurred in these institutions, but it was a spirit-killing experience for many teachers and students that did not originate with them. The thought inspired my interest in the formative years of the U.S. Department of Education and its early effects as an agent of teaching and learning.[5] A creature of Reconstruction, the department was modeled after the newly established Department of Agriculture, the Freedmen's Bureau, and efforts by states to design offices responsible for school supervision and collecting related statistics. Postwar American schools were acquiring a vertical policy environment. An era of transition was underway, edging schools almost imperceptibly away from immediate constituents. Causes and effects merged obliquely, and they resisted early identification or easy interventions. In Louis Menand's subsequent analysis the Civil War changed the ways Americans thought about almost everything, morally, religiously, politically, and intellectually, a point driven home in Drew Gilpin Faust's documentation of pervasive Civil War death. At the time, new directions remained far from clear. Looking back on the 1860s, we can appreciate the confusion as a kind of educative stew.[6]

Compelling histories of education, even when narrowed to institutional themes, nonetheless confront economic, cultural, and psychological distances to be measured. They attend to matters of context if only to settle uncertainty about institutions' relative significance. Equally important, they protect human dimensions, personalities who add spice and accountability to summaries of actions taken. It is in this regard that I remember Elsa Baldwin, director of the Cambridge Neighborhood House. A self-described "girls college" graduate, she worked the local court system and social services bureaucracies with intense, magical skill, often a grin, and, it must be added, not always suppressed fury. When loosed, her tongue could turn to acid. Then as now, I think of her as an educator. But her Cambridge Neighborhood House no longer exists, the building demolished probably in anticipation of its physical collapse. As anyone could see, it was not aging well, and the costs of repair surely would have exceeded the available budget. It is the nature of certain institutions, including schools, because of the changing cultures sustaining them, to confront such disruptions. They evolve or devolve, vanishing with limited traces of their histories left behind or adapting along various continuums systemically, sometimes into unrecognizable forms. Progressive narrative structures cannot capture the dynamics. Upon discovery, the conundrums advise education historians to look beyond familiar perspectives and territories for different markers of educative situations, always on the alert for ships flying under false colors: those more accurately labeled noneducative or, in more subtly dangerous guises, miseducative. We reconstruct the past, and we read it. No resurrection occurs. The "key to the interpretation of history is historical activity," Tillich argued, "a unity of experience and interpretation," criticism and creation, joined within ever "broader" and more "realistic" frames. The process stretches, is inherently painful, and "transforms" perceptions of history and its authors. It does not prefer "security to truth" and to inch toward the latter draws energy and insight from principled criticism and "prophetic challenge."[7]

PEOPLE

Donald Warren: Favorite Works
Albert Camus, *The Myth of Sysiphus and Other Essays*, trans. Justin O'Brien (New York: Vintage Books, 1960).
John Dewey, *Interest and Effort in Education* (Carbondale: Southern Illinois University Press, 1975 [1913]).
Patricia Galloway, ed., *The Hernando de Soto Expedition: History, Historiography, and "Discovery" in the Southeast* (Lincoln: University of Nebraska Press, 1997).
Preston Holder, *The Hoe and the Horse on the Plains: A Study of Cultural Development among North American Indians* (Lincoln: University of Nebraska Press, 1970).
Edward P. Jones, *The Known World* (New York: Amistad, 2003).

I took my first education courses at the University of Chicago, learning afterwards they were atypical. The faculty fashioned an intellectually rich setting, each grounded in a discipline but teaching and writing across boundaries. Charles Bidwell, Robert Havighurst, and Robert McCaul, for example, offered joint seminars blending history, sociology, and sociocultural development in studies of school reform amid social change. Learning of my still forming interests, McCaul sent me to the history department for seminars in urban, Civil War, Reconstruction, and intellectual history. Slavery and race emerged as common threads. For research on teaching and learning, I went to Philip Jackson, then working on an ethnographic investigation of life in classrooms. Graduate study at Chicago proved to be less about a regimen of courses than about "taking" faculty. The lesson has guided my teaching and administrative assignments at Chicago State University (previously the Cook County Normal School), University of Illinois at Chicago Circle, also now with a shortened name, University of Maryland at College Park, and Indiana University. Educational research and teacher preparation, I concluded early on, needed entwined disciplinary roots.

The history of teachers offers a case in point. I left Cambridge with a bias against the profession, fed by observation and ample evidence, but Jackson's ethnographic study revealed teachers' workplaces in a sobering light. They imposed exhausting labor unrelieved by fixed schedules, and he found teachers working in diverse settings simultaneously, discoveries promising only modest surprise to insiders. Geraldine Clifford and Barbara Finkelstein added historical substance. Both pioneered in the search for teachers in the American past, succeeding in finding flesh and blood people, not stereotypes. They kept subjects in their family, community, and school contexts and reconstructed the nexus of individuals and settings with warts on full display. Whether situated in schools or elsewhere, the stories resisted prettification. Unsurprisingly, given demographic factors, teachers fell within the emerging scope of women's history. Polly Welts Kaufman, among other historians, joined the fray. It became something of a fight largely over the use of autobiography, biography, and other personal history sources. Clifford even devoted her History of Education Society presidential address to the necessity and reliability of such materials in projects of a certain ilk.[8] Teachers qualified for innovative historical methods in large part because they proved hard to find, their lives scattered in obscure archives or, worse, in moldy boxes consigned to attics. Even the focus on teachers provoked controversy. They lacked status in their own times and currently as subjects of historical investigation. Basic problems blocked progress. The old historical literature could be described charitably as thin; new work remained uncollated and conceptually fragmented. At Bill Reese's suggestion, five of us (Clifford, Reese, David Tyack, Linda Perkins, and I) gathered to discuss strategies for correcting the failures. We proposed the publication of a book to the American Educational Research Association, with invited chapters on teachers' policy environments, career lines, formal preparation and licensure, and related reform issues. To our surprise, the plan was accepted. The resulting volume, with an exhaustive (as of 1988) bibliography appended, provided the first comprehensive exploration of teachers' history since Willard Elsbree's *The American Teacher* had appeared 50 years earlier.[9] And it corrected a damaging omission in his book: not a single citation of sources reflecting teachers' perspectives on their own history.

A decade later, I attempted to gauge methodological and substantive progress through a search for my first grade teacher, a woman who had affected me personally. In the interim considerable work had been completed, propelled by ongoing discoveries of personal history documents. With Geraldine Clifford leading the way, it turned out that various archives and families had retained materials on teachers, waiting as it were to be rescued. My project required a different approach. I had a name - Gertrude Baldwin - but not a person. She left no papers or other clues on her family, ideas, values, and teaching experiences. Her college records had been destroyed in a fire. What remained were the personnel files of her school districts; archives of Beaumont's First Baptist Church where for two decades she had volunteered as a Sunday school teacher; factual but impersonal data in school surveys conducted by teams of outside experts; and memories of her by surviving colleague teachers and former students, including me. At best, I could triangulate the evidence to reveal her workplaces in schools, church, and Mexican-American neighborhoods, where the city's other minority of color was concentrated. Bilingual in English and Spanish, she had achieved, as I learned, subterranean fame in these communities as a translator, intermediary, and advocate. A front-page newspaper report on her death described her as a saint. Nonetheless, like most past teachers, I suspect, she now teeters on the brink of oblivion, increasingly beyond historical reach.[10]

Recent research depicts similar conceptual and evidentiary problems in the history of slavery. After longstanding disputes, Civil War and Reconstruction historians lately seem agreed on slavery's pivotal role in nineteenth-century American social formation. It was the leading cause of the nation's bloodiest and most destructive military engagement and bequeathed the color line that still distorts race relations and attitudes across the country. The new research suggests pointedly that slavery functioned as a purveyor of cultural teaching and learning, an educational institution of a different sort. Its impact did not cease with emancipation in 1863 or two years later, for that matter, but in Douglas Blackmon's telling phrase persisted in the form of "slavery by another name" arguably into the present. The resulting agenda of inquiries runs a gamut from slaves' political struggles and those of their descendants to the concomitant deferential aspirations and structurally low social status of southern white yeomen and the rampant racially prompted anti-intellectualism among southern whites of all classes. The agenda also includes probes into durable faith-based rationales for racism along with the contributions of evangelical Protestantism to their persistence, and the uneven generation of social capital, North and South, skewed by ingrained racial attitudes. At issue in the new and contentious literature is the matter of agency, that exerted by whites and African Americans. As George Frederickson has noted, giving it too much weight risks diluting the horrendous conditions under which slaves lived and understates slavery's crippling, masochistic effects on whites. Emphasizing agency also threatens to transform the Mason-Dixon Line from a trope into a wall beyond which other regions escaped slavery's poisons relatively unaffected. Denying or qualifying agency, on the other hand, discounts available evidence and renders a life-changing episode in United States history as little more than a victimization tale.[11]

Historians of education have tended to watch this substantive and methodological dispute in the parent discipline from the sidelines. We have focused on the schooling of slaves and subsequent issues of black formal education, more or less ignoring the educative power of slavery itself. With a few exceptions, that work is being conducted by historians outside our specialization, many of whom have no trouble grasping how social formation can metastasize with debilitating, destabilizing, even fatal consequences for the body politic. They also exhibit a quarantine of their own, often omitting details of schools' impact on literacy and social capital levels in the North and the South during the mid-nineteenth century. We may be uniquely prepared to link these themes as nuanced inclusive narratives.[12]

Donald Warren: Favorite Works (cont'd)

Michael Lewis, *Moneyball: The Art of Winning an Unfair Game* (New York: W. W. Norton & Company, 2003).

Charles C. Mann, *1491: New Revelations of the Americas before Columbus* (New York: Alfred A. Knopf, 2005).

Louis Menand, *The Metaphysical Club: A Story of Ideas in America* (New York: Farrar, Straus and Giroux, 2001).

Richard Storr, "The Education of History: Some Impressions," *Harvard Educational Review* 31, no. 2 (Spring 1961): 124–35.

Paul Tillich, *The Protestant Era*, trans. James Luther Adams (Chicago: The University of Chicago Press, 1948).

Within the estate Americans have inherited from slavery, urban race riots could be of particular interest to education historians. They occurred during the second half of the nineteenth century and well into the twentieth as though on a schedule – North, South, and West. Sparked by wars, shortages, crimes or more commonly rumors of crime, and a host of other local problems, they tended to pit low-wage whites against outnumbered blacks, who fought back strategically. One occurred in Beaumont, Texas at the height of World War II. Ten years old at the time, I harbored vague yet unforgettable memories of the event. Details proved readily available in local archives. Thinking to enliven the account, I interviewed a casually constructed sample of African Americans, whites, and Mexican-Americans who, save for one, had lived in the city at the time of the riot. Three sets of memories surfaced. Blacks remembered the event vividly, adding stories of resistance not to be found in newspaper reports; whites did not. They required prompting that the riot had occurred. Mexican-Americans could only outline the event but unbidden offered details about the Zoot Suit Riot in Los Angeles as though they had witnessed it. On one level, the interviewees merely confirmed human memory as a wavering resource. On another, they testified to distinct reservoirs of meaning that can be deposited by personalized social upheavals.[13] Beaumont experienced the most destructive race riot in the South during World War II. There were some 80 others, plus the longer, more devastating, and more thoroughly reported racial disturbances in Detroit, Harlem, Chicago, and Los Angeles. Nevertheless, it seemed to have left local whites unfazed. Some may have suppressed their memories, but just as probable for others, the event did not register. Blacks constructed a different narrative of enduring civic scars and distrust of whites. An 11-year-old boy sharpened the hypothesis. I interviewed him on a whim as he played in an interviewee's yard. He recalled the riot without prompts, repeated stories I had just heard from his grandmother and parents, and drew the same grim lessons. He, of course, had missed the event by a half century. Hypothetically, the riot had become an exercise in cross-generational, street-level civic education. That proposition warrants case studies by education historians that dig deeply enough to tap written or oral personal reflections.

Similar methodological challenges arise in the history of American Indians. Here too education historians have not occupied the front lines of research. With few exceptions we have settled for concentrations on the schooling imposed on Indians by Europeans, colonists, and by the end of the eighteenth century, Americans. Important as that project is, if fully contextualized, it tacitly assumes that outsiders introduced education to the "New World" and leaves historians bereft of sturdy reference points to assess the costs and benefits of enforced schooling from indigenous perspectives. In the hands of scholars determined to complicate the narrative, such as David Wallace Adams, Vine Deloria Jr., Donald Fixico, Preston Holder, and Adrea Lawrence, multiple story lines take shape.[14] Native Americans, after all, have always been diverse peoples, socially, politically, and axiologically. North of the Rio Grande River, many of their nations and federations achieved what archaeologists and historical anthropologists describe as advanced civilizations. They developed complex economies and adapted the exacting science of maize agriculture to local climates and soils. (Originating in Mesoamerica, corn horticulture took root in the heartland centuries before Euro-Americans arrived as the sophisticated, influential Arikara Nation broke away from the Caddo alliance to migrate north during the long precontact era, armed with agricultural and commercial expertise and grounded religious commitments.) Long before encountering Europeans, American Indians devised refined tool and weapons technologies and traded among themselves across wide distances and difficult terrains, with neither horses nor wheels, it should be added. They enjoyed a unique, differentiated spirituality and produced aesthetically impressive art, encoding cultural achievements in oral traditions and mnemonic totems.[15] Without written materials, reconstructing this past using American Indian sources leads us inevitably into the realm of human memory. We may debate its frailty, but there can be no disagreement that education played a prominent role in Native history, even though it never acquired institutional forms that Euro-Americans could recognize easily. On the lookout for significant omissions in education history, we should consider Patricia Galloway's stern advice regarding research on American Indians. It must be multidisciplinary, she insisted, with the crucial partners coming from anthropology, archaeology, history, and now several scientific fields. Vine Deloria Jr. added that oral traditions, the languages freighting them, and spirituality, in consultation with tribal elders, are required sources as well. These are not literatures typically searched by education historians. What they reveal are processes and forms of teaching and learning that have occurred in the American past outside the influence of schooling and, as evidence confirms, at least partly in defiance of it. As David Shorter demonstrated in depth and detail, Native history, reached ethnographically, posits education as an integral element in cultural maintenance and change.[16] It was the means by which Indians have managed to survive and adapt across millennia and through recent centuries of repeated direct and indirect assaults on their societies. Pieced from diverse materials, the narratives imply a core, generational resilience. It is legitimate to imagine American Indians' pasts as essentially histories of education.

METHODS

That cannot be said of all peoples or all histories. Searching for evidence of teaching and learning, we need to know who did what to whom, where, and with what consequences. We need to know other things too, and reconstructing contexts to depths and ranges permitted by quantitative and qualitative sources helps us name them. Almost from the self-conscious beginnings of our field, say with Henry Barnard in the mid-nineteenth century, we and our predecessors have worked with the aid of definitions and tacit assumptions. We knew what education meant and assumed schools and other formal institutions met the standard. Their personnel; related laws and policies; the enacting legislatures, boards, and councils; allied governmental and voluntary organizations; and countless generators of ideas, plans, and reform proposals fell into place, although not always neatly. A frequent error omits details on relevant taxes, budgets, and expenditures, thus encouraging inclinations to ignore or mismeasure exertions of covert economic power.[17]

If something fresh is now in the wind, we may be indebted to Richard Storr. Fifty years ago, he proposed a methodological innovation in polite response to Cremin's definitional approach.[18] What if we worked without a net? Rejecting even the implication that we can know fully and in advance what education is or ought to be, he thought the history of education might move to more fertile ground through inquiries conducted inductively. Otherwise we can never be sure what significant educative events have been overlooked or what measures should be applied in determining whether a self-declared educational institution functioned in ways that justified its claim.

Recent contributions suggest merit in Storr's proposal. Consider A. J. Angulo's path-breaking work that charts slavery's dampening effects on scientific advancement as racial dynamite stockpiled in the South.[19] Then there is Mary Niall Mitchell's fascinating analysis of mid-nineteenth-century racial history made possible by the author's discovery of documents penned by African American school children.[20] Dionne Danns explores what black leaders, teachers, and students learned as activists in social protest movements in Chicago during the 1960s.[21] Eileen Tamura writes cogently about the Japanese American internment camps during World War II as educational institutions.[22] Her analysis focuses on the camps themselves, not merely the schools they contained, and on durable "value lessons" acquired by internees. David Setran parses religious experiences and theological canons as he probes the transition of the "College Y" from a muscular nineteenth-century evangelical Christianity into an era of twentieth-century secularization.[23] Milton Gaither exposes inconsistencies in Bailyn's critique of the history of education and Ellwood P. Cubberley, specifically, through an exegesis of U.S. history literature of the nineteenth and early twentieth centuries.[24] In effect he reveals Bailyn's isolated context - school historiography - as too small. Joshua B. Garrison performs a similar expansion in searching for origins of the idea of adolescence and G. Stanley Hall's thinking in rarely consulted late nineteenth-century scientific literature, including that produced by racially benumbed anthropologists working in Africa.[25] In searching for relevant sources Garrison adapted methods resembling those employed at an archaeological dig. Consider too Glenn P. Lauzon's inquiry on nineteenth-century agricultural history and the roles of county fairs, grange clubs, and town/county associations in the forming of civic consciousness, notably in the rural Midwest.[26] His conceptual framework is similar to Nicholas V. Longo's in a collection of case histories on education in democracy that demonstrate socially constructed civic learning.[27] In a review of the book Scott J. Peters emphasizes antecedents to this approach in the early twentieth-century work of Joseph Kinmont Hart, who argued that communities etched political lessons more indelibly than schools.[28] Apparently, Richard Storr stood on the shoulders of others. Cited above, Adrea Lawrence's study of federal education policy in a Pueblo community at the turn of the twentieth century delineates the multiple social roles played by a Bureau of Indian Affairs teacher and her supervisor. Their educative effects and those of the policies they were expected to implement were neither constrained by her classroom assignments nor channeled through them. Standing Bear Kroupa moves completely beyond the realm of Euro-American schooling in a reconstruction of his Arikara Nation's past as an arc of spiritual mastery sustained by traditional teaching and learning.[29]

The examples share certain features in common. The authors follow the trail of evidence not a pre-existing definition of education. They establish thick contexts, moving authoritatively into an array of disciplinary literatures, including oral traditions. The expansions augur renewable vitality, a field inquiring wildly beyond the repetition of one familiar thing after another toward history's main stage.

NOTES

1 Sol Cohen, *Challenging Orthodoxies: Toward a New Cultural History of Education* (New York: Peter Lang, 1999).

2 Richard Storr, "The Education of History: Some Impressions," *Harvard Educational Review* 31 (Spring 1961): 124–35.

3 See, e.g., Daniel Walker Howe, *What Hath God Wrought: The Transformation of America, 1815–1848* (New York: Oxford University Press, 2007), 451–455.

4 Michael B. Katz, *The Irony of Early School Reform: Educational Innovation in Mid-nineteenth Century Massachusetts* (New York: Teachers College Press, 2001 [1968]).

5 Donald R. Warren, *To Enforce Education: A History of the Founding Years of the United States Office of Education* (Detroit: Wayne State University Press, 1974).

6 Drew Gilpin Faust, *This Republic of Suffering: Death and the American Civil War* (New York: Vintage Books, 2009); Louis Menand, *The Metaphysical Club: A Story of Ideas in America* (New York: Farrar, Straus and Giroux, 2001).

7 Paul Tillich, *The Protestant Era*, trans. James Luther Adams (Chicago: The University of Chicago Press, 1948), x–xxix.

8 Geraldine Jonçich Clifford, "Home and School in 19th-Century America: Some Personal-History Reports from the United States," *History of Education Quarterly* 18 (Spring 1978): 3–34; Barbara Finkelstein, *Governing the Young: Teacher Behavior in Popular Primary Schools in Nineteenth*

Century United States (Philadelphia: Falmer Press, 1989); Polly Welts Kaufman, *Women Teachers on the Frontier* (New Haven: Yale University Press, 1984).

[9] Willard Elsbree, *The American Teacher: Evolution of a Profession in a Democracy* (New York: American Book, 1939); Donald Warren, ed., *American Teachers: Histories of a Profession at Work* (New York: Macmillan, 1989).

[10] Donald Warren, "Looking for a Teacher, Finding Her Workplaces," *Journal of Curriculum and Supervision* 19 (Winter 2004): 150–68.

[11] George M. Fredrickson, "America's Original Sin," *New York Review of Books* 51 (March 25 2004): 34–36; Annette Gordon-Reed, *The Hemingses of Monticello: An American Family* (New York: W. W. Norton & Company, 2008); Steven Hahn, *A Nation Under Our Feet: Black Political Struggles in the Rural South from Slavery to the Great Migration* (Cambridge: Belknap Press of Harvard University Press, 2003).

[12] Douglas A. Blackmon, *Slavery by Another Name: The Re-enslavement of Black Americans from the Civil War to World War II* (New York: Doubleday, 2008); Erskine Clarke, *Dwelling Place: A Plantation Epic* (New Haven: Yale University Press, 2005); Steven Hahn, *The Political Worlds of Slavery and Freedom* (Cambridge: Harvard University Press, 2009).

[13] John Bodnar, "Generational Memory in an American Town," *Journal of Interdisciplinary History* 26 (Spring 1996): 619–37.

[14] David Wallace Adams, *Education for Extinction: American Indians and the Boarding School Experience* (Lawrence: University Press of Kansas, 1995); Vine Deloria Jr., *God is Red: A Native View of Religion* (Golden, CO: Fulcrum Publishing, 2003); Donald L. Fixico, *The American Indian Mind in a Linear World* (New York: Routledge, 2003); Preston Holder, *The Hoe and the Horse on the Plains: A Study of Cultural Development among North American Indians* (Lincoln: University of Nebraska Press, 1970); Adrea Lawrence, "Unraveling the White Man's Burden: A Critical Microhistory of Federal Indian Education Policy Implementation at Santa Clara Pueblo, 1902-1907," (PhD diss., Indiana University, 2006).

[15] Charles C. Mann, *1491: New Revelations of the Americas before Columbus* (New York: Alfred A. Knopf, 2005); Jeffrey Ostler, *The Plains Sioux and U.S. Colonialism from Lewis and Clark to Wounded Knee* (New York: Cambridge University Press, 2004); Patricia Galloway, ed., *The Hernando de Soto Expedition: History, Historiography, and "Discovery" in the Southeast* (Lincoln: University of Nebraska Press, 1997).

[16] David Delgado Shorter, *We Will Dance Our Truth: Yaqui History in Yoeme Performances* (Lincoln: University of Nebraska Press, 2009).

[17] See, e.g., Matthew T. Gregg and David M. Wishart, "The Economic Significance of the 'Trail of Tears': Estimating the Cost of Cherokee Removal," (Paper presented at the annual meeting of the Social Science History Association, Chicago, IL, November 2007).

[18] Storr, "The Education of History: Some Impressions."

[19] A. J. Angulo, "William Barton Rogers and the Southern Sieve: Revisiting Science, Slavery, and Higher Learning in the Old South," *History of Education Quarterly* 45, no. 1 (Spring 2005): 18–37; Angulo, *William Barton Rogers and the Idea of MIT* (Baltimore: Johns Hopkins University Press, 2009).

[20] Mary Niall Mitchell, *Raising Freedom's Child: Black Children and Visions of the Future after Slavery* (New York: New York University Press, 2008).

[21] Dionne Danns, *Something Better for Our Children: Black Organizing in Chicago Public Schools, 1963–1971* (New York: Routledge, 2003).

[22] Eileen H. Tamura, "Value Messages Collide with Reality: Joseph Kurihara and the Power of Informal Education," *History of Education Quarterly* 50, no. 1 (February 2010): 1–33.

[23] David P. Setran, *The College "Y": Student Religion in the Era of Secularization* (New York: Palgrave Macmillan, 2007).

[24] Milton Gaither, *American Educational History Revisited: A Critique of Progress* (New York: Teachers College Press, 2003).

[25] Joshua B. Garrison, "Ontogeny Recapitulates Savagery: The Evolution of G. Stanley Hall's Adolescent," (PhD diss., Indiana University, 2006).

[26] Glenn P. Lauzon, "Civic Learning through Agricultural Improvement: Bringing the 'Loom and the Anvil into Proximity with the Plow' in Nineteenth-century Indiana," (PhD diss., Indiana University, 2007).

[27] Nicholas V. Longo, *Why Community Matters: Connecting Education with Civic Life* (Albany: SUNY Press, 2007).

[28] Scott J. Peters, "Book Review," *History of Education Quarterly* 49, no. 3 (August 2009): 396–99.

[29] Standing Bear Kroupa, "With Arikara Eyes: History of Education as Spiritual Renewal and Cultural Evolution" (Paper presented at the annual meeting of the American Educational Research Association, Denver, CO, May 2010).

HAROLD S. WECHSLER

EIGHT SUBWAY STOPS ON THE BRIGHTON
LINE—AND WHAT HAPPENED IN BETWEEN

I decided to study the history of American higher education shortly after May 1, 1968.[1] Early that morning, over a thousand New York City police officers cleared the Columbia University campus of demonstrators and the occupants of five university buildings. Upwards of 800 were arrested; perhaps the same number of students, faculty, and police needed medical attention. The next afternoon, the leaders of Students for a Democratic Society gathered on the balcony of the Columbia Law School building, looking at over a thousand demonstrators protesting the police action. The images of the police action initiated by the Columbia administration still haunt me. But so does the brief triumph of "manipulatory democracy" practiced by SDS members.

It did not take a criminal justice specialist to predict what would happen if the police came onto the campus. The Columbia administration, having lost touch with students, faculty, and the surrounding community, could think of nothing to end the crisis short of bringing predictable violence to the campus. Conversely, SDS exposed its hand when sociologist Allan Silver asked its leaders if they found anything at Columbia precious, even indispensable, and if so, would their answer place any restraints on their actions. The leaders huddled, but came up with no answer. Neither side was willing to assume responsibility for its acts.[2]

Shortly after the police bust, I joined the staff of a faculty committee charged with reforming the governance of the university.[3] I spent the summer attending committee meetings, discussing the university's past and future relationships with its students, faculty, and surrounding community, and writing about university governance. This was my way of helping to rebuild a flawed university to which I owed much. Columbia had opened new intellectual and social worlds during my undergraduate years, so much so that I had decided to stay there for graduate work in history after receiving a BA in 1967. When staff colleagues learned that I majored in history, they asked questions about prior student demonstrations and protests at Columbia and elsewhere. No one knew much about Columbia's recent history, much less its formative years, or about the history of student protest or campus governance.

At that time Columbia possessed an unequalled faculty of historians of higher education including Walter Metzger, who became my thesis adviser, Lawrence Cremin, Richard Hofstadter, and Douglas Sloan. *The Development of Academic Freedom in the United States*, published in 1955 by Hofstadter and Metzger served as an invitation to study the history of higher education.[4] Sloan demonstrated the

W. J. Urban, Leaders in the Historical Study of American Education, 313–321.

centrality of religion for understanding American history.[5] Cremin insisted we look beyond the classroom to understand educational processes. All four taught tolerance for, even appreciation of, different points of view—a difficult lesson in politicized times. The Columbia History Department and Teachers College also attracted a cadre of graduate students destined to shape our understanding of the history of American education—Alison Bernstein, Paula Fass, James Fraser, Sheila Gordon, David Hammack, Ellen Lagemann, David Ment, Deborah Dash Moore, and Steven Schlossman—all of whom became lifetime friends and colleagues.

While studying for doctor's orals in 1969, I noted a prescient sentence in the bibliographic essay in Frederick Rudolph's *The American College and University: A History*: "Thus far, we have little more than educated guesses as to what a history of college preparation in the United States might tell."[6] The previous spring, Black and Puerto Rican students staged a sit-in at City College of New York (CCNY). Their key demand: admit more students of color to this college, known historically for promoting educational opportunity.

My Favorite Books and Articles:

"An Academic Gresham's Law: Group Repulsion in American Higher Education," *Teachers College Record* 82 (Summer, 1981): 576–588.

Access to Success in the Urban High School: The Middle College Movement (New York: Teachers College Press, 2001).

"Brewing Bachelors: The History of the University of Newark," *Paedagogica Historica* 46 (February, 2010): 229–249.

Jewish Learning in American Universities: The First Century (Bloomington and Indianapolis: Indiana University Press, 1994), (with Paul Ritterband).

The Qualified Student: A History of Selective College Admission in America 1870–1970 (New York: John Wiley-Interscience, 1977).

New York's demographics changed rapidly during the postwar years, but the city's four-year municipal colleges—short of space, and reliant solely on SATs and GPAs as admissions criteria—excluded many working class and minority students. The City College sit-in forced the parent City University of New York (CUNY) to open admission to *all* New York City high school graduates. Supporters and opponents debated the history and politics of college admission—open and selective. State universities, Open Admissions advocates asserted, traditionally opened their doors to all high school graduates. But this was done only to flunk out many of the entrants before the end of their first year, opponents charged. Better politically and educationally, advocates replied, to give all high school graduates a chance at college than to alienate students and their taxpaying parents and to intensify a contentious racial climate. The times are different, they added. Unlike the state universities of old, CUNY sought to provide admitted students with the academic support needed to succeed.

During the 1960s and 1970s, debates over admissions policies frequently invoked the word "quota," usually in the context of the Ivies and Seven Sisters. Quotas were also debated when contemplating changes in CUNY's admissions policies to accommodate racial and ethnic minority students.[7] It was to avoid the use of quotas that CUNY officials opted to find a place in the university for all. I heard about quotas while growing up in Brooklyn, New York. I had Jewish friends who graduated in the top one percent of the senior class of James Madison High School. Madison—located near the Kings Highway station on the Brighton Beach subway line that connected Brooklyn to Manhattan—was among the "best" high schools in the country, our teachers told us. The academic demands made upon we Madisonians put the Ivies to shame, they added. Yet when the time came, in spring 1963, Harvard, Yale, and Princeton rejected the applications of my friends.

Intrigued by Rudolph's bibliographic comment, watching the CUNY admissions controversy from the West Side of Manhattan just a year after the Columbia demonstrations, and asking if Jewish quotas still existed despite many denials, I proposed to write a history of admission to American colleges and universities. The thesis would place racial and ethnic factors in the context of 20th century efforts to define relations between secondary schools and colleges.

I spent a semester in Columbia's Low Library reading "active" files dating to 1890.[8] Columbia's leaders, it turned out, played key roles in standardizing college entrance requirements, creating the College Entrance Examination Board, and devising "selective admissions" policies intended to keep out Jews. Besides Columbia, my thesis discussed other colleges and universities where changes in admissions policies had significant social implications—including Open Admissions at CUNY. I defended the thesis in 1973 and resolved to continue research on access to US higher education.[9]

*

The centrality of Jewish students to my story—their quest for higher education, and their exclusion by college gatekeepers—led me to take on a second research theme: the Jewish encounter with American higher education. This research often overlapped with my studies of access. The "Jewish problem" often exemplified issues relevant to other groups (and vice versa). I worked for a year at CCNY where sociologist Paul Ritterband and I began research on the history of Jewish learning in American universities.

In 1976, I began a decade of teaching in the Department of Education of the University of Chicago. The university had obtained a Spencer Foundation grant allowing a younger generation, largely from the academic disciplines, to overlap with the scholars recruited by Ralph Tyler during the 1940s—including Benjamin Bloom, Harold Dunkel, Robert Havighurst, Cyril Houle, and Herbert Thelen. I became director of the department's higher education program upon Houle's retirement, taught courses in contemporary issues in higher education, and continued my historical research, focusing on a draft of *Jewish Learning in American Universities: The First Century*.[10]

The book explored the effect of Judaica scholars, their subjects, and the concerned community on American universities, and the effect of American academic life on practitioners and on American Jewry. The field of Judaica tempered the Christian orientation of universities, especially the Christological focus of humanities departments, while strengthening the Jewish role in American higher education. Academics in this field and concerned Jewish-community members tried to force Gentile university authorities to adhere to professed norms of merit and objectivity even when they were inconvenient, or conflicted with other goals. Indeed, forcing adherence to professed norms by Americans and their institutions became a key strategy for Jewish accommodation to American life.

> **Books that Influenced Me:**
>
> F. N. Cornford, *Microcosmographia Academica* (London: Bowes and Bowes, 1908).
>
> Paula Fass, *The Damned and the Beautiful* (New York: Oxford University Press, 1977).
>
> Lynn D. Gordon, *Gender and Higher Education in the Progressive Era* (New Haven: Yale University Press, 1990).
>
> David C. Hammack, *Power and Society: Greater New York at the Turn of the Century* (New York: Russell Sage Foundation, 1982).
>
> Richard Hofstadter and Walter P. Metzger, *The Development of Academic Freedom in the United States* (New York: Columbia University Press, 1955).
>
> Max Weber, "Science as a Vocation," in Hans Gerth and C. Wright Mills *From Max Weber: Essays in Sociology* (New York: Oxford University Press, 1946), 129–156.

By using the same criteria to judge the work of Judaica practitioners and other subjects and by legitimating the field for Gentiles as well as Jews, American universities attempted to separate devotion from scholarship. They also shaped a research and curricular agenda congruent with "parent" disciplines, not around Jewish books or modes of internal organization. The shift in the field's dominant outlook from universalism to pluralism and to particularism during the 20th century permitted comparisons with other fields— ethnic and women's studies, for example—that might affect, and be affected by, communal norms and behavior.

I complemented this research on Jewish learning by examining the rationales used to restrict the access of Jewish students. How valid were oft-articulated administrative concerns that too many Jews (or members of any "distinctive" group) would induce other (more "desirable") groups to depart from the college? Colleges and universities, I found, often did not wait to find out. Instead they invoked a desire for "diversity" to limit enrollment of a "distinctive" faction liable to "overwhelm" a more favored group, irrespective of the qualities of individual members. They interpreted "democracy" to mean majority rule, even at the expense of minority rights (including access). This and similar rationales for imposing social restrictions on admissions, I concluded, were disingenuous.

I also examined the fate of Jewish faculty members working in non-Judaic departments. Dilemmas of exclusion, I suggested, led to subsequent dilemmas of inclusion. Circumspection helped Jewish academics navigate through pre-World War II anti-Semitic currents. But this same characteristic, which persisted among some Jewish faculty members during my years at Columbia, led to subsequent communal charges of faculty indifference—even alienation—affecting the religious and ethnic identity of Jewish college youth.[11] I balanced my research on the Jewish encounter with secular universities by writing essays on the history of Jewish seminaries in America, focusing on how mainstream practices, including accreditation, influenced these institutions.[12]

*

Then and now, many academic couples experience difficulties finding jobs in the same geographic area. Lynn D. Gordon, my spouse, and I were no exception. We faced an additional dilemma since Lynn also studied the history of higher education.[13] We thought that my experience teaching courses in higher education, and Lynn's ability to teach courses in women's history would work in our favor. But we endured 14 years of commuting between several city pairs: Boston-Chicago, Princeton-Chicago, Rochester-Chicago, Rochester-Washington, D.C., and Rochester-Evanston, Illinois. The airlines finally lost the Gordon-Wechsler revenue stream in 1991. We spent the next 14 years at the University of Rochester with offices down the hall from each other.

In 1987, I had attempted to end our commuting by accepting an off-campus job: director of higher education publications at the National Education Association in Washington.[14] *Thought & Action: The NEA Higher Education Journal*—now with a 150,000 circulation—became a forum for communication among two-and four-year college faculty and staff members—not as chemists or engineers, but as members of academic communities. Editing the journal allowed me to apply a lesson learned during the 1968 Columbia demonstrations: faculty, staff, and students, having an institutional stake equal to trustees and administrators, merit a voice in campus affairs—and not only during crises.

Ironically, my NEA work advanced my research, instead of diverting me from it. The Reagan administration, especially Secretary of Education William Bennett, constantly attacked NEA as a barrier to its version of educational reform. Those attacks produced considerable tension in NEA's communications department and in the Washington higher education establishment, itself often at odds with NEA. One response around which all could unite: counterattacks on the Reagan administration for ignoring a decline in the number of African American college students.[15] A request by colleagues at the Association of American Colleges to write a monograph on how four-year colleges and universities could increase minority student transfers from two-year colleges led me to resume my research on access.[16]

I built on my research on Open Admissions at CUNY by studying the planning and growth of the first Middle College High School (MCHS). Opened in 1974, MCHS is a public high school for at-risk students located on the campus of Fiorello H. LaGuardia Community College in Long Island City, New York. The limited number of minority students at CUNY, argued some observers, had stemmed not so much from the use of "objective" admissions criteria, as from the significant dropout rate at New York City high schools with substantial minority enrollments. Would at-risk students, asked the designers of MCHS, benefit from the presence and influence of older community college students who had overcome similar obstacles? Would these students prosper in a collegiate environment with fewer restrictions than the traditional urban high school? Could the designers adopt an innovation originally aimed at academically and socially elite students—beginning college work while in high school—to the needs of at-risk students?

Dismantling barriers between secondary school and college, MCHS planners concluded, would encourage at-risk 10th through 12th graders to continue their education while helping to assure adequate college preparation. A high school with access to community college faculty and facilities would also reduce the need for developmental courses at the postsecondary level. Conversely, MCHS students could enroll in—and receive college credit for—LaGuardia's college-level courses while still in the secondary grades, an incentive to engage in and expedite postsecondary work.

MCHS and its replications emerged just as educators and policy makers were rethinking the viability of the comprehensive high school and the transition between high school and college. The prospect of a 14-year educational norm for all students, a goal that President Obama considers feasible and desirable, portended substantial increases in college enrollments. Community colleges may want to—or have to—intervene in preparing academically at-risk to average high school student populations. The Middle College movement addressed the complexities involved in educating at-risk students "at the border."[17]

*

While at work on the Middle College book, I noted a significant omission in the literature on the history of higher education, given the intensity surrounding contemporary debates on admissions. We lacked a comprehensive history of racial, ethnic, and religious relations at those predominantly white colleges and universities where minority students overcame hesitations, applied, and *got in*—colleges offering relatively low tuition, ease of commuting, and the promise of a career.

The accommodating colleges included flagship and regional state universities, such as Ohio State University (African American students), the University of Washington (Asian-American students), and Northeastern State Normal School (now Northeastern State University) in Tahlequah, Oklahoma, the capital of the Cherokee Nation (Native American students). They also included private streetcar colleges and universities, such as the University of Newark and the University of Buffalo, and municipal colleges, such as the College of the City of New York and Wayne University, which accommodated substantial numbers of first and second-generation Americans. Some colleges attracted multiple nationalities, such as American International College in Springfield, Massachusetts, and Valparaiso College in Indiana. Other colleges attracted students from a single nationality or ethnic group. Alliance College in Cambridge Springs, Pennsylvania (1912–1986), for example, recruited Polish-Americans. One last sub-group consisted of colleges opened, in part at least, as responses to discrimination, such as Long Island

University in Brooklyn and Roosevelt University in Chicago.[18] I decided to write the book myself, beginning with essays on individual colleges.[19]

Educators still debate questions of access and articulation more than a century after the publication of the Committee of Ten Report and the founding of the College Board. Where should high school end and college begin? What kinds of high school preparation bode well for college success? Who should go to college? What role does the community college play in promoting or impeding access to higher education?[20] Is there a difference between the use of selective admissions and quotas when considering the credentials of minority students?[21] What are the uses and misuses of standardized college entrance tests? How should we educate students who cannot or do not enter postsecondary institutions? I hope my research provides a context in which scholars and policy makers can offer educational, not polemical answers to these questions.

*

While at Rochester, I continued my research on the Jewish encounter with American colleges and universities. I focused on two topics: the history of attempts to reduce prejudice against Jews on the college campus, and the academic and vocational decision-making, along with the moral and religious growth of Jewish college students.[22] I put the knowledge gained to immediate use in my next institutional move. In 2000, the Steinhardt School at New York University—eight express stops from Kings Highway on the Brighton Beach subway line—established a doctoral program in "Education and Jewish Studies." I sat on the external planning committee for this program and accepted its co-directorship several years later. *Jewish Learning in American Universities* provided useful insights for developing this program in a secular university. Bringing together a diverse group of future Jewish leaders around educational questions may help to unify an otherwise factionalized Jewish community. A university location also helps to guard the study of Jews and Judaism against insularity.

My department at NYU, Humanities and Social Sciences in the Professions, founded by historian Ellen Lagemann, serves as a program incubator by promoting strengthened student knowledge of historical context, academic content, and educational process. It allows students to explore the aims of Jewish education in a world of choices.[23]

*

Election to the presidency of the History of Education Society (2007–2008) provided an opportunity to contemplate the direction of the field. I defined five initiatives: First, identify, and make available, important but fugitive historical records. Second, strengthen the teaching of the history of education.[24] Third, reverse the elimination of the subject from the curricula of schools of education and from accreditation requirements in teacher education programs. Fourth, increase the public visibility of the field and of the society. Fifth, convey a sense of the field's excitement and importance to a new generation of scholars, and help these scholars succeed.

The last lines of my HES presidential address summarize the thinking behind these initiatives: "As for that question posed to Mark Rudd: Is there anything about academic life that's precious, even indispensable? Yes. We historians of education must complement our commitments by bringing reason and rigor to subjects about which there is all-too-often only heat and passion in the public square. If we don't, who will?"[25]

I hope that I've helped to advance these goals though my scholarship, my teaching, and my associational work.

NOTES

[1] The following paragraphs are drawn from "Presidential Address: How Getting into College Led Me to Study the History of Getting into College," *History of Education Quarterly* 49 (February, 2009): 1–38.

[2] See Allan Silver, "Orwell, Thou Should'st Be Living at This Hour," in Immanuel Wallerstein and Paul Starr, eds., *The University Crisis Reader*, volume 2: *Confrontation and Counterattack* (New York: Random House, 1971), 85–92.

[3] The staff was known as the Project on Columbia Structure. The faculty group, the Executive Committee of the Faculty, governed Columbia de facto during the 1968–69 academic year and oversaw the formation of the Columbia University Senate.

[4] Richard Hofstadter and Walter P. Metzger, *The Development of Academic Freedom in the United States* (New York: Columbia University Press, 1955).

[5] Douglas Sloan, *Faith and Knowledge: Mainline Protestantism and American Higher Education* (Louisville, Ky.: Westminster/John Knox Press, 1994).

[6] Frederick Rudolph, *The American College and University: A History* (New York: Vintage, 1962), 502.

[7] One of the few exceptions: Ernest Cummings Marriner, *The History of Colby College* (Waterville, ME.: Colby College Press, 1963) frankly discussed the ethnic politics of college admission.

[8] Most folders remained untouched for a half-century or more. The university would archive its documents in the 1990s.

[9] Wechsler, *The Qualified Student: A History of Selective College Admission in America 1870–1970* (New York: John Wiley-Interscience, 1977).

[10] Paul Ritterband and Harold S. Wechsler, *Jewish Learning in American Universities: The First Century* (Bloomington and Indianapolis: Indiana University Press, 1994).

[11] "The American Jewish Academic: Dilemmas of Exclusion and Inclusion," in Mayer I. Gruber, ed., *The Solomon Goldman Lectures*, volume 6 (Chicago: Spertus College of Judaica Press, 1993), 183–209, and "Academe," in Jack Fischel and Sanford Pinsker, eds., *Jewish-American History and Culture: An Encyclopedia* (New York: Garland Publishing, 1992), 3–13. My studies of the tension between academic and communal norms informed my service as a trustee of Spertus College of Judaica in Chicago and as a member of local and national boards of Hillel: The Foundation for Campus Jewish Life.

[12] "Jewish Seminaries," in Thomas C. Hunt and James C. Carper, eds., *Religious Seminaries in America: A Selected Bibliography* (New York and London: Garland Publishing, 1989), 128–139: "Jewish Seminaries and Colleges," in Thomas C. Hunt and James C. Carper, eds., *Religious Higher Education in the United States: A Source Book* (New York: Garland Publishing, Inc., 1996), 413–436; and "The Jewish Theological Seminary of America in American Higher Education," in Jack Wertheimer, ed., *Tradition Renewed: A History of the Jewish Theological Seminary*, volume 2 (New York: Jewish Theological Seminary of America, 1997), 767–825.

[13] Both of us have served as presidents of the History of Education Society (U.S.).

[14] I edited *Thought & Action: The NEA Higher Education Journal*, *The NEA Almanac of Higher Education*, and *The NEA Higher Education Advocate*. I still edit the *Almanac*. Two lessons: First, advocacy publishing can coexist with high academic standards. Second, scholars, especially historians, must continually communicate with the public. I also edited the *History of Higher Education Annual* (now entitled *Perspectives on the History of Higher Education*) during these years.

[15] See American Council on Education, *One-Third of a Nation: Minorities in the United States* (Washington, D.C.: ACE, 1988) and Wayne J. Urban, *Gender, Race, and the National Education Association: Professionalism and its Limitations* (New York: Taylor & Francis, 2000).

[16] *The Transfer Challenge: Removing Barriers; Maintaining Commitment: A Handbook for Four-Year Colleges* (Washington, D.C.: Association of American Colleges, 1989), and *Meeting the Transfer Challenge: Five Partnerships and their Model: The Report of the Vassar/AAC National Project on Community College Transfer* (Poughkeepsie, N.Y. and Washington, D.C.: Vassar College and the Association of American Colleges, 1991).

[17] Wechsler, *Access to Success in the Urban High School: The Middle College Movement* (New York: Teachers College Press, 2001).

[18] John Rury's research on the student demographics of DePaul was an inspiration. See John L. Rury and Charles S. Suchar, eds., *DePaul University: Centennial Essays and Images* (Chicago, Il.: DePaul University. 1998). Rury also facilitated project funding while a Spencer Foundation program officer. Over coffee at an O'Hare Airport cafeteria, Jeff Mirel insisted that I write a dispassionate history of minority access to higher education.

[19] "Brewing Bachelors: The History of the University of Newark," *Paedagogica Historica* 46 (2010): 229–249, and "One Third of a Campus: Ruth Crawford Mitchell and Second-Generation American Students at the University of Pittsburgh," *History of Education Quarterly* 48 (February, 2008): 94–132.

[20] See my review of *The Diverted Dream: Community Colleges and the Promise of Educational Opportunity in America 1900–1985*, by Steven Brint and Jerome Karabel, in *Science* 250 (December 21, 1990): 1755–1756.

[21] See "The Rationale for Restriction: Ethnicity and College Admission in America 1910–1980," *American Quarterly* 36 (Winter, 1984): 643–667.

[22] I studied the National Conference of Christians and Jews, the largest organization of its kind in mid-century. That research led to a Ford Foundation invitation to examine the applications to its *Difficult Dialogues* program. The goal: to identify themes common to colleges experiencing racial and ethnic strife. The Ford Foundation will publish an essay based on this research.

[23] See "Belonging Before Belief," and "Promoting a Counterculture," in Jack Wertheimer, ed., *Learning and Community: Jewish Supplementary Schools in the 21st Century* (Lebanon, N.H.: Brandeis University Press; University Press of New England, 2009), 113–144, 207–235 (both essays with Cyd Beth Weissman).

[24] The annual meeting of the History of Education Society now features a workshop on teaching in this field. See also the curriculum developed at the LaGuardia and Wagner Archives at LaGuardia Community College, New York City: http://www.cuny.edu/cc/higher-education.html.

[25] "Presidential Address…," 38.

KATE ROUSMANIERE

AFTERWORD

The history of education is a peculiarly circular field: we study the processes and patterns of education in the past, driven by questions raised in our own educational experience as students, teachers, parents, or community members. We live and work in academic institutions, teach courses that engage in educational issues, and research education in the past while observing education in the present. Inevitably, our scholarly questions about the history of education spiral back to our own experiences as students and teachers: how did education work or not work for me? What happened to my friends who didn't make it? Why did that teacher or that book have such an influence on me? What is it about my own education that set a seed that then grew into a tough nut that I continue to try to crack?

Given the continually reflective nature of our work, it is ironic how rarely we hear about the educative experiences of our colleagues. As historians, we usually begin our analysis with other's scholarship and historical data as framing devices, but quickly move on to the analysis of primary data. Personal motivations sometimes appear in forewords or acknowledgements, but we leave the historical narrative to tell its own tale. As scholars, we tend to stay out of the way of our work.

This collection turns our normal practice upside down. Here the founding scholars of the field take a deep breath and tell us their intellectual autobiography, tracing their personal and professional development in the history of education. They refract their scholarly work through their self-portraits, from which we learn about both individual development in the field and a broader story about education in the last half of the 20th century. As both biography and history, these memoirs provide a number of lessons for historians and educators alike, and are especially instructive for junior scholars who are preparing to chart their own career paths.

First, the medium of memoir allows us in most of the cases to see the texture and complexity of academic work through to retirement. Common themes emerge, the most notable of which is the accidental nature of our field: we stumble into this corner of scholarship through different serendipitous paths, and are surprised to find a body of literature and a cast of characters that speak directly to questions that intrigue us. We are guided by other individuals: advisors, faculty, friends and fellow readers. We work in a great variety of life and professional patterns, balancing between history and education and between humanities and social science. Our intellectual work develops through teaching and research, and also, less obviously, through service in editorial ventures, educational administration, faculty governance, and engagement in communities, politics and schools.

It is also interesting to note the impact of historical context on our colleagues' work and life. Historians are no less affected by history than those we study, and in this collection we see the role of national events on career and life paths: for example the opportunities offered by the NDEA and funding for higher education; the rise of the AAUP and teacher unions; the attraction of alternative and progressive schooling, civil rights, feminist, and peace movements, and national wars. Junior scholars may also note the timelessness of concerns about jobs and the state of the field, and the universal anxiety about publishing, tenure, and finding time to research.

Notable too is the common experience that good work takes a long time, many drafts, and many readers. The best work has been reviewed and criticized often, tried out in public settings, talked over, played over, practiced, and re-written. Co-authorship, cohort relationships as graduate students, and collegial relationships as faculty inspire the co-construction of research. The History of Education Society and other organizations become places to sort through ideas, to be mentored, and in turn to mentor others.

Common to all of the memoirs is a deep engagement with major scholarship in the field, reminding us that the best way to write history is to read history. The best history speaks to critical questions that resonate with the present, so that a classroom teacher struggling with student alienation in a modern school is inspired by a study of schooling inequality in colonial New England. Since at least the 1960s, history students have made the reverse connection between past and present by applying contemporary reports on the failure of public schooling to their own historical questions. The best history is, in one way or another, in conversation with the present.

These memoirs shine with the excitement of individual intellectual growth and the collective construction of a body of literature and norms of scholarly practice during the first fifty years of the American History of Education Society. The narratives of founding scholars in the formative years of the field can elicit a romanticized longing for a "golden age" of the field when academics worked in unison toward a common goal. But the image of unified progress in the past can be deceptive. Certainly historians of education were a smaller and more homogenous group in the past, and their memoirs are often self-referential, referring to interconnected webs of contacts and the powerful dynamic of sponsored mobility. Yet there are occasional hints of the conflict that moved the field forward, as individuals argued for the legitimacy of new quantitative and qualitative research methods, critiqued traditional academic norms, and debated the significance of education policy, the role of theory, and the political dynamics of class, race, and gender in historical analysis. The battle over the revisionists may be the most notorious of these collective debates about the shape of the field, and although remembered as an exciting time, it was also a period marked by some bitter personal and professional divisions. Communities of common work also experience internal conflict.

My own experience is as a member of a middle generation, a student of many of these founding leaders and a peer colleague of others. These memoirs lead me to look backward and forward, appreciating the foundation on which my own work is based, and remembering the anxiety of arguing for new perspectives and questions.

I recall the moment as a doctoral student when I understood that to develop my own work, I had to move beyond and even critique my mentors. And I recall the gentle advice of those same mentors who encouraged such ventures, thereby modeling the behavior that innovation is constructive and does not have to be an intellectual hostile takeover. Over my own professional career, I have learned that what ultimately matters is not single individual accomplishments but the cumulative work of both intersecting and divergent research paths.

Historians lead strangely individual and collective lives, driven by our solitary work in the archive and at our desks even as we draw on the scholarship of others through historiography and rely on our colleagues' editorial comments. As these memoirs poignantly reveal, historians of education also have a third eye, one that looks to the real world of education, beginning with the meaning of our own educational experiences. The illustrations of the work of that third eye in the essays in this volume testify to its acuity in indicating the power of many of the challenges the writers have confronted, though not necessarily conquered, during their careers. The same challenges, as well as new ones yet to be specified, confront my own generation, and its successors.

CPSIA information can be obtained at www.ICGtesting.com
Printed in the USA
BVOW010637270412

288790BV00004B/30/P

9 789460 917530